The *Realia* Jesus

"This beautifully illustrated, carefully researched, and up-to-date book answers many of the questions that ordinary Bible readers (and scholars) ask but don't know where to look for answers. David Fiensy carefully but charitably surveys a range of approaches and accessibly synthesizes years of research in ways that even students newest to the discipline can grasp. I HIGHLY recommend this book to anyone interested in learning more about the Gospels and Jesus's life and ministry."

—**Craig S. Keener**, professor of biblical studies, Asbury Theological Seminary

"*Realia* is a look at the cultural backdrop and the archeological evidence of the first century that helps us to understand the world of Jesus in the first century. This is a solid survey and up-to-date discussion of what we have and what it may show about Jesus' life. It is full of fascinating observations. Read it for a better glimpse of Jesus' ministry."

—**Darrell L. Bock**, senior research professor of New Testament studies, Dallas Theological Seminary

"A remarkable and unique resource that will be valuable to anyone who wants to appreciate more fully the stories and teachings of our Third Gospel. David Fiensy relates data and insights from recent archaeological studies to principal texts and motifs from Luke's Gospel in a way that makes the findings accessible and relevant. His emphasis is on realia—documents, artifacts, structures, objects, and even human remains that emerge from the soil to help us understand the environment in which Jesus lived, ministered, and died."

—**Mark Allan Powell**, retired professor of New Testament, Trinity Lutheran Seminary

"This book is a wonderful, thorough survey of the archaeological discoveries that impact the story of Jesus. Though David Fiensy, of necessity, also appeals to the contemporary written accounts left by the elite social class, he does not neglect the conditions of average people understood through the fossil record they left behind. Profusely illustrated, this book should prove a boon to scholars, students, and educated non-specialists looking for a comprehensive yet readable introduction to the historical context of the Gospel accounts."

—DAVID CHRISTIAN CLAUSEN, adjunct lecturer in
Christian origins, University of North Carolina at Charlotte

"There has been a longstanding need for accessible archaeological information that is relevant to the study of Jesus and the Gospels. David Fiensy meets this need with a book that is readable and approachable while also being rigorous, comprehensive, and steeped in ongoing conversations in the archaeology of Jewish Galilee in the early Roman period. This book will be the go-to reference on the shelf that we reach for when looking for reliable and accessible information on the archaeological and historical context of Jesus and the Gospel of Luke."

—JORDAN J. CRUZ RYAN, associate professor
of New Testament, Wheaton College

The *Realia* Jesus

An Archaeological Commentary on the Gospel of Luke

DAVID A. FIENSY

CASCADE *Books* • Eugene, Oregon

THE *REALIA* JESUS
An Archaeological Commentary on the Gospel of Luke

Copyright © 2024 David A. Fiensy. All rights reserved. Except for brief quotations in critical publications or reviews, no part of this book may be reproduced in any manner without prior written permission from the publisher. Write: Permissions, Wipf and Stock Publishers, 199 W. 8th Ave., Suite 3, Eugene, OR 97401.

Cascade Books
An Imprint of Wipf and Stock Publishers
199 W. 8th Ave., Suite 3
Eugene, OR 97401

www.wipfandstock.com

PAPERBACK ISBN: 978-1-6667-7257-9
HARDCOVER ISBN: 978-1-6667-7258-6
EBOOK ISBN: 978-1-6667-7259-3

Cataloguing-in-Publication data:

Names: Fiensy, David A., author.

Title: The realia Jesus : an archaeological commentary on the gospel of Luke / David A. Fiensy.

Description: Eugene, OR: Cascade Books, 2024. | Includes bibliographical references and index.

Identifiers: ISBN 978-1-6667-7257-9 (paperback). | ISBN 978-1-6667-7258-6 (hardcover). | ISBN 978-1-6667-7259-3 (ebook).

Subjects: LCSH: Bible. Luke—Criticism, interpretation, etc. | Bible—Gospels—Antiquities. | Excavations (Archaeology)—Israel. | Jesus Christ—History. | Jews—Social life and customs. | Palestine—History–To 70 AD.

Classification: BS621 F54 2024 (print). | BS621 (epub).

VERSION NUMBER 06/11/24

Contents

List of Tables | vii
List of Figures | ix
List of Sidebars | xiii
List of Maps | xv
Acknowledgments | xvii
List of Abbreviations | xix
Introduction | xxix

1. The Birth Narratives | 1
2. John the Baptist | 24
3. Jesus' Youth | 44
4. Capernaum | 61
5. The Male and Female Disciples | 82
6. Village Life | 99
7. Three Towns around the Lake | 114
8. Two Parables | 127
9. Two Controversies | 146
10. Disease and Death | 164
11. Jericho | 181
12. The Upper City, Eleona, and Gethsemane | 201
13. The Last Supper and the Arrest | 225
14. The Crucifixion | 240
15. Jewish Burials and the Tomb of Jesus | 266

Appendix A: Archaeological Periods of Palestine | 293
Appendix B: Glossary | 295
Bibliography | 297
Subject Index | 329
Scripture Index | 333

Tables

Introduction: How archaeology informs biblical study | xxx–xxxi

1.1: Marriage documents | 3

1.2: Age at marriage | 5

1.3: Life expectancy | 20

1.4: Life expectancy—various findings | 22

4.1: A sampling of house sizes in late second temple Israel | 72

5.1: Jesus' twelve apostles | 86–88

5.2: Named women disciples | 89–90

5.3: Women in the Gospels compared with archaeological sources | 91–92

5.4: Fifteen individuals from the "ninety percent." | 93–6

5.5: Economic standing of persons in Luke's Gospel | 98

6.1: Village sizes | 102

6.2: Village and city contrasts | 106

6.3: Features in ancient Palestinian villages | 107–8

6.4: Luke's references to Herod the Tetrarch (Antipas) | 110–11

8.1: Large estates | 129

9.1: Sources of impurity | 148–49

9.2: Levels of purity in late Second Temple Israel | 156

9.3: References to *Archisynagōgoi* in the New Testament and inscriptions | 158

10.1: Child mortality in ancient Israel | 175–76

10.2: Youth mortality in the Greco-Roman world | 176

11.1: Stature in Israel | 188

11.2: Average stature in Greece | 188

11.3: Dining terminology in Luke | 194

12.1: Chief priests in the Lukan narratives | 201–2

12.2: The four priestly houses | 212

Figures

1.1: Archaeological plan of the Church of St. John | 8

1.2: Plan of excavations west of the Church of St. John | 10

1.3: Grotto under the Church of the Nativity | 17

1.4: Underground stable | 18

1.5: Nave of the Church of the Nativity | 19

2.1: Replica of 1QS manuscript | 28

2.2: Qumran Cave 4 | 29

2.3: Artist's depiction of the Cave of John the Baptist | 34

2.4: Summit of Machaerus | 38

2.5: Plan of Fortress Macharus | 39

2.6: Herodium | 42

2.7: Artist's reconstruction of Fortress Machaerus | 43

3.1: Nazareth: Churches of Anunciation and St. Joseph | 45

3.2: Wine press | 47

3.3: House in Nazareth | 49

3.4: Kokhim tomb in Nazareth | 49

3.5: Scenes from Nazareth | 51

3.6: Ossuary of Simon | 53

3.7: Model of Sepphoris | 55

3.8: Sepphoris theater | 57

3.9: Sepphoris aqueduct | 58

3.10: Cardo at Sepphoris | 60

4.1: Model of the Galilee Boat | 62

4.2: The octagonal church, Capernaum | 65

4.3: Plan of 1st century BCE house, Capernaum | 68

4.4: Artist's reconstruction of the "House of Peter" | 71

4.5: Standing back wall of synagogue, Capernaum | 77

4.6: Layout of Capernaum | 78

4.7: Two types of stone, Capernaum synagogue | 79

5.1: Ossuaries | 85

6.1: Gamla synagogue | 105

6.2: Model of typical village | 106

7.1: Seat of Moses in the synagogue of Chorazin | 115

7.2: House of the Fisherman, Et-Tell | 118

7.3: Temple plan at Et-Tell | 120

7.4: Mikveh at Magdala | 125

7.5: Synagogue at Magdala | 126

8.1: Artist's reconstruction of palatial mansion, Ramat ha-Nadiv | 131

8.2: Ruins of the mansion | 132

8.3: Hypocaust of the bath | 132

8.4: Swimming pool | 133

8.5: Plan of Horvat Aqav | 134

8.6: Mikveh at agricultural center | 134

8.7: Olive crusher | 135

8.8: Model of Scythopolis | 141

8.9: Scythopolis city center | 142

8.10: Colonnaded street | 143

8.11: Theater in Scythopolis | 144

9.1: Ritual bath, Yodefat | 150

9.2: Pool of Siloam | 152

9.3: Stoneware vessels | 155

9.4: Theodotus inscription | 160

11.1: The mouth of Wadi Qelt | 182

FIGURES   xi

11.2: Herod's winter palace at Jericho | 183

11.3: Date palms at Jericho | 185

11.4: Balsam pressing pool | 185

11.5: A couch | 193

11.6: *Triclinium* | 196

11.7: Great Hall at Herod's third winter palace | 198

12.1: The Old City of Jerusalem | 203

12.2: Model of first-century Jerusalem | 204

12.3: Excavation plan, Jewish Quarter | 205

12.4: Menorah graffito | 207

12.5: Isometric of the Palatial Mansion | 208

12.6: The Reception Hall | 209

12.7: Frescoed walls | 210

12.8: Stone tables and jar | 211

12.9: Stone weight with inscription | 212

12.10: Plan of Gethsemane | 217

12.11: Olive trees near Gethsemane | 218

12.12: The rock of agony | 219

12.13: Plan of Gethsemane cave | 220

12.14: Olive press | 221

13.1: The Madaba Map | 225

13.2: Caiaphas's ossuary | 235

13.3: The Church of Saint Peter in Gallicantu | 238

13.4: Under the Church of Saint Peter in Gallicantu | 239

14.1: Model of the Praetorium | 241

14.2: Golgotha (Jerusalem model) | 250

14.3: Rock inside Church of the Holy Sepulcher | 252

14.4: Golgotha according to Corbo | 253

14.5: Golgotha according to Taylor | 254

14.6: Alexamenos worships god | 258

14.7: Sketch of crucified Alkimila | 259

14.8: Magical gem, intaglio | 260

15.1: Map of Jerusalem | 267

15.2: Monumental tombs | 271

15.3: Loculus tomb interior | 272

15.4: *Arcosolium* tomb interior | 273

15.5: Stone blocking entrance to a tomb | 275

15.6: Entrance to the Church of the Holy Sepulcher | 280

15.7: Christian Quarter in Old Jerusalem | 283

15.8: Edicule inside the Church of the Holy Sepulcher | 285

15.9: Gordon's Calvary | 286

15.10: Plan of Constantine's Church of the Holy Sepulcher | 291

Sidebars

Introduction: Pilgrims and natives, informants about biblical sites | xxxii–xxxiv

1.1: Church of Saint John | 7

1.2: Herod the Great | 11

1.3: Constantine's Church of the Nativity | 14

1.4: Emperor Hadrian | 21

2.1: Jesus' birth year and his year of death | 31

2.2: The Dead Sea Scrolls | 32–33

2.3: Josephus | 36

2.4: Josephus on John the Baptist | 37–38

2.5: Herodian fortresses | 40–41

2.6: Herod's children | 42–43

4.1: The Galilee Boat | 62–63

4.2: Synagogues from the first century CE | 80–81

6.1: Herod Antipas | 112–13

9.1: The Mishnah | 154

10.1: Fever amulet | 173

11.1: Diners in a *triclinium* | 197

12.1: Caliph Hakim | 209

12.2: The high priestly dynasty of the house of Annas | 222

12.3: Annas the high priest | 224

13.1: The size of the Holy Sion Church | 229

13.2: Where was Caiaphas's house? | 239

14.1: Pontius Pilate mentioned in two inscriptions | 244–45

14.2: Ossuary of Simon (of Cyrene?) | 247–48

14.3: Heel bones of two crucifixion victims | 263

14.4: Jesus' crucifixion reported in other sources | 265

15.1: Four reasons to conclude Jesus was buried | 277–78

15.2: Timeline of the Holy Sepulcher Church and vicinity | 287

15.3: Emperor Constantine | 289

15.4: Helena (mother of Constantine) | 290

Maps

Map 1: Palestine under Herod the Great | 2
Map 2: Lower Galilee | 100

Acknowledgments

No work of this nature happens with just one person's effort. I have been the recipient of several gracious offers to use images, site plans, and maps in an effort to illustrate and explain to the reader the subject matter of this monograph.

- A. D. Riddle generously allowed me to use two of his maps which are Maps 1 and 2 in this volume.
- Shimon Gibson kindly granted me the reuse of his images for Figures 1.1 and 2.3
- The Studium Biblicum Franciscanum, Jerusalem generously granted me the reuse of several plans from their publications:
  - Figure 1.2 came from Saller, *Discoveries*.
  - The plan in Sidebar 1.3 came from Hoade, *Guide*.
  - Figure 4.3 came from Corbo, *Capharnao I*.
  - Figures 12.10 and 12.13 came from Corbo, *Richerche Archeologische*.
  - Figures 14.3 and 15.10 came from Corbo, *Sepolcro II*.
- Győző Vörös graciously allowed me to use two images from *Machaerus I*, which became Figures 2.5 and 2.7.
- Bethsaida Excavations kindly granted publication of the artist's conception of the House of the Fisherman and the plan of the alleged temple at Et-Tell (Figures 7.2 and 7.3).
- C. Thomas McCollough granted me use of his fever amulet image (SIDEBAR 10.1)
- *Biblical Archaeology Review* granted the image used in Figure 12.14.

- The Israel Antiquities Authority kindly allowed me the use of their photograph and sketch of the Pilate finger ring (SIDEBAR 14.1)
- Joan Taylor kindly permitted me to reuse her map of Golgotha, which became my Figure 14.5.
- Albion Archaeology granted me permission to republish their photograph of a crucifixion victim's heel bone (SIDEBAR 14.3) and clarified their view on its date.
- David Christian Clausen graciously read a portion of the manuscript and offered helpful advice.
- McFarland Books kindly granted me the right to reuse one of their maps (Figure 15.1).
- Billy Grantham sent me valued observations.
- Yonatan Adler gave me an up-to-date calculation of *mikva'ot* in Israel.
- Steven Notley and Motti Aviam each helped clarify, through correspondence, their position on El-Araj.
- The Kentucky Christian University library staff deserves thanks for their timely assistance in interlibrary loan.

Most importantly, I thank my wife—my great love and best friend—for her support and partnership in life.

All Scripture translations are the author's. All uncredited figures are the author's.

Abbreviations

GENERAL ABBREVIATIONS

Aram.	Aramaic language
ASOR	American Schools of Oriental Research
Byz	Byzantine
ER	Early Roman
ESA	Eastern Terra Sigilata A (see glossary)
Gk.	Greek language
Heb.	Hebrew language
Hell	Hellenistic
IAA	Israel Antiquities Authority
Lat.	Latin language
LH	Late Hellenistic
LR	Late Roman
MR	Middle Roman
SBL	Society of Biblical Literature

ABBREVIATIONS OF SECONDARY SOURCES

AASOR	Annual of the American Schools of Oriental Research
AB	Anchor Bible
ABD	David Noel Freedman, ed. *The Anchor Bible Dictionary*. 6 vols. New York: Doubleday, 1992
ABRL	Anchor Bible Reference Library
ABS	Archaeology and Biblical Studies
ADAJ	*Annual of the Department of Antiquities Jordan*
AGJU	Arbeiten zur Geschichte des antiken Judentums und des Urchristentums

AJR	Hillel Geva, ed. *Ancient Jerusalem Revealed*. Jerusalem: Israel Exploration Society, 1994
ANF	Alexander Roberts and James Donaldson, eds. *The Ante-Nicene Fathers. Translations of the Writings of the Fathers down to A.D. 325*. 10 vols. Buffalo: Christian Literature, 1885–1896
ANRW	*Aufstieg und Niedergang der römischen Welt*
AOAT	Alter Orient und Altes Testament
ASAWSS	Eric M. Meyers et al., eds., *The Architecture, Stratigraphy, and Artifacts of the Western Summit of Sepphoris*. 2 vols. Duke Sepphoris Excavation Reports 3. University Park, PA: Eisenbrauns, 2018
BA	*Biblical Archaeologist*
BAIAS	*Strata: Bulletin of the Anglo-Israel Archaeological Society*
BAR	*Biblical Archaeology Review*
BASOR	*Bulletin of the American Schools of Oriental Research*
BBR	*Bulletin for Biblical Research*
BECNT	Baker Exegetical Commentary on the New Testament
Bethsaida	Rami Arav and Richard A. Freund, eds. *Bethsaida: A City by the North Shore of the Sea of Galilee*. 4 vols. Kirksville, MO: Thomas Jefferson University Press, 1995–2009
BibOr	Biblica et Orientalia
BJPES	*Bulletin of the Jewish Palestine Exploration Society*
BJS	Brown Judaic Studies
BN	*Biblische Notizen*
BNP	Hubert Cancik and Helmuth Schneider, eds. *Brill's New Pauly: Encyclopedia of the Ancient World*. 15 vols. Leiden: Brill, 2002–2010
BR	*Bible Review*
BSac	*Bibliotheca Sacra*
BTB	*Biblical Theology Bulletin*
CahRB	Cahiers de la Revue biblique
CIJ	*Corpus Inscriptionum Judaicarum*. Edited by Jean-Baptiste Frey. 2 vols. Rome: Pontifical Biblical Institute, 1936–1952
Diodorus of Sicily, LCL.	Walton, Francis R., ed. *Diodorus of Sicily*. 12 vols. New York: Putnam, 1933–1967
DJD	Discoveries in the Judaean Desert
DSD	*Dead Sea Discoveries*
ECL	Early Christianity and Its Literature
EncJud1	Cecil Roth, ed. *Encyclopedia Judaica*. 16 vols. Jerusalem: Keter, 1972

EncJud2	Fred Skolnik, ed., *Encyclopedia Judaica*. 2nd ed. 22 vols. Detroit: Thomson/Gale, 2007
ETZ	Susan L. Cohen, ed. *Excavations at Tel Zahara (2006–2009): Final Report*. BAR International Series 2554. Oxford: Archaeopress, 2013
Eusebius, *Vita Const.*	*The Life of the Blessed Emperor Constantine*. London: Aeterna, 2014.
GLSTMP	David A. Fiensy and James Riley Strange, eds. *Galilee in the Late Second Temple and Mishnaic Periods*. 2 vols. Minneapolis: Fortress, 2014–2015
GBS	Guides to Biblical Scholarship
GRBS	*Greek, Roman, and Byzantine Studies*
HA-ESI	*Ḥadashot Arkheologiyot: Excavations and Surveys in Israel*
HSCP	*Harvard Studies in Classical Philology*
HTR	*Harvard Theological Review*
IDB	George Arthur Buttrick, ed. *The Interpreter's Dictionary of the Bible*. 4 vols. New York: Abingdon, 1962
IDBSup	*Interpreter's Dictionary of the Bible: Supplementary Volume*. Edited by Keith Crim. Nashville: Abingdon, 1976
IEJ	*Israel Exploration Journal*
IJP	*International Journal of Paleopathology*
Int	*Interpretation*
IRT	Issues in Religion and Theology
JA	James H. Charlesworth, ed. *Jesus and Archaeology*. Grand Rapids: Eerdmans, 2006
JAC	*Jahrbuch für Antike und Christentum*
JAJ	*Journal of Ancient Judaism*
JBL	*Journal of Biblical Literature*
JDS	Judean Desert Studies
JE	*Jewish Encyclopedia*
JJS	*Journal of Jewish Studies*
Josephus, LCL	H. St. J. Thackeray et al., trans. *Josephus*. 10 vols. Cambridge: Harvard University Press, 1926–1965
JPFC	Samuel Safrai et al., eds. *The Jewish People in the First Century*. 2 vols. Compendia Rerum Iudaicarum ad Novum Testamentum. Assen: Van Gorcum, 1974–1988
JQE	Hillel Geva and Oren Gutfeld, eds. *Jewish Quarter Excavations in the Old City of Jerusalem Conducted by Nahman Avigad, 1969–1982*. 8 vols. Jerusalem: Israel Exploration Society, 2000–2021

JR	Yigael Yadin, ed. *Jerusalem Revealed*. New Haven: Yale University Press, 1976
JRA	*Journal of Roman Archaeology*
JRASup	Journal of Roman Archaeology Supplement Series
JRS	*Journal of Roman Studies*
JSHJ	*Journal for the Study of the Historical Jesus*
JSJ	*Journal for the Study of Judaism*
JSJSup	Supplements to the Journal for the Study of Judaism
JSNTSup	Journal for the Study of the New Testament Supplement Series
JSOT	*Journal for the Study of the Old Testament*
JSOTSup	Journal for the Study of the Old Testament Supplement Series.
JTS	*Journal of Theological Studies*
LAI	Library of Ancient Israel
LCL	Loeb Classical Library
LSJM	Henry George Liddell, Robert Scott, Henry Stuart Jones, and Roderick McKenzie. *A Greek-English Lexicon*. Oxford: Clarendon, 1968
MECW	Dennis E. Smith, *Meals in the Early Christian World: Social Formation, Experimentation, and Conflict at the Table*. Edited by Hal Taussig. New York: Palgrave MacMillan, 2012
MOG	Richard Bauckham, ed. *Magdala of Galilee: A Jewish City in the Hellenistic and Roman Period*. Waco, TX: Baylor University Press, 2018
NEA	*Near Eastern Archaeology*
NEAEHL	Ephraim Stern, ed. *The New Encyclopedia of Archaeological Excavations in the Holy Land*. 4 vols. Jerusalem: IES, 1993. (Volume 5, Supplementary, 2008).
NICNT	New International Commentary on the New Testament
NIGTC	New International Greek Testament Commentary
NIDB	Katharine Doob Sakenfeld, ed. *The New Interpreter's Dictionary of the Bible*. 5 vols. Nashville: Abingdon, 2006–2009
NovT	*Novum Testamentum*
NTL	New Testament Library
NTS	*New Testament Studies*
OCD	N. G. L. Hammond and H. H. Scullard, eds. *Oxford Classical Dictionary*. 2nd ed. Oxford: Clarendon, 1970
OCD3rev.	Simon Hornblower and Antony Spawforth, eds. *The Oxford Classical Dictionary*. 3rd ed. rev. Oxford: Oxford University Press, 2003

ODCC	F. L. Cross and E. A. Livingstone, eds. *The Oxford Dictionary of the Christian Church*. 2nd ed. repr. Oxford: University Press, 1974
OEANE	Eric M. Meyers, ed. *The Oxford Encyclopedia of Archaeology in the Near East*. 4 vols. New York: Oxford University Press, 1997
OEBA	Daniel M. Master, ed. *The Oxford Encyclopedia of the Bible and Archaeology*. 2 vols. Oxford: Oxford University Press, 2013
OHJDL	Catherine Hezser, ed. *The Oxford Handbook of Jewish Daily Life in Roman Palestine*. Oxford Handbooks in Classics and Ancient History. Oxford: Oxford University Press, 2010.
OeO	Oriens et Occidens
OTL	Old Testament Library
OTP	James H. Charlesworth, ed. *The Old Testament Pseudepigrapha*. 2 vols. Garden City, NY: Doubleday, 1983–1985
PEQ	*Palestine Exploration Quarterly*
PJ	*Palästina-Jahrbuch*
PRSt	*Perspectives in Religious Studies*
RevQ	*Revue de Qumran*
SBF	Studium Biblicum Franciscanum
SBFCMa	Studium Biblicum Franciscanum, Collectio major
SBFCMi	Studium Biblicum Franciscanum, Collectio minor
SBLSP	Society of Biblical Literature Seminar Papers
Seneca, LCL	Gummere, Richard M., trans. *Lucius Annaeus Seneca. Moral Epistles*. Cambridge: Harvard University Press, 1967
SFSHJ	South Florida Studies in the History of Judaism
SJLA	Studies in Judaism in Late Antiquity
SNTSMS	Society for New Testament Studies Monograph Series
STDJ	Studies on the Texts of the Desert of Judah
SUNT	Studien zur Umwelt des Neuen Testaments
SVM	Emil Schürer et al. *The History of the Jewish People in the Age of Jesus Christ (175 B.C.–A.D. 135)*. 3 vols in 4 parts. Edinburgh: T. & T. Clark, 1973–1987
TANZ	Texte und Arbeiten zum neutestamentlichen Zeitalter
TDNT	Gerhard Kittel et al. *Theological Dictionary of the New Testament*. 10 vols. Grand Rapids: Eerdmans, 1964–1976
TSAJ	Texte und Studien zum antiken Judentum
USQR	*Union Seminary Quarterly Review*

WHJP	Michael Avi-Yona, ed. *The Herodian Period*. The World History of the Jewish People: Ancient Times, 1st ser., 7. London: Allen, 1975
WUNT	Wissenschaftliche Untersuchungen zum Neuen Testament
YJS	Yale Judaica Series
ZDPV	*Zeitschrift des deutschen Palästina-Vereins*
ZNW	*Zeitschrift für die neutestamentliche Wissenschaft*

ABBREVIATIONS OF PRIMARY SOURCES

1QapGen	Genesis Apocryphon from Qumran Cave 1
1QS	Qumran Community Rule
1QSa	Qumran Rule of the Congregation
11QT	Qumran Temple Scroll
11QTa	Qumran manuscript "a" of the Temple Scroll
4QMMT	Qumran Miqṣat ma'aseh ha-Torah (or Halakhic Letter)
4QpNah	The Qumran Pesher (commentary) on Nahum
4QSama	Qumran manuscript "a" of the Book of Samuel
Abod. Zar.	Abodah Zara
Ahil.	Ahilot
Ant.	Josephus, *Antiquities*
Ant. rom.	Dionysius of Halicarnassus, *Roman Antiquities*
Apion	Josephus, *Against Apion*
'Arak.	'Arakin
Arist.	Letter of Aristeas
b.	Babylonian Talmud
B. Batra	Baba Batra
Bell. civ.	Appian, *Bella civilia*
Ber.	Beracot
B. Metzia	Baba Metzia
B. Qama	Baba Qama
Bik.	Bikkurim
Cant. R.	Canticles (or Song of Solomon) Rabbah
CD	Cairo Damascus Document
Cels.	*Against Celsus* (Origen)
Clem.	Clement
Comm. Isa.	Jerome, *Commentary on Isaiah*
Congr.	Philo, *De congressu eruditionis gratia*
Cyr.	Xenophon, *Cyropaedia*

Decl.	Quintilian, *Declamationes*
Dial.	Seneca, *Dialogues*
Dial. meretr.	Lucian, *Dialogue of the Courtesans*
De Ira	Seneca, *On Anger*
Dem. ev.	Eusebius, *Demonstratio evangelica*
Eccl. R.	Ecclesiastes Rabbah
ʿEd.	Eduyyot
ʿErub.	Erubin
Ep.	Horace, *Epistles*
Exod. R.	Exodus Rabbah
Flacc.	Philo, *In Flaccum*
Gen. R.	Genesis Rabbah
Gitt.	Gittin
Gos. Ebion.	Gospel of the Ebionites
Gos. Mary	Gospel of Mary
Gos. Phil.	Gospel of Philip
Gos. Thom.	Gospel of Thomas
Hist. rom.	Dio Cassius, *Historiae romanae*
Haeres.	Epiphanius, *Haereseis*
Ḥag.	Ḥagigah
Ḥall.	Ḥallah
H.E.	Eusebius, *Ecclesiastical History*
Herm. *Vis.*	Shepherd of Hermas, *Vision*
Ḥev.	Text from Naḥal Ḥever
Ḥull.	Ḥullin
Hypoth.	Philo, *Hypothetica*
j.	Jerusalem (or Palestinian) Talmud
Jdt.	Judith
Jos. Asen.	Joseph and Asenath
Jub.	Book of Jubilees
Kel.	Kelim
Keri.	Keritot
Ket.	Ketubbot
Kil.	Kilayim
L.A.E.	*Life of Adam and Eve*
Lam. R.	Lamentations Rabbah
Legat.	Philo, *Embassy to Gaius*
Lev. R.	Leviticus Rabbah
Liv. Pro.	The Lives of the Prophets
Luct.	Lucian, *On Funerals*
LXX	The Greek translation of the Old Testament

m.	Mishnah
Ma'as.	Ma'aserot
Ma'as. S.	Ma'aser Sheni
Macc.	Book of Maccabees
Maksh.	Makshirin
Meg.	Megillah
Metam.	Apuleius, *Metamorphoses*
Mid.	Middot
Mikv.	Mikva'ot
Mil. glor.	Plautus, *Miles gloriosus*
Mo'ed Qat.	Mo'ed Qatan
Mur	text from Wadi Muraba'at
Ned.	Nedarim
N.H.	Pliny, *Natural History*
Nidd.	Niddah
Ohol.	Oholot
Pan.	Epiphanius, *Panarion*
Parah	Parah
Pausanias, *Descr.*	Pausanias, *Graeciae descriptio*
Pes.	Pesaḥim
Pesiq. Rab.	Pesiqta Rabbati
Pliny, *N.H.*	Pliny, *Natural History*
POxy.	Papyrus Oxyrhynchus
Prot. Jac.	Protevangelium of James
Ps.-Mantheo	Pseudo-Mantheo, *Apotelesmatica*
Ps. Philo	Pseudo Philo (also called *Liber Antiquitatum Biblicarum*)
Ps.-Phoc.	Pseudo-Phocylides
Qidd.	Qiddushin
Rosh H.	Rosh Ha-Shanah
Sanh.	Sanhedrin
Se	Text from Naḥal Ṣe'alim
Sem.	Semaḥot
Shabb.	Shabbat
Sheb.	Shebi'it
Sib. Or.	Sibylline Oracles
Soṭah	Soṭah
Spec. Leg.	Philo, *De Specialibis Legibus*
Sheq.	Sheqalim
Sir	The Wisdom of Jesus ben Sira
Strabo	Strabo, *Geography*

Sukk.	Sukkah
Sus	Book of Susanna
Syr. Men.	Sentences of the Syriac Menander
t.	Tosephta
Ta'an.	Ta'anit
Tacitus, *Ann.*	Tacitus, *Annales*
Ter.	Terumot
Test. Iss.	Testament of Issachar
Test. Jud.	Testament of Judah
Tohor.	Tohorot
Trypho	Justin Martyr, *Dialogue with Trypho*
T. Yom	Tevul Yom
Virt.	Philo, *De virtutibus*
Vit. Const.	Eusebius, *Life of Constantine*
War	Josephus, *Jewish War*
Yad.	Yadayim
Yebam.	Yebamot
Yoma	Yoma (= Kippurim in Tosephta)

ABBREVIATIONS OF SCRIPTURAL BOOKS

1 Chr	1 Chronicles
1 Cor	1 Corinthians
1 Sam	1 Samuel
2 Sam	2 Samuel
Deut	Deuteronomy
Eccl	Ecclesiastes
Ezek	Ezekiel
Exod	Exodus
Gen	Genesis
Hab	Habakkuk
Heb	Epistle to the Hebrews
Isa	Isaiah
Jas	Epistle of James
Jer	Jeremiah
Judg	Judges
Kgs	Kings
Lam	Lamentations
Lev	Leviticus
Mal	Malachi

Matt	Matthew
Neh	Nehemiah
Num	Numbers
Prov	Proverbs
Ps	Psalm
Rev	Revelation
Rom	Romans
Sam	Samuel

Introduction

REALIA ARE "OBJECTS OR activities used to relate classroom teaching to the real life especially of peoples studied."[1] The word means the actual finds—some object you can hold in your hand, touch, or see—as opposed to literary sources, socioeconomic models, hypotheses, or theories. Of course, sometimes the finds *are* new literary sources, whether inscriptions (on coins or stone) or documents (on animal skins or papyrus). The material remains emerge from the soil—ranging from entire cities to microscopic items—with data we can use in understanding the people and events of our period of study. Understandably, those interpreting the remains always have an agenda. Therefore, in our appeal to the *realia* to shape our study in this volume, we sometimes will find that archaeologists disagree on what the remains mean.

Such disagreement is especially expected when dealing with the historical Jesus. We want to carefully distinguish between the "real Jesus," a loaded and controversial term,[2] and our title "the *realia* Jesus." The two are by no means the same. What the title of this volume implies is an assessment of objects that illustrate and clarify history. This endeavor hopes to bring more understanding—through archaeology—to the environment in which Jesus was born, grew up, ministered, and died. But no monograph ever captures a "real" person.

Archaeology, simply put, is "the scientific study of material remains of past human life and activities."[3] Or, one could say that archaeology is

---

1. Merriam-Webster.com/, s.v. "relia," https://www.merriam-webster.com/dictionary/realia/.

2. See e.g., Johnson, *Real Jesus* for a survey; and Levy (prod./dir.) et al., *Smithsonian: The Real Jesus of Nazareth*, a television series (https://www.smithsonianchannel.com/shows/the-real-jesus-of-nazareth/).

3. Dever, "Archaeology," 44. This definition is very similar to Hoppe, *Biblical Archaeology*, 3; and the official definition in a glossary on the Archaeological Institute of America's website: "The scientific excavation and study of ancient human material

a "way of making inferences about 'how it was in the past' by examining material culture remains . . . [it is an] ethnography of the dead."[4] Archaeologists study "bits and pieces of other peoples' garbage";[5] they "[deal] with the wreckage of antiquity."[6] Archaeology focuses on what is left over after wars, natural disasters, and time have had their effects. Obviously, only the most durable objects (stone, fired clay, metal, and bones) survive with any regularity although sometimes more perishable treasures are found—such as cloth, texts written on animal skins or papyri, or wooden objects—if the climate allows it.

We distinguish three broad categories in archaeology: (1) written remains (on clay, stone, coins, potsherds, papyrus, or vellum), (2) nonwritten remains including (a) large structures (fortifications, villages, gates, religious buildings, and domestic structures); (b) small finds (jewelry, weapons, pottery, animal bones, and glass),[7] and (3) human remains.[8] We will be dealing with all three categories of remains in this work; we are pressing for a "holistic approach"[9] which considers as many *realia* as possible.

These are the sources of our information which I will supplement and interpret by using appropriate primary texts as well. The question always arises, however, how one uses these remains to understand the text of the Gospel of Luke. Several have weighed in on the appropriate use of archaeology in interpreting the Bible (or any ancient text):

Uses of archaeology	1	2	3	4	5	6	7	8	9	10
Illustrate/visualize		X		X					X	
Supplement the text	X		X	X			X	X	X	
Clarify the text	X		X					X		X
Correct the text	X			X			X	X		
Confirm the text	X		X	X			X	X		X
Reconstruct the social/religious world		X			X	X		X	X	X

remains" (https://www.archaeological.org/).

4. Hoppe, *Biblical Archaeology* 54.
5. Dever, *What Did the Biblical Writers Know*, 53.
6. Wright, "What Archaeology," 76.
7. See Lance, *Old Testament*, 5; and Gibson, *Cave of John the Baptist*, 3.
8. "We argue that bones of those long dead can be 'read' for clues that will reveal how the people lived, adapted, and died" (Grauer and Armelagos, "Skeletal Biology," 109). I have added the third category due to my investigation of skeletal remains and latrine remains from the ancient world. See Fiensy, *Daily Life*.
9. On the holistic approach, see Lev-Tov, "Upon What Meat."

Uses of archaeology	1	2	3	4	5	6	7	8	9	10
Reconstruct a practice					X					
Allow us to hear voices left out of the literature									X	
Reconstruct the biblical text										X

Table illustrating Several Scholars' Articulations of
How Archaeology Informs Biblical Study:
KEY: 1= Meyers and Strange; 2 = Charlesworth; 3= Hoppe; 4 = Starbuck; 5 = J. F. Strange; 6 = Reed; 7 = Levine; 8 = Dever (2X); 9 = Moreland et al.; 10 = McRay[10]

As the reader can quickly see, there is essential agreement on the uses of archaeology in biblical interpretation, although some scholars offer a unique perspective. These historians focus on using the remains to clarify the text, to supplement the text, to confirm the text, and to correct the text. Most of the contributions to New Testament interpretation from the field of archaeology, however, are in reconstructing the political, social, economic, health, or religious world in order to place the New Testament texts in their context. This is where the present volume will focus. This book will often illustrate an object (for example, the so-called Jesus Boat or the fortress where John the Baptist was executed). Nevertheless, this volume will mostly seek to reconstruct practices such as ritual purity, living on a large estate, and crucifixion. It will also endeavor to reconstruct the religious, social, economic, and pathological world as they influenced—and today help us understand—the history of the Jesus-movement.

New Testament scholars are steadily (and slowly) realizing that we must consult not just the texts but also the artifacts. This is the point made by Felicity Harley in a recent review essay on crucifixion:

> We can no longer study religion as an exclusively textual phenomenon, but must be able to use images and objects, as well as archaeological evidence, to effect fuller historical reconstructions of ancient practice and thought . . . [We need] a systematic analysis of the visual evidence from late antiquity.[11]

---

10. Table is based on Meyers and Strange, eds., *Archaeology, the Rabbis, & Early Christianity*, 28–29; Charlesworth, "Archaeology, Jesus and Christian Faith?" 8–9; Meyers and Meyers, "Holy Land Archaeology"; Hoppe, *Biblical Archaeology*, 4–8; Starbuck, "Why Declare"; Strange, "Sayings of Jesus," 296–97; Reed, *Archaeology*, 18; McRay, *Archaeology*, 17–19; Levine, "Archaeological Discoveries," 76; Dever, *Recent Archaeological Discoveries*, 32–35; Dever, *What Did the Biblical Writers Know*, 83, 271; Moreland et al., "Introduction," 1–2.

11. Harley, "Crucifixion," 323.

What follows in the subsequent chapters will be "visual evidence." Either by photograph, by drawing, or by mere verbal description, we hope to bring forth those archaeological remains that enhance our understanding of the life and ministry of Jesus as presented to us in the Gospel of Luke.

Sidebar

Introduction

The Pilgrims and the Natives: Beginning in the fourth century, after the Constantinian takeover, Christian pilgrims started to journey to Palestine. Their descriptions of venerated sites are today valuable in assisting archaeologists and historians to piece together the interpretation of the material remains. Additionally, those Christian scholars and leaders born in Palestine, or those who immigrated to Palestine, serve as helpful informants. We will cite several of these witnesses in the remaining chapters of this volume.

Pilgrims	Date of pilgrimage	Brief description
Bordeaux Pilgrim[12]	333	He was from Gaul. His writing chronicles his journey from Gaul through Italy to Constantinople, then to Syria and down to Palestine.
Aetheria (also called Etheria and Egeria)[13]	381–86	A woman, perhaps a nun, from Spain who visited Egypt, Palestine, and Syria and made one of the earliest pilgrim accounts.
Piacenza Pilgrim[14]	6th century	From Italy. Often gives fabulous stories which historians today find incredible. Nonetheless, his reports of visiting sites are often valuable.

12. Wikipedia, s.v. "*Itinerarium Berdigalense*, https://en.wikipedia.org/wiki/Itinerarium_Burdigalense/. For a translation, see Jacobs, "Bordeaux Pilgrim."

13. Wikipedia, s.v. "Egeria (pilgrim)," https://en.wikipedia.org/wiki/Egeria_(pilgrim)/; and Cross and Livingstone, "Etheria." See McClure and Peltoe, *Pilgrimage*, for a translation.

14. Wikipedia, s.v. "Anonymous pilgrim of Piacenza." https://en.wikipedia.org/wiki/Anonymous_pilgrim_of_Piacenza/. For translation, see Wilkinson, *Jerusalem Pilgrims*, 79–89.

Pilgrims	Date of pilgrimage	Brief description
Theodosius[15]	sixth century	A German archdeacon who wrote a brief but valuable account of his trip to the Holy Land.
Arculf[16]	seventh century	A French bishop who after his journey to Palestine related his experiences to Adamnan, Irish abbot of Iona, Scotland, who wrote of them in three volumes. These volumes also have sketches of some of the Byzantine churches.
Saewulf[17]	1103	One of the first English pilgrims to Palestine following the First Crusade. Many details about the geography of Jerusalem.
Daniel[18]	1106	A Russian abbot

Native (or immigrant) informants	Dates of life span	Brief description
Justin[19]	100–165	Born in Neapolis (Shechem) in Samaria.
Origen[20]	185–254	Born in Egypt but moved to Caesarea on the Palestinian coast.

15. Wikipedia, s.v. "*De situ terrae sanctae*" (https://en.wikipedia.org/wiki/De_situ_terrae_sanctae/). For translation, see Wilkinson, *Jerusalem Pilgrims*, 63–71.

16. *Catholic Encyclopedia*, s.v. "Arculf" (https://www.newadvent.org/cathen/01699b.htm/); Wilkinson, *Jerusalem Pilgrims*, 9–10 (translation 93–116).

17. Wikipedia, s.v. "Saewulf" (https://en.wikipedia.org/wiki/S%C3%A6wulf); Sobecki, "Seawulf's Lost Arabic Map."

18. Finegan, *Archaeology*, 60.

19. Cross and Livingstone, "Justin."

20. Cross and Livingstone, "Origen."

Native (or immigrant) informants	Dates of life span	Brief description
Eusebius[21]	260–340	He became bishop of Caesarea on the Palestinian coast. Wrote the *Onomasticon*, a list of towns and cities in Palestine and their approximate locations, and *The Life of Constantine*, a panegyric on the first Christian emperor, which also describes several sites in Jerusalem.
Cyril of Jerusalem[22]	c. 315–86	He was the bishop of Jerusalem from about 349 CE. In his *Catechetical Lectures*, he described the Church of the Holy Sepulcher and other sites.
Epiphanius[23] of Salamis	315–403	He was a native of Palestine who became bishop of Salamis.
Jerome[24]	342–420	He was born in Italy but in 386 moved to Bethlehem where he lived in a cave adjoining the Church of the Nativity.
Paulinus Bishop of Nola[25]	353–431	He was from Bordeaux, France, but settled in Spain where he became bishop. He did not journey to Palestine but through correspondence with others has information on several sites.
The Madaba Map[26]	600	In the Byzantine Church of Saint George in Madaba, Jordan, is a mosaic map of Palestine. It is especially valuable for its map of Jerusalem. See Figure 13.1 (p. 225).
Epiphanius the Monk[27]	750–800	He was a Jerusalem monk who wrote a guidebook to Jerusalem.

21. Cross and Livingstone, "Eusebius."
22. Cross and Livingstone, "Cyril, St."
23. Cross and Livingstone, "Epiphanius, St."
24. Cross and Livingstone, "Jerome, St."
25. Cross and Livingstone, "Paulinus, St."
26. Wilkinson, *Jerusalem Pilgrims*, 7; Avi-Yonah, *Madaba*.
27. Wilkinson, *Jerusalem Pilgrims*, 11 (translation, 117–21).

1

The Birth Narratives

LUKE'S GOSPEL IS THE most comprehensive in terms of biography. It begins not only with the birth story of Jesus but of John as well. Luke opens his story with the annunciation of the birth of John in the village of Ein Kerem in Judea. After that announcement to Zacharias, an angel appears in Nazareth of Galilee to a teenage girl named Mary.

BETROTHAL

> And in the sixth month (of Elizabeth's pregnancy) the angel Gabriel was sent from God to a city in Galilee named Nazareth to a maiden betrothed to a man named Joseph of the house of David and the maiden's name was Mary. (Luke 1:26–27)

The text of Luke (and Matt 1:18–19) indicates that Mary is betrothed to Joseph at the time of the annunciation. How did one become betrothed and does archaeology offer any insights?

We have a rather full accounting in the Mishnah in the tractate *Ketubbot* ("marriage documents") of the process for marriage in the second century CE. In the first place, the prospective bride and groom did not choose each other; the parents chose for them. In the Mishnah (as also in Josephus[1]), the whole thing is a business transaction. The Mishnah indicates that there were three ways for a man to "acquire" a bride: by oral agreement, by written document, and by the couple entering a room together.[2]

---

1. Josephus, *Apion* 2.200.
2. m. Qidd. 1:1; m. Ket. 4:4. "Entering a room"? Literally, by sexual intercourse but

The parents negotiated a bride or groom for their child and sealed the deal before witnesses in one of those three ways.

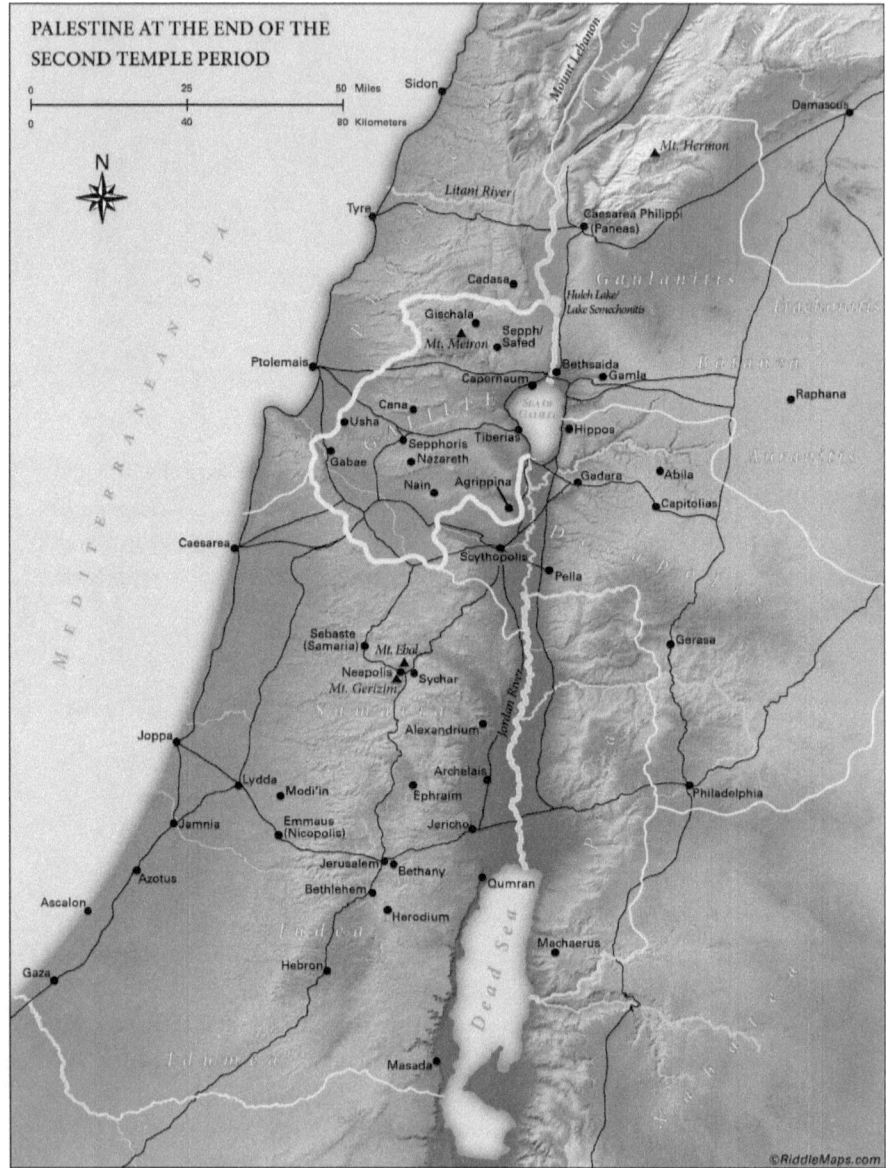

Map 1: Palestine under Herod the Great (map courtesy A. D. Riddle)[3]

---

they assumed if a couple was alone in a room, it had taken place. See Kehati, *Kiddushin*, 1–2; Kehati, *Ktubot*, 4; Mayer, *Jüdische Frau*, 60.

3. www.RiddleMaps.com.

The reader familiar with some of the Old Testament marriage practices might be surprised to find some new customs by the first century CE. A change had taken place decades before Joseph and Mary were wed. Simeon ben Shetach, great scribe and brother of Queen Salome Alexandra (reigned 76–67 BCE) had added the rule of the *ketubbah*. In this ruling—not at all hinted at in the Old Testament—the groom pledged a divorce or widow-settlement to be paid to the bride should the marriage dissolve. This settlement was called the *ketubbah* (the word can mean the document or the sum specified in the document).

Not only do we have a rabbinic tractate with rules for this process, but now we also have actual marriage contracts from near our period of time. They were discovered in caves on the west side of the Dead Sea, two from Wadi Muraba'at and one from Naḥal Ḥever (see Sidebar 2.2), and date from the early second century CE. Among these documents are three marriage contracts in the Aramaic language in which the groom promise to pay an amount of money to the bride if the marriage dissolves (one promises 400 denarii, about $24,000 by my calculation), confirming that the Mishnaic regulation was in effect.

Document[4]	Date[5]	Ketubbah Amount	
Mur 20	117 CE	Fragmentary, some denarii plus maintenance	
Mur 21	122–125 CE[6]	Maintenance	
5/6 Ḥev 10	125–128 CE	400 denarii	Naḥal Ḥever (Photograph by Benno Rothenberg)[7]

Table 1.1: Summary of the content of three Aramaic marriage documents from the Dead Sea area

4. The text abbreviations are from Tov, *Texts*.

5. For these dates, see Benoit, Milik, and DeVaux, *Grottes de Muraba'at*; Lewis, *Documents from the Bar Kokhba Period*; Yadin et al., *Documents from the Bar Kokhba Period*.

6. Benoit, Milik, and DeVaux hesitated to date this one but Cotton ("Cancelled Marriage Contract") assigns the dates as 122–25 CE.

7. Wikimedia Commons: https://commons.wikimedia.org/wiki/File:Nahal_Hever_(997009858484705171.jpg/.

When a couple entered a marriage, the groom wrote up a document—or orally agreed—and submitted the agreement to the bride's family. In the document or oral agreement, the groom promised to pay the bride, in the event the marriage dissolved, a dissolution payment. If the family approved the contract, the couple was betrothed. Since Mary and Joseph were "betrothed," Joseph must have had such a written or oral contract with Mary's parents. He, or his parents, would have pledged a sum of money (the *ketubbah*) in the event of his divorcing her later or in the event of his death. During the betrothal period, the exclusivity of the bride to the groom was the same as after the marriage had been consummated. The presumed situation we find in the Gospel of Matthew is supported by texts in both Philo and Josephus.[8] When Joseph found that Mary was pregnant, he decided initially to "divorce" her according to Matthew's Gospel (Matt 1:19). For a betrothed girl to have sex with a man other than her future husband was adultery.

AGE AT MARRIAGE

How old were they? The girls were usually married off by their parents by the time they were teenagers. The rabbinic texts advise that a young girl—*naʿarah*,[9] a "prepubescent girl"—should be betrothed at age twelve to twelve and a half and married about one year later.[10] The rabbis urged parents to marry their children close to the age of puberty.

There is also archaeological evidence of age-at-marriage for Jewish girls in the first century CE. This evidence is in the form of tomb inscriptions and other documents. A woman's tombstone would sometimes indicate how old she had been when she married. An investigation of these sources shows that most Jewish girls married between the ages of twelve and seventeen with the greatest number marrying at age thirteen. They would have been betrothed about a year earlier than the wedding. We should probably think of Mary in this age group.[11] What about the boys? Again, parents preferred to marry them young. An idealized text recommended age eighteen (m. Avot 5:21). Other rabbinic texts suggested around the time of puberty like the girls (b. Yebam. 62b). We should imagine Joseph in the same age group as Mary.

---

8. For Philo: *Spec. Leg.* 3.72. For Josephus: *Apion* 2.201.

9. Luke has used the Gk. word *parthenos* (1:27 twice), which means the same thing. She is just approaching puberty and the age in which they usually betrothed the girls.

10. m. Ket. 5:2.

11. See the evidence in Fiensy, *Archaeology of Daily Life*, 108-9.

Age when married	12 years	13 years	14 years	15 years	16 years	17 years	18 years	20 years	23 years	25 years	27 years
Number in this category	3	7	2	6	2	5	1	1	1	1	1

Table 1.2: Age at marriage for Jewish girls in Palestine and the diaspora (sample size 29)[12]

What about the suggestion by some[13] in the ancient church that Joseph was older than Mary and had children by a previous marriage? That is possible. But it need not mean Joseph was in his fifties or even older. The Gospels never give an age for Joseph. They married so young back then that Joseph in his late twenties already could have been a widower with six children (see Mark 6:3) especially in light of the brief life-spans of women.

Whom would they marry? The villages were probably endogamous. Endogamy seems to have been the norm in the Old Testament (Gen. 28:2) as it is today in the Middle East.[14] There are strong indications also that in the late Second Temple period Jewish families preferred their children to marry either a cousin or a niece/uncle.[15]

Further, archaeology offers strong hints of village endogamy. At Meiron in Upper Galilee (Map 2 p. 100), those examining the skeletal remains of the former inhabitants found an "extremely high" number of skeletal anomalies (genetically caused), indicative that those buried in the tomb were "an endogamous group."[16] Therefore, it is probable that Joseph and Mary were relatives even if we credit the medieval tradition[17] that Mary grew up in nearby Sepphoris and not in Nazareth.

---

12. See Fiensy, *Archaeology of Daily Life*, 109 for further explanation of this table. These data derive from tombstones and papyri.

13. See the second century Prot. Jac. 9.2.

14. Endogamy seems to be the preference throughout the Middle East today in rural villages. See Kramer, *Village Ethnoarchaeology*, 21; Tannous, "Arab Village Community," 539; Lutfiyya, *Baytin*, 130. In the Jordanian village Lutfiyya reports on, they preferred to marry paternal cousins. Lancaster and Lancaster ("Jordanian Village," 39) report the same. Tannous, ("Arab Village Community," 539) reports that Muslims marry first cousins while Christian Arabs prefer second or third cousins.

15. Philo, *Spec. Leg.* 2.126; Tobit 4:12–13; 7:10–11; t. Qidd. 1:4. See Mayer, *Jüdische Frau*, 54–55; and Fiensy, *Archaeology of Daily Life* 110 for details.

16. Smith et al., "Skeletal Remains," 118.

17. Wikipedia, s.v. "Sepphoris."

THE *REALIA* JESUS

EIN KEREM

> "And Mary rose up in those days and journeyed in haste to the hill country to a city of Judah and she entered the house of Zacharias and greeted Elizabeth" (1:39–40).

Next comes the visit of Mary to Elizabeth and the wonderful poem, The Magnificat (Luke 1:39–56). Luke 1:39 does not give us the name of the "city," i.e., village, where Zacharias and his wife, Elizabeth, lived. It only tells us it was a village in the hill country of Judah (1:39, 65). We are, however, not totally in the dark regarding where John's home village was.

The historian and exegete often must compare Christian "tradition" (either the witness of pilgrims to the Holy Land or that of natives; see Sidebar: Introduction) with archaeology to ascertain the location of certain events. Ancient veneration of a site along with archaeological evidence that the site was in use in the first century offers at least a plausible case for the site's authenticity. The thesis is that the local Jewish Christians often remembered the locations of events important to their faith and pointed these out to the pilgrims, who, in turn, kept diaries or itineraries of their pilgrimage.[18]

Christian tradition has celebrated the village of Ein Kerem (4.5 miles west of Jerusalem) as the village of Zacharias and Elizabeth and the birthplace of John. The tradition is both direct and indirect:

- The earliest *indirect* evidence for this being a sacred Christian site is the discovery of two fragments of a marble statue of Aphrodite. These may have been part of a pagan shrine which Hadrian erected to supplant the Christian site as he allegedly did in the place of the Jewish Temple and Jesus' tomb in Jerusalem. In the second century, Emperor Hadrian (see Sidebar 1.3), according to Jerome, wanted to remove Jewish and Christian venerated sites from Palestine and to replace them with pagan sacred sites. Again, this is indirect but early (second-century) evidence.[19] If Hadrian in the early second century CE wanted to replace a Christian site, it means that it was being visited and venerated at least in the late first century.

- The earliest *direct* Christian tradition is from the fourth century CE followed by other authors from the sixth through the twelfth centuries:[20] Serapion (fourth century), Theodosius (sixth century), Epiphanius the

---

18. This thesis has been challenged in the last thirty years, notably by Joan Taylor. This volume will interact with her argument at appropriate intervals. See below.

19. See Gibson, *Cave*, 38; and Finegan, *Archaeology*, 5.

20. See Gibson, *Cave*, 30–31; Finegan, *Archaeology*, 3–4; Hoade, *Guide*, 587–88.

Monk (eighth century), and Daniel (twelfth century). They mention the name Ein Kerem, and that John the Baptist was born there in the house of Zacharias (allegedly, the modern Church of Saint John).[21]

Sidebar 1.1

The Church of Saint John, looking west[22]

The village of Ein Kerem has not been completely excavated, but there was definitely a Second Temple period occupation. In 1941–1942 the Franciscans did an excavation of the Church of Saint John and the adjacent area. The Church of Saint John (see Sidebar 1.1) was originally built in the fifth century, destroyed, rebuilt in the Crusader period, destroyed again, and rebuilt in the seventeenth century. In the eastern end of the church is a stairway leading to a cave which is celebrated as the birthplace of John the Baptist. On the western end of the church are two small chapels which rest

---

21. Saller, *Discoveries*, 1–50.

22. Photograph at Wikimedia Commons: https://commons.wikimedia.org/wiki/File:Ein_Karem_with_the_church_of_St._John_the_Baptist_in_the_Mountains.jpg/. The photo has been cropped.

on ruins from the Herodian period (hence the time of Jesus and John). The chapels cover ancient wine presses with potsherds in them dating from the first century CE. Just south of the southern chapel was a *mikveh* (ritual bath) from the first century. Excavations of the courtyard, west of the church (Figure 1.1), also revealed a *mikveh*. Some of the tombs in the area are from the ER period containing ossuaries, a feature of Jewish burial introduced in the first century BCE and largely ended in the early second century CE (see Chapter 5). Some of the agricultural terraces have been dated to the first century BCE. Thus, the village was certainly in existence at the time John was born.[23]

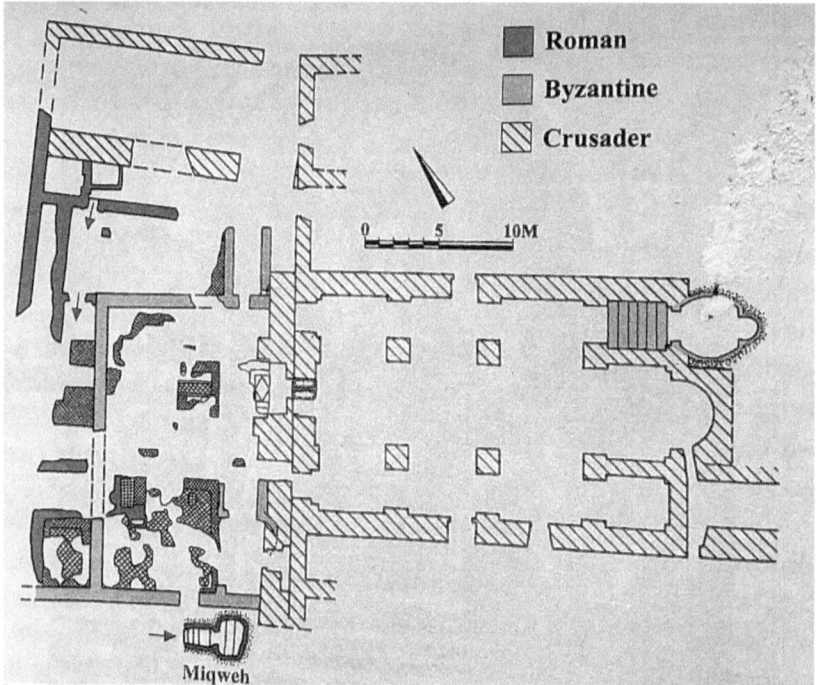

Figure 1.1: Archaeological plan of Church of Saint John. In the northeast corner of the church is the grotto celebrated as the birthplace of John. Two rooms west of the church are small chapels that sit on Herodian-period constructions. A small installation southwest of the building is a *mikveh* (ritual bath). (Figure courtesy Shimon Gibson)[24]

23. See Saller, *Discoveries*; Gibson, *Cave*, 34–42; Finegan, *Archaeology*, 4; Hoade, *Guide*, 587–90; Wikipedia, s.v. "Ein Kerem"; and Zissu and Amit, "Classification," 246–61 (247).

24. See Gibson, *Cave*, 38; Hoade, *Guide*, 589–91. For an additional installation (south of the church) as a *mikveh*, see Zissu and Amit, "Classification," 247.

The Christian traditions combined with the archaeology show that the local Jewish Christians remembered this village as the home village of John. The archaeological remains show there was a village there at least by the first century BCE and that the village was Jewish (the *mikva'ot*). Further evidence is the so-called John the Baptist cave (see Chapter 2), some one and one-half miles to the west of Ein Kerem, where John was venerated from the first century to the Byzantine era. Ein Kerem was such a small and insignificant village that one struggles to imagine people inventing it as John's home. Although this location has not been the only suggestion for John's village,[25] it has the best and oldest evidence. This identification as John's home village, therefore, is plausible. That does not necessarily mean, of course, that the grotto identified in the northeast corner of the Church of Saint John was the actual spot where John was born.

---

25. Other suggestions have been two different locations on the Mount of Olives in Jerusalem—in the village of Hebron, and in a village called Yatta. See Finegan, *Archaeology*, 5; and Hoade, *Guide*, 587. Murphy-O'Connor seems to have been skeptical that Ein Kerem was the home village of John. See Murphy-O'Connor, *Holy Land*, 169.

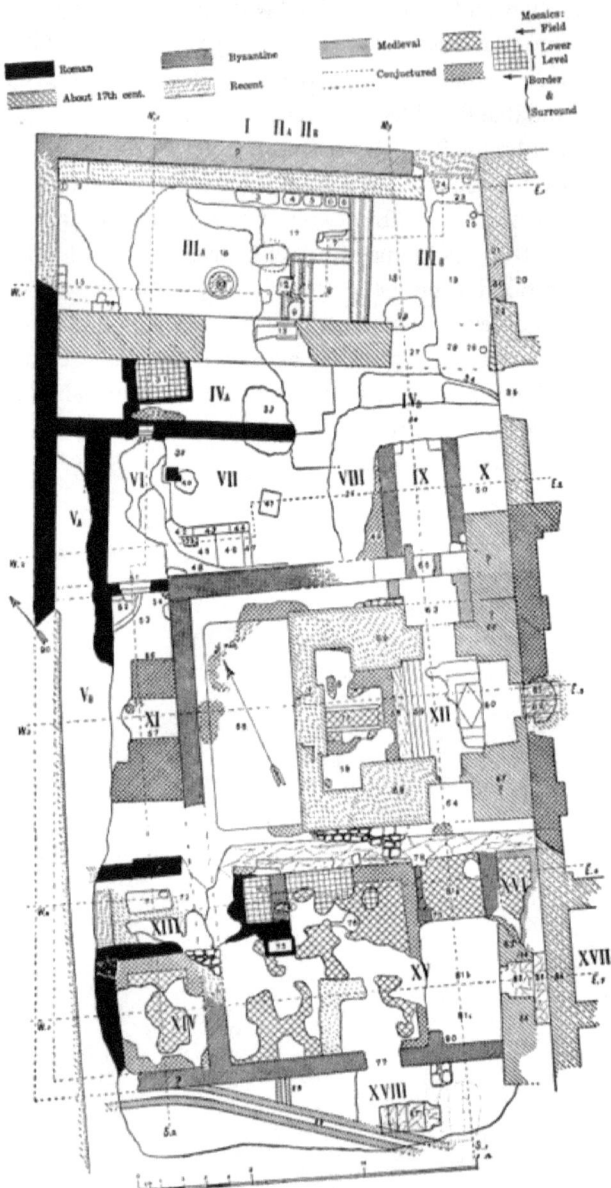

Figure 1.2: Plan of excavations west of the Church of Saint John. Number 87 (at bottom) was a plastered chamber with ER ceramics. Number 16 at the top of the figure is a terrace dating to the first century BCE. Number 41, in the middle of the plan, was a pit holding two fragments of a statue of Aphrodite.(Figure courtesy Studium Biblicum Franciscanum, Jerusalem)[26]

26. Plan in Saller, *Discoveries at St. John's*, foldout.

Sidebar 1.2

Herod the Great

Herod reigned over a kingdom composed of Idumea, Judea, Samaria, Galilee, Perea, and Gaulanitis from 37 to 4 BCE. He is the Herod of Luke 1:5 and Matt 2:3, 16. A great builder of cities and monuments (including the Temple in Jerusalem), he was also a cruel and brutal tyrant. The Jewish historian Josephus (see Sidebar 2.4), wrote in detail about his reign. In addition, we have archaeological references to his name in the form of the bronze coins he minted (below) and in inscribed jar handles found at Masada.[27]

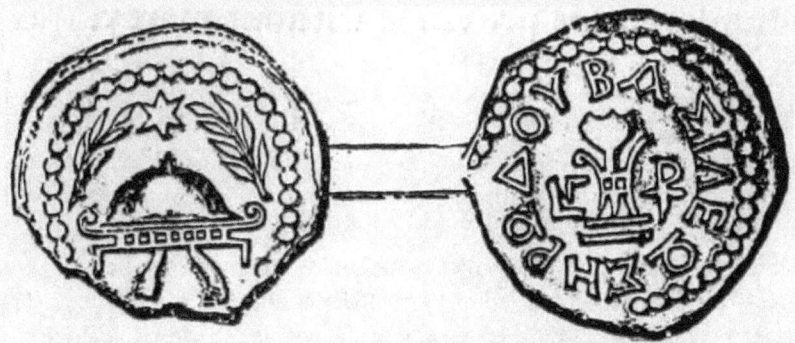

COIN OF HEROD THE GREAT.

Sketch of a coin of Herod the Great: On the left (obverse) a tripod with ceremonial bowl and helmet topped by palm branches and a star. On the right (reverse) inscription: "of Herod the King," with symbols indicating the coin was struck in "the year three" and other symbols showing the coin's value. Herod's image never appears on his coins. (Sketch by James Dabney McCabe[28])

---

27. The jars held *garum*, a fish sauce the Romans valued. On some of the handles is inscribed in Lat.: "of king Herod of Judea." See Cotton et al., "Fish Sauces"; and Netzer and Stiebel, "Masada."

28. Available on Wikimedia Commons: https://commons.wikimedia.org/wiki/File:Coin_of_Herod_the_great.jpg/.

BETHLEHEM

> And Joseph went up from the city of Nazareth into Judea to the city of David called Bethlehem because he was from the house and family of David (Luke 2:3-4).

Luke, Matthew (2:1, 6, 8), and, possibly, John (7:42[29]) affirm that Jesus was born in Bethlehem of Judea even though Joseph and Mary lived in Nazareth (Luke 1:26). Although some argue that Jesus was born in Nazareth because he was called Jesus of Nazareth,[30] Christian tradition from the second century on insists his birth took place in Bethlehem of Judea.[31]

Whatever one wants to conclude about Luke's narrated taxation of the entire world under Augustus (Luke 2:1),[32] that a Galilean like Joseph would be "from the house and family of David" is not surprising. That a family living in Galilee might have—indeed probably would have—kinship ties with a village in Judea can now be confirmed by archaeology.

There are today three hypotheses as to the origin of the inhabitants of Galilee. Some suggest that they were the remnants of the old Israelites, that is, those left over after the deportations into Assyria in the eighth century BCE.[33] Others offer that these folk were converted Iturians, that is, Gentiles, who became Jews when Aristobulus (reigned 104-103 BCE) or Alexander Jannaeus (reigned 103-76 BCE) conquered the territory (first century BCE).[34] Finally, others posit that the people were Jewish colonists—immigrants from Judea—who settled in Galilee after Alexander Jannaeus annexed the territory for Judea. Which view does archaeology support?

Jonathan Reed has presented the data, pulled from archaeological surveys of Galilee, in support of the third view. In a survey, a team visits a site, randomly collects ceramics (potsherds) from the surface (no excavating), and then records the dates of the finds.[35] Reed points out, first, that there was an absence of any Galilean settlements for over a century after

---

29. In its enigmatic and ironic way. See Brown, *John* 2:330.

30. See, e.g., Spong, *Jesus*, 16; Mason, "Little Town"; Theissen and Merz, *Historical Jesus*, 164. Others surmise that the association of Jesus' birth with a cave originated from pagan myths of the birth of gods. See the discussion in Taylor, *Christians and the Holy Places*, 112; Bacci, *Mystic Cave*, 30.

31. See, e.g., Murphy-O'Connor, "Bethlehem."

32. See SVM 1:399-427 on the historical problems of the census of Quirinius mentioned in Luke 2:1.

33. Alt, *Kleine Schriften*, 2:363-435; Horsley, "Archaeology and the Villages of Upper Galilee."

34. SVM 1:142, 217.

35. See Herr and Christopherson, *Excavation Manual*, 51.

the Assyrian conquest in the eighth century BCE (thus hypothesis 1 seems improbable). Second, the rule of Alexander Jannaeus coincides with an increase of population. This looks to Reed like Jewish immigration, not forced conversion of Gentiles. Reed suggests that the Galilean Jews originated as colonists from Judea. This view seems to be the consensus today.[36] Thus, it is plausible that Joseph—as the son or grandson of Judean immigrants—had kinship ties with the village of Bethlehem in Judea, and therefore—whether one wishes to credit the reference to a census/tax or not—finding Joseph and his family visiting there is not a surprise.

Bethlehem was famous in the Old Testament as the home village of King David (Ruth 4:11; 1 Sam 16:1–13) and was celebrated in prophecy by Micah (5:2). After the Babylonian exile, 123 persons from Bethlehem returned to Judea (Ezra 2:21, cf. Neh 7:26), presumably, to the original village. It was an Israelite village, then, with a long history.

The spot revered as the birthplace of Jesus has some ancient support. In Bethlehem, according to Jerome, Hadrian (reigned 117–38) consecrated a grove to Adonis (Tammuz), just above the cave revered as Jesus' birthplace. He was, according to Jerome, attempting to replace Christian sacred places with pagan content. Jerome (395 CE) wrote a letter to Paulinus of Nola, noting that Hadrian, two hundred sixty years before his time, had placed a statue of Jupiter over the tomb of Jesus and one of Venus on the hill where the cross had stood. He went further to mention a similar replacement shrine in Bethlehem:

> [Hadrian] supposed that by polluting our holy places [he] would deprive us of our faith in the passion and in the resurrection . . . Even my own Bethlehem, as it now is, that most venerable spot in the whole world . . . was overshadowed by a grove of Tammuz . . . and in the very cave where the infant Christ had uttered his earliest cry lamentation was made for the paramour of Venus.[37]

Likewise, Paulinus of Nola (353–431 CE) wrote:

> For the emperor Hadrian, in the belief that he could destroy the Christian faith by the dishonoring of a place, dedicated a statue of Jupiter on the place of the passion, and Bethlehem was profaned by a grove of Adonis.[38]

---

36. Reed, "Galileans." See also Meyers et al., "Meiron Excavation Project"; Aviam, "Galilee"; Freyne, "Archaeology and the Historical Jesus," 133–34; Root, *First Century Galilee*, 99, 112–13, 148–50 (who also gives New Testament evidence); and Jensen, "Political History," 52–57.

37. Translation in Finegan, *Archaeology* 35–36 of Jerome, *Letter 58 to Paulinus*.

38. Translation in Finegan, *Archaeology*, 36 of Paulinus of Nola, *Epistle* 31.

Sidebar 1.3

Constantine's Church of the Nativity (Bethlehem)

The altar (number 1) stands over the cave of the nativity. The underground caverns are shown in dotted lines.[39]

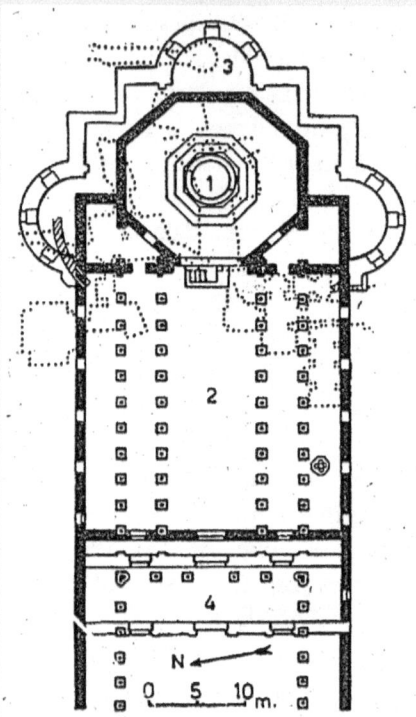

(Image courtesy Studium Biblicum Franciscanum, Jerusalem)

Thus, fourth century authors maintained that Hadrian embarked on a somewhat thorough replacement of Christian venerated localities. *If* that was true, one could conclude from these quotations that the Christian community must have been venerating this site at least by the end of the first century CE. Indeed, Bacci asserts, based on a statement by Origen in the third century (see below), that the grotto was a Christian cult site frequented and revered by Christians and non-Christians alike.[40] That the cave had become a cult center witnesses to the possibility that the memory of the

---

39. Plan from Hoade, *Guide*, 363.
40. Bacci, *Mystic Cave*, 32.

location of Jesus' birth "may have been almost uninterruptedly cultivated by local Jewish-Christian groups."[41]

Later, Emperor Constantine (reigned 306–37 CE) destroyed the pagan shrine and built his Church of the Nativity[42] as a replacement of the replacement. Around two hundred years after that, Emperor Justinian (reigned 527–65 CE) dismantled Constantine's church and built his own, larger building, essentially the church we see today.[43]

In addition to the *indirect* evidence of Hadrian's attempt to stifle Christian reverence for this spot, there is possible *direct* testimony of their belief that Jesus was born here. Christian authors from the second century onward insisted that Jesus was born in a cave:[44]

- Justin, who was born in the late first or early second century CE in Neapolis (in Samaria), knew that Christians venerated this site: "When Jesus was born in Bethlehem . . . [Joseph] took up his quarters in a certain cave near the village . . ." (Justin Martyr, *Trypho* 78; 140 CE)[45]

- Origen, who frequented Palestine after 215 CE seems to have visited the cave: "If anyone wishes to have further proof to be convinced that Jesus was born in Bethlehem besides the prophecy of Micah and the story recorded in the Gospels by Jesus' disciples, it can be remarked that, in accordance with the story in the Gospel about his birth, a cave is shown in Bethlehem where he was born and the manger in the cave where he was wrapped in swaddling clothes. What is demonstrated there, namely that the Jesus who is worshipped and admired by Christians was born right in that cave, is well known in those parts even among people alien to the faith." (Origen, *Cels.* 1.51; 220 CE)[46]

- Around one hundred years after Origen's statement, Eusebius wrote: "It is agreed by all that Jesus Christ was born in Bethlehem as even a

---

41. Bacci, *Mystic Cave*, 30.

42. One of four churches built in Palestine by Constantine, the others being the Church of the Holy Sepulcher in Jerusalem, the Eleona Church on the Mount of Olives, and a church in Hebron (see Chapters 12 and 15).

43. See Avi-Yonah, "Bethlehem"; Bacci, *Mystic Cave*, 39–55, 59–109.

44. See, in addition to these two quotes, the second-century Prot. Jac., which refers repeatedly to the cave of Jesus' birth: 18:1, 19:1, 2, 3, 20:4, 21:3; Eusebius, *Vit. Const.* 3.43 (fourth century); Jerome, *Epistle* 58 (fourth century; quoted above); the Piacenza Pilgrim (sixth century); and the account of Arculf (seventh century).

45. Translation by Alexander Roberts and James Donaldson in *ANF* 1:237.

46. Translation in Bacci, *Mystic Cave*, 30–31.

cave is shown by the local inhabitants there to those who come from elsewhere for a look."[47]

Thus, the argument is that there is a chain of evidence that Christians at least from the late first century CE venerated this cave as the place of Jesus' birth. There are several caves under the church, in two of which Jerome (342–420 CE) and two women were later buried.[48] But the main cave (Figure 1.3), along with a highly decorated manger, is the spot celebrated as the birthplace of Jesus.

That a cave near or under a house might be used as an animal stable (Luke 2:7) was not unusual. Murphy-O'Connor[49] observed that there are many houses in Bethlehem even today built above caves, and it was common in the nineteenth century (in premodern times) in this region to house small animals in caves under the house.[50] In ancient Palestine/Israel, houses often had subterranean stables. If there was an excavated area under the floor of the house, it was usually for the livestock.[51] We know from excavations (see, e.g., Figure 1.4, below) that the ancients utilized all available space, including the space under the floor of their house to give shelter to their livestock.

Thus, there is ancient Christian testimony that they venerated a cave as the place of Jesus' nativity, and it is a well-known fact from archaeological sites and from Middle Eastern custom that residents often had subterranean stables for small animals. The testimony and the customs fit together to offer at least weak support for this site as the actual place of Jesus' birth.

This way of reasoning, based on the ancient testimony of the church fathers, is commonly presented regarding Bethlehem as the location of Jesus' birth. But other voices have joined the discussion with different conclusions. Joan Taylor, for example, gives no credence to Justin's witness that the church celebrated Jesus' birth in a cave. She opines that Justin was merely guessing that Jesus was born in a cave since most houses had underground stables for small animals. It is doubtful that Justin ever visited Bethlehem, she argues, although he grew up in Samaria, not far away. Further, the testimony of Origen shows only that a cave sacred to Tammuz-Adonis came to be identified by local Christians as Jesus' nativity cave. If Origen visited the cave of the nativity, he would have viewed a site under the shrine of Tammuz-Adonis.

---

47. Quotation in Taylor, *Christians and the Holy Places*, 106.

48. See Murphy-O'Connor, *Holy Land*, 233 for a plan of the caves. He shows eight caves.

49. Murphy-O'Connor, *Holy Land*, 230.

50. Taylor, *Christians and the Holy Places*, 100.

51. See Bacci, *Mystic Cave*, 29, who refers to stables in caves in the region.

Taylor concludes there is no evidence that Jewish Christians venerated this cave before Hadrian's time, and when they did begin to frequent it, it was because it was already sacred to the pagan devotees of Tammuz-Adonis.[52]

Figure 1.3: Grotto under the Church of the Nativity, Bethlehem

Taylor's argument certainly bears consideration. The testimony about the cave is sparse and can be questioned. But there is no valid reason to conclude that Justin merely assumed Jesus was born in a cave. Just as reasonable is that he had heard this while living in Palestine. Further, Origen writes that many people venerated the nativity cave in his day, both Christians and non-Christians. Origen makes no mention of a shrine to Tammuz-Adonis, which could mean Christians visited one cave and devotees of Tammuz-Adonis a different one. At any rate, one can just as easily reason that pagans joined the Jewish Christians in venerating Jesus' birth-cave as that Jewish Christians followed pagans in venerating the Tammuz-Adonis cave (as the nativity cave).

52. Taylor, *Christians and the Holy Places*, 112.

Figure 1.4: Underground stable for small animals.
Nazareth, Church of the Annunciation

Most of the archaeological investigation in Bethlehem has focused on the Church of the Nativity. No extensive archaeological excavations have been made of the village itself. Archaeological surveys, however, have shown that the village was occupied as early as the Bronze Age.[53]

Some examination of archaeological remains under the Justinian church was done in 1934 by William Harvey.[54] He was able, he believed, to locate the Constantinian ruins about 2½ feet below the present floor. There he identified mosaics as those from the fourth-century church. Thus, the archaeology supports only the literary testimony that there was a Constantinian church built over a cave revered as the birthplace of Jesus. No archaeological remains confirm that a first-century house and stable lie under the church.

---

53. Avi-Yonah, "Bethlehem"; Bacci, *Mystic Cave*, 33–34.
54. See Finegan, *Archaeology*, 37.

Figure 1.5: Left: Nave of the Church of the Nativity in Bethlehem. Right: Beneath the floor of the nave, revealing presumed Constantinian mosaic. (Photograph of the nave by Abraham; photograph of the mosaic by Britchi Mirela[55])

There is no convincing argument leading to the conclusion that Jesus was not born in Bethlehem and that he was not born in a cave. Yet, one cannot be certain as to *which* cave; identification of the exact spot is now impossible. The alleged nativity cave of Jesus, though possible, is not convincing. The cave under the church of the Nativity is as good a place as any to venerate.

AVERAGE LIFE SPANS

We read in Luke 2 that Mary had to wait (40 days) for her purification after giving birth to a male child (see Chapter 9), and then they brought him into the temple for his redemption. Every firstborn male child had to be redeemed with a sacrifice. They have brought two doves for this purpose. There in the temple they meet Simeon, who was promised in a prophetic oracle (2:26) that he would not die before he saw the Messiah. According to Luke, Simeon broke into a song when he saw Jesus. Then a "prophetess" named Anna saw him:

> And there was a prophetess, Anna, daughter of Phanouel and of the tribe of Asher. She was advanced in many days, having lived with her husband seven years from her virginity and she was a widow until 84 years. (Luke 2:36–37a).

---

55. The images are available at Wikimedia Commons—Nave: https://commons.wikimedia.org/wiki/File:Bethlehem_Church_of_the_Nativity_main_nave.jpg/; Mosaic: https://commons.wikimedia.org/wiki/File:Palestine,_Bethlehem,_Church_of_the_Nativity_or_Birthplace_of_Jesus_(mosaics).jpg/.

Anna saw Jesus, and her prophetic Spirit moved her to confess that Jesus was the long-awaited Messiah. How old was Anna? Some read the somewhat confused wording as saying she was 84 years old; others that she had been a widow for 84 years.[56] Hence, if she married at age 13, was widowed after seven years, and now has been a widow for 84 years, she would be 104. That would be very rare for this time and place but not unheard of.

That raises the question, what was the average life expectancy for a woman at this time? To answer this question—and many others in subsequent chapters—we will appeal to the field of osteoarchaeology: the study of skeletal remains. The field of physical anthropology is the study of human bones. A person skilled in this discipline can learn much about a dead person by a thorough examination of his/her remains. One can discover: how tall people were, if they suffered from chronic illnesses, how long they lived,[57] if they were well nourished, to what ethnic group they belonged, whether they died of natural causes or violently, genetic affinities, the state of bodily development, wear and tear from labor, and social conditions.[58] The bones record many things.

We can calculate age-at-death from skeletal remains analyzed from roughly the time period of Jesus and his movement. Physical anthropologists assign an age to the individuals buried or entombed and one can then add these ages. To arrive at an average life expectancy, one divides the number of individuals into the total number of years of life.[59] The results will indicate how exceptional Anna's age was.

Cohort	Sample size	Average life span
Men	190	37 years
Women	118	32 years

Table 1.3: Life expectancy in late Second Temple Israel from biological adulthood (age 20) based on the data from sixteen tombs/cemeteries[60]

56. For the former, see the New American Standard Bible translation. For the latter, see Marshall, *Luke*, 123; Branch, "Anna."

57. Grmek, *Diseases*, 383, n. 40: "The determination of age at death from these skeletal remains is based on tooth eruption, formation of long bones, cranial suture closure, metamorphosis of the public [sic] symphysis, radiographic translucency of proximal femur and humerus, dental wear, and a variety of minor indicators."

58. Smith, "Skeletal Analysis"; Eakins, "Human Osteology and Archeology"; Grmek, *Diseases*, 51; Nagar and Sonntag, "Byzantine Period Burials"; and Steckoll, "Preliminary Excavation Report."

59. See Frier, "Roman Life Expectancy," 219 for the method of computing average life expectancy. Also cf. Grmek, *Diseases*, 105.

60. The table is compiled from Arieli, "Human Remains"; Steckoll, "Preliminary

Sidebar 1.4

Emperor Hadrian[61]

Hadrian (reigned 117–38 CE) is today famous for two things: his wall in northern England and his war of extermination (132–35 CE) against the Jews in Palestine, who were led by Bar Kokhba (aka. Simon bar Kosiba). After the war, he prohibited Jews from entering Jerusalem, renamed the city Aelia Capitolina, and replaced several Jewish and Christian holy sites with pagan shrines.

Hadrian (bust in Palazzo dei Conservatori)
(Photograph by Marie-Lan Nguyen[62])

We get the average of 37 years life expectancy for any male reaching adulthood and 32 years life expectancy for females reaching adulthood in Israel in the late Second Temple period. In other words, if a man was able to

---

Excavation Report" (Qumran); Sheridan, "Skeletal Remains" (Qumran); Broshi and Eshel, "Whose Bones?" (Qumran); Smith, "Skeletal Remains" (Abba cave); Smith and Zias, "French Hill" (French Hill [LH]); Hachlili, "Goliath Family"; Hachlili and Smith, "Genealogy"; Smith et al., "Skeletal Remains" (Meiron); Zias, "Caiaphas'"; Haas, "Anthropological Observations" (Giv'at ha-Mivtar); Zias, "Armona"; Zias, "Mount Scopus"; Arieli, "Human Remains"; and Zias, "Anthropological Analysis" (Akeldama); Nathan, "Naḥal Ḥever"; Arensburg and Belfer-Cohen, "En-Gedi"; Hadas, "En-Gedi"; Kahana, "Wadi-Ḥalaf"; Tendler et al., "Typical and Atypical Burial"; and Grauer and Armelagos, "Skeletal Biology," (Tel Hesban). One is unable to use much of the osteoarchaeological data in this calculation due to (1) some publications not calculating the ages beyond the most general observation: "child, adult, etc." (e.g., Arensburg and Rak, "French Hill" [ER]; and Arensburg and Smith, "Appendix") and (2) some not giving the sex of the individual (e.g., Nagar and Torgeé, "Biological Characteristics").

61. See Sutherland and Hammond, "Hadrian."

62. Wikimedia Commons: https://commons.wikimedia.org/wiki/File:Bust_Hadrian_Musei_Capitolini_MC817.jpg/.

survive childhood and reach the age of twenty, he could expect, on average, to live seventeen more years. A woman at age twenty could expect twelve more years.

If these results seem too low, one may compare them with various calculations made by other historians of Greece, Rome, and Israel:

HISTORIAN	AGE
Angel[63] (Greece)	Males: 40.2; Females: 34.3 (Roman Period) Males: 42.6; Females: 36.6 (Hellenistic Period)
Gallant[64] (Greece)	Males: 40; Females 38
Grmek[65] (Greece)	Males: 40; Females 34
Burn[66]	Males: 38; Females 33 (Carthage) Males: 40; Females 33 (Provinces of the Danube)
Zias[67]	Males: 34 years (Qumran)
Nagar and Torgeé[68]	All: 38 years (8 Judean/Samaritan tombs)
Mayer[69]	Females: 41.25 years (Palestine and Diaspora)

Table 1.4: Life expectancy—various findings

The calculations above in Table 1.3, then, are a bit lower than most of those in Table 1.4 but still within their range. From these data, one can immediately realize how exceptionally old Anna would have seemed. The table also allows making the following observations.

There was a significant gender gap in life expectancy for those reaching early adulthood. Wells affirmed that on average one could demonstrate a gap using both osteological and epigraphic evidence of five years life expectancy;[70] Table 1.3 agrees.

Why the disparity in life expectancy by sex? Most point to the dangers of childbirth in this nonmedical age.[71] Demand maintains that childbirth before the modern age was perilous. The main causes of death in mothers

---

63. Angel, "Ecology," 94.
64. Gallant, *Risk*, 20.
65. Grmek, *Diseases*, 104.
66. Burn, "Hic breve vivitur," 16.
67. Zias, "Cemeteries of Qumran."
68. Nagar and Torgeé, "Biological Characteristics."
69. Mayer, *Jüdische Frau*, 95–96.
70. Wells, "Ancient Obstetric," 1235.
71. Russell, *Late Ancient*, 35; Gallant, *Risk*, 20; Eakins, "Human Osteology," 95.

before giving birth, during delivery, and, also, in the days after giving birth were puerperal fever, toxemia, hemorrhage, and malaria.[72]

There is archaeological evidence of the dangers to mothers in childbirth. J. Naveh describes the ossuary (see Table 5.4) of a young woman, found just north of Jerusalem and dating to the first century CE, which states, in an inscription on one end, that she failed to give birth. Inside the ossuary were the bones of a woman with a fetus still in the birth canal. Her pelvis was curved and she was, therefore, unable to deliver. Had she a midwife, Naveh opines, she would not have died.[73] Tal Ilan cites in addition five inscriptions that seem to indicate that mother and baby often both died in childbirth.[74] The archaeological data seem to help explain the gap in longevity between men and women.[75]

THE FEW ELDERLY

All of this is not, of course, to say that all died in their thirties or forties. There is further archaeological evidence as to the age-at-death of some women in antiquity. Günter Mayer has included a study of tombstones in his work on Jewish women. He lists 130 individuals in his study. Of these, fifty-one (39 percent) died before age nineteen. Fourteen (11 percent) lived past age sixty. Four were in their seventies when they died and six were in their eighties. The oldest was ninety-six.[76] Thus, though they were rare, there were elderly women like Anna in the ancient world.

---

72. Demand, *Birth*, 76–86. S. R. Llewelyn gives the text of a letter (second century CE) from a husband to his wife who states how happy he is that is wife escaped the dangers of childbirth. See *Review of Greek Inscriptions*, 57.

73. Naveh, "Ossuary Inscriptions." For the osteological information, see Haas, "Anthropological Observations."

74. Ilan, *Jewish Women*, 118. These inscriptions may indicate—it is not always clear to me that they do—that the mother and baby died in childbirth.

75. Given the dangers of childbirth, it is no wonder that the midwife was an honorable and valued profession. See m. Shabb. 18:3; m. Rosh H. 2:5; Horsley, *New Documents*, 23.

76. Mayer, *Jüdische Frau*, 93–97. Mayer gleaned his data entirely from *CIJ*.

2

John the Baptist

ZACHARIAS AND ELIZABETH, John's parents, were an elderly and godly couple that lived in the hill country of Judea (Luke 1:39) in a village only a few miles west of Jerusalem. Zacharias was a priest; thus, we might expect John to have been raised to fulfill his priestly obligations as well. Instead, we find a singular character out in the desert preaching a strange message to passersby. Luke had anticipated this surprising story by ending his birth narratives with puzzling words.

JOHN'S YOUTH

> The boy grew and became strong in the Spirit and was in the lonely places[1] until the day that he was presented to Israel. (Luke 1:80)

The word that intrigues readers is the word *erēmoi* "deserts" (i.e., lonely places or deserted places). What was the boy doing in the desert(s), i.e., "lonely places"? How could a mere boy live there? Then, when John reappears on the narrative scene, he is once again in the desert:

---

1. Gk.: *erēmois*, "lonely places" (Danker, *Lexicon*). Luke sometimes uses the plural in such a way: 5:16, 8:29. This is, according to Marshall, *Luke*, 95, from the influence of the Septuagint version of the Old Testament. The term *erēmos* can mean simply uninhabited areas or can refer specifically to the region around the Dead Sea (Danker, *Lexicon*). The Heb. *midbar* similarly can refer generally to uncultivated areas (the steppe) or to a specific region in Israel (west of the Dead Sea or the Negev, south of Judea). See Holladay, *Lexicon*.

The word of the God came to John, son of Zacharias, in the desert[2] (Luke 3:2b).

Following the list of important men (Luke 3:1), Luke introduces John the Baptist. Luke writes that John went all over the region of the Jordan preaching "a baptism of repentance for the remission of sins" (3:3) then quotes Isa 40:3–5 (Luke 3:4–6). Like the reference in Luke 1:80, this reference to the desert (3:2b) catches our eye immediately. John both grew up in the desert—or "lonely places"—and conducted his ministry there. Why there? Thus far, scholars—those who deign to comment on it—offer two hypotheses for John's affinity for the "desert" even as a boy: the Essene connection at Qumran and the newer suggestion of the John the Baptist cave one mile west of Ein Kerem.

The Essene Association

The discovery of the Qumran scrolls sparked much reflection on previously puzzling scripture texts. One of those was Luke 1:80. What was the boy John doing out in the desert? Several scholars[3] suggested, soon after the discovery of the Dead Sea Scrolls, that John had lived at Qumran with the Essenes (or with a sect like the Essenes) until he began his ministry. Others followed their hypothesis in subsequent years.[4] The hypothesis has not been without its critics, however.[5] Why would anyone surmise that John the Baptist had ever had anything to do with the Qumran covenanters?

---

2. The word *erēmos* is here singular, unlike in Luke 1:80.

3. Brownlee, "John the Baptist"; Robinson, "Baptism of John"; Geyser, "Youth of John the Baptist."

4. Betz, "Was John the Baptist an Essene?"; VanderKam, *Dead Sea Scrolls Today*, 170. Fitzmyer, *Luke*, 1:389; and Fitzmyer, *Dead Sea Scrolls*, 19 thought it "plausible" that John had been associated at one time with the Qumran community. Although Meier (*Marginal Jew*, 2:27) thought it "not impossible that John was 'educated' at Qumran," he inclined against the view. Marcus, *John the Baptist*, 45 concludes: "It is likely that the period prior to the Baptist's public ministry was shaped by his membership in the Qumran community."

5. Pryke, "John the Baptist"; Klawans, *Impurity*, 141; Bock, *Luke*, 1:198; Marshall, *Luke*, 96. Hutchison, "John the Baptist" 187 writes: "[T]he evidence supports little or no historical connection between the two." Taylor, *Immerser*, 22–48, 77–88: There is no reason to suggest the Essenes influenced John though "we cannot conclusively say they could not have done so" (88). Steggeman, *Library of Qumran*, 225 concluded: "John the Baptist was neither an Essene nor a spiritual pupil of the Essenes. Were he ever to have made the effort to walk over to Qumran, as a non-Essene he would have been denied entry, and at best provided with enough food and drink for the long walk back."

Jamal-Dominique Hopkins offers a list of comparisons between John the Baptist and the Qumran Essenes that explain why some have drawn the above conclusion. Both John the Baptist and the Qumran Essenes, he writes:

1. practiced a type of ritual immersion (1QS 3:4–5; 5:7–15; Matt 3:5; Mark 1:4–5; Luke 3:7; John 1:25),

2. interpreted Isaiah 40:3 as self-fulfillment (1QS 8:12–16; 9:19–20; Matt 3:1–3; Mark 1:2–4; Luke 3:2–6; John 1:23),

3. stressed the expectation of eschatological judgment and of an eschatological divine figure,

4. were situated in the same geographical (Judean wilderness) area,

5. demonstrated a type of ascetic nature,

6. displayed a critical attitude toward the temple establishment in Jerusalem,

7. had a conscious awareness of the Holy Spirit, and

8. had priestly backgrounds.[6]

Let us explore a few of the above comparisons: numbers 1, 2, 4, and 8. First, both John and the Qumran community emphasized ritual immersion. John demanded it at the Jordan River, and the Qumran community offered ten large *mikvaʾot* for this purpose.[7] Even Taylor, who is disinclined to find a connection between John and Qumran, notes "there is one curious similarity that deserves attention," namely the association of ritual immersion, accompanied by repentance, with atonement. Both John and the Qumran scrolls connected initial (or initiatory) immersion with repentance, with the remission of sins (Mark 1:4, Luke 3:3; *Ant.* 18.116–17; 1QS 3:4–12).[8]

---

6. Hopkins, "Essene Filled with the Holy Spirit?" Cf. the lists of similarities in Meier, *Marginal Jew*, 2:25; and Taylor, *Immerser*, 22. Marcus opines on the expression "brood of vipers" as possibly having a Qumran connection (*John the Baptist*, 31–32). Some also point to a similarity in diet between the Qumran people and John, namely, eating locusts (CD 12:14–15 and Mark 1:6). But the similarity may only be coincidental. See Kelhoffer, "Did John the Baptist Eat Like a Former Essene?"

7. Galor ("Qumran's Plastered Pools") informs that there are twenty-six plastered installations at Qumran, all of which could have been used for ritual purification: "the dividing line between pools that were used for ritual immersion and those that were used for water storage was not as clear as previously assumed and may sometimes not be applicable."

8. Taylor, *Immerser*, 77–88 (quote on page 77). See also Marcus, *John the Baptist*, 28. Taylor's insight disagrees with Rousseau and Arav, *Jesus and His World*, 80. They maintain that, for John, baptism was a one-time event as part of the conversion process; for the Qumran/Essene people, as a twice daily ritual purification before meals, according

Second, Qumran is only a few miles from the Jericho area where John later stationed himself to preach and baptize (Luke 3:2–3). John plausibly baptized in the region of Bethabara (3.6 miles east of Jericho, on the east bank of the river) at the fords of the Jordan River.[9] Some manuscripts of John 1:28 read "Bethabara" (instead of Bethany),[10] and several church fathers and pilgrims insisted that Bethabara was the baptismal location.[11] At any rate, the fords of the Jordan would have been a logical place for John to station himself. Qumran is in the Judean wilderness where Luke says John spent his childhood. Therefore, John must have often been near Qumran. How could he not have known about it? One might even ask how he could possibly have avoided encounters with the Qumran residents and how he could have eschewed interacting with them.

Third, John preached (Matt 3:2–3; Mark 1:3; Luke 3:4–6; John 1:23) that he was the voice in the desert preparing the way of the Lord, a text from Isaiah (Isa 40:3), which the Qumran community also applied to itself:

> As it is written, "In the wilderness prepare the way of ****,[12] make straight in the desert a roadway for our God." (1QS 8:14, quoting Isa 40:3; cf. 1QS 9:19b–21a)

True, the Qumran sect applied this text to their sectarian residence and Torah observance in the desert around Qumran as preparation for the Messiah. John the Baptist understood the Isaiah text as referring to his eschatological ministry of preaching and baptism as preparation for the Messiah. Yet, the fact that both John and the Qumran community saw an eschatological meaning for Isa 40:3 is suggestive that there was at one time a connection between them.[13]

---

to Josephus (*War* 2.129–31).

9. The Gospels narrate that John is in the desert (Mark 1:4; Matt 3:1; Luke 3:2) but also baptizing in the Jordan river (Mark 1:5; Matt 3:6; John 1:28). This would put him near Jericho.

10. Papyrus 66 (c. 200 CE) and uncial Sinaiticus (fourth century) read Bethany. The second corrector of Sinaiticus and many translations (Syriac, Coptic, Armenian) read Bethabara. The United Bible Society text 4th ed. gives this reading a "C" rating. Brown, *John* 1:44 doubted the reading "Bethabara."

11. See Gibson, "On John the Baptist," 221. Origen, Eusebius, and the Piacenza Pilgrim identify Bethabara as the place of John's baptizing activities.

12. The four asterisks are dots in the manuscript and stand for the Tetragrammaton: YHWH.

13. Taylor, *Immerser*, 25, however, requires "precisely the same" interpretation of the Isaiah text in order to accept an influence.

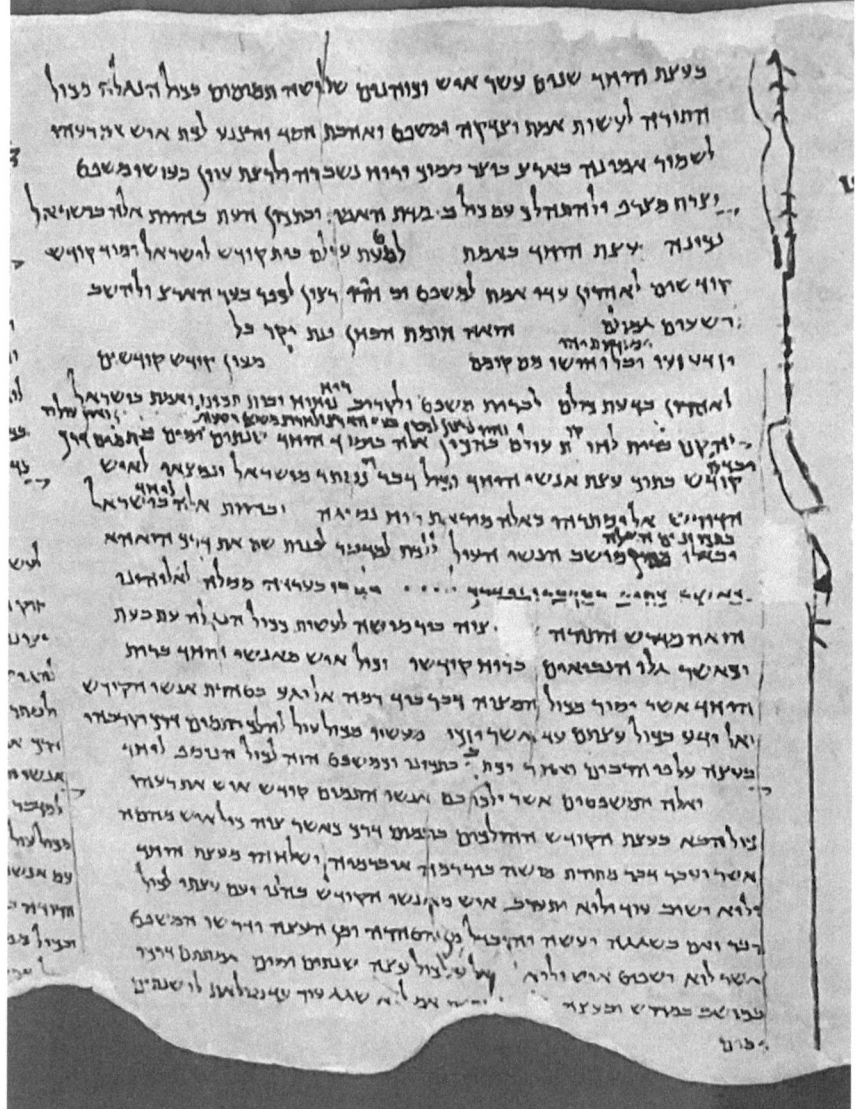

Figure 2.1: Author's replica of 1QS (also called the Community Rule) column 8, which interpreted Isa 40:3 similarly to John the Baptist. Notice the four dots in the middle of the column for the Tetragrammaton.

Figure 2.2: Qumran Cave 4 (to the right) and Wadi Qumran
running up the middle of the photograph

Fourth, the Qumran community was strongly associated with priests (e.g., 1QS 5:1–3; 1Q28a 1:1–3). Its founder, the Teacher of Righteousness, was a priest,[14] and the literature of the Dead Sea Scrolls often refers to priests at Qumran. Thus, a priestly family might have connections there. John's parents were already elderly when he was born (Luke 1:7) and therefore may have died while he was quite young. The Essenes often took in orphaned children to rear (*War* 2.120) so they could easily have given John a home at Qumran. His parents, though not Essenes themselves, may have admired the strict lifestyle of the Essenes and asked for their son to be taken by this group when they saw their deaths approaching. They knew the Essenes kept strict food laws and would rear their son as he was supposed to be (Luke 1:15, i.e., as a Nazarite).[15]

Yet, as Otto Betz[16] cautioned, one must bear certain facts in mind: John is never mentioned in the Qumran scrolls. John was never called an Essene

14. See Pesher on the Psalms (4Q171) 3:15–16; and Schiffman, *Reclaiming*, 114–15, 120.

15. Betz, "Was John the Baptist an Essene?" sketches the story this way.

16. Betz, "Was John the Baptist an Essene?" Bock, *Luke*, 1:198 lists five differences between John and the Qumran community.

either in the New Testament or by Josephus. The Essenes drank wine and ate meat, items missing and even forbidden from John's diet (Luke 1:15). Finally, John stood at the fords of the Jordan to preach and call all Israel to repentance. The Qumran members took an oath to hate all the nonmembers (1QS 1:3). If John ever had been around the Qumran covenanters (or Essenes), he was not one of them when we encounter him in the Gospels, argued Betz. Thus, adherents of the "Qumran hypothesis" must presume a breaking point between John and the Dead Sea community.

This is precisely what John Pryke described, although he was skeptical of an association between John and the Qumran community:

> The suggested adoption by the sectarians of the Baptist as a child is conjectural. His later history and views do not support it—rather the contrary. If he was trained as an Essene brother, he must have apostasized [sic] and revolted.[17]

Why would John have separated from the Qumran community—his boyhood home if the hypothesis is correct? Marcus offers three suggestions:

1. John had a developing sense of his own mission as opposed to the community's mission.
2. John desired to break from the "self-enclosed world of Qumran" to invite all Israel to repent.
3. John developed a different attitude toward Gentiles.[18]

How should one conclude? As Fitzmyer offered, one can neither prove nor disprove this connection.[19] Fitzmyer was inclined, however, to regard it as plausible. His wisdom seems appropriate. Thus, the archaeological remains, in the form of texts written on animal skins and found in caves, *might* help us discover the nature of John's childhood.

---

17. Pryke, "John the Baptist," 495.
18. Marcus, *John the Baptist*, 35–36.
19. Fitzmyer, *Dead Sea Scrolls*, 19.

Sidebar 2.1

Jesus' Birth Year and His Year of Death

Luke 3:23 states that Jesus was "something like thirty years old" when he began his ministry, and it was in the fifteenth year of the reign of Tiberius, emperor of Rome. We need not insist on Jesus' being exactly thirty, however, as the Lukan *hosei* ("something like") is frequently used in both the Gospel of Luke and the book of Acts to express approximate numbers.[20]

Most commentators decide on a birthdate range of 6–4 BCE. Herod the Great died in 4 BCE, and both Matt and Luke name him as the ruling "king" at that time.[21] Some like a date a bit earlier (7 BCE) because of astral configurations that might have excited astrologers from Babylon or Parthia.[22] The two most commonly cited dates for the crucifixion are 30 CE and 33 CE.[23] Thus, if Jesus was born in 6 BCE and crucified in 33 CE (assuming a three-year ministry), he would be at the beginning of his ministry (31 CE) around thirty-seven years old. Alternatively—at the other extreme—had he been born in 4 BCE and crucified in 30, he would have been (in the year 28 CE) around thirty-two years old.[24]

---

20. E.g., Luke 9:14; Acts 1:15, 2:41.

21. Meier, *Marginal Jew*, 1:375, 377 opts for a few "but only a few" years before the death of Herod (in 4 BCE) as the birth year of Jesus. Most accept the range of 6–4 BCE: Donfried ("Chronology," 1016), Theissen and Merz (*Historical Jesus*, 160), Brown (*Introduction*, xxxviii); Finegan, *Handbook*, 232 (who prefers 5–4 BCE); Bock, *Luke*, 1:75.

22. Goldsworthy, *Augustus*, 487; and Parpola, "Magi." Finegan, *Handbook*, 245 gives several possibilities for astral phenomena at the time of Jesus' birth.

23. See Meier, *Marginal Jew*, 3:402, 431; Theissen and Merz, *Historical Jesus*, 160; Donfried, "Chronology," 1016; Brown, *Introduction*, xxxviii; and Humphreys, *Mystery*, 71 (who insists the date of Jesus' crucifixion *must* have been 33 CE);

24. Meier, *Marginal Jew*, 3:402, tends toward the year 28 as the start year for Jesus' ministry (evidently, shortly after John the Baptist began his ministry). He maintains that the year 30 as the date of Jesus' death is supported by a "wide range of scholars" (431). Bock, *Luke*, 1:285 likes the year 29 CE as the start of Jesus' ministry. Donfried ("Chronology," 1016) suggests that Jesus was about 35 years old when he began his ministry.

Sidebar 2.2

The Discovery of the Dead Sea Scrolls

The phrase "Dead Sea Scrolls" "can be used in both a broad and a narrow sense. Broadly, it refers to the manuscripts discovered in at least eighteen locations in the Judean desert since 1947 ... More narrowly, the 'Dead Sea Scrolls' refers to the manuscripts from eleven caves near Qumran, close to the northwest shore of the Dead Sea."[25]

The chance discovery of ancient documents stashed in a cave just west of the Dead Sea in Israel has revolutionized New Testament studies, especially our investigation of the ministry and teachings of Jesus. The details of the discovery are somewhat uncertain. They involve a Bedouin shepherd boy and his family, a shoe cobbler in Bethlehem, an archbishop of the Syriac Orthodox Church, and various Israeli archaeologists. When the scholarly community finally realized what had been found, more scientific excavations and searches were done. The result is that thousands of manuscript fragments and over eight hundred texts are now available for comparison with the New Testament, the Hebrew Bible, and other Jewish documents previously known.[26]

The Dead Sea area

25. Penner, "Dead Sea Scrolls," 173.

26. See VanderKam and Flint, *Meaning of the Dead Sea Scrolls*, 3–19; Cook, *Solving the Mystery*, 11–30; Schiffman, *Reclaiming*, 3–19; Vermes, *Complete Dead Sea Scrolls*, A1–5.

The expression "Dead Sea Scrolls" covers any documents that have come to light from various locations west of the Dead Sea. These locations include Wadi Muraba'at, Naḥal Ḥever, Masada, Naḥal Se'elim, and Qumran, the source of most of the documents. The Qumran documents may be placed into three categories: biblical manuscripts (texts of the Hebrew Bible), nonbiblical Jewish texts (such as the Apocrypha and Pseudepigrapha), and sectarian texts (those texts written by the Qumran people). All three categories of texts are extremely valuable, but the most excitement has been reserved for the last category since these texts tell us about the organization and theology of the Qumran sect—usually today identified with the Essenes. But other documents referred to above, not associated with Qumran, are also important for our study of Luke.

Cave of John the Baptist

A new suggestion for understanding the youth of John the Baptist was offered by Shimon Gibson based on his archaeological discovery. In 1999 Gibson and his team discovered a cave in the hill country of Judea southwest of Jerusalem (and just west of Ein Kerem, John's home village) in which ritual activity had been carried out beginning in the Late Hellenistic period. The cave, measuring 79 by 11 feet, is situated in the Wadi Esh-Shemmarin, about 1.2 miles from Ein Kerem. In the cave are crude drawings, one of a man whom Gibson concluded represents John the Baptist because the figure resembles John the Baptist as depicted in Byzantine art. Although the cave was in use as early as the Iron Age as a water reservoir and later in the Early Hellenistic period as a place of ritual washing, it was sometime in the first century CE that a religious sect took it over and practiced occasional (he opines yearly) ritual immersions and foot washings. There are a *mikveh* (ritual bathing installation; see Chapter 11) and a place evidently used for foot washings (marked by a carving of a foot on the cave floor) that were used in the first century.[27]

Evidently no one lived in the cave since there were almost no material remains recovered from the floor except broken pottery. Further, the pottery was mostly one-handled jugs instead of a full range of vessels that one might use in a house. Gibson surmises that the jugs were used in the ritual washings. Then, after the rituals, they evidently smashed the jugs into

---

27. Gibson, *Cave*, 4, 11–13, 207, 173, 170, 161–62.

many pieces. Not a single intact vessel was found while over one hundred thousand sherds were recovered. The sherds date from the late first century BCE to the early second century CE.[28]

Fast-forward from the first century to the Byzantine era when the drawings were etched into the plastered cave walls. Among the images depicted on the walls are a crude figure of a man, a severed head, and a severed arm. Gibson believes the man to be John the Baptist, the head to represent his beheading, and the arm to point to a relic kept somewhere in the cave (perhaps an arm bone attributed to John the Baptist). He thinks the Byzantine monks gathered there for special worship services in which the leader told the story of John the Baptist by referring to the cave drawings.[29]

Figure 2.3: Artist's depiction of the "John the Baptist Cave"[30]
(Image courtesy Shimon Gibson)

But why, asks Gibson, did the Byzantine monks regard the cave as a holy site? Here he looks at some patristic texts and medallions which talk about John the Baptist's association with nearby Ein Kerem and about his mother Elizabeth's flight from Herod the Great with the infant John (Prot. Jac. 22:3) just as Joseph and Mary fled with Jesus. Gibson opines that Elizabeth hid in the cave to escape Herod's men, that later the boy John lived in the cave while he tended sheep in this "wilderness" (deserted) area, and that

28. Gibson, *Cave*, 155–59.
29. Gibson, *Cave*, 59–67.
30. The image appears in Gibson, *Cave*, 66.

still later John used the cave as a place of baptism for those hearing his message. This cave (and not Qumran), argues Gibson, is the "lonely places" of Luke 1:80. John's association with the cave was remembered and celebrated in the Byzantine era.[31]

Though historians may question some of Gibson's conclusions—his hypothesis would mean that the *erēmois* (deserted or lonely places) of Luke 1:80 (which he identifies as a cave in a deserted area west of Ein Kerem) and the *erēmos* of Luke 3:2 (i.e., near Jericho) were different localities—one can certainly admire his careful collection of both artifacts and texts. In bringing objects and texts together, he may well have expanded our knowledge of the youthful life of an important New Testament character. It is possible that Elizabeth might have retreated to the cave to hide her son, that John as a young boy came there for solitude, and that after John's death, his disciples met there to remember their former teacher. Can one fit both hypotheses—the Qumran connection and the cave west of Ein Kerem—together into a coherent narrative? It would be a bit of a strain but perhaps conceivable.

---

31. Gibson, *Cave*, 30–31, 80–83, 213.

Sidebar 2.3

Josephus

Facts about his life[32]

- He was born in Jerusalem 37 CE (some say 30).
- Full name (Heb.): Yoseph ben Mattityahu.
- He was of priestly descent and descended from the Hasmoneans on his (great grand-) mother's side.
- At age sixteen, he tried all three main Jewish sects and ended up a Pharisee.
- After the war began in 66 CE, he was put in charge of defense of Galilee
- He recruited and trained an army of 60,000 foot soldiers.
- He made a stand at Jotapata (Yodefat).
- He surrendered (68 CE).
- The Roman general Vespasian kept him as war captive.
- He remained in Palestine and vicinity until Jerusalem was destroyed and then traveled to Rome with Titus. He never returned to Palestine as far as is known.
- He was made a Roman citizen; his new Roman name was (Titus?) Flavius Josephus.
- He was given an annual stipend.
- He wrote four works: *War; Antiquities; Life; Against Apion*.
- Josephus refers in his writings to Jesus twice and John the Baptist once (*Ant.* 18.63–64, 18.116–19, 20.200).

Josephus on John's Preaching

"Herod had put [John] to death, though he was a good man and had exhorted the Jews to lead righteous lives, to practice justice towards their fellows and piety towards God, and so doing to join in baptism ... When others too joined the crowds about him, because <u>they were aroused to the highest degree by his sermons</u>, Herod became alarmed" (*Ant.* 18.116–17).[33]

---

32. See Feldman, "Josephus"; and *Flavius Josephus Primer Home Page*.
33. Translation by Feldman in Josephus, LCL (underlining added).

JOHN'S MARTYRDOM

After summarizing John's message to the masses, Luke adds:

> Herod the Tetrarch, after he was reprimanded by him [John] because of Herodias, his brother's wife[34] and because of all the evils which Herod did, added this to them: he locked John up in prison. (Luke 3:19–20)

All four Gospels (cf. Matt 14:3–12; Mark 6:17–29; John 3:24) remember the imprisonment of John by Antipas; Mark and Matthew narrate that John died during a banquet. Luke and John seem to have known of his imprisonment and execution by Antipas but gave the story only a brief mention. Matthew and especially Mark give many more details of the martyrdom. But we also have two additional sources of information for John's imprisonment and death: Josephus and the archaeological remains of his prison. Josephus was fairly impressed with what he had heard about (and read about?) John. He calls him a just man who taught people to live righteous lives. He contrasts John's righteous life with Antipas's immoral and sinful life (see Sidebar 2.4).

Sidebar 2.4

Josephus on John the Baptist

"Herod became alarmed. Eloquence that had so great an effect on mankind might lead to some form of sedition, for it looked as if they would be guided by John in everything that they did. Herod decided therefore that it would be much better to strike first and be rid of him before his work led to an uprising, than to wait for an upheaval, get involved in a difficult situation and see his mistake. Though John, because of Herod's suspicions, was brought in chains to Machaerus, the stronghold that we have previously mentioned, and there put to death, yet the verdict of the Jews was that the destruction visited upon Herod's army was a vindication of John, since God saw fit to inflict such a blow on Herod" (*Ant.* 18.118–19; translation by Feldman in Josephus, LCL)

---

34. See Lev 18:16, 20:21, which forbid taking the divorced wife of a brother. Although Mark and Matt (Mark 6:17, Matt 14:3) give a brother of Antipas named Philip as the former husband of Herodias, we should not conclude that it was Philip the Tetrarch (see Sidebar 2.6). Josephus writes that Herodias was married to a son of Herod the Great who was also named Herod (*Ant.* 18.109, 136). Was this Herod called Herod Philip? See Herion, "Herod Philip"; Lane, *Mark*, 216.

View of Machaerus, one of the fortresses built by Herod the Great and inherited by Antipas. It was in Perea, East of the Dead Sea (Map 1 p. 2).

Figure 2.4: The summit of Machaerus, standing columns

Josephus informs us that John was held prisoner in one of Herod the Great's old fortresses (see Sidebar 2.5 for others), a fortress called Machaerus. This fortress was first constructed by the Hasmonean king Alexander Jannaeus, probably around 90 BCE. It was then destroyed by the Romans in 57 BCE, rebuilt by Herod the Great, and lasted from 30 BCE to 72 CE (*War*

7.171–72). Excavation results have agreed with the history of Josephus: There are two periods of occupation, according to the pottery and other datable finds: Hell II and ER I, that is, the Hasmonean and the Herodian. The fortress stood on a hill rising to 3600 feet above the level of the Dead Sea. The fortress itself covers an area of 1 ½ acres. The ruins consist of a palace including a courtyard, a Roman bath, a Jewish ritual bath,[35] a large *triclinium*[36] (2,550 square feet), and a somewhat larger colonnaded courtyard. It may have been in the *triclinium*, in the courtyard—or both—that the infamous dance of Herodias's daughter (Matt 14:3–12; Mark 6:17–29; named Salome, *Ant.* 18.136) took place leading to John's beheading.[37]

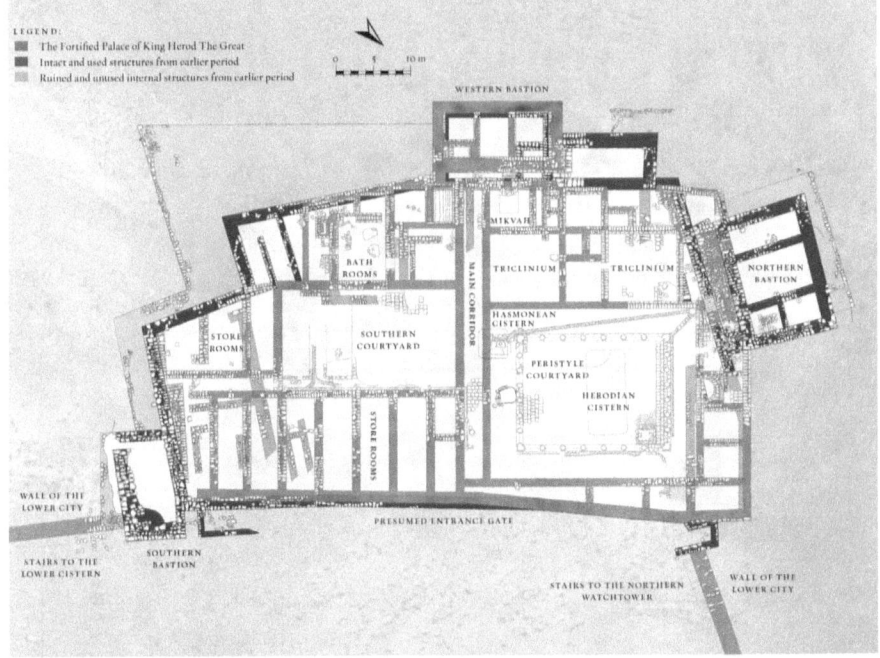

Figure 2.5: Machaerus, the fortress where John was held prisoner by Antipas. Plan of the palace indicating the colonnaded courtyard and *triclinium*.[38] See Figure 2.7, below, for the artist's reconstruction of the palace. (Image courtesy Győző Vörös)

35. See Vörös, "Machaerus: A Palace-Fortress."

36. See Chapter 11 for *triclinia*.

37. See Finegan, *Archaeology*, 17–19; Loffreda, "Machaerus"; Loffreda, "Preliminary Report." Vörös (*Machaerus II*, 80) believes the banquet was held in the courtyard, the largest space in the fortress.

38. Plan in Vörös, *Machaerus I*, 289.

How long John was imprisoned at Machaerus before he was executed we cannot tell, but evidently for a few months to a year or so. John was in prison long enough to hear about Jesus' words and deeds, to send his disciples to question Jesus (Matt 11:2–6//Luke 7:18–23), and to receive their answer. Evidently, John died somewhere in the middle of Jesus' (three-year?) ministry. At this point, after Jesus' ministry is well advanced, Antipas also heard of Jesus' deeds and began to fear that John had been raised from the dead (Matt 14:1–2//Mark 6:14–16//Luke 9:7–9). Thus, we could conclude that John was executed at some time between six months and one year of the beginning of Jesus' ministry.

Sidebar 2.5[39]

Herodian Fortresses

Herod the Great built *at least*[40] two new fortresses (named after himself) and repaired six Hasmonean fortresses that had been destroyed by the Romans. Six of the fortresses were located west of the Jordan River and two (Machaerus and Herodium 1) east.

NEW FORTRESSES			
Name	Location	Josephus reference	Relevance for Gospel of Luke?
Herodium 1[41]	In the mountains "toward Arabia"	*War* 1.419	No
Herodium 2[42]	Ten miles south of Jerusalem (Map 1, p. 2)	*War* 1.419–21	Yes, Herod the Great was buried there.[43]
REBUILT HASMONEAN FORTRESSES			
Name	Location	Josephus reference	Relevance for Gospel of Luke?

---

39. See SVM 1:306–7; Netzer, "Herod's Building Program"; Richardson, *Herod*, 179–83; Roller, *Building Program*.
40. Richardson, *Herod*, 179, 181 gives other possible fortress constructions.
41. Roller, *Building Program*, 168–69.
42. Netzer, "Herodium"; Roller, *Building Program*, 164–68.
43. Netzer, "In Search of Herod's Tomb."

Cypros[44] (the name of Herod's mother)	West of Jericho (Tell el-Aqaba)	*War* 1.417; *Ant.* 16.143	No
Alexandrium[45]	North of Jericho (Map 1 p. 2)	*War* 1.308; *Ant.* 14.419	No
Hyrcania[46]	In the Judean wilderness (Khirbet Mird) eight miles SE of Jerusalem	*War* 1.364, 664	No
Machaerus[47]	Fifteen miles southeast of the mouth of the Jordan River (Map 1 p. 2)	*War* 7.171–72	Yes, John the Baptist was executed there.
Masada[48]	West of the Dead Sea (Map 1 p. 2)	*War* 7.275–303	Not directly, but several ostraca have been found that explain the Gospel of Luke.
Arttaba[49]	Northern Judea	None	No

44. Netzer, "Cypros"; Roller, *Building Program*, 182–83.

45. Tsafrir and Magen, "Sartaba-Alexandrium"; and Gutfeld, "Hyrcania's Mysterious Tunnels"; Roller, *Building Program*, 129–31.

46. Patrich, "Hyrcania"; Gutfield, "Hyrcania"; Roller, *Building Program*, 170–71.

47. Vörös, *Machaerus I*; Vörös, *Machaerus II*.

48. Yadin, *Masada*; Netzer and Stiebel, "Masada"; Roller, *Building Program*, 187–90.

49. Raviv, "Artabba Fortress."

Figure 2.6: Herodium where Herod the Great was buried (see Map 1 p. 2).

Sidebar 2.6

Some Children of Herod the Great[50]

Herod the Great (74–4 BCE)			
Mariamme I (wife)	Mariamme II (wife)	Malthace (wife)	Cleopatra (wife)
Alexander and Aristobulus (sons of Herod; both d. 7 BCE)	Herod Philip (son of Herod, married Herodias initially)	Archelaus and Antipas (sons of Herod; both became his heirs. Archelaus deposed in 6 CE; Antipas divorced his Nabatean wife and married Herodias)	Philip (son of Herod; his third heir; married Salome, daughter of Herodias)

50. See *Ant.* 17.19–22. Josephus writes that Herod the Great had nine wives.

Agrippa I (son of Aristobulus) and Herodias (daughter of Aristobulus; at first married to Herod Philip, then to Antipas. Her daughter by Herod Philip was Salome, evidently the one who danced for Antipas and who later married Philip the Tetrarch.)			

Figure 2.7: Reconstruction of Herod's fortress at Machaerus. The courtyard is in the upper center; the *triclinium* to its left.[51] (Image courtesy Győző Vörös)

---

51. Reconstruction in Vörös, *Machaerus I*, 331.

3

Jesus' Youth

GALILEE

> And Jesus returned in the power of the Spirit into Galilee and his fame spread to every region. And he was teaching in the synagogues and being honored by everyone. (Luke 4:14–15).

THE JEWISH HISTORIAN JOSEPHUS (first century CE; see Sidebar 2.3) divided Galilee into two sections: Upper Galilee and Lower Galilee (*War* 1.22, 3.35–39). The rabbinic collection called the Mishnah (collected in 200 CE; see Sidebar 9.1) divided Galilee into three parts: Upper Galilee, Lower Galilee, and the Great Plain (m. Sheb. 9:2). A steep slope separates the Upper and Lower Galilee. To determine where the one ended and the other began, the reader may draw an imaginary line from the northern end of the Sea of Galilee westward toward the Mediterranean Sea.[1] The mountains of Upper Galilee reach a height of 3,000 feet while those of Lower Galilee rise to just under 2,000 feet. Lower Galilee is intersected by four valleys running east to west and finally drops in the south from a height of 1,500 feet at Nazareth to the Jezreel Valley, which is 492 feet above sea level. Upper Galilee extends over 180 square miles; Lower Galilee 470 square miles.[2]

Archaeologists have confirmed that there was also a bit of a cultural divide between Upper Galilee and Lower Galilee. Upper Galilee was

---

[1]. This is only an approximate division. For a more precise dividing of the two Galilees, see Avi-Yonah, *Holy Land*, 133–35.

[2]. See Aharoni, *Land of the Bible*, 27–28; E. M. Meyers, "Cultural Setting of Galilee"; and Reed, *Archaeology*, 115.

more conservative and isolated, speaking mostly Hebrew and Aramaic (as evidenced by the inscriptions found so far). It had only villages and small towns, and no major trade routes dissected its region. Lower Galilee has produced more Greek inscriptions and had two fair-sized cities: Sepphoris and Tiberias, plus one small city, Magdala/Taricheae.³ It was more open to outside influences because important trade routes (such as the Via Maris) ran through it. The differences between the two Galilees have sometimes been exaggerated, but that there were differences few would deny today. Jesus' hometown, Nazareth, was located in Lower Galilee.

NAZARETH

We have only one reference, found in Luke, to the boyhood of Jesus. There, he and his family attend the Passover in Jerusalem, and Jesus is left behind as the family heads home (Luke 2:41–52). The story ends with the family returning to Nazareth where Jesus finishes growing up intellectually, socially, physically, and spiritually (v. 52). But what sort of life did Jesus and his family have in Nazareth? We can only speculate, but the archaeological remains give us important hints.

Figure 3.1: Modern Nazareth. On the right (domed), the Church of the Anunciation. On the left (square tower) the Church of Saint Joseph. These parameters roughly define the ancient village. (Photograph by Anan Maalouf)⁴

> And he went down with them and came to Nazareth and lived in submission to them. (Luke 2:51)

---

3. See E. M. Meyers, "Galilean Regionalism"; E. M. Meyers, "Jesus and His Galilean Context"; and Vale, "Literary Sources in Archaeological Description."

4. Wikimedia Commons: https://commons.wikimedia.org/wiki/File:Laang-Nazareth_View.jpg/.

> And he came to Nazareth where he had been brought up . . . (Luke 4:16).

All four Gospels agree that the village of Nazareth—an agricultural village about three miles from the city of Sepphoris and around fifteen miles from Tiberias—was Jesus' hometown (Matt 2:23; Mark 1:9; Luke 4:16; John 1:45–46). Excavations in and around Nazareth have focused on six locations:

- under the Church of the Annunciation and the Church of Saint Joseph;
- at Mary's Well, which has revealed coins from the Hasmonean and Herodian periods;
- in the area between Nazareth and Sepphoris (Naḥal Zippori);
- at the Nazareth Village Farm Project;
- at the International Marian Center;
- and under the Sisters of Nazareth Convent.[5]

So far, the excavations under the two churches in modern Nazareth (the Church of Saint Joseph and the Church of the Annunciation) and on the Nazareth Village Farm have revealed many agricultural installations: grottoes, granaries, pits, vaulted cells for storing wine and oil, wine presses, rock quarries, cisterns, silos, and oil presses.[6] Only slight traces of the houses have been left, leading some archaeologists to suggest that the houses must have been made of fieldstones and mud.[7] The pottery from these sites (under and around the two churches) ranges from Hellenistic to Roman to Byzantine. Excavators found one *mikveh* under the Church of the Annunciation and one under the Church of Saint Joseph.[8] Several caves were used as houses. Excavators found twenty-three tombs encircling the area of the churches, evidently circumscribing the boundaries of the ancient village. Eighteen of these tombs were of the *kokhim* type (having burial niches; see Chapter 15), known in Palestine from 200 BCE and the standard type in the first century CE. Two of the tombs contained burial objects (lamps, ceramic vases, and glass) which dated from the first century to the fourth century CE. In all, the pottery—associated with the houses, with the agricultural installations, and with the tombs—and the types of tombs indicate that Nazareth was a Jewish village beginning in the first century BCE.[9]

---

5. See Jenks, "Historical Nazareth."
6. Bagati, "Nazareth, Excavations"; and Pfann et al., "Nazareth Village Farm."
7. Reed, *Archaeology*, 132; Jenks, "Historical Nazareth."
8. Strange, "Nazareth."
9. Finegan, *Archaeology*, 45–46.

The area between Nazareth and Sepphoris (on the south side of Naḥal Ẓippori nearest to Nazareth) has revealed "low-status" farms and very small villages. The area was apparently densely farmed during the first century CE. The remains from the south side of the wadi (nearest Nazareth) are locally made pottery and stoneware vessels, indicating conservative Jewish occupation. On the north side of the wadi (nearest Sepphoris), were found some fragments of ESA (imported) ware.[10]

The Nazareth Village Farm Project excavations (west of Nazareth) have discovered ancient terraces with ER pottery in them, thus dating the original construction of the terraces. The terraces and other farming installations such as wine presses (see Figure 3.2) indicate an agricultural community.[11]

Figure 3.2: first-century wine press, Nazareth

One first-century house was recently excavated across the street from the Church of the Annunciation at the International Marian Center.[12] The lead excavator uncovered a courtyard house occupied from the Hell II to the late second century CE. It yielded ER pottery and stoneware fragments.

10. Jenks, "Historical Nazareth"; Dark, "Jesus' Nazareth House."
11. Pfann et al., "Nazareth Village Farm"; Jenks, "Historical Nazareth."
12. Dark, "Archaeology of Nazareth."

There were storage pits under the house like those under the Church of the Annunciation and the Church of Saint Joseph.

An additional first-century house was excavated under the convent of the Sisters of Nazareth (Figure 3.3).[13] It was a typical first-century courtyard house yielding first-century cookware, Roman glass, one spindle whorl, and possible stoneware vessel fragments. The structure of the building, itself was typical of first-century Galilean dwellings. Also under the convent were two ER *kokhim*-type tombs. This house is now famous because of one archaeologist's hypothesis that it was the house where Jesus as a boy lived with his parents and siblings.[14] Leaving aside that sensational claim, we can confidently conclude that this was a first-century CE domestic building. Based on the finds and the house size and construction, one archaeologist described the family inhabiting it as "low-status (but far from impoverished)."[15]

Another archaeological find related to Nazareth comes not from the village, itself but from Caesarea on the Mediterranean coast. In 1962, an inscription (in three fragments) was found on gray marble in the ruins of a Jewish synagogue. The inscription dates from the late third—early fourth century CE. It was a list of the twenty-four courses of priests (cf. Luke 1:5)[16] and where they had settled after the Jewish War of 66–73 CE. A similar list was found near Ascalon and other lists of priestly courses from the sixth and seventh centuries were already known from the rabbinic liturgical poems.[17]

---

13. The Sisters of Nazareth convent is near the Marian Center.

14. Jenks, "Historical Nazareth"; Dark, "Early Roman-Period Nazareth"; and Dark, "Jesus' Nazareth House."

15. Dark, "Early Roman-Period Nazareth," 57.

16. See also 1 Chr 24:10; Neh 12:17.

17. See Avi-Yonah, "Priestly Courses."

Figure 3.3: House under the convent of the Sisters of Nazareth. Was this Jesus' boyhood home?

Figure 3.4: Kokhim tomb niches under the Sisters of Nazareth convent

One fragment had the name Natsrat (i.e., Nazareth) on it in the second line. Here is a translation of the full reconstruction of the three fragments:

The 17th course Hezir MA]MLIAH
The 18th course Hapizzez[18] NAZARETH
The 19th course Pethahiah AKHLAH Arab
The 20th course Ezekiel MI]GDAL Nunaiya[19]

This is the first mention of Nazareth in an inscription known to date. But if priests fled to and settled in Nazareth after the war, it must have been (a) in existence in 70 CE, and (b) well enough known to have deserved settlers.[20]

The Carpenter

The Nazareth villagers do not seem to have been as prosperous as those at other villages in Lower Galilee, e.g., Yodefat and Khirbet Qana. Nor do they seem to have had any industry or means to make a living beyond farming.[21] Thus, one might conclude that if a villager from Nazareth did not own a significant amount of land, he might wander afar in search of employment at certain times of the year. Many have speculated that the family of Jesus did exactly that. But where could Jesus' family have found lucrative occupation?

We should consider it probable that Jesus was a *tektōn*, a carpenter or builder.[22] Although this assertion is found only in Mark 6:3 (while in the parallel passage in Matt 13:55, he is called "the son of the carpenter" and Luke 4:22 merely calls him the son of Joseph), nevertheless, the historical probability that Jesus was a carpenter remains high. In the first place, all the major Greek manuscripts—except one[23]—and many of the early versions have the reading: "Is not this the carpenter?"[24]

Second, the passage in Matthew ("Is not this the son of the carpenter?")—even if one were to argue that it is more accurate or authentic—actually supports the meaning of Mark, since fathers usually taught their

---

18. 1 Chr 24:15.

19. This reconstruction and translation are from Avi-Yonah, "Priestly Courses." For the fully reconstructed text of the inscription found at Caesarea listing Nazareth, see Avi-Yona, "Caesarea."

20. See Finegan, *Archaeology*, 46.

21. See Strange, "Nazareth"; Fiensy, *Archaeology of Daily Life*, 181–83.

22. On this see Fiensy, *Christian Origins*, 23–33; Fiensy, *Jesus the Galilean*, 66–83.

23. Papyrus 45 from the third century CE has the text of Mark 6:3 read like that of Matt 13:55.

24. See Metzger, *Textual Commentary*, 88–89; and Cranfield, *Mark*, 194–95. But for an opposing view, see Taylor, *Mark*, 299–301.

craft to their sons.[25] Third, these words are found in a text describing Jesus' rejection at his hometown—which all four Gospels record or at least allude to[26]—a narrative unlikely to have been invented by the early church (using the criterion of embarrassment[27]).

Fourth, Jesus was remembered widely in the early church and beyond as a carpenter. Several apocryphal and patristic texts affirm or assume that Joseph or Jesus was a carpenter. The most important patristic text is that of Justin Martyr (*Trypho* 88), who maintained that Jesus was a carpenter who made yokes and ploughs. The pagan detractor of Christianity Celsus (second century CE) knew that Jesus was a carpenter (Origen, *Cels.* 6.36). Thus, we should conclude that Jesus came from the artisan class.[28]

Nazareth was a small agricultural village with a population of around 500. Excavations show no signs of industry.

Figure 3.5: Scenes from the old city of contemporary Nazareth; on the left, the Suk; on the right, a street

As a carpenter, Jesus would have been skilled in fashioning wood products such as furniture, tools, agricultural implements, and waterwheels for irrigation, and would probably have been skilled in building houses.[29] It is also possible that he would have been able to work in stone. The philosopher

25. Burford, *Craftsmen*, 82; Klausner, *Jesus of Nazareth*, 178; and Cooper, "Crafts, Trade."

26. Matt 13:53–58//Mark 6:1–6//Luke 4:16–30//John 4:44, 6:42. Cf. Gos. Thom. 31.

27. See on this criterion, Meier, *Marginal Jew*, 1:168–71.

28. The Aram. term for carpenter sometimes is used in the Talmud metaphorically of a scholar (see Vermes, *Jesus the Jew*, 21–22) just as the Gk. word for carpenter was occasionally used for any master of an art, such as a gymnast, poet, or physician (see LSJM). But the term in Mark 6:3 clearly is not used in that sense. Mark's point is that because Jesus was *only* a carpenter, the residents of Nazareth refused to listen to him. Otherwise, the passage makes no sense.

29. See McCown, "O TEKTŌN"; Furfey, "Christ as *tektōn*"; Blümner, *Technologie und Terminologie*, 2:311–47; and Brewster, *Roman Craftsmen*, 77–79.

Epictetus (1.15.2; first century CE) defined a *tektōn* as one that worked in wood as opposed to one that worked in bronze. But Aelius Aristides (46; second century CE) said that a *tektōn* was a worker in stone. Thus, these craftsmen seem to have worked in both materials as builders.

Historians agree that most artisans labored long and hard days but were able to earn enough to live simply.[30] They were not usually wealthy, but neither were they destitute. Dio Chrysostom (late first—early second century CE, *Discourse* 7.112–13) says that those who know a trade will never worry about a living and will lack nothing needful and useful. Lucian (*Dial. meretr.* 6.293, second century CE) has a mother say to her daughter that as long as her husband, Philenus the smith, was alive, his family had plenty of everything. The Talmud (b. Sanh. 29a) says that as long as one knows a trade, he need have no fear of famine. Another rabbinic work (t. Qidd. 1:11) compares knowledge of a trade to a vineyard with a wall around it. The early second century CE Christian text Didache 12:3–4, assumes that a person without a craft may need financial assistance. In sum, craftsmen lived simply, but they lived without anxiety and without want.

Nonetheless, craftsmen could at times attain a modest level of affluence if their skills were especially in demand, or if they could afford extra workers (either enslaved or paid day laborers) to mass-produce their goods. There were, for example, affluent tanners, weavers, and bakers in classical Athens.[31] Skilled labor, on average, earned one and one-half times the income of unskilled labor in fourth-century BCE Greece.[32]

Archaeologists have discovered a family of artisans in Jerusalem: the family of Simon the Temple builder (see Table 5.4), buried in Tomb I on Givat ha-Mivtar, north of the city.[33] Simon's name and occupation had been chiseled on the end and side of his ossuary (Figure 3.6). This was a family of laboring craftsmen—evidently constructing the temple—as can be seen from a pathological examination of the skeletal remains. They were builders like Jesus, yet they attained enough surplus to afford a tomb in a rather

---

30. Burford, *Craftsmen*, 138–43; Mossé, *Ancient World at Work*, 79; Hock, *Social Context*, 35; Cooper, "Crafts, Trades" 906. Cf. also Glotz, *Ancient Greece at Work*, 359, who notes that craftsmen at Delos earned twice as much per day as unskilled laborers in the fourth and third centuries BCE.

31. Mossé, *Ancient World at Work*, 90–91; Burford, *Craftsmen*, 141; Hock, *Social Context*, 34; Glotz, *Ancient Greece at Work*, 359; Cooper, "Crafts, Trade," 906.

32. Jevons, "Some Ancient Greek."

33. This tomb and its contents are described in Tzaferis, "Jewish Tombs"; Haas, "Anthropological Observations"; Naveh, "Ossuary Inscriptions."

high-priced area. Destitute persons were not usually buried in tombs, certainly not tombs in this vicinity.³⁴

Thus, the family, if not wealthy—being comfortable and perhaps even "middling" economically—was able either to purchase or, more probably, to excavate their own family tomb. We might suggest that the family of Simon the Temple builder typifies Jesus' own family's economic standing. They were not destitute; they were not wealthy. They were somewhere in between, at least living a simple yet comfortable lifestyle and perhaps in the "middling" economic range (see Table 5.5).

Figure 3.6: Ossuary of "Simon Builder of the Temple" (Israel Museum). See Table 5.4. Compare his ossuary with Figure 13.2 p. 235, the ossuary of Caiaphas. (Photograph by Gary Todd)³⁵

What sort of business would a carpenter in Galilee in the first century CE have done? The traditional concept is of a simple village carpenter who

34. See Smith and Zias, "French Hill," 115. They note that this was an expensive area to purchase a tomb. Cf. Chapter 15 on affording a tomb. Tzaferis, "Jewish Tombs," 3 believed that only the well-to-do could afford ossuaries. This conclusion, however, needs some refinement. Most now conclude that ossuaries were made of cheap, soft limestone and could have been easily afforded. See Chapter 5.

35. Wikimedia Commons: https://commons.wikimedia.org/wiki/File:Limestone_Ossuary_of_%22Simon,_builder_of_the_Temple%22_Jerusalem,_1ˢᵗ_Century_AD_(43218142621).jpg/.

made mostly yokes and ploughs for the local peasantry.[36] According to this view, he would seldom, if ever, have left the village.

The Greek historian Xenophon describes the work of a village carpenter: he must be skilled at many tasks and still may make only barely enough to sustain his family (*Cyr.*, 8.2.5). The traditional understanding of Jesus' background has been that of the small-village artisan described by Xenophon. But did Jesus' skill as a carpenter ever take him out of the village and into the city, where he would have learned about and participated in urban life? If so, could his urban employment have elevated his economic status? Was Jesus a village woodworker, or did he also work in the building trade? A carpenter family ambitious for more business than making "yokes and ploughs"[37] would need to travel to nearby villages and cities.

SEPPHORIS

Almost one hundred years ago, Shirley Jackson Case suggested an alternate view regarding Jesus' background.[38] Although Nazareth was probably a small village, it stood only three or four miles from Sepphoris, one of the largest cities in Galilee (see Map 2 p. 100). Case opined that Jesus as a youth had worked in the reconstruction of Sepphoris and later in the construction of Tiberias. Sepphoris had been destroyed by the Romans in 4 BCE and was then magnificently rebuilt by Antipas (*Ant.* 18.27). Since it would take many years to reconstruct a city such as Sepphoris, Case reasoned that a carpenter's family could have found important and lucrative work there for a sustained period of time. Richard A. Batey has more recently taken up Case's thesis and supported it from his own work on the excavation of Sepphoris.[39]

That artisans in antiquity would travel from their home villages to work on large construction projects is well known. It is also quite plausible that Jesus and his family worked in other towns in Galilee, such as Tiberias, which began construction somewhere between 18 and 23 CE.[40] They may

---

36. This is the view of, e.g., Furfey ("Christ as *tektōn*"), Klausner (*Jesus of Nazareth*, 233), and Stewart S. Miller ("Sepphoris").

37. See the discussion in Fiensy, *Christian Origins*, 25–29.

38. Case, *Jesus*, 199–212.

39. See the following publications by Batey: "Is Not This the Carpenter?"; Batey, "Sepphoris"; and Batey, *Jesus and the Forgotten City*, 65–82.

40. For the date in which construction began on Tiberias, see Overman, "Who Were the First Urban Christians?"; Weiss, "Josephus and Archaeology"; Shulamit Miller, "Tiberias"; Cytryn-Silverman, "Tiberias"; and Bonnie, "Tiberias."

even have worked in Jerusalem or some of the Decapolis cities for short periods of time.[41]

There are clear examples in the Mediterranean world of artisans traveling to distant building sites. Building temples and other public works almost always required importing craftsmen from surrounding cities. There was a general shortage of craftsmen in the building trades—carpenters, masons, sculptors—especially from the fourth century BCE on. The shortage necessitated that craftsmen travel from city to city.[42] This shortage of craftsmen was especially acute in the Roman period.

Figure 3.7: Model of the city of Sepphoris at the visitors' center, Sepphoris National Park (Looking from west to east): The "Western Domestic Quarter" is in the foreground and the theater is in the upper left.

Since this was the case throughout the Mediterranean world, we should expect that in Palestine in the Herodian period artisans from surrounding cities and villages were used for large building projects. This expectation is confirmed by a passage in Josephus. Josephus related that Herod the Great

---

41. See Applebaum, "Economic Life in Palestine"; Ze'ev Safrai, *Economy*, 215; and Stauffer, *Jesus and His Story*, 44 for traveling craftsmen in Palestine.

42. For *architektōnes*, see Cooper, "Crafts, Trade," 904.

(ruled 37 to 4 BCE) made the following preparations to build his Temple in 20 BCE:

> He made ready 1,000 wagons which would carry the stones. He gathered 10,000 of the most skillful workers . . . and he taught some to be masons and others to be carpenters. (*Ant.* 15.390)

Josephus's description of Herod's collection and training of carpenters and builders in preparation for building his Temple implies there was a shortage of artisans in Jerusalem for this massive construction project. Furthermore, according to Josephus (*Ant.* 20.219–20), the completion of the temple, which did not occur until the procuratorship of Albinus (62–64 CE), put 18,000 artisans out of work.

What *might* Jesus' family have helped construct in ancient Sepphoris? The visitor to the site of Sepphoris today will see many ruins of what must have been fabulous constructions. Most of these did not exist in the time period we are interested in. The following have been suggested to have been there in the first century CE:

1. The western domestic quarter (houses of the well-to-do; everyone agrees on this dating)
2. A "villa"[43]
3. The basilical building (debated)
4. The theater (debated)
5. Streets laid out in a Hippodamian grid (with Cardo and Decumanus; debated)
6. An aqueduct bringing fresh water to Sepphoris from two springs

---

43. See Chancey, "Cultural Milieu," 134.

Figure 3.8: Theater of Sepphoris; lower part is restored. It could seat 4,000 persons.[44] Did it exist in the first century CE?

The city of Sepphoris had a large public building built in basilica fashion (i.e., with a nave and apse) measuring 118 X 131 feet (15,000 square feet) in the interior area. This building, according to James F. Strange, was probably where the bureaucrats had offices and ran the government, the tax system, and the courts. In addition, some of the rooms were undoubtedly shops; in other words, the building served as a forum. The question debated by archaeologists is whether this building was built by Antipas or toward the end of the first century CE.[45]

There may have been (gravel) *Cardo* and *Decumanus* streets in Sepphoris in the early first century but this is debated.[46] There may have been a

---

44. Chancey and E. M. Meyers, "How Jewish Was Sepphoris," 26.

45. For the argument that this building existed only in the later part of the first century, see Weiss, "Josephus and Archaeology," 397–400. See also the discussion in Schumer, "Population Size of Sepphoris." On the other hand, Chancey, *Myth*, 76; Chancey, "Cultural Milieu," 134; and Strange, "Eastern Basilical Building," say it was there in the early part of the century (and thus during the time of Jesus). See additionally on the basilica Strange, "Sepphoris."

46. See Weiss, "Josephus and Archaeology," 397, who maintains that the Cardo and Decumanus streets, the Hippodamian grid pattern of city planning, was a late first-century, early second-century CE innovation. For a contrary view, see Chancey, "Cultural

theater built in the time of Antipas and Jesus, but the date of this structure is also disputed.[47] An aqueduct was also necessary in the early first century to provide adequately for the large populace. One was constructed to bring water from the Ein Genona and Amitai springs.[48]

Figure 3.9: One of the Sepphoris aqueducts

What were certainly in Sepphoris—or were being built in Sepphoris—in the early decades of the first century CE were the domestic structures on the western hill. These "moderately sized courtyard houses" measured on average c. 1900 square feet on the first story. They were constructed of "roughly cut, squat ashlars," laid in a header-stretcher fashion. A family

---

Milieu," 134; Chancey, *Myth*, 76; and Crossan and Reed, *Excavating Jesus*, 104.

47. For a date in the early first century (thus the time of Antipas and Jesus), see Strange, "Six Campaigns at Sepphoris," 342; Strange, "Sepphoris," 28; and Batey, *Jesus and the Forgotten City*, 83–103. For a date of late first century or early second century for the theater, see Weiss and Netzer, "Hellenistic and Roman Sepphoris"; C. Meyers and E. M. Meyers, "Sepphoris"; E. M. Meyers, "Jesus and His World," 198–90; Weiss, "From Galilean town to Roman City"; and Weiss, "Josephus and Archaeology," 400–402.

48. See Tsuk, "Aqueducts of Sepphoris"; Tsuk, "Bringing Water to Sepphoris"; and Strange, "Sepphoris Aqueducts."

of builders from nearby Nazareth could plausibly have been employed in building such dwellings.[49]

This is not to say, of course, that we know the family of Jesus did work at these sites. I only suggest the kind of work available for carpenters in Galilee that would take Jesus and his brothers beyond their home village.[50]

Given the urbanization of Lower Galilee (Sepphoris and Tiberias), the Decapolis (see Chapter 8), and also of the tetrarchy of Philip (Caesarea Philippi and Bethsaida Julias), one can well imagine that an artisan in the building trade would be in demand.[51] Since such was the case in the Greco-Roman world in general, causing artisans to move frequently from job to job, we should expect the same to have been true in Galilee. It is even possible that Jesus and his family worked on the Temple in Jerusalem from time to time.[52] Thus, even before Jesus began his ministry,[53] his social circle, which served as the base of his movements during his ministry, was established.

Therefore, we can say with certainty that there were several continuous and massive building projects during Jesus' youth and early adulthood. Second, we can be reasonably confident that these projects necessitated the services of skilled carpenters from distant cities and villages. Jesus and his extended family could easily have worked in Sepphoris, Tiberias, or other Galilean cities, and even in Jerusalem. Opportunities were there for this family to experience urban culture and to rise to the same level of economic comfort as the artisan family of Simon the Temple builder, perhaps to a kind of "middling" economic status.[54] The common understanding that Jesus grew up in dire poverty is unfounded and implausible.

---

49. See Meyers et al., "Chronological Summary," 21-23.

50. In Tiberias, they could have worked on (after around 20 CE) the gate with its two large towers. See Foerster, "Tiberias."

51. Overman, "Who Were the First Urban Christians?"

52. Oakman, *Economic Questions of His Day*, 186-93 argues that Jesus' social contacts with people in Jerusalem indicate that he was there many times before his ministry began. Oakman points to Jesus' friends in Bethany (near Jerusalem, Mark 14:3; Luke 10:38-42; John 11:1) and to the owner of the upper room (Mark 14:12-16).

53. Jesus' later detractors made much of his travels to Egypt where he allegedly acquired magical powers. Could this tradition testify to Jesus' travels as a carpenter? Stauffer has suggested that it does (*Jesus and His Story*, 44). See also Origen, *Cels.* I.28; b. Shabb. 104b (referring to Ben Stada).

54. For the fairly recent suggestion that there existed in the Greco-Roman world an economic "middling class," see Scheidel and Friesen, "Size of the Economy"; and Longenecker, *Remember the Poor*, 45. They maintain that 15 to 30 percent of the population consisted of workers with moderate surplus.

Figure 3.10: The Cardo Maximus street, Sepphoris.
Was it there in the early first century CE?

4

Capernaum

JESUS AND HIS DISCIPLES are often found in the Gospels traveling around the Sea of Galilee (or Lake Gennesaret) by boat.[1] Perhaps that is one reason Jesus decided on Capernaum as his ministerial base. He could more quickly travel from town to town (e.g., between Magdala/Taricheae, Tiberias, Bethsaida, and Capernaum; see Map 2 p. 100).

THE GALILEE BOAT

> One day when the crowd was pressing him to hear the word of God and he was standing next to the lake of Gennesaret, he saw two boats near the shore. Fishermen who had walked away from them were washing their nets. And embarking on one of the boats—the one belonging to Simon—he asked him to put out a bit from the land. Sitting (there) he taught the crowd from the boat. (Luke 5:1–3)

But what sort of boats did they use? We now have an actual ancient (first century BCE—first century CE) Galilee boat. The boat was discovered in the winter of 1986 on the northwest side of the Sea of Galilee when a drought caused the shoreline of the sea to recede. Buried in the mud was the hull of a boat that turned out to be from the time of Jesus (see Sidebar 4.1). It measured 26 ½ feet long and 7 ½ feet wide and could carry up to fifteen persons. Many consider this boat to be typical of the fishing boats used on

---

1. Matt 8:18, 23–27, 9:1, 14:13–14, 22–32, 15:39, 16:5; Mark 4:35–41, 5:18, 21, 6:32–34, 45–51, 8:9, 10, 13–14; Luke 5:2–11, 6:1, 8:22–25, 37, 40; John 6:16–21.

the Sea of Galilee in the first century and therefore similar to boats (though likely not one) that Jesus and his disciples actually used.

Several have constructed a model of what the boat would have looked like based on clues from the hull:

Figure 4.1: Model of the Galilee Boat reconstructed from the hull (Ginosar Museum, Israel).

Sidebar 4.1

The Galilee Boat[2]

- When discovered: 1986
- Where: Northwest shore of Sea of Galilee
- Size of boat:
    - 26½ feet long
    - 7½ feet wide

2. See Wachsmann, "Galilee Boat"; Wachsmann, *Sea of Galilee Boat*.

- 4½ feet high
- Full capacity—fifteen persons
• Date of the boat:
  - C14 test: 40 BCE (+ or –80 years)
  - Construction type: first cent. BCE–second century CE
  - Pottery found in the boat:
    ♦ Lamp: first century BCE–first century CE
    ♦ Cooking pot (casserole): first century BCE–first century CE
    ♦ Sherds of storage jar: first century BCE–first century CE
    ♦ Jugs and juglets: first century BCE–second century CE
  - Conclusion: The boat was probably built in the late first century BCE or early first century CE and used until the event in 68 CE near Magdala described in Josephus's writings (*War* 2.632–46; *Life* 155–78).
• Historical significance: may have been one of those commandeered by Josephus

The Hull

Photo by Konrad Summers[3]

3. Wikimedia Commons: https://commons.wikimedia.org/wiki/File:2,000_year-old_Galilee_Boat_(25891224685).jpg/.

THE HOUSE OF "SAINT PETER"

After Jesus' experience at his hometown of Nazareth, he went to Capernaum (Luke 4:31) to reside. Capernaum was a medium-sized fishing and agricultural village (of between 1,000 and 2,000 inhabitants) located on the north side of the Sea of Galilee. We read in Luke 4:38 (cf. Matt 8:14, 17:24–25; Mark 1:29, 9:33) that Jesus stayed at the house of Simon (Peter) in Capernaum, and that he healed Peter's mother-in-law of a high fever (probably malaria). In Chapter 5 of Luke's Gospel, we see how, because of the crowds pressing into Peter's house, four helpers (so Mark 2:3) had to resort to extreme means to bring their afflicted relative to Jesus for healing.

> Some men carrying a paralyzed man on a stretcher tried to bring him into (the house) to place him before (Jesus). But when they could not find a way in because of the crowd, they went up on the roof and lowered him on his cot—through the clay roof[4]—into the middle (of the house) and right in front of Jesus. (Luke 5:18–19)

Luke (and Mark 2:3–4) describes the scene during which Jesus was teaching inside a house (Mark 2:1) in Capernaum, presumably, the house of Peter, where Jesus stayed. Why were so many persons crowded into this house? How large was the house? Can we imagine what it looked like?

Italian archaeologists discovered in their excavations of Capernaum the remains of an octagonal church (see Figures 4.2 and 4.6, below). At first, they were puzzled as to the building's function. It had three concentric octagonal walls. When they uncovered a baptistry and an apse, both facing east, they knew it must be a church. They dated the church to the fifth century CE.[5]

Under the octagonal church was another, earlier church. Its central hall measured 27 X 25 feet. It was plastered and painted with several colors (reds, yellows, greens, blues, browns, white, and black). The wall decorations included geometric designs, pomegranates, flowers, and figs. A wall had been built around an entire block of earlier dwellings, evidently to form a distinct precinct. The structure was in use from the first century BCE to

---

4. This word (*keramos*) could be translated "ceramic tiles." See Danker, *Lexicon*. There were such tiles found in a village in Judea (Khirbet el-Maqatir; see Chapter 6), but they are usually only found in upscale houses in cities such as in Sepphoris in the western domestic quarter and in Jerusalem in the upper city. Bock, *Luke*, 1:481 maintains, however, that the word can mean simply "clay" as in Herm. *Vis.* 22:6.

5. Strange and Shanks, "House Where Jesus Stayed"; Finegan, *Archaeology*, 110.

the fourth century CE, originally having been a courtyard house. There were, then, three main phases of occupation of this site.[6]

Visitors to the church, apparently religious pilgrims, scratched many inscriptions (graffiti) on the walls. They were mostly in Greek but also in Aramaic, Syriac, and Latin.[7] One inscription was typical: "Christ have mercy." The numerous graffiti in so many different languages informed the excavators that pilgrims were coming to worship at this church (which was originally a house).

Figure 4.2: The octagonal church at Capernaum: the house of Peter?

The house, from which the first church was constructed, had been built simply of "wadi stones" (stones found lying about in the streambeds). The roof was "probably"[8] beams, branches, and earth. The house was actually a compound of buildings consisting of two courtyards, one large room, and several smaller rooms (see Figure 4.3, below). The "venerated room" alone

6. Loffreda, "Capernaum," 295. There were actually four phases, counting the Islamic phase of ninth to eleventh century CE (see De Luca, "Capernaum"), but only the first three concern the identification of the "House of Peter."

7. See the differing lists in Corbo, *House of Saint Peter*, 68; Strange and Shanks, "House Where Jesus Stayed"; and Meyers and Chancey, *From Alexander to Constantine*, 193. The last work lists 151 Gk. graffiti, 10 Aram., 13 Syriac, and 2 Lat.

8. Strange and Shanks, "House Where Jesus Stayed"; Finegan, *Archaeology*, 107.

(locus #1 on Carbo's plan [Figure 4.3, below]), that had been the focus of the house church, was c. 490 square feet.[9] But the southern door of this room opens into other rooms (certainly, room #8 in Figure 4.3, below) which may have been part of the house. This additional room makes the entire house c. 600 square feet plus shared courtyards. It was a substantial house/room. By way of comparison, the two rooms (7 and 18) made together another residence, which covered around 300 square feet.

The original house was constructed around 63 BCE at the time the Romans took possession of Palestine from the Seleucids. The excavators used pottery sherds[10] and coins embedded in the floor to date the original house.[11] Below is Corbo's plan of Insula I of Capernaum (cf. Figure 4.4, below), which contains the alleged House of Peter:

Why, then, would some suggest that this house belonged to Peter and that therefore Jesus, himself, resided there for several years? The argument is similar to that applied to the Church of Saint John in Ein Kerem: archaeological evidence of first-century occupation as well as Christian tradition about the site. There are, as stated above, three phases as attested by archaeology and Christian pilgrimages:

1. First, there is an ancient structure (built in the first century BCE). It was a simple house with an unusually large room compared with others in Capernaum. At some point, Peter and Andrew would have gained ownership of the house and perhaps the entire courtyard-compound associated with it. A floor laid on a fresh bed of stones at the end of the first or beginning of the second century CE remained in use until at least the third century,[12] attesting to the continuous occupation of the house.

2. The second stratum had two subphases.

    a. Subphase A: At some point, the ordinary house became a house church, followed by a church building, according to Strange. The floors and walls were plastered, and the pottery changed from household vessels to storage jars, "suggesting that the building ceased to be a simple domicile."[13] At this point, pilgrims were making journeys from all over the region (evidenced by the

---

9. Corbo, *House of Saint Peter*, 42; Loffreda, "Capernaum," 295; Strange and Shanks, "House Where Jesus Stayed."

10. I.e., fragments of cooking pots, pans, jars, and lamps. See Finegan, *Archaeology*, 107.

11. Strange and Shanks, "House Where Jesus Stayed."

12. See Taylor, *Christians and the Holy Places*, 282.

13. Meyers and Chancey, *From Alexander to Constantine*, 192.

multilingual graffiti) to visit the site. Taylor[14] maintains that the site never became an actual church (no items of worship or initiation have been found, such as a baptistry) but morphed into a pilgrim destination. A fourth-century woman named Aetheria (traveled 381–86 CE) visited the site and wrote: "In Capernaum, moreover, out of the house of the first of the apostles a church has been made, the walls of which still stand just as they were. Here the Lord cured a paralytic."[15]

  b. Subphase B: Then in the late fourth to early fifth century, the site, whether a house church or pilgrimage spot, was enlarged.

3. During the third stratum (the fifth century through the eighth century) an entirely new church building (the octagonal church) was erected. James F. Strange has observed that octagonal structures at this time were used for monument churches.[16]

Pilgrims continued to visit the site and the new church building. The Piacenza Pilgrim wrote around 570 CE: "We went to Capernaum into the house of the Blessed Peter, which is now a basilica."[17]

Was this, then, the actual location of Peter's house? It may well have been the residence of Jesus during his three-year ministry, but such identifications are usually tentative.[18]

A second issue—whether one accepts the identification of the venerated room with Peter's house—is the size of the house. One may question how much of this housing compound or *insula* actually belonged to Peter. Fred Strickert maintained that the entire complex (3,500 square feet) belonged to one person, and that it is therefore unlikely that Peter the poor fisherman could have afforded it. He suggested the house in Capernaum might have belonged to wealthier residents such as Jairus (Luke 8:40–42, 49–56) or the centurion (Luke 7:1–10).[19]

---

14. Taylor, *Christians and the Holy Places*, 274–76, 282.

15. Translation in Finegan, *Archaeology*, 110.

16. Strange and Shanks, "House Where Jesus Stayed," modified somewhat in De Luca, "Capernaum."

17. Translation in Wilkinson, *Jerusalem Pilgrims*, 81.

18. The conclusion of Meyers and Chancey is less sanguine: "The site could mark where Peter's house actually stood, or it could mark where later Christians mistakenly thought it stood, or it could even be associated with a church altogether distinct from the House of Peter mentioned in literary sources" (*From Alexander to Constantine*, 193). Likewise, Becker ("Jesus and Capernaum," 120) "cannot exclude the possibility" that the house was Peter's.

19. Strickert, *Bethsaida*, 25–28.

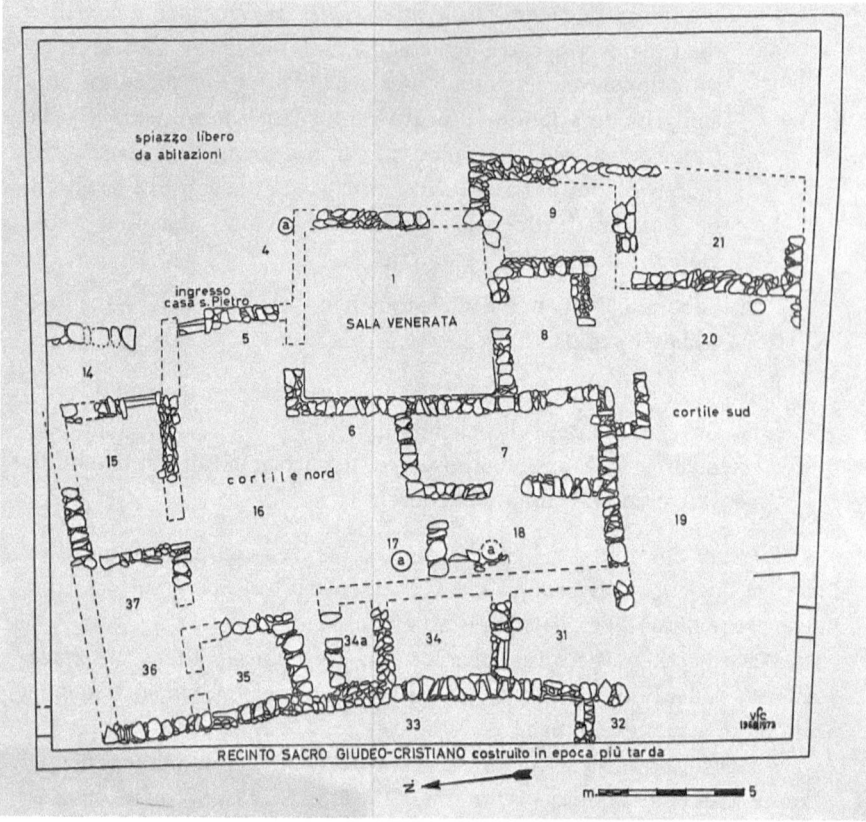

Figure 4.3: Plan of the first-century BCE house under the church and adjoining houses/rooms. Locus #1, the venerated room, was the alleged house of Peter.[20] Compare Figure 4.4, below. (Image courtesy Studium Biblicum Franciscanum, Jerusalem)

Others seem to have assumed multiple families or, more likely, multiple family members shared the courtyards and inhabited one- or two-room dwellings. Peter's part of the *insula*, under this understanding, would have been only the venerated room of 490 square feet (but I suggest 600 square feet). Corbo, for example, assumed that the *insula* was a "clan house," i.e., that the complex was owned by the wider family of Peter and Andrew. In this arrangement, Peter would have owned one or more rooms of the complex or *insula* and shared one or more courtyards with other extended family members that inhabited the other rooms.[21] In the latter case, Peter need not have been wealthy to afford to live there.

20. Plan is scanned from Corbo, *Capharnao I*, Tav. IX.
21. Corbo, "Capernaum," 867.

A third debate concerns whether Peter ever lived in Capernaum at all. Even before recent archaeological discoveries, those excavating at what they have claimed was the village of Bethsaida (i.e., at Et-Tell, see Chapter 7) maintained that the actual house of Peter was not in Capernaum. Thus, Fred Strickert suggested that this house in Capernaum actually belonged to Peter's mother-in-law (if not to Jairus or the centurion, see above) and not to Peter himself. Peter's (and Andrew's) house was in Bethsaida, affirmed Strickert.[22] An eighth-century Bavarian pilgrim to the Holy Land, Willibald, reported seeing a church in a village identified then as Bethsaida. He further noted that the locals claimed this church had been constructed over the first-century house of Peter and Andrew:

> From [Capernaum], they went to Bethsaida, the city of Peter and Andrew; there is now a church there in the place where originally their house stood.[23]

Several sixteenth-century pilgrims, perhaps quoting Willibald, maintained the same.[24] Thus, some of the Holy Land pilgrims believed that Peter's and Andrew's house was in Bethsaida, not Capernaum, and Strickert and others excavating Et-Tell believed the house was there (somewhere).

But what about Aetheria's fourth-century report (quoted above) that she visited the house of Peter at Capernaum? Steven Notley observes that this quotation comes to us through the twelfth-century CE author Peter the Deacon. Notley further maintains that Peter the Deacon was a "notorious forger and liar." Thus, he hopes to dispense with Aetheria's testimony. What of the word of the Piacenza Pilgrim (sixth century), whose statement is also quoted above? Notley suggests that the pilgrim hinted that he visited Capernaum "and then" moved on to Bethsaida where the house of Peter stood, and was not indicating that he visited Peter's house in Capernaum.[25]

Now, we possibly have further evidence. Due to excavations in the summer of 2022, excavators believe they have found a Byzantine basilica—perhaps the very church mentioned by Willibald—built over the house of Peter and Andrew in a different village that they identify as Bethsaida. The excavations of El-Araj (on the northeast shore of the Sea of Galilee) may cause several paradigm shifts in the coming years. Archaeologists associated

22. Strickert, *Bethsaida*, 25–28.
23. Translation in Wilkinson, *Jerusalem Pilgrims*, 128.
24. Newswire, "New Inscription"; Steinmeyer, "Discovering Biblical Bethsaida"; Aviam and Notley, "In Search of the City"; McNamer, "Pilgrim Accounts," 399–400.
25. Notley, "Byzantine Bethsaida," 540, 546–47. The Lat. words "et inde" appear in one manuscript of the Piacenza Pilgrim. There is no mention explicitly of Bethsaida in the Pilgrim's account.

with these excavations claim that they have discovered both the true village of Bethsaida (see Chapter 7) and the true location of the house of Peter and Andrew. Their discovery, in the ruins of the fifth-century so-called Church of the Apostles, is a mosaic inscription in Greek asking for intercession from Peter, the "chief and commander of the heavenly apostles."[26]

This new evidence will take time to process and evaluate. We must always be open to new information and to changing our conclusions. Yet, the evidence for the Capernaum house—both archaeological and literary (Aetheria's and the Piacenza Pilgrim's reports)—is not easily set aside. The site in Capernaum was continuously occupied and/or visited from the first-century BCE to the eleventh century CE. There were numerous pilgrims to the site as the inscriptions show. The site at El-Araj had a 200-year gap in its occupation (from the third to the fifth centuries, see Chapter 7), during which time it silted over from river floods. Under those conditions, could the Byzantine builders have known where Bethsaida was, and especially where the original house of Peter and Andrew stood if it was at El-Araj?[27]

We await further investigation. It is possible that the church in El-Araj rests on the birth-house of Peter and Andrew (or in that vicinity) and that the two brothers moved into Galilee (from the Golan) to Capernaum to marry and seek better economic opportunities.[28] One fourth-century church father offered:

> Peter was from Bethsaida but had married a woman from Capernaum, for the two places are not far apart.[29]

That statement might imply that Peter had moved to Capernaum from the village of his birth, Bethsaida.

Thus, we have two debates happening at the same time: First, was Peter's (and Andrew's) house in Capernaum or Bethsaida? Second, at which

---

26. Newswire, "New Inscription"; Steinmeyer, "Discovering Biblical Bethsaida."

27. Aviam and Notley answer (private correspondence): "We assume that the name of the site, and ruins in some parts [of] it were visible on [the] surface. There is no need to pinpoint exactly to the "house of Peter" (Aviam). "No one on the excavation team is suggesting that the church is in fact built over the house of Peter . . . While Byzantine traditions are often questionable, we must bear in mind that in the East memories are tenaciously long" (Notley).

28. Other scholars, commenting on Willibald's testimony, have suggested that he confused Bethsaida with Capernaum. See Aviam and Notley, "In Search of the City" 8; McNamer, "Pilgrim Accounts," 400.

29. Epiphanius, *Panarion* 51.15.5. Translation in Notley, "Byzantine Bethsaida," 543.

site—Et-Tell or El-Araj[30]—can one find the ruins of biblical Bethsaida? We will speak further of the second controversy in Chapter 7.

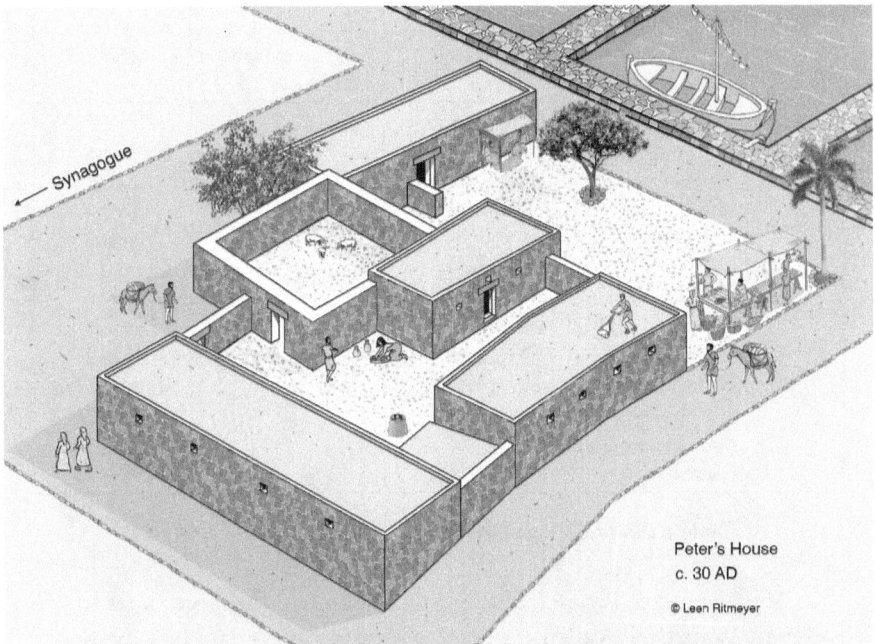

Figure 4.4: Artist's reconstruction of the "House of Peter," looking southeast. The venerated room is unroofed in the drawing. Notice the drawing does not indicate a second story on any of the rooms. Did Peter own the entire *insula*, just the venerated room, or the venerated room plus an adjoining room?[31]

HOUSE SIZES

It is instructive to compare the size of this house with others featured in this volume. It is not so much the raw square footage of a domicile but more so the comparative size that indicates level of wealth. The following table collects some of the evidence:

---

30. See the debate in: Notley, "Et-Tell is Not Bethsaida"; and Arav, "Bethsaida."
31. Drawing purchased from https://www.ritmeyer.com/. The drawing in Corbo, *Capharnao I*, Tav. X was also one story.

Location of living space	The "House of Peter" at Capernaum and adjoining house	Two houses from Et-Tell (possibly Bethsaida; see Chapter 7)	Average size of houses in the western domestic quarter in Sepphoris (see Chapter 3)	Three houses in the Upper City of Jerusalem (see Chapter 12)
Size in square feet	1. Peter's house: minimally 490, probably c. 600 plus two shared courtyards 2. House adjoining on southwest side (loci 7 and 18, see Figure 4.3, above): c. 300 plus a shared courtyard[32]	1. A "Simple house": 255 plus a shared courtyard 2. House of the Fisherman 4,300 including its own private courtyard	1900	1. Palatial mansion: 13,000 2. Herodian House: 1,400 3. House near Church of Saint Peter in Gallicantu: 1,600

Table 4.1: A sampling of living space in first-century CE Israel

The "House of Peter" in Capernaum is among the larger ones in the southern (sometimes called the "sacred") *insula* or compound. The house (loci #7 and #18) sharing a courtyard with "Peter's" house, on the other hand, was much smaller, and there were evidently several other smaller dwellings connected to the two courtyards that Peter's house used. There are two cautions, however. First, we actually have remains at Capernaum of very few houses from this period.[33] Many of the dwellings date to the Byzantine period.

Second, the excavations have not been able to clearly delineate all the housing units around the venerated house.[34] There may have been a first-century house in the *insula* between the venerated house and the synagogue (see Figure 4.6 below). This excavated area is disputed, however. Matillah

---

32. Corbo, *House of St. Peter*, 42–50 gives the size of rooms/houses sharing the north courtyard with the alleged house of Peter. His loci 7 and 18 were 178 and 121 square feet respectively. But these loci look like two rooms of one house, thus 299 square feet for the house. I accept the principle presented in Matillah, "Capernaum," 229: the independence of a unit is defined by its lack of accessibility from other units. If one needs to exit his/her own unit and walk into neutral space in order to enter another unit, they are separate habitations.

33. Matillah, "Capernaum," 224 identifies twelve large houses on the Capernaum site. Of these, she dates only two to the time of Jesus.

34. Corbo, *House of St. Peter*, 39; Matillah, "Capernaum," 245.

contends that the ruins between the venerated insula and the synagogue formed three large houses, of which, house #1 (covering an area of 3,400 square feet) was first century, the other two being Byzantine.[35] Murphy-O'Connor, on the other hand, saw in this area (which would include all three of the houses identified by Matillah) fifteen small units sheltering around one hundred persons.[36] By Matillah's standards, Peter's house would be on the small size for this village. By Murphy-O'Connor's, his house would be larger but not extravagant.

Compared to the houses of the well-to-do in Sepphoris, to the House of the Fisherman at Et-Tell, and to the houses in Jerusalem's upper city, the venerated house—which may have been Peter's house—is of small to middling size. If we can make any judgments based on living space, Peter was not a poor man but certainly not in the same economic class as those inhabiting the Palatial Mansion of Jerusalem (see Chapter 12) or the House of the Fisherman at Et-Tell. Capernaum's House of Peter is neither as small as the other two-room house sharing his courtyard nor as small as the "simple house" of Et-Tell described in Chapter 7.

One other factor must be mentioned. These houses in the two *insulae* (around the alleged House of Peter and the one to the north of it) gave no evidence of luxury goods. The walls were unworked, basalt stones (no frescoed walls and no mosaic floors), and the contents of the houses were modest. Thus, they were comfortable but not wealthy residents.[37]

HOW TO BUILD A HOUSE

Whether this particular house belonged to Peter (and Andrew his brother, Mark 1:29), to Peter's mother-in-law, to Jairus, the centurion, or to someone totally unknown to us, it shows typical building techniques for houses in Capernaum and probably is a good illustration of the houses most Galilean villagers owned in the first century CE. Peter's house—wherever it was—would have been at least similar to this one.

Learning how they built these houses may help us understand this scene in Luke 5. We have the ancient references to house-building and the contemporary Palestinian/Arab village builders to inform us. The first task in building a house was to gather materials. The main materials were stone, mortar (clay soil mixed with water), and wood (for the roof). Builders of houses in contemporary traditional Palestinian villages will pile up the soil

35. Matillah, "Capernaum," 221, 230.
36. Murphy-O'Connor, *Holy Land*, 252.
37. Corbo, *House of St. Peter*, 37–39.

in huge heaps and bring in the quarried or wadi stones to stack in storage while waiting for the beginning of the construction. The stones may then be cut into "worked stones" (flat-surfaced blocks) or into "hammered" stones (either hewn stones from a quarry that were not dressed, or fieldstones with minimal dressing). The stones may also not be worked at all but merely picked up from the ground, especially from a wadi bed, and used as they are (the way the so-called House of Peter was built).[38]

Most houses in Herodian-period Palestine were made of stone, either the white limestone so abundant in much of Palestine or the black basalt found north and east of the Sea of Galilee and used in Capernaum and at Et-Tell. The exception was in the Sharon Plain and other lower-lying areas, where houses were built of mud brick.[39] The use of bricks in building houses seems to have been both a necessity for those living in certain regions where stones were not readily available and also a local tradition as the following text from the Mishnah indicates.

> A place where people are accustomed to build with rough stones, hewn stones, rafters, or bricks, they build [that way]. Everything is done according to the custom of the region.[40] (m. B. Batra 1:1)

The roofs in ancient Palestine—the more expensive ones[41]—were often made of limestone slabs like those in the traditional contemporary Palestinian houses.[42] Such roofs were, for obvious reasons, very strong but could only stretch a certain length without a support column on the first floor.

But those families of more modest means used wooden beams woven with smaller branches and then covered with mortar (clay soil and water). These flat roofs are common in contemporary traditional sites in Israel today and were also the standard in ancient Palestine/Israel. Houses, such as those at Capernaum, apparently had roofs of wooden beams and smaller tree branches covered with clay-plaster and straw.[43] Luke describes the four

---

38. Hirschfeld, *Palestinian Dwelling*, 217-19, 222.

39. Safrai and Brunner, "Home and Family," 732; and Hirschfeld, *Palestinian Dwelling*, 24. See m. Soṭah 8:3 and m. B. Batra 1:1 for mud-brick houses. For the technology of ancient brick building see Homsher, "Mud Bricks."

40. Translation from the Heb. text in Mi-Bartenura, *Six Orders*, 2:67.

41. Krauss, *Talmudische Archäologie*, 1:27; Beebe, "Domestic Architecture" 101; Safrai and Brunner, "Home and Family," 732; Yeivin, "Survey of Settlements," xiv. Yeivin, "Ancient Chorazin," 25 describes the basalt roofs of ancient Chorazin.

42. Hirschfeld, *Palestinian Dwelling*, 120-34; Sweet, *Tell Toqaan*, 114-15; Thompson, *Land*, 1:132, 386; 2:434.

43. Strange and Shanks, "House Where Jesus Stayed"; Corbo, *House of St. Peter*, 37.

men taking up the clay (tiles? Luke 5:19) from the roof of the house. Mark says they "removed the roof" by "digging" it out (2:4).

Since many of the dwellings at Capernaum had external staircases,[44] it is possible they had a second story, at least a partial one, although the drawing (see Figure 4.4, above) does not show them. We must also bear in mind, however, that stairs may only demonstrate a need to ascend to the roof. Although some of the houses may have had a full second story—something most excavators up to now have doubted due to the rather weak walls[45]—most, if they had a second story at all, had covered only part of their flat roof with another room (see Chapter 13 for upper rooms). Therefore, it seems that the four men (Mark 2:3) carrying the disabled man may have climbed the exterior stairs (no trace of them is left at this house, but one of the other rooms in this *insula* had stairs) to the second story and pulled up the clay-mud roof of the first story. If Peter's house had a second story, it may not have been a complete covering of the first story's roof.

These waddle-and-daub roofs required continual maintenance especially during and just after the rainy season to keep the mud smoothed down. To maintain the roofs in contemporary traditional houses, there is a stone roller left in place on the roof to flatten it on occasion.[46] Undoubtedly the ancients had the same technique. Archaeologists have found stone roof rollers in the ruins of some houses, indicating the ancient method of maintaining their roofs was identical to the traditional Arab method.[47]

Since so many persons on this day were crammed into this house (the four could not get the disabled man into the house because of the crowd; Mark 2:4, Luke 5:19), it is likely that this scene took place in the rainy season. People pushed into the house to get out of the rain while listening to Jesus teach. Otherwise, it is inconceivable that they would not meet out of doors. If so, the work of the four men—on the rain-soaked mud of the waddle-and-daub roof—may have been less strenuous.

---

44. Several dwellings in the *insula* of the alleged house of Peter had staircases. See Corbo, *House of St. Peter*, 50; and De Luca, "Capernaum," 176.

45. Finegan, *Archaeology*, 107; Strange and Shanks, "House Where Jesus Stayed"; Corbo, *House of St. Peter*, 35–52.

46. Hirschfeld, *Palestinian Dwelling*, 120–34, 244; Canaan, *Palestinian Arab House*, 48, 54–55; Sweet, *Tell Toqaan*, 114–15; and Thompson, *Land*, 1.132, 386; 2.434.

47. Dever, *Lives of Ordinary People*, 131; Borowski, *Daily Life*, 20; Wright, "Israelite Daily Life," 60.

SANITATION

Lawrence E. Stager suggested that livestock was usually brought into a room close to the living quarters at night, either underneath in a dug cave (see Chapter 1, Church of the Nativity), in the living quarters, or in a room next to it (e.g., room # 8 in Figure 4.3, above). He suggested that side rooms found at Capernaum with "fenestrated walls" actually contained not windows but storage niches for animals. If Stager is correct, then animals often slept on the ground floor or in a room adjoining the living quarters.[48] Josephus writes about a prohibition of butchering animals which "take refuge in our houses" (*Apion* 2.213),[49] evidently referring to these nocturnal guests.

Further, this practice was still being done (and perhaps is continuing today in very traditional villages) up to the mid-twentieth century in the Middle East. Western travelers to Palestine in the nineteenth and early twentieth centuries often remarked on the smell and unsanitary conditions of the village houses: "The houses are not fit to put pigs in, and every dooryard is full of mire and filth."[50]

Masterman, a physician practicing in Palestine in the early twentieth century, also noted the extreme filth of the houses and the presence of every sort of vermin. He wrote that in their dwellings:

> lice, mosquitoes, and other insect-pests are found in abundance ... Most dwellings swarm with vermin ... There are, with very few exceptions, no sanitary arrangements ...[51]

Were the houses similarly filthy in first-century Israel? Was Peter's house, in which Jesus resided for a while, that unsanitary? One would think so.

Thus, in Peter's house may have been, not only his own family, but also his brother Andrew's family, Peter's mother-in-law, Jesus, a few of his disciples—and some animals. The venerated room (plus the side room) no longer seems large.

---

48. Stager, "Archaeology of the Family" 11–14. For animals sleeping either in the living quarters of the family or under the living quarters see Hirschefeld, *Palestinian Dwelling*, 120–34, 149, 158–59; Amiry and Tamari, *Palestinian Village Home*, 25–29.

49. Translation by Thackery, in Josephus LCL.

50. Thompson, *Land*, 2:544 (quotation from a nineteenth-century speaker).

51. Masterman, "Hygiene and Disease in Palestine," 15–17.

THE SYNAGOGUE

Figure 4.5: Standing back wall of the LR–Byz limestone synagogue at Capernaum

> And it happened on another Sabbath that he went into the synagogue and was teaching. (Luke 6:6)[52]

In Capernaum Jesus often taught in the synagogue (Mark 1:23; Luke 4:33, 38; John 6:59), on one occasion casting a demon from a man. We learn later (Luke 7:5) that this synagogue was the benefaction of a residing "centurion" who asked Jesus to heal his son/slave (see Chapter 10). In the text above, while Jesus was teaching, he encountered and healed a man with a crippled right hand.

---

52. See parallels in Matt 12:9–14; Mark 3:1–6.

Figure 4.6: Capernaum today (western side), looking south. The octagonal building at the top of the photo covers the Byz church ruins and the alleged House of Peter. The large, unroofed building below is the LR–Byz synagogue allegedly standing over the first-century synagogue. (Photograph by AVRAMGR)[53]

Visitors to the ruins of Capernaum today will encounter immediately the white limestone remains of a second–fifth-century CE synagogue (figures 4.5 and 4.6). This was not, of course, the synagogue in which Jesus taught frequently. But those excavating around and inside the current ruins may have found the first-century building in which Jesus taught.

First, excavators noticed that the white limestone ruins of the LR–Byz synagogue were resting on a black basalt base (Figure 4.7). Upon investigation, they found that the base was not just the foundation of the later synagogue but an actual wall, four feet thick and still extant to a height of three feet.

53. Wikimedia Commons: https://commons.wikimedia.org/wiki/File:KFAR_NA-HUM_AERIAL_V.JPG/. For explanation of this site, see Loffreda, "Capernaum," 291.

Figure 4.7: Limestone LR–Byz synagogue sitting on a basalt base.

Next, they excavated beneath the floor of the nave of the LR–Byz synagogue. They discovered four strata beneath the pavers: Just beneath was a layer of mortar. Beneath that was a thick layer of limestone chips, undoubtedly laid down by the builders of the LR–Byz synagogue. Beneath this stratum were three feet of fill. Finally, the lowest level consisted of a cobbled pavement of basalt stones. On top of and in between the stones were pottery sherds dating from the first to the fourth centuries CE. Further, excavators noticed basalt walls which were associated with this basalt pavement. Thus, the walls and pavement were part of an earlier building. Under the cobbled pavement they found sherds dating from the third–second century BCE. There was at that time general agreement that they had found the first century CE synagogue in which Jesus had preached.[54] The dimensions

54. See Strange and Shanks, "Synagogue"; Loffreda, "Capernaum," 294; Runesson et al., *Ancient Synagogue*, 32; and Hachlili, *Ancient Synagogues*, 23.

of this synagogue make it one of the largest from the first century discovered so far (see Sidebar 4.2). Thus, although one can no longer step inside the actual synagogue where Jesus taught in Capernaum—because it is several feet below the present ruins—one can visit the site which stands over that synagogue.

There have been further developments since the Franciscan excavations in the 1960s and 1970s and the other excavations on the eastern side of the site of Capernaum in the 1970s and 1980s.[55] One of the debates, as indicated above, is whether the constructions between the octagonal church and synagogue represent an *insula* or block of apartment-like dwellings of rather poor persons, or larger houses of the well-to-do (see above). Additionally, there is an ongoing investigation into both the octagonal church and the synagogue to determine dates and construction.[56] Conclusions about Capernaum may remain in flux for some time.

SIDEBAR 4.2

Below is a table of synagogues from the first century CE[57] in descending order of size.[58] There certainly were synagogue buildings in existence during the ministry of Jesus.[59] Some of these synagogues, however, although dating from the first century, may have originated after Jesus' time (i.e., after 33 CE).[60]

---

55. See Laughlin, "Capernaum."

56. The investigation is being led by Rina Talgam of Hebrew University.

57. This list keeps growing. It will undoubtedly be outdated soon. See Bauckham, "Magdala," 42–44; Tessler, "Ancient synagogue"; Levine, "Synagogues of Galilee"; Onn et al., "Khirbet Umm el-'Umdan"; Netzer, "Masada"; Foerster, "Herodium"; Netzer, "Jericho: Exploration since 1973"; Leibner, "Kirbet Wadi Hamam"; Runesson et al., *Ancient Synagogue*; and Hachlili, *Ancient Synagogues*; Ryan, "Recent Archaeological Discoveries"; Ryan, "Jesus and the Synagogue"; Osband and Arubas, "Majduliyya"; "Tel Rekhesh"; Hasegawa, "Tel Rekhesh"; Gross, "Other Side of Beth Shemesh"; Har-Even, "Ḥorvat Diab"; Netzer, "Synagogues."

58. But compare the dimensions given by Haber, "Common Judaism, 67; Strange and Shanks, "Synagogue," 206; Runesson et al., *Ancient Synagogue*, 25–75. Their differing figures are evidently the result of measuring the interior space as opposed to the entire space, or measuring the entire space as opposed to just the hall.

59. "It is not uncommon to see statements in New Testament scholarship to the effect that there are no or very few synagogues [*sic*] buildings that date to the time of the New Testament that have been discovered in the Southern Levant. I wonder whether such statements are still appropriate in light of the new discoveries," (Ryan, "Recent Archaeological Discoveries.").

60. I do not include in this list the synagogues of Khirbet Qana and Shikhin since they are, at best, late first and probably second century CE. See McCollough, "Khirbet Qana," 141; James Riley Strange, "Kefar Shikhin," 105. For maps of all synagogues

Synagogue location	Size in square feet
Capernaum (Galilee)	4,931
Gamla (Golan)	4,050 (hall: 1,345)
Majduliyya (Golan)	3,100
Jericho (Judea)	2,042
Herodium (Judea)	1,765 (hall: 1,689)
Masada (Judea)	1,410
Khirbet Umm el-ʿUmdan (near Modiʾin in Judea)	c. 1,312
Magdala I (Galilee)	1,291 (main hall)
Ḥorvat Burnat (Judean Shephelah)	1,140
Qiryat Sefer (NW of Jerusalem)	992
Ḥorvat ʿEthri (SW of Jerusalem)	980 (the hall)
Tel Rekhesh (Galilee near Mt. Tabor)	850
Beth Shemesh (Judean Shephelah)	693
Magdala II[1] (Galilee)	635
Shuafat (N of Jerusalem)	538
Ḥorvat Diab (Judea)	272 (hall)
Khirbet Wadi Hamam (near Magdala)[2]	?
Chorazin (north of Capernaum)[3]	?
Ḥorvat er-Tuwani (in Hebron mountains)	26[4] X ?

(dating from the first to the fifth centuries CE) excavated in Israel, see Rousseau and Arav, *Jesus and His World*, 271; Clausen, *Upper Room*, 170–71; Meyers and Chancey, *From Alexander to Constantine*, 218; Hachlili, *Ancient Synagogues*, 22.

1. See "Second Synagogue Found in Magdala."

2. There was a public building, similar to the synagogue at nearby Magdala, but whose dimensions could not be ascertained since one end of it was destroyed and removed. See Leibner, "Kirbet Wadi Hamam," 348–49; Leibner and Arubas, "Area A," 29, 91.

3. Explorers in 1926 found what was evidently a first-century synagogue 200 meters west of the later synagogue, but these remains are evidently now lost. See Hachlili, *Ancient Synagogues*, 30; and Netzer, "Synagogues."

4. Only the west side of the synagogue survived. See Hachlili, *Ancient Synagogues*, 26.

5

The Male and Female Disciples

> And it happened that he went out onto a mountain to pray. He spent the night in prayer to God and when the (next) day came, he called his disciples to choose twelve of them whom he called apostles: Simon whom he named Peter, Andrew, his brother, James,[1] John, Philip, Bartholomew, Matthew, Thomas, James[2] son of Alphaeus, Simon called the Zealot, Judas son of James,[3] and Judas Iscariot who became the betrayer. (Luke 6:12–16)

THUS READS THE LIST of disciples in Luke, the identical list of Acts 1:13 though in a different order, and the closely parallel lists of Matt 10:2–4 and Mark 3:16–19.[4] One understandably wants to know more about these men but often has only their names to investigate. To tease out more information of the men on the list (and the women on a later list) this chapter will first consider the names themselves in comparison with names of others from this region and time and then, second, offer osteopathic analysis of persons presumed to be typical—i.e., take a look at the skeletal remains of

---

1. I.e., Jacob.
2. I.e., Jacob.
3. I.e., Jacob.
4. The lists of Matt and Mark substitute Thaddeus for Judas son of James. Why the difference? Bauckham, *Jesus and the Eyewitnesses*, 99–100 maintains that this disciple had two names, a Gk. one (Thaddeus) and a Heb. one (Judas). Meier, *Marginal Jew*, 3:131, argues, however, that the original disciple, Thaddeus, left the group (perhaps he was expelled by Jesus or became ill), and that Judas son of James took his place. Fitzmyer, *Luke*, 1:620, affirmed that by the time Luke and Matt wrote their Gospels, the early church could no longer remember all the names of the original twelve disciples.

working-class persons—to offer insights into the lives of the first members of the Jesus-movement. We present below a table with comparative information about names gleaned from both the Dead Sea Scrolls (see Sidebar 2.2) and from the burial boxes called ossuaries. We ask how common these names were and whether the names indicate anything about the origins of these men and women. Later, we present a list of persons—some named—from three cemeteries as representatives of first-century Jews in Palestine/Israel. The study then offers a socioeconomic hierarchy and places Jesus' first followers—somewhat speculatively—within it.

OSSILEGIUM

First, let us say a word about ossuaries. Many families living in Judea (but not usually Galilee) practiced secondary burial in ossuaries, a burial custom beginning in the first century BCE and ending sometime in the second century CE. First, they placed the deceased in a tomb, stretched out on a stone slab or in a niche. Then, about one year later (see b. Qidd. 31b), they went to the tomb, gathered the bones, and placed them in a box, usually constructed of stone but sometimes of clay or wood. This practice is called ossilegium.

The oft-quoted words of Rabbi Eleazar bar Zadok summarize the process:

> My son, bury me at first in a fosse [trench]. In the course of time, collect my bones and put them in an ossuary.[5]

The Mishnah (see Sidebar 9.1) further discusses the practice:

> A man may gather together the bones of his father or his mother [during midfestival] since this is to him an occasion for rejoicing (m. Mo'ed Qat. 1:5).[6]

> When the flesh had wasted away, they gathered together the bones and buried them in their own place (m. Sanh. 6:6).[7]

In Jerusalem and Jericho in the first century BCE families transitioned from primary burials for their loved ones in wooden coffins to secondary burials in ossuaries, first placing the deceased in a tomb and then, one year later, collecting the bones and putting them into a box (see Figures 3.6,

---

5. Sem. 12.9. Translation in Zlotnick, *Semaḥot*, 82.
6. Translation in Danby, *Mishnah*.
7. Translation in Danby, *Mishnah*. See further m. Pes. 8:8.

above (p. 53); 5.1, and 13.2 (p. 235), and Sidebar 14.2 (p. 248)).[8] Although this change took place in Judea, it did not become popular in Galilee until the second century CE. To date only two ossuaries from the first century have been found in Galilee.[9]

Why Jews in Judea initiated the practice of secondary burial in ossuaries is something of a mystery. There are at least four hypotheses as to the origin and rationale for using ossuaries or secondary burials.[10] Whatever the origin of the practice, the use of ossuaries has been found across most class levels. Most of the ossuaries would have been cheaply made of soft limestone[11] and so affordable for the working class. There seems, then, to have been no correlation between one's wealth and the use of stone boxes to contain one's bones.[12] Thus, there was a kind of democratization in burial, especially in Jerusalem and Jericho. Many wanted a rock-cut tomb, even those of modest means (those in the working class but not destitute), and they also wanted to use ossuaries in secondary burial. That is not to say, however, that the extremely poor and destitute could afford a rock-cut tomb and ossuaries for the family (see Chapter 15).[13] But increasingly, it seems, the working class—the 90 percent—had a tomb and a cheaply made stone box for their bones.

The fact that ossuaries were introduced often helps us glean information about the deceased persons. This information comes in the form of inscriptions on the box which might include the name (and nickname), occupation, an unusual feature, and/or an event from the life of the departed. To date, between nine hundred and a thousand tombs have been discovered in the Jerusalem area from our period. In these tombs around six hundred ossuaries were inscribed.[14] We will see some of this information in Table 5.4 below. These ossuaries sometimes present us with a miniature history of the persons contained in them.

8. Hachlili, "Burial Practices," 449; Hachlili, *Jewish Funerary Customs*, 75, 94.

9. Aviam, "Distribution Maps," 125–26 knew of none. But a tomb was recently discovered which contained one stone and one clay ossuary. See Leibner and Amitzur. "Roman-Period Burial Cave."

10. See Magness, *Stone and Dung*, 151–52; Rahmani, "Jewish Ossuaries," 30–31; Rahmani, "Ancient Jerusalem's Funerary Customs," 110; Hachlili, "Burial Practices," 450; Evans, *Jesus and the Ossuaries*, 27–29; Fine, "Death," 447–51.

11. But there are a few hard limestone ossuaries in some of the tombs. According to Rahmani ("Jewish Ossuaries," 31–33), these would have been quite expensive and were the work of expert stone masons.

12. Magness, *Stone and Dung*, 151; Hachlili, "Burial Practices," 450. On the other hand, Ilan, "Ossuaries," 64 writes: "even the simplest ossuaries at our disposal do not represent the paupers of Jerusalem."

13. Paupers were buried in the ground and did not practice secondary burial.

14. See Price, "Languages of the Jews."

Figure 5.1: Ossuaries (boxes for human bones) from the Israel Museum. Some of them are painted and/or decorated with rosettes. (Photograph by Tamara[15])

THE LISTS OF MALE DISCIPLES

The ossuaries, then, may offer helpful hints about a person's family and background as the table below, listing the names of the Twelve alongside information from the Dead Sea Scrolls (DSS) and the ossuaries, demonstrates:

---

15. Wikimedia Commons: https://commons.wikimedia.org/wiki/File:Ossuaries_of_Jesus_son_of_Joseph_and_more.JPG/. For photographs of finely crafted, ornate ossuaries from our time period, see Sussman, "Jewish Burial Cave."

Name	Number of times the name occurs in the ossuaries	Number of times the name occurs in the DSS	Nickname (if any)	Comments[16]
Simon	59	72	Peter ("rock")	The name occurs 257 times in all sources. It is the most common man's name during the time of Jesus.
Andrew	0	0		His name occurs 3 times in the New Testament and writings of Josephus. It is a Greek name.
Jacob (James)	5	10	"Son of Thunder" (Mark 3:17; along with his brother John)	The name occurs 45 times in all sources. The Greek, *huioi brontēs*, "sons of thunder," stands for the Hebrew *benei* regesh,[17] "sons of restlessness" or *benei ra'am*[18] "sons of thunder." The name Jacob is usually rendered in English translations of the New Testament as James.
John	25	40	(see above)	(see above) The name (Heb. Yoḥannan) occurs 128 times in all sources.
Philip	0	0		His name occurs 7 times in all the sources. It is a Greek name. Since Philip came from Bethsaida (see Chapter 10), a town under the jurisdiction of Philip the Tetrarch, perhaps he was named for him.

16. Ilan, *Lexicon*, investigated other sources of names including: the Pseudepigrapha, Josephus, the ostraca, the rabbinic literature, the New Testament, the early noncanonical Christian literature, papyri, inscriptions, coins, and jars.

17. Danker, *Lexicon*.

18. Ilan, *Lexicon*, 18.

Name	Number of times the name occurs in the ossuaries	Number of times the name occurs in the DSS	Nickname (if any)	Comments[16]
Bartholomew	1	0		His name means "son of Ptolemy,"[19] a Greek-Aramaic hybrid name. We do not know this disciple's personal name. The name Ptolemy appears 10 times in the sources.
Matthew	17	15		The name is found 63 times in all sources.
Thomas	0	0	(This is his nickname)	His name is the Aramaic word for "twin." John's Gospel gives the Greek equivalent "Didymus" (11:16, 20:24, 21:2)[20]
Jacob (James), son of Alphaeus	5	10		See above for the name Jacob/James
Simon	59	72	The Zealot	See above for the name Simon. Matt and Mark give the Aramaic term for his nickname: "the Cananaean."[21] Zealot means he was zealous for the law as was Paul of Tarsus (Gal 1:14).[22]

19. Fitzmyer, *Luke*, 1:618 notes that there is a Talmai, king of Geshur, mentioned in 2 Sam 3:3. Thus, it might be conceivable that this man is a "son of Talmai," a Syrian. But this identification is improbable and far removed chronologically (*pace* Bock, *Luke*, 1:544).

20. See Nolland, *Luke*, 1:270; Danker, *Lexicon*. There was a Gk. name similar to Thomas. The Grecized form of the Aram. "twin" came to "coincide" (Danker, *Lexicon*) with the original Gk. name.

21. I.e., *qan'an*: "enthusiastic, zealous, revengeful." See Danker, *Lexicon*; Jastrow, *Dictionary*.

22. Bock, *Luke*, 1:545, accepts the older view that "zealot" is to be identified with those later leading the Jewish rebellion. Thus, Simon would have been a kind of revolutionary, even a terrorist. On this see, however, Horsely and Hanson, *Bandits*, 217. The Zealots as terrorists were a result of the outbreak of the war, not the cause. The earlier

Name	Number of times the name occurs in the ossuaries	Number of times the name occurs in the DSS	Nickname (if any)	Comments[16]
Judas, son of Jacob (James)	44	35		The name Judas appears 179 times in all sources. See John 14:22 for this disciple.
Judas	44	35	Iscariot (The Betrayer)	See above for the name Judas. Iscariot means "man of (the village of) Keriot." The Gospel of John (6:71) calls him "Judas, son of Simon Iscariot."

Table 5.1: The Twelve "Apostles" according to Luke[23]

The table gives the frequency with which the names appear in ancient sources (with focus on the Dead Sea Scrolls and ossuaries) as well as a little about the background of some of the disciples. According to Tal Ilan,[24] the name Simon is the most frequently attested Jewish man's name from antiquity, appearing in all sources 257 times. Both men named Simon get a nickname, the first one (Peter) given by Jesus himself, and the second one (the Zealot), presumably one that followed him. Other frequently appearing names are Judas (the third most common Jewish man's name), John (the fifth most common), Matthew (the ninth most common), and Jacob (i.e., in English, James, the eleventh most common). There is nothing in these names themselves, then, to distinguish these men. Ilan calls them biblical names. They derive from the Hebrew Bible, are attested elsewhere in the New Testament, but are also frequently on the ossuaries and in the Dead Sea Scrolls. Thus, most of the first disciples, based on their names, were ordinary Jews named after figures in the Hebrew Bible.

Three disciples have Greek names (Andrew, Philip, and Bartholomew), indicating the cultural mix of Palestine in the first century CE. In all, about

---

persons called zealous were devoted to Torah, not to violence.

23. The table is compiled from information in Ilan, *Lexicon*; Bauckham, *Jesus and the Eyewitnesses*, 85–91; and Meier, *Marginal Jew*, 3:128–41.

24. Ilan, *Lexicon*, 218–26; Bauckham, *Jesus and the Eyewitnesses*, 102.

15 percent of the names in Ilan's database are Greek names.[25] One must ponder why observant Jewish parents would give a son a Greek name.

Their epithets or nicknames may tell us a little about them. The "Rock" or "Zealot" as nicknames are revealing. That Iscariot is the home village of Judas the Betrayer may or may not have significance beyond distinguishing him from Judas son of James.

THE FEMALE DISCIPLES

Luke also gives a list, albeit a shorter one, of women disciples of Jesus. The New Testament makes it clear that there was an active women's ministry associated with the Jesus-movement:

> Also with him were certain women that had been healed of evil spirits and sickness: Mary called Magdalene (from whom he cast out seven demons), Joanna, wife of Chuza, the finance manager of Herod (Antipas), Susanna, and many other (women) who ministered to them out of their own finances. (Luke 8:2–3)

Martin Hengel maintained that these women disciples formed a "separate group" from the male disciples and had their own distinctive ministry.[26] Nolland surmises that "Luke establishes a deliberate parallel between the apostles and the women."[27] The ministry of the women disciples of Jesus was significant, though somewhat muted by the biblical accounts which give preeminence to the twelve men. Luke emphasizes multiple times (8:3, 23:49, 55, 24:10) and Mark and Matthew once each (Mark 15:41; Matt 27:55) that many women followed Jesus (i.e., traveled on his itinerant teaching campaigns) and eventually came with him to Jerusalem for the final days of his life. These women were probably present in the upper room for the Last Supper (see Chapter 13). In the verses translated above, we have the names of three of them. We know of others from references elsewhere in Luke and in the other three Gospels:

Matt 27:56, 61, 28:1, 11	Mark 15:40, 47, 16:1	Luke 8:1–3 10:38–39, 24:10	John 19:25, 20:1
Mary Magdalene	Mary Magdalene	Mary Magdalene	Mary Magdalene

---

25. Ilan, *Lexicon*, 11.
26. Hengel, "Maria Magdalena," 243. Similarly, Bock, *Luke*, 1:712.
27. Nolland, *Luke* 1:365.

Matt 27:56, 61, 28:1, 11	Mark 15:40, 47, 16:1	Luke 8:1–3, 10:38–39, 24:10	John 19:25, 20:1
Mary, mother of Jacob (James) and Joses	Mary, mother of Jacob (James) the less and Joses	Mary, mother of Jacob (James)	
The "other Mary" same as above?			
Mother of Zebedee's sons			
	Salome (mother of Zebedee's sons?)		
		Joanna	
		Susanna	
		Mary, sister of Martha (of Bethany)	
		Martha	
			Mary, mother of Jesus
			Mary's sister
			Mary, wife of Cleopas (same as Mary's sister?)

Table 5.2: Named women disciples of Jesus in the four Gospels.[28]

Joel Green[29] suggests that those women whose names are given without reference to a male relative (husband or son), i.e., Mary Magdalene and Susanna, were unmarried. Given the cultural tendency to assign women to the nearest male kin, that suggestion seems reasonable. There is no reason, however, to think that Mary Magdalene (or Susanna, for that matter) was a former prostitute. Such a tradition is the erroneous result of conflating several Gospels' stories onto the person of this Mary.[30]

We can discern that the women's ministry was significant even though the culture of the day tended to emphasize the contribution of the male disciples. We have several named female disciples who obviously played a large role in the ministry as well as the "many others," the unnamed women who traveled and ministered.

28. See Brown, *John* 2:905; Hengel, "Maria Magdalena," for details.
29. Green, *Luke*, 318.
30. See Schaberg, "Mary Magdalene."

As we did above, we can here compare these names with archaeological sources to ascertain how common they were and if we can learn anything about them based on their names and epithets.

Name	Number of times the name occurs in the ossuaries	Number of times the name occurs in the DSS	Epithet or Nickname	Comments
Mary	42	9	Magdalene (her town of birth)[31]	Mary is the most common woman's name in the New Testament era and the most common woman's name in both the New Testament (six times) and Josephus (seven times). In all sources the name appears 80 times. See Table 5.4 for the name on an ossuary.
Mary	42	9	Mother of Jacob (James) and Joses	See above
Mary	42	9	The "other"	See above
Mary	42	9	Mother of Zebedee's sons	See above
Mary	42	9	Mother of Jesus	See above
Mary (?)	42	9	Mary's sister	See above
Mary	42	9	Wife of Cleopas	See above
Mary	42	9	Martha's sister	See above
Salome	41	8		See Table 5.4 for this name (twice) on ossuaries. In all sources the name Salome appears 63, Shelamzion 25 times. Salome means "peace." Shelamzion means "peace of Zion."

31. Like the name Judas Iscariot (i.e., Judas, man from the village of Iscariot). For men called Magdalene, see Bauckham, "Additional Note B," 359: Rabbi Isaac the Magdalene; and Rabbi Yudan the Magdalene.

Name	Number of times the name occurs in the ossuaries	Number of times the name occurs in the DSS	Epithet or Nickname	Comments
Martha	17	0		See Table 5.4 for the name on an ossuary.
Joanna	7	3	Wife of Chuza	Hebrew Yoḥannah. The masculine form is Yoḥannan (John, see Table 5.1).
Susanna[32]	1	0		The name occurs in Josephus, in a Christian apocryphal book and in the Old Testament apocrypha (the name of a heroic woman). Altogether it appears 5 times.

Table 5.3: Women in the Gospels compared with archaeological sources[33]

These twelve men in addition to an unknown number of women, formed the nucleus of the Jesus-movement. Although we cannot know much more about most of them than what is revealed in the tables above, we can learn about the population from which these men and women emerged. To meet these persons, we will introduce individuals unknown to us before the discovery of their skeletal remains. For some we can now even know their names (through inscriptions on their ossuaries). These are the people from the 90 percent, or, in other words, the working class.[34] They were not

32. The Heb. name Shoshanna means "lily" or "rose."

33. Created based on Ilan, *Lexicon*, 9–37; and Bauckham, *Jesus and the Eyewitnesses*, 89. In addition to the ossuaries and the Dead Sea texts, Ilan consulted the New Testament, Josephus, ostraca, jars, coins, and rabbinic literature.

34. I.e., minus the 1 to 2% in the elites and the 5 to 8% in the destitute classes. Lenski (*Power and Privilege*, 281–83) estimated that the group at the very bottom of the socioeconomic classes in agrarian societies, the "expendables," composed from 5 to 10% of the total population. But Lenski included in this class criminals, who were not necessarily wretchedly impoverished. The other two groups in the bottom category (beggars and underemployed itinerant workers), however, might have lived well below subsistence. Other calculations (e.g., Scheidel and Friesen, "Size of the Economy") estimate the group below subsistence at 10–22%. The higher figure seems to me, although perhaps not far off for the large urban areas in the empire, not realistic for first-century Palestine/Israel.

the wealthy elites who were leisured because of large landholdings. Nor were they the desperately poor, unemployed because of bodily weakness (like Lazarus in Luke's parable, 16:19-31). They all earned a living through labor, some by skilled or intellectual labor, others by manual work. Although some evidently lived through difficult times judging by the pathological evidence on their remains, they could work to receive a living, whether meager or well above adequate. Some of them—c. 10 percent—might have earned a comfortable surplus income, others barely enough to survive.[35] These are the kind of people with whom Jesus interacted on a daily basis and probably the crowd from which he called his disciples.

We will cull our evidence from the skeletal remains of fifteen individuals buried in three tomb complexes and cemeteries: a tomb at Jericho, a tomb complex in Jerusalem, and the Qumran cemetery. The table also indicates the economic situation of each cemetery within the 90 percent:

#	Tomb/grave location	Sex	Age at death	Pathology	Inscription on the ossuary	Comments
Upper-level working class						
1.	Jericho	F	40		"Mariah daughter of Nat[an]el daughter of Shlomsion"	The inscription is in an Aramaic/Hebrew linguistic mix
2.	Jericho	M	50–60		"Theodotus Freedman[36] of Queen Agrippina"[37]	The inscription is in Greek. His Greek name (the only one in the tomb) means "given by God" and is expressed elsewhere in the tomb (see #1) by the Hebrew equivalent "Nathanel" He was evidently a re-patriate into Israel

---

35. See Scheidel and Friesen, "Size of the Economy."

36. As a freedman, Theodotus/Nathanel would have been granted Roman citizenship.

37. The Agrippina alluded to was probably the mother of Emperor Nero and wife of Emperor Claudius. So, Hachlili, "Goliath Family." See Chapter 11.

#	Tomb/grave location	Sex	Age at death	Pathology	Inscription on the ossuary	Comments
3.	Jericho	F	50–60	Fused thoracic vertebrae (One of three with this condition in this tomb of 31 individuals)	"Shelamsion mother of Yehoezer Goliath"	Her name was inscribed on her ossuary in both Greek and Aramaic. Her name ("peace of Zion"; see also #1) is expressed in Greek as "Salome" (Mark 15:40; 16:1 and #13 below). Who was Yehoezer nicknamed Goliath? Probably #4 below.
4.	Jericho	M	25–35			Very tall for this region and period: 6'2". Was he "Goliath"?[38]
Midlevel working class						
5.	Giv'at ha-Mivtar	F	50–60	Lost most of her teeth. Well-developed muscles in left arm. Significant evidence of hard work.		Her head had been smashed by a blunt weapon, perhaps a mace. 4'8" tall
6.	Giv'at ha-Mivtar	F	23–25	Osteoporosis, periodontitis. One leg 3 cm. shorter than the other. Very slight bones.	"Martha"	Inscription in Aramaic. Perhaps had endocrine disorder. 4'9" tall
7.	Giv'at ha-Mivtar	Child	3–4	Small round hole on left occipital bone		Child died from arrow wound to the head. Death was not immediate.

38. For average stature in the first century CE, see Chapter 11.

THE MALE AND FEMALE DISCIPLES 95

#	Tomb/grave location	Sex	Age at death	Pathology	Inscription on the ossuary	Comments
8.	Giv'at ha-Mivtar	F	30–35	Deformed right side of the pelvis. Hunchbacked. Full term fetus in pelvis. Unable to deliver child without help. Died in childbirth.	"The ossuary of Salome daughter of Saul who failed to give birth"	Inscription in Aramaic. A midwife could have saved her and her baby. 4'11" tall.
9.	Giv'at ha-Mivtar	M	45–48	Bones well developed. Very strong hands. Robust and strong individual. Some arthritis.	"Simon the Temple builder"	Inscription in Aramaic. 5'6" tall. See Figure 3.6 (p. 53).
10.	Giv'at ha-Mivtar	Child	7–8	Cribrosis		Starved to death
Lowest-level working class						
11.	Qumran	M	22	Bones in hands and feet thick and gnarled.		Did hard physical labor with his hands from an early age. Went barefooted all his life.
12.	Qumran	F	25			Buried with 2-year-old child
13.	Qumran	M	65	Skeletal structure of shoulders and legs deformed		Did hard labor. Carried heavy burdens on shoulders causing changes to skeletal structure of shoulders and legs.

#	Tomb/grave location	Sex	Age at death	Pathology	Inscription on the ossuary	Comments
14.	Qumran	M	65	Severe head wound; fractured right clavicle		Wounded in head with sling stone. Wound would have taken a long time to heal and would have caused severe pain. Broken clavicle also took a long time to heal.[39]
15.	Qumran	F	14–16			The cause of this teenage girl's death is unknown.

Table 5.4: Fifteen individuals from "the 90 percent"[40]

We cannot read the diaries and literary works of the lower classes, but we can meet them in their remains. We introduce the reader to fifteen individuals from this time period (some of them by name) completely unknown from any literary source. These forgotten persons represent the working-class population. Some of them show evidence of this social stratification in the pathology of their bones. I have selected individuals from these three burial sites because these remains had been pathologically examined. Let us here make four observations:

First, individuals 5, 9, 11, and 13 demonstrate what it was like for the unskilled working class. They did hard labor—some from childhood (individual 11)—and it shows in their bones. Individual 13 was evidently a day laborer who carried around heavy objects. It caused deformity to his skeletal structure. The left-handed woman (individual 5) worked at something requiring significant manual labor with one arm. Individual 9 was a construction worker who worked on the building of the Temple in Jerusalem.

Second, several of them had bone disorders, either as a result of pathology (individuals 3, 6, 8, and 10) or hard labor (individuals 11 and 13). Two suffered from tooth pathology (individuals 5 and 6).[41]

39. See Chapter 10.

40. Information gleaned from Hachlili and Smith, "Genealogy," 68; Hachlili, "Goliath Family"; Steckoll, "Preliminary Excavation," 335; Haas and Nathan, "Anthropological Survey"; Haas, "Anthropological Observations"; and Naveh, "Ossuary Inscriptions."

41. Cf. Arensberg and Smith, "Appendix," 192–94. Out of a total of 185 individual skeletal remains in the tombs of Jericho they examined pathologically, thirteen had osteoporosis, osteophyles, or spina bifida (7%). The same bone diseases were also in

Third, four of the seven women on the list died young. We described this feature in Chapter 1 in contrast to the elderly Anna. Frequently, a young mother would be (re)buried in an ossuary with her child (see individual 12).[42]

Fourth, some of these individuals suffered violent attacks, evidently during war. Individual 14 survived a head wound after a long recovery. Individuals 5 and 7 died from head wounds, the former from a mace, the latter by an arrow. Two died from critical circumstances: individual 10, a child, starved to death; individual 8 died in childbirth, unable to deliver because of the lack of a midwife.[43]

We can speculate that the Jericho tomb served an extended family on the upper end of the working class (see Chapter 11), that the Qumran graves were for the poorest workers, and that the Giv'at Ha-Mivtar tomb was the final resting place for a skilled-craft family. The pathologies seem to reflect this assessment.

Table 5.4 can serve as a template to understand the persons featured in the Gospel of Luke, both the historical characters and the fictional figures appearing in Jesus' parables. It may help one to visualize those in the working class. The table below explains the individuals in Luke's Gospel in light of Table 5.4. Some of the table is necessarily speculative but fits reasonably well with evidence presented in this chapter:

---

evidence at Meiron. See Smith et al., "Skeletal Remains."

42. Sometimes the entire family would be placed in the same ossuary. See the Caiaphas tomb in Chapter 14.

43. Two other children in this tomb died of starvation. Since the individuals in the tomb showed no signs of extreme poverty and since several of them met violent deaths, we presume that the children starved in a time of danger such as during the Roman siege and later destruction of Jerusalem (70 CE). The Giv'at ha-Miv'tar tomb also contained a woman who died in her early twenties by burning, a teenaged man who was burned to death on a rack, and a crucified man (see Chapters 11 and 14).

Elites		Antipas; the man wearing purple and fine linen (Luke 16); the father of the prodigal son (Luke 15); Caiaphas; Annas; Sadducees; the Rich Man (Luke 18); the chief priests
Working class (the 90 percent)	Upper-level working class	Zaccheus (Luke 19); the scribes; the lawyers; the centurion (Luke 7); Chuza/Joanna; Jairus (Luke 8); the *archisynagōgoi;* the estate stewards (e.g., Luke 16, some may have been slaves); Levi (Luke 5)
	Midlevel working class	Mary/Joseph and children (Jesus, James, Joses, Jude, Simon, and sisters); Peter and Andrew; James and John; Susanna; Mary Magdalene; Zebedee/the mother of Zebedee's sons; Zachariah/Elizabeth; Simon of Cyrene; ordinary priests; Levites; Mary/Martha; Cleopas/Mary
	Lowest-level working class	Enslaved persons; tenants (Luke 20); day laborers; the sinful woman (Luke 7)
Completely without means (*ptōchos*) or disabled		John the Baptist; Lazarus (Luke 16); the blind man (Luke 18); the paralytic (Luke 5); lepers (Luke 5); the widow at Nain (Luke 7)

Table 5.5: Economic standing of persons in Luke's Gospel

6

Village Life

VILLAGES AND CITIES

> In the following days, he traveled around from one city and village to another preaching and evangelizing about the kingdom of God along with the Twelve. (Luke 8:1)

As JESUS AND THE Twelve moved from one center of habitation to the other, they found many more villages than they did cities. If we calculate the Jewish population of first-century Palestine/Israel as 1.5 million,[1] and if we add the populations of the cities—Jerusalem (60,000–100,000 population), Caesarea Maritima (15,000), Sebaste (capital of Samaria, 25,000), Sepphoris in Galilee (10,000), Tiberias in Galilee (10,000), Banias in the tetrarchy of Philip (later called Caesarea Philippi, 28,000), and the diminutive city of Magdala/Taricheae (around 4,000 souls)[2]—then that leaves 1,312,000 persons living in villages and towns in Judea, Idumea, Samaria, Perea, the Golan, and the Galilee. Clearly, the overwhelming majority of persons lived in villages.

---

1. See Fiensy, *Archaeology of Daily Life*, 21 on the total population estimates. For Galilee, see E. M. Meyers, "Jesus and His Galilean Context," 59; and Hoehner, *Herod Antipas*, 53. Hoehner prefers the figure 200,000, and Meyers prefers 150,000 to 175,000. Meyers accepts Josephus's figure of 204 villages in Galilee and multiplies this number by 500 residents per village. That number plus the populations of the two cities give his final population figure. McCown cites an older figure of 400,000 for Galilee ("Density of Population," 426). His own estimate was 100,000 (436) based on an estimate of 150 persons per square mile. This estimate he derives from comparing with other population densities in the modern period.

2. For population of the Palestinian cities, see Fiensy, *Archaeology of Daily Life*, 22, 35, 52–53; Table 6.1, below; and Avigad, "Samaria (City)."

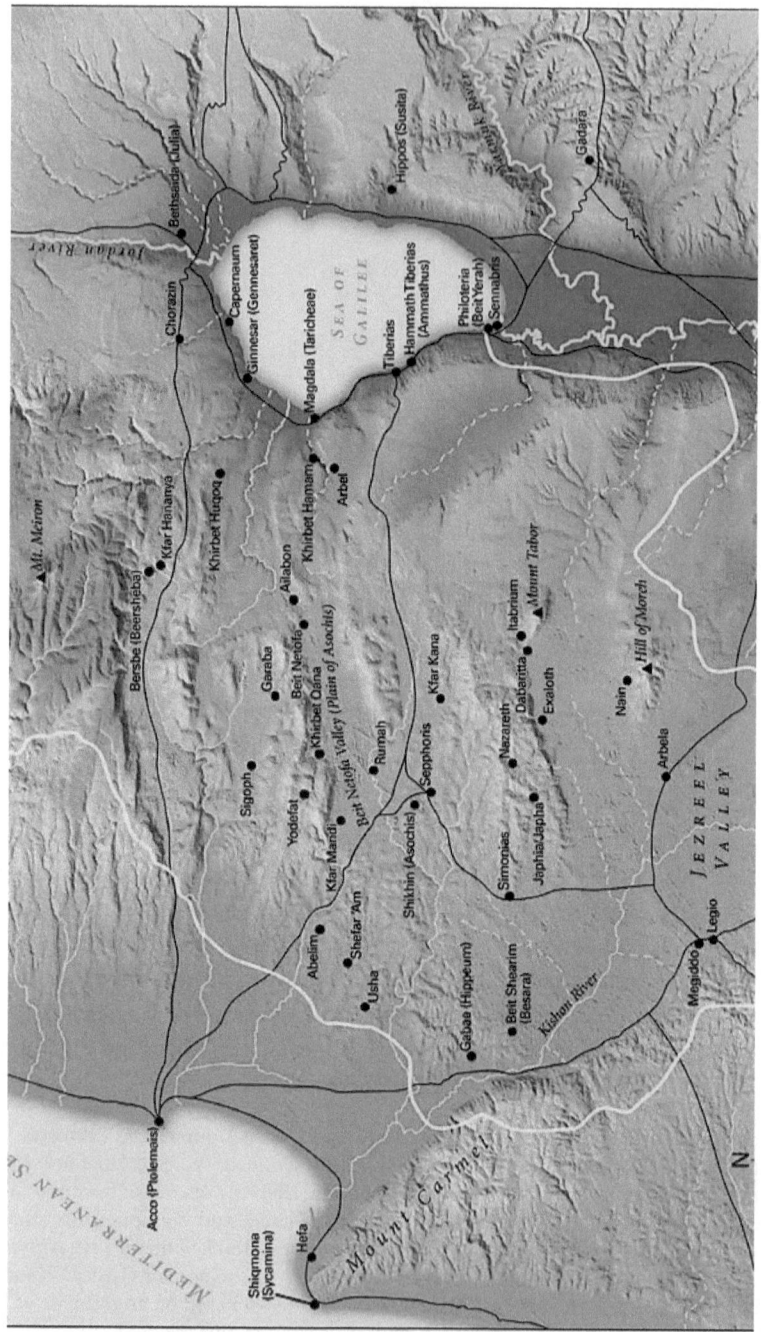

Map 2: Lower Galilee[3] (Map created by A. D. Riddle)

3. www.RiddleMaps.com. Used with permission.

What was it like to live in one of the villages? How large were they? What would you see in them? In a previous era of scholarship, we were dependent on Josephus and the Mishnah to describe for us life in Palestine/Israel in the time of Jesus. More recently, scholars have turned to archaeological work that has been done in the region. This work sometimes confirms the older views and sometimes leads to a reassessment. The survey below relies mostly on the material remains to draw a picture of village life in the New Testament period.

Technically, a *polis* ("city") had its own constitution, coinage, territory, and town council.[4] But others defined cities by what they saw, that is, by the architecture. An architectural description from Pausanias[5] gives one perspective. He declared that no center could justify calling itself a true city unless it had government buildings, a gymnasium, a theater, a market square, a fountain, and a few large mansions (i.e., an urban elite). Table 6.2, below, will compare the architectural features of ancient cities with villages. On the other hand, those less inclined to glamorize city life described cities not only by what they saw but also by what they heard and smelled. To them cities were full of noisy, muddy streets, crumbling tenement houses, and dirty people.[6]

HOW LARGE WERE VILLAGES?[7]

We will appeal to the archaeological remains to answer the question, How large were most villages in Palestine/Israel during our time period? Most of the remains studied to determine village size and economic activities have come from the archaeological surveys[8] (not excavated villages). We will compare villages surveyed (and some excavated) in the regions of Galilee, the Golan, Samaria, and Judea. The surveys reveal a usual range of village space and its concomitant population from less than 2.5 acres to 10 acres. Table 6.1 has averaged the village sizes from several first-century sites in

---

4. See SVM 2:86-87; Jones "Urbanization"; Ehrenberg "Polis." Sherwin-White suggested considering the city (*polis*) in both Josephus and the Gospels as a capital of a toparchy (or region), even if the place was not technically a city. See Sherwin-White, *Roman Society*, 129-30. *Cf.* SVM 2:188. See also Goodman, *State and Society*, 27.

5. Pausanias, *Descr.* 10.4.1.

6. Seneca, *De Ira* 3.35.5; Juvenal, *Satires* 3.232-38.

7. The Israeli scholars measure space in dunams (4 dunams = c. 1 acre). Europeans use hectares (1 hectare = 2.47 acres). I will usually convert all measurements into acres.

8. In surveys, the researchers pick up surface sherds and note architectural features but do not dig.

Palestine/Israel. As the reader can discern, most villages were in the 4–9-acre range with an average population between 600 and 1,100 souls.[9]

Location of site group and acreage of site group	Total number of sites in site group	Total number of acres in all sites within site group	Average size of villages in site group	Average population per site/village (160 persons per acre)
Urman (Golan) [range was less than 2.5 acres to 50 acres]	133	935	7 acres	1,120 residents per village
Frankel et al. (Upper Galilee) [range: 2.5 acres to 30 acres]	74	306.25	4.1 acres	656 residents per village
Leibner (Eastern Lower Galilee) [range: .5 acre to 18.7 acres]	40	233.3	5.8 acres	928 residents per village
Dar (Samaria) [range: 4 acres to 10 acres]	6	33.15	5.5 acres	880 residents per village
Western Lower Galilee Sites	4	37.5	9.3 acres	1488 residents per village
Judea [range: 2.5 acres to 10 acres]	5	23	4.6 acres	736 residents per village

Table 6.1: Villages in Galilee, Golan, Samaria, and Judea[10]

---

9. I have eliminated the cities from the survey information: Caesarea Philippi, Magdala, and Sepphoris.

10. Table composed from: Urman, *Golan*, 87–88, 93; Dar, *Landscape and Pattern*, 51, 53, 42, 47, 36, 231; Frankel et al., *Settlement Dynamics*; Leibner, *Settlement and History*, 102–306; Crossan and Reed, *Excavating Jesus*, 34; James F. Strange, "Nazareth"; Loffreda, "Capernaum," 292; Reed, *Archaeology*, 83; Richardson, *Building Jewish*, 81; Edwards, "Khirbet Qana," 106; McCollough, "City and Village," 58; Magen et al., "Qiryat Sefer"; Hirschfeld, "En-Gedi"; Zissu and Ganor, "Horbat 'Ethri"; Onn et al., "Khirbet Umm el-'Umdan"; and Peterson and Stripling, "Kh. El-Maqatir." For more information on these village sizes and populations, see Fiensy, *Archaeology of Daily Life*, 61–62.

One method of determining population is to multiply the number of acres of the site times the supposed number of people that, on average, lived on one acre in antiquity. This method appears to be the most common one used by historians.[11] This method too is problematic since, in the first place, surveyors cannot always tell exactly the total area an ancient village covered; and, in the second place, the estimates of population density vary. Wolfgang Reinhardt, who has done a detailed study of ancient population calculations, notes that one should not expect all villages/cities to have had the same population density.[12] Nevertheless, calculating populations can be a helpful heuristic exercise to compare villages. Table 6.1 does not offer a literal head count; it presents figures as a good guess to help the reader picture what an ancient village was like.

The density figure accepted by both Magen Broshi and Yigal Shiloh is 160 to 200 persons per acre.[13] Certainly the population figures obtained by this method are speculative, but they are often the only figures we have. At least they offer some comparisons among contemporaneous villages from the late Second Temple period.

The higher number (200 persons per acre) seems to posit too dense a population[14] since there must have been, in most villages, spaces for threshing floors, perhaps gardens, and even areas where nomadic folk and travelers stayed in tents.[15] Thus, using the lower number, we obtain the population figures given in Table 6.1. If most villages ranged in occupied space from c. 4 acres to 9 acres, then their population ranged from c. 600 to 1,500 individuals. These are the villages Jesus and the Twelve frequently entered on their teaching tours.

---

11. See Reinhardt, "Population Size," 241: "The most common method is calculation by means of the product of area and density."

12. Reinhardt, "Population Size," 241.

13. I.e., 40 to 50 persons per dunam. See Broshi, "Estimating the Population"; Shiloh, "Population."

14. Dever, *Lives of Ordinary People,* 48-49 has calculated populations of eighth-century BCE towns and villages using a slightly lower estimate of population density. His estimate appears to be 100 persons per acre. Ze'ev Safrai (*Economy*, 65) speculates that ten families could live on a dunam (or 40 families on an acre) of ground in the Talmudic period (200-500 CE). He arrives at a figure of 120 to 160 persons per acre (125). Thus, his upper limit matches Broshi's lower limit.

15. See the work on a modern village in the Middle East: Sweet, *Tel Toqaan,* 52.

WHAT WAS IN A VILLAGE?

First, the villages had narrow, unpaved streets arranged in haphazard patterns and no gates or walls.[16] The exception to the haphazard streets may have been some parts of Khirbet Qana and Yodefat where they resemble the grid patterns of the cities. But for most villages the streets were haphazardly determined, often leaving open areas which became public domain. This haphazard village arrangement can be observed in several of the ancient villages in Palestine/Israel[17] and is often noted by observers of contemporary Middle Eastern villages. The description by Tannous of premodern Arab villages is common:

> A compact, nucleated form of structure is the first striking impression one gets of the Middle Eastern village. It is a conglomeration of houses standing close to each other, divided by winding alleys and paths that do not seem to have any regular design.[18]

Second, most villages had no gates or fortified walls. There were at least two exceptions to this pattern from our period. One Galilean town—Yodefat—was fortified (given walls) in preparation for the revolt of 66–73 CE as was Gamla[19] in the Golan. But these were special preparations and not the usual feature for villages.

Third, several villages had a synagogue and a public building (see Sidebar 4.2 (p. 80) and Figures 6.1 and 6.2, below. Also, near the village was of course the cemetery/tomb complex.

---

16. See, e.g., Capernaum (Crossan and Reed, *Excavating Jesus*, 81); and Nazareth (Reed, *Archaeology*, 131, 152–53).

17. E.g., in Capernaum. See Crossan and Reed, *Excavating Jesus*, 81. Cf. Killebrew, "Village and Countryside," 196: "Natural topography, and not a master plan that typified the *polis*, played a key role in the general layout and network of streets of these unfortified 'medium-sized cities.'" Cf. also Ze'ev Safrai, *Economy*, 46: "The Jewish city or town was not planned. Therefore its streets and thoroughfares often meandered with no clear purposes." For open areas as public domain, see also Sweet, *Tell Toqaan*, 55. But contrast Loffreda, "Capernaum," who sees some order to the streets of Capernaum.

18. Tannous, "Arab Village Community," 528. For other ethnographic references to the haphazard arrangement of streets and alleys in Middle Eastern villages see Kramer, *Village Ethnoarchaeology*, 85, 88; McGarvey, *Lands of the Bible*, 105, 108; Lutfiyya, *Baytin*, 20; Sweet, *Tell Toqaan*, 51, 54 (The streets [of contemporary Palestinian villages] are mere "cow paths."). These authors speak of "winding alleys," crooked and narrow streets, and of paths in the village "twist[ing] around corners of long blocks of compounds."

19. Adan-Bayewitz and Aviam report that the excavations of Yodefat revealed that its walls were begun in the Hellenistic period but strengthened by Josephus. Thus, this town had walls—at least in some areas—from the beginning. See Adan-Bayewitz and Aviam, "Iotapata." Gamla, in the Golan, was also fortified during the revolt.

Figure 6.1: Synagogue at Gamla

By way of contrast, the cities were planned with streets in a grid pattern and with entertainment facilities. This was especially true of the gentile Decapolis cities (see Chapter 8) but even to some extent for the more Jewish cities. Jerusalem, e.g., had a theater, a hippodrome (a track for horse races), an amphitheater, and paved streets;[20] Caesarea had a theater and hippodrome; Tiberias had a theater, a stadium for athletic games, and a monumental gate; Magdala had a hippodrome, baths, and a *palaestra* (a building for exercise).[21]

The cities had spacious streets, formally designated marketplaces, large public buildings, large domestic quarters, and more comforts of life such as entertainment. To go from village to city was to cross into a new subculture. The following table contrasts the cities and villages in late Second Temple Israel:

---

20. These architectural features of entertainment, built by Herod the Great, may have been only wooden, temporary constructions. See Lichtenberger, "Jesus and the Theater"; and Chapter 12.

21. See Crossan and Reed, *Excavating Jesus*, 60–67; Dothan, *Hamath Tiberias*, 16; and Weiss, "Theatres."

Villages	Cities
Most were unwalled. Exceptions: Yodefat and Gamla (walled for the war).	Walled.
No formal marketplaces but open spaces may have served informally.	Clearly designated marketplaces.
Topography determined how the streets were laid out. They were done in "traditional ways."	The cities were laid out in Hippodamian (i.e., checkerboard) grids.
Cisterns were the main source of water.	The cities had aqueducts.
There was no architecture for entertainment.	There were theaters, stadiums, hippodromes, and amphitheaters.

Table 6.2: Village and city contrasts[22]

Figure 6.2: Model of a typical village in Galilee in the Mishnaic period (Yigal Allon Museum, Ginosar, Israel). Notice how close together the houses are and how haphazardly the streets are arranged. The large structure on the right is the synagogue.

Table 6.3, below, must be read with discretion. It indicates what has been discovered and cannot be used to demonstrate what was not in the

---

22. The table was constructed based on ideas in Richardson, "Khirbet Qana," 127–28.

villages. At most, it can only show what has not yet turned up in the excavations. But common sense will tell that virtually all the villages planted grain, olives, and grapes, and most of them (except for those located on the Sea of Galilee) had cisterns.

Features	1	2	3	4	5	6	7	8	9
first cent. Synagogue		X	Perhaps						X
House(s) of the wealthy	X	X	X	X					
Olives	X	X	X	X	X	X	X		X
Vines			X	X	X	X	X		
Other crops									
Pottery production				X	X			X	
Grain production	X	X		X	X	X		X	X
Wool (spindle whorls or sheep pens)		X		X				X	X
Other industry	Cooperage		Dyeing, glass production						Fishing
Quarries			X	X	X	X			X
Columbaria			X						
Tombs found	X	X	X		X	X	X	X	X
Ritual baths	X		X	X	X	X	X	X	
Stone vessels	X	X	X	X	X	X	X	X	X
Water reservoir			X	X					
Cisterns	X		X	X	X	X			
Public building			X						

Table 6.3 continued

Features	10	11	12	13	14	15	16	17
first cent. Synagogue	X		X	X			X	X
House(s) of the wealthy	X	X	X	Herodian winter palaces		X		
Olives	X		X				X	X
Vines		X	X				X	X
Other crops				Dates, balsam	Dates, balsam		Figs	
Pottery production								
Grain production								
Wool (spindle whorls or sheep pens)		X						
Other industry		Fishing		Date wine, balsam oil				
Quarries							X	
Columbaria							X	
Tombs found	X		X	X	X	X	X	X
Ritual baths	X		X	X	X	X	X	X
Stone vessels	X	X	X	X	X	X	X	
Water reservoir					X			
Cisterns	X		X			X	X	X
Public building	X	X						

Table 6.3: Features in ancient Palestinian villages[23]

23. The table has been constructed based on information from Edwards, "Khirbet Qana"; Richardson, "Khirbet Qana"; Matillah, "Capernaum"; McCollough, "City and Village"; Bagatti, "Nazareth"; Adan-Bayewitz and Aviam, "Iotapata"; Reed, *Archaeology*, 131–32, 143–59; Pfann et al., "Nazareth Village Farm"; E. M. Meyers and C. Meyers, "Digging the Talmud"; E. M. Meyers et al., *Excavations at Ancient Meiron*, xviii, 44, 107–20; Loffreda, "Capernaum"; "Capernaum: the town of Jesus"; James Riley Strange, "Kefar Shikhin"; Magen et al., "Khirbet Badd'isa"; Hirschfeld, "En-Gedi"; Netzer, "Jericho: Exploration since 1973"; Alexandre, "Karm er-Ras"; Grey and Spigel, "Ḥuqoq"; Magness et al., "Ḥuqoq"; Aviam, "Distribution Maps"; Adler, "Archaeology of Purity," 321–43; Magen, *Stone Vessel Industry*; Aviam, "Socio-Economic Hierarchy"; Peterson and Stripling, "Kh. el-Maqatir"; Zissu and Ganor, "Horvat 'Ethri"; Onn et al., "Khirbet

Table 6.3 KEY:

Upper Galilee: 1 = Meiron
Lower Galilee: 2 = Capernaum; 3 = Khirbet Qana; 4 = Yodefat; 5 = Shikhin;
6 = Nazareth; 7 = Ḥuqoq; 8 = Karm er-Ras; 9 = Khirbet Wadi Hamam
Golan: 10 = Gamla; 11 = Et-Tell (Bethsaida?)
Judea: 12=Qiryat Sefer; 13=Jericho; 14=En Gedi; 15=Kh. el-Maqatir; 16 = Ḥorvat ʿEthri; 17 = Khirbet Umm el-ʿUmdan

The villages indicate common patterns. When Jesus, the Twelve, and the women ministers roamed Galilee, the Golan, and Judea for their teaching activities, they usually would have entered villages of 600–1,500 inhabitants. The village would have consisted of simply made houses, haphazardly planned and unpaved streets, with a few open areas used on market day or by nomadic visitors for their tents. They might have had a building dedicated exclusively to synagogue study and prayer. Most villagers were probably engaged in agriculture, but certain kinds of industry were also present (pottery production, glass manufacturing, the making of clothing from wool, the making of barrels), and those villages positioned near the lake engaged in fishing. The village would usually have had stepped pools (*mikvaʾot*) at various spots especially for use by those engaged in producing agricultural liquids (olive oil and wine). The villages located on the lake, however (Capernaum, Et-Tell, and Khirbet Wadi Hamam), had no ritual bath installations (at least none found so far), the residents evidently using the lake for that purpose. Almost all the villages investigated for Table 6.3 showed that the households invested in cheaply made stone vessels to avoid using cups, bowls, and cooking pots of impurity (see Chapter 9).

HEROD THE TETRARCH IN GALILEE

> Herod the Tetrarch heard all that was happening and he was perplexed because it was being said by some that John (the Baptist) had been raised from the dead, by others that Elijah had appeared, and by still others that one of the prophets of old had risen (from the dead). Herod said, "I decapitated John; who is this about whom I hear such things?" And he sought to see him. (Luke 9:7–9)

Umm el-ʿUmdan"; Arav and Savage, "Bethsaida," 265–76; Leibner, "Summary and Discussion."

Herod the Great (see Sidebar 1.2) changed his will several times, finally settling on three sons, two by the mother Malthace (Archelaus and Antipas) and the third by Cleopatra of Jerusalem (Philip), as his heirs (Sidebar 2.6). Although he willed that Archelaus be granted the title of king over Idumea, Judea, and Samaria, Rome changed his title to ethnarch (ruler of a nation).[24] He gave Philip rule over the Golan[25] and put Antipas in charge of Galilee and Perea. Both Philip and Antipas were to have the titles tetrarch (ruler over a fourth).[26]

Each of the heirs appears in the Gospels. Archelaus is named in Matt 2:22 and alluded to in a parable in Luke 19:12–27. Philip is named in Luke's chronological designation (Luke 3:1). Philip is of some importance to students of the New Testament since three of Jesus' disciples originated from Bethsaida (see Chapter 10), which was a small town on the northeast shore of the Sea of Galilee in the territory of Philip. All three of the heirs, like their father, are mentioned not only in the New Testament and Josephus but also archaeologically as well (Sidebar 6.1).

Antipas[27] shows up frequently in the Synoptic Gospels, especially in Luke, under the name "Herod the Tetrarch." To interpreters of the Gospels and the early Jesus-movement, Antipas is the most important of the three heirs because he ruled over Galilee, where Jesus ministered most of the time. The Gospel of Luke has more references to Antipas than any of the other Gospels:

Lukan texts	Quotation of the text	Parallel texts
Luke 3:1	The word of God came to John during the tetrarchy of Herod the Tetrarch	
Luke 3:19	Herod the Tetrarch, after he was reprimanded by him (John) because of Herodias, his brother's wife, and because of all the evils which Herod did, added this to them: he locked John up in prison.	Matt 14:1–6; Mark 6:14–22; John 3:24
Luke 8:3	Joanna, wife of Chuza, Herod's finance (or estate) manager	

24. The Romans changed his title to ethnarch when a Jewish delegation traveled to Rome to ask that he be dethroned. See SVM 1:330–31; and Josephus *War* 2.80–100; Josephus, *Ant.* 17.299–320.

25. That is, the regions of Batanaea, Trachonitis, Auranitis, Gaulanitis, Panias, and Ituraea. See SVM 1:336.

26. See SVM 1:326.

27. For Antipas, see the works by Hoehner, *Herod Antipas*; and Jensen, *Herod Antipas*.

Lukan texts	Quotation of the text	Parallel texts
Luke 9:7–9	Herod the Tetrarch heard all that was happening and he was perplexed because it was being said by some that John (the Baptist) had been raised from the dead, by others that Elijah had appeared, and by still others that one of the prophets of old had risen [from the dead. Herod said, "I decapitated John; who is this about whom I hear such things?" And he sought to see him.	Matt 14:1–2; Mark 6:14–16
Luke 13:31	In that very hour, some of the Pharisees came to (Jesus) saying, "Get out and go away from here for Herod wants to kill you."	
Luke 23:6–8	When Pilate heard this, he asked if he was from Galilee. Knowing that (Jesus) was under the authority of Herod, he sent him to Herod since he also was in Jerusalem in those days. Herod, when he saw Jesus, was very glad. He had for some time wanted to see him because he had heard about him and hoped to see some sort of sign done by him.	
Luke 23:11–12	Herod and his soldiers treated (Jesus) with contempt. After mocking him and putting expensive clothes on him, he sent him back to Pilate. And Herod and Pilate became friends with one another on that day.	
Acts 13:1	There were in the church in Antioch prophets and teachers, namely, Barnabas, Simeon called "the Dark Skinned," Lucius the Cyrenian, Menahem the boyhood friend[28] of Herod the Tetrarch, and Saul.	

Table 6.4: Luke's references to Herod the Tetrarch (Antipas)

---

28. The term (*syntrophos*) means "to be brought up together." It is often used of intimate friends or boyhood companions (Danker, *Lexicon*).

Sidebar 6.1

Herod Antipas (governed 4 BCE–39 CE)

- He was one of Herod the Great's three heirs
- He was given title "Tetrarch" (Luke 3:19)
- He was usually referred to as "Herod" (rather than as Antipas) by Josephus, by the New Testament, and on his coins.
- His territory included Galilee and Perea (see Map 1 p. 2).
- He rebuilt the (destroyed) city of Sepphoris in the beginning of his reign and later the new cities of Tiberias in Galilee and Livias in Perea.
- He executed John the Baptist (see Chapter 2)
- He later feared that Jesus was John the Baptist resurrected (Matt 14:1–2; Mark 6:14–16; Luke 9:7–9).
- He was deposed and banished to Gaul in 39 CE by Emperor Caligula.[29]

Archaeological references to Antipas

In addition to the New Testament and Josephus, both of which have numerous references to Antipas, there are inscriptions—on stone and on bronze coins (see below)—that refer to him. Here is one on stone from the island of Delos:

- "The people of Athens and those inhabiting the island [honor] Herod the Tetrarch, the son of king Herod, because of his virtue and benevolence."[30]

---

29. SVM 1:340–53.

30. Gk. text in SVM 1:341. They quote another inscription, similar to this one, found on the island of Cos.

VILLAGE LIFE   113

Photo of coin of Herod Antipas. On the right (obverse): palm branch, the date of coin (34th year of his reign, i.e., 29–30 CE), and "(coin) of Herod tetrarch" (in Gk.). On the left (reverse): a wreath surrounding "Tiberias," the city in Galilee where the coin was struck. No images of persons or animals appear on the coins of Antipas.[31] (Photo from Classical Numismatic Group, Inc.[32])

---

31. For an analysis of the coins of Antipas, see: Meshorer, *Treasury*, 81–84, 226, 325; Reinach, *Jewish Coins*, 33; and SVM 1:343 (n. 16).

32. Available at Wikimedia Commons: https://commons.wikimedia.org/wiki/File:Herod_Antipas.jpg/.

7

Three Towns around the Lake

"Woe to you, Chorazin! Woe to you, Bethsaida!" (Luke 10:13).

IN THE COURSE OF sending his disciples on a preaching/teaching trip, Jesus reflected on the lack of faith (cf. Matt 11:21) in the villages of Bethsaida and Chorazin (see Map 2 p. 100). The last village lay 2 ½ miles north of Capernaum and is only mentioned in the New Testament here and in the parallel passage in Matthew (11:21–24). The village also shows up in the rabbinic literature (b. Men. 85a). The two villages plus Capernaum have been called the "evangelical triangle"[1] due to their proximity to one another. Based on this text, one can imagine that Jesus and his disciples made frequent trips to nearby Bethsaida and Chorazin while they lodged in Capernaum.

CHORAZIN

Chorazin is most famous among students of the New Testament for its illustration of the "seat of Moses," the ornate stone chair that was evidently the teaching seat (Matt 23:2) and/or the "chief seat" (Luke 11:43, 20:46; Matt 23:6; Mark 12:39) in the synagogue. Whether it was the chair of the guest preacher/teacher (as in Luke 4:20), the seat of the regular *archisynagōgos*, i.e., "ruler of the synagogue" (see Chapter 9), the seat of honor for visiting dignitaries, or all the above, one can imagine the honor accorded to anyone occupying the chair during the synagogue service.

---

1. Pixner, *With Jesus through Galilee*, 33.

Figure 7.1: The ornate seat (the Seat of Moses) in the synagogue of Chorazin. (For the inscription on the seat, see Chapter 9) (Photograph by Pikiwikisrael)[2]

Excavations of Chorazin took place from 1964 to 1984. There are scant remains to testify to the village's existence in the first century CE.[3] It seems to have flourished from the second to fourth centuries CE as a typical Galilean village with oil presses, houses, and a ritual bath. The village from this period is marked by two domestic complexes with multiple rooms (one had 14 rooms) surrounding courtyards. Ze'ev Yeivin believed these complexes were domestic quarters for an extended family (evidently each room housing a nucleated family), the same arrangement Virgilio Corbo believed was in the complex of rooms (which he called an *insula*) of the alleged House of Peter at Capernaum (see Chapter 4). The synagogue (with ornate chair)

---

2. Wikimedia Commons: https://commons.wikimedia.org/wiki/File:Chorazin_Seat_of_Moses.jpg/.

3. McRay, *Archaeology*, 170–71 reports there is no evidence of a habitation from the time of Jesus. Yeivin ("Chorazin") noted that he found potsherds dating from "either the late first or early second century CE." So far, then, we have only the New Testament evidence for a habitation from the early first century.

dates to the fourth century.[4] There are also reports of finding a first-century synagogue, though all traces of it have now disappeared (see Sidebar 4.2).

BETHSAIDA

The village of Bethsaida ("place of the fish[net]") was an important fishing village on the north side of the Sea of Galilee, just east of the Jordan River. It lay just inside the tetrarchy of Philip and thus was not politically a part of Galilee even though it had close ties to Galilee economically, being only a few miles from Capernaum. According to the Gospel of John (1:44, 12:21), it was the home village of the brothers Simon Peter and Andrew as well as of Philip. Near the village on one occasion Jesus encountered a blind man and healed him in two stages (Mark 8:22–26). To Bethsaida on two occasions Jesus withdrew with his disciples to find refuge from the crowds (Luke 9:10; Mark 6:45). The village possibly appears in the rabbinic literature under the name *tsaidan*.[5] In several places, rabbis decide civil law based on cases in *tsaidan* (Bethsaida?), indicating that it was a Jewish village living according to Torah.

In 29–30 CE came a new phase of its history. In this year, Philip, tetrarch of the Golan area in which Bethsaida was located, decided to advance the village to the status of *polis* (city). He renamed it Julias after the wife of the late Emperor Augustus (*Ant.* 18.28). Julia[6] was also the mother of the current emperor, Tiberius. Changing this sleepy fishing village of mostly very observant Jews into a Greco-Roman *polis* with pagan shrines and statues could have been a shock to its residents.

Even though the village (now officially a "city") probably had hated symbols of both paganism and the Roman Empire now showing up, it must have remained a deeply Jewish settlement. Thus, one can understand Jesus' and his disciples' retreating there away from the crowds. Three of his disciples had connections there (relatives and friends) who could provide sanctuary for a few days for the small group.[7]

---

4. Yeivin, "Ancient Chorazin"; Yeivin, "Chorazin"; Finegan, *Archaeology*, 94–96.

5. *Tsaiidan* (*tsaiiad*) means "fisher." The word *tsaidan* is rendered by Jastrow (*Dictionary*) and Neusner (e.g., in his translation of t. Nidd. 4:6) as "Sidon," the Phoenician city on the Mediterranean Sea coast. Freund argues, based on context, that this word means more likely the village of Bethsaida. See Freund, "Search for Bethsaida"; and, also Notley, "Et-Tell is Not Bethsaida."

6. Her given name was Livia, but after Augustus died, she was adopted into the Julian clan and renamed Julia.

7. The parallel accounts in Matt and Mark say the place of refuge was a "deserted place" (Matt 14:13; Mark 6:32; cf. Luke 9:12).

Later, during the Jewish War with Rome (66–70 CE), Josephus fortified the area "one stade"[8] from Julias near the Jordan River" with two thousand men and earthworks. He won a battle there at the expense of falling from his horse and breaking an arm (*Life* 399–403). That he defended the city might further indicate its continued Jewishness.

We know approximately where Bethsaida was, but since the nineteenth century there have been two sites identified as the first-century village: Et-Tell and El-Araj, about one and one-half miles apart from each other.[9] Rami Arav and associates have excavated the site called Et-Tell for several decades and have maintained in a series of publications that Et-Tell was ancient Bethsaida.[10] Whether Et-Tell or El-Araj (or both[11]) was the biblical Bethsaida, both locations were first-century BCE–first century CE Jewish fishing villages.

We have, to date, more archaeological information from Et-Tell (but this situation is changing). Et-Tell, Stratum II,[12] was a first-century Jewish village, perhaps slightly larger than Capernaum, with fishing persons and farmers. Rami Arav describes the residential quarter of Et-Tell from the time of Jesus as a "humble community of country people who lived in poor dwellings and were occupied in fishing, viticulture, livestock raising.[13] The houses were constructed in similar fashion to those at Capernaum.

---

8. A stade (Gk. *stadion*) was c. 192 meters or one-eighth mile. See Danker, *Lexicon*.

9. See Notley, "Et-Tell is Not Bethsaida."

10. See Arav and Freund, *Bethsaida*, volumes 1–4.

11. It is possible, as one nineteenth-century explorer (Gottlieb Schumacher) suggested, that "el-Araj marks the fishing village [and] et-Tel . . . the princely residence [i.e., Julias]." See Notley, "Et-Tell is Not Bethsaida," 220. It is also logically possible that neither site preserves ancient Bethsaida.

12. Excavators have identified seven strata at Et-Tell: pre–Iron age, Iron IIA, Iron IIB, Assyrian/Babylonian, Persian, Hellenistic-Roman, and Medieval to recent times. See Arav, "Final Report," 3.

13. Arav, "Preliminary Report: 1994–1996," 11.

Figure 7.2: Artist's reconstruction of the House of the Fisherman, the residence of a well-to-do family built in the Hellenistic period and reused in the Early Roman (first century) period. The house and courtyard covered c. 4,300 square feet.[14] (Image courtesy of Bethsaida Excavations)

The town, in Stratum II, went through three historical and archaeological phases. First, it was a Hellenistic town under the power of either the Ptolemies of Egypt or, later, the Seleucids of Syria. The residents were prosperous Phoenicians who built nice courtyard houses, two of which the excavators have named "House of the Fisherman" (Figure 7.2) and "House of the Winemaker."[15]

Next, in the first century BCE, Jewish immigrants arrived and displaced the original inhabitants. There is no evidence of destruction; hence, there was evidently no battle over the village. Apparently, the Hasmoneans pushed out most of the Phoenicians and resettled the village with Jews from Judea. Thus, the "House of the Fisherman," pictured above, was a Phoenician house taken over later by Jewish immigrants and still in use in the days of Jesus. The occupation of the villagers as fishermen seems clear based on the numerous lead weights (for the fishnets), hooks, iron and bronze needles (for mending nets), and stone anchors not only on the premises of the House of the Fisherman but throughout the village.[16]

---

14. Strickert, *Bethsaida*, 69.
15. See the account in Arav and Savage, "Bethsaida."
16. Arav and Savage, "Bethsaida," 266. Fortner, "Fishing Implements" lists from the Et-Tell finds seventy-four lead sinkers, twenty-three stone sinkers, thirteen fishhooks, seven bronze and iron needles, and an unspecified number of basalt anchors. Strickert, *Bethsaida*, 50–57 adds one fish seal used to stamp jar handles.

The coinage during this phase changes from Seleucid into Hasmonean, suggesting a political change from local population to Jewish immigrants. Other material remains point toward Jewish immigrants as well: the use of stone vessels and the employment of simple lamps (no images of people or animals) made from clay coming from the Jerusalem area. From the mid-first century BCE to the mid-second century CE, Jews in Judea and then in other Jewish regions began to favor stone vessels (plates, bowls, cups, jars, and pots) because stone could not become ritually unclean, unlike clay vessels (see Chapter 9).[17] Therefore, when an excavator finds stoneware or fragments of stoneware in a site (see Table 6.3), he/she will usually conclude that the residents were Jewish.

The lamps without images were in obedience to the second of the Ten Commandments prohibiting graven images (Exod 20:4). The Jewish inclination to prefer lamps made with clay from Jerusalem or the area near Jerusalem was entirely a new development which did not derive from any teaching in the Hebrew Bible.[18]

A fourth indication that the village was Jewish in the first century BCE is not as conclusive as the coins, stoneware, and clay lamps but still suggestive. Villagers appear to have used locally manufactured pottery rather than imported (as in phase I), namely pottery from the famous Galilean pottery villages of Kefar Ḥananya and Shikhin (see Map 2 p. 100).[19]

Thus, Et-Tell was a thoroughly Jewish village by the time of Jesus (and the three disciples Simon Peter, Andrew, and Philip, who came from Bethsaida). Like the other villages described in Chapter 6, Et-Tell had no street planning (i.e., no checkerboard streets) and no Greco-Roman architectural structures of entertainment. The Jewish settlers took over some of the courtyard houses from their Phoenician predecessors, such as the House of the Fisherman, but others built their own simpler dwellings in other parts of the settlement. The excavators describe these Jewish constructions as "simple rural houses built of fieldstones, with plastered and whitewashed walls."[20] Fred Strickert describes an excavated two-room house of 255 square feet as typical of the first-century dwellings of Et-Tell.[21]

Then came the third historical/archaeological phase of stratum II. Excavators of Et-Tell have discovered the ruins of a building which they believe

---

17. According to the Mishnah: m. Kel. 4:4, 10:1, m. Ohol. 5:5, m. Parah 5:5, m. Yad. 1:2.
18. See Fiensy, *Archaeology of Daily Life*, 287–89.
19. Arav and Savage, "Bethsaida," 265–76.
20. Arav and Savage, "Bethsaida," 277.
21. Strickert, *Bethsaida*, 66.

to be a pagan temple, perhaps a temple dedicated to Livia/Julia after whom the village was now named Julias. The temple was actually the restoration of an old Phoenician temple (c. 66 X 16 feet; Figure 7.3, below) that stood on a mound in the center of the village. The structure was identified as a temple because it had an east-west orientation, a porch in the *antae* in both east and west ends, remains of a column foundation, a room that looks like a *pronaos*, a room that appears to have been a *cella*, and a porch that "can be viewed as the *adyton*"; (see Glossary). Yet, Rami Arav has noted that if this was a pagan temple, it was not constructed on a podium (as usual), nor was it a very elaborate temple, especially compared with the pagan temples Philip's father, Herod the Great, built at Samaria and Caesarea Philippi.[22]

Near the structure they found two bronze incense shovels, indicating ritual activity, and several clay figurines. One of the figurines was a "veiled woman with curly hair" and another "the upper torso of a female wearing a veil and a tiara or diadem." The excavators surmise that the Phoenician temple was reused in 29–30 CE when Philip the Tetrarch elevated the village to a city and named it Julias. The reconstructed temple would have been dedicated to the divine Livia/Julia.[23]

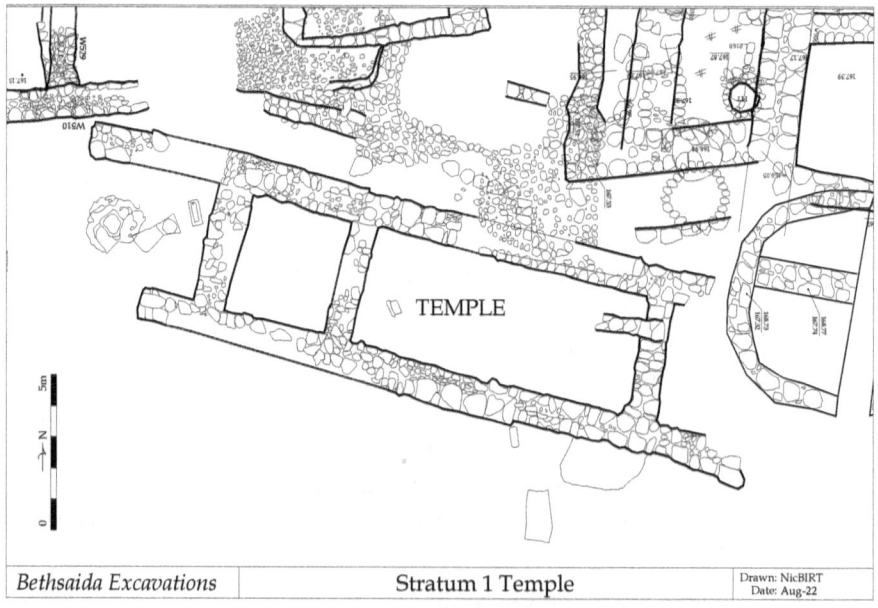

Figure 7.3: Temple plan at Et-Tell. (drawing by Nik Birt; used with permission of Bethsaida Excavations)

22. Arav, "Preliminary Report, 1994–1996," 22, 24.
23. Arav and Savage, "Bethsaida," 263, 266–67.

If Et-Tell is the ancient Bethsaida, Philip's elevating it to *polis* status did not cause a major Hellenization of the village. There are not, except for the temple, architectural features of Greco-Roman cities such as gridded streets, theaters, hippodromes, or agoras (marketplaces). In spite of its new status, it remained a small, Jewish—and not very prosperous—village.[24]

The archaeology of Et-Tell, then, somewhat fits what we know about the history of Bethsaida. The main problem, as observers have pointed out, is that this village is rather far (one and one-half miles) from the shore of the Sea of Galilee. Historians debate whether this situation prevailed in antiquity or whether geological shifts have taken place to account for the possible movement away from the shore. At any rate, this village was clearly: (1) Jewish and (2) a fishing village.

Lately, El-Araj is getting more attention since excavations are now taking place. Excavators of El-Araj have found ruins of Jewish habitation from the first century BCE (stoneware vessels) and some evidence of Romanization (a Roman bath and a silver denarius with Emperor Nero's image).[25] The village has three archaeological strata: an ER stratum (dated from coins and pottery), a layer of silt (coinciding with the village's abandonment), and an upper Byzantine stratum in which has been found a Christian basilica, allegedly built over the first-century house of Peter and Andrew (See Chapter 4).

This ER village, contemporaneous with the ministry of Jesus, yielded the following small finds:

- Stoneware vessels (for Jewish ritual purity as at Et-Tell; see Chapter 9)
- Knife-pared Herodian lamps with no pagan decorations and no images of animals and humans of any kind (like Et-Tell)
- The Kefar Hananya ware (like Et-Tell)
- Lead weights for fish nets (like Et-Tell).[26]

The two villages, then, are mirror images of each other. Finding a Roman-style bath argues that the Romans at some point had an influence on the fishing village now named El-Araj. It would be rare for a small Jewish village to have had a Roman bath in the first century. On the other hand, if the structure uncovered at Et-Tell was a pagan temple dedicated to Livia/

---

24. Arav and Savage, "Bethsaida," 277. The inhabitants were not as wealthy as those in the upper city of Jerusalem but better off than—so the excavators maintain—those from En-Gedi.

25. Notley and Aviam, "Searching for Bethsaida"; Shpigel and Schuster, "Lost City of Jesus' Apostles."

26. See Aviam and Notley, "In Search of the City."

Julia, that would argue that Bethsaida was at what is now Et-Tell and became the tiny *polis* of Julias in the year 29–30 CE.

Thus, the archaeological evidence from each site, so far, seems to be able to argue either way. Both were Jewish villages engaged in fishing. The small finds alone cannot determine which village—if either—was the New Testament and rabbinic village of Bethsaida. We need a Roman milestone or another sort of inscription naming one of the sites as Bethsaida. Until that happens, there will continue to be differing opinions. Yet both were certainly Jewish villages contemporaneous with the ministry of Jesus, and therefore archaeological information about both is valuable to the interpreter of the Gospel of Luke.

MAGDALA

> Also with him were certain women that had been healed of evil spirits and sickness: Mary called Magdalene (from whom he cast out seven demons) . . . (Luke 8:2)

In every list of women disciples, Mary Magdalene appears first.[27] The reason for this placement is beyond the scope of our archaeological commentary. She obviously was a leader. Why that was the case we are left to speculate. But her epithet, "Magdalene," tells us a little about her in addition to the brief notice that Jesus cast seven demons out of her. There has been a suggestion—since the Aramaic word *magdala* is the equivalent of the Hebrew word *migdol* "tower"—that the term means that Mary was a tower of strength, a "tower-ess,"[28] and does not indicate anything about her hometown. Nevertheless, the notion that her name identifies her place of origin (like Judas Iscariot) seems to have general support.[29]

The Aramaic Magdala "tower," was perhaps the place the rabbis called Magdala Nuniya ("tower of the fish," b. Pes. 46a) and Magdala Ṣab'ayya ("tower of the dyers," j. Ma'as. S. 56b).[30] The Greek authors referred to this location as Taricheae (*War* 2.252). The location of the two named sites, as with several other sites mentioned in the Gospel of Luke, is sometimes

---

27. Luke 8:2; Mark 15:47; Mark 16:1//Matt 28:1//John 20:1; Luke 24:10; John 20:2, 11–18.

28. See the discussion in Joan Taylor, "Missing Magdala"; Taylor, "Magdala's Mistaken Identity"; and Evans, *Jesus and the Remains*, 23–24.

29. See Danker, *Lexicon*, on the term "Magdalene"; Theissen and Merz, *Historical Jesus*, 222; Fitzmyer, *Luke*, 1:697; Marshall, *Luke*, 316; Bauckham, "Additional Note B."

30. See Bauckham, "Magdala in Rabbinic Traditions."

debated. Do the two names, Magdala and Taricheae, refer to the same town, or were they two separate locations?[31] The debate is not over the archaeology of the alleged town but over geographical references from antiquity. This discussion will probably continue, but for now the conclusion of Richard Bauckham is preferable: "The scholarly consensus . . . is that Taricheae and Magdala . . . were names for the same place."[32]

The nature of the small city of Magdala/Taricheae is only now, because of excavations, being clarified. Magdala/Taricheae was located on the western shore of the Sea of Galilee, approximately 3.5 miles north of Tiberias (see Map 2 p. 100). Uzi Leibner informs us that the area covered 22.5 acres.[33] That area would calculate to 3,600 persons populating this town or small city. That figure, or perhaps slightly more, is about right. It was not as large at Sepphoris or Tiberias (8,000–10,000), but it was larger than the average village.

In spite of its size, Magdala was a genuine *polis* in the cultural sense (of Pausanias). Scholars point to the monumental buildings and other urban features as markers of the city-like atmosphere of Magdala. Here is a summary of them:

1. The city was laid out in an organized manner (Hippodamian grid) with a *Cardo Maximus* (32 feet wide) and several *decumani*.

2. There were urban buildings: fountains, baths, a *stoa*-shaped fountain house,[34] a *palaestra* (exercising building), and a hippodrome (horse-race track). See Josephus, *War* 2.599 and *Life* 132, 138.

3. There was a water system bringing fresh water into the city, and a latrine system.

4. There was a mixed Jewish/gentile population.[35]

With these features, one is hard-pressed to call Magdala a village since it had many of the architectural features of a city.

---

31. For a challenge to the identification of the two names, see Kokkinos, "Location"; Joan Taylor, "Missing Magdala"; and Taylor, "Magdala's Mistaken Identity." For the argument for the identity of the two locations, see Bauckham, "Magdala as We Now Know It," 7–10.

32. Bauckham, "Magdala as We Now Know it," 7.

33. Leibner, *Settlement and History*, 214.

34. See Bonnie and Richard, "Building D1."

35. Bauckham, "Magdala as We Now Know it," 23–37; De Luca and Lena, "Magdala/Taricheae," 304, 327; Leibner, *Settlement and History*, 215; Bonnie and Richard, "Building D 1," 73–74.

Based on its Greek name, Taricheae ("fish salting factories"[36]), historians universally agree that the small city lived from the fish industry, both catching the fish and preparing them for shipment to the far reaches of Palestine and beyond. Not only do we have the literary references to the pickled fish of the Sea of Galilee (Strabo 16.2.45;[37] m. Abod. Zar. 2:6; m. Ned. 6:4), but we also have in the Magdala ruins two indicators of the importance of fishing: numerous lead weights (for the fishnets) and water installations. With regard to the latter finds, it is possible that excavators have discovered some of the fish vats where the fish were pickled/salted as well as aquaria where live fish were kept until ready to be killed and processed.[38] The pickled fish were well known in antiquity and were transported at great distances.

Roman historians considered Magdala/Taricheae an important small city. It is listed by Pliny the Elder alongside Tiberias, Hippos, and Bethsaida Julias as the principal towns around the Sea of Galilee (Pliny, *N.H.* 5.71). Both the archaeological remains and the literary references indicate the importance of this city.

Magdala was populated by a large percentage of Jews as indicated by three sorts of archaeological finds:

1. Four *mikva'ot* (see Figure 7.4, below)
2. Numerous fragments of stone vessels
3. Two synagogues (see Figure 7.5, below)

These "markers of Judaism" make it certain that most of the residents were Jewish, although a significant minority must have been gentile. This latter conclusion is based on iconic finds (lamps and other items with depictions of erotic and animal scenes).[39] Thus, it was a mixed population like Jerusalem, Sepphoris, and Tiberias. The Jewish villages were more homogeneous, however.

---

36. De Luca and Lena, "Magdala, Taricheae," 283; and LSJM.

37. "At the place called Taricheæ, the lake supplies the best fish for curing." Translation of Strabo in *Perseus Digital Library*: http://www.perseus.tufts.edu/hopper/text?doc=Perseus:text:1999.01.0239:book=16:chapter=2&highlight=/.

38. De Luca and Lena, "Magdala, Taricheae," 309.

39. See De Luca and Lena, "Magdala, Taricheae," 329; Bauckham, "Magdala as We Now Know It," 39-45; Reich and Zapata-Meza, "Domestic Miqva'ot"; Aviam, "Synagogue"; Zapata-Meza, "Domestic and Mercantile Areas."

Figure 7.4: One of the four *mikva'ot* at Magdala

As in the other cities where we have enough exposed to tell, there were ritzier sections of Magdala. Some of the houses were constructed of better materials and with better workmanship than others. These houses also had mosaic floors similar to those in the upscale houses of Jerusalem. The excavators emphasize, however, that the size of the Magdala houses was "modest in comparison" with the Jerusalem dwellings of the wealthy.[40]

Thus, one is inclined to surmise that, as in the cities of Sepphoris and Tiberias,[41] there were three main socioeconomic classes in Magdala: the wealthy class (the owners of the upscale houses), the working class (fishing families and those in the fish pickling business), and the destitute persons (always present but leaving scant evidence of themselves). The interesting question is, from which class did Mary Magdalene come? Without further information, we presume she came from one of the three tiers within the working class (see Table 5.5).

40. Zapata-Meza, "Domestic and Mercantile Areas," 93; De Luca and Lena, "Magdala, Taricheae," 306.

41. Both the Talmud (b. Ḥull. 92a, for Sepphoris) and Josephus (*Life* 32–39, for Tiberias) indicate three socioeconomic classes in the cities: the elites, the working class (*am ha-aretz*), and the "empty ones" (Talmud) or "most insignificant persons" (Josephus). See Fiensy, *Archaeology of Daily Life*, 43.

Figure 7.5: Interior of first-century Synagogue at Magdala

8

Two Parables

PARABLES ARE FICTIONAL STORIES that illustrate a religious message. The stories originated from the everyday life of the people who heard them and told them. When Jesus told his parables, how would the local village residents have imagined them? The archaeological remains of a large agricultural estate and of a non-Jewish city will help us gain a clearer picture of the setting for two of them.

THE PARABLE OF THE RICH FOOL

> He told a parable to them, "The land of a rich man produced abundantly. He thought about it and said, 'What can I do? I don't have anywhere to gather my produce.' Then he said, 'I'll do this: I'll tear down my granaries and build bigger ones. I'll gather there all my wheat and my goods. I'll say to myself, "Self, you have many goods laid aside for many years. Take it easy, eat, drink, and have fun."' But God said to him, 'Fool! This very night I'm calling in the debt of your life. Who's going to get what you have prepared?'" (Luke 12:16–20)

Aside from the important moral lesson of sharing our bounty with the less fortunate and living for more than just our own entertainment, this parable and others inform us of certain economic conditions in Palestine/Israel during the time of Jesus. This "fool" has a lot of land and it produces a bumper crop. He has the financial ability to tear down the existing granaries and build bigger ones. The wheat he has stored has made him wealthy beyond his fondest dreams, and he intends to kick back and take it easy for the rest of his life. What sort of economic system is at play here? Does archaeology inform us?

Large Estates in the Parables

Large land estates, some of them huge even by modern standards, were a phenomenon in the Early to Late Roman period. One in Spain was allegedly 270,000 acres; one in Italy topped 226,000 acres, and an estate in North Africa was 75,000 acres.[1] Such economic cities-unto-themselves required a skilled manager, a suitable physical plant to store the produce, and, of course, a large and dependable workforce. No estate approaching these sizes existed in Palestine/Israel in the late Second Temple Period, but there certainly were estates of 2,000 to 3,000 acres.

Since the publication of Johannes Herz's "Large Estates in Palestine at the Time of Jesus" in 1928, it has been assumed that Jesus' parables were alluding to real economic conditions in Lower Galilee.[2] Whether historians have accepted that all, or even most, of these parables originated from the historical Jesus, they nonetheless have seen in the parables genuine reflections of economic life in Palestine/Israel. Several of Jesus' parables assume that there were large agricultural estates. Although these estates were not as large as the celebrated ones listed above, they were large enough to require tenant farmers, agricultural slaves, and bailiffs to care for the landowner's farm.

---

1. See the references in Fiensy, *Social History*, 23; and Stegemann and Stegemann, *Jesus Movement*, 43.

2. Herz, "Grossgrundbesitz."

Parable/event	Large estates in Luke	Large estates in other Gospels
The two debtors	7:41-43	Matt 18:24-34
The rich fool	12:16-21	
The shrewd steward	12:42-43	
The prodigal son	15:11-32	
The unjust steward	16:1-7	
The rich man and Lazarus	16:19-31	
The unworthy servant	17:7-10	
The talents	19:11-27	Matt 25:14-30
The wicked tenants	20:9-19	Mark 12:1-12; Matt 21:33-46
The rich man's question	18:18-23	Mark 10:17-22; Matt 19:16-22
The workers in the vineyard		Matt 20:1-15

Table 8.1: Large estates alluded to in the Gospels

Some parables depict scenes on a large estate. The Parable of the Rich Fool, featured above (Luke 12:16-21), for instance, describes an estate owner hoarding grain in a manner reminiscent of an account in Josephus (*Life* 119) about the granary of Queen Berenice. Luke 17:7 refers to a man's servant plowing his field for him. Matt 20:1-15 narrates about a landowner who has so much land that he must hire day laborers to work it. Luke 12:42-43 alludes to a wealthy man who has a bailiff to run his estate.

Based on the New Testament, Josephus, the papyri, and the Talmud, several scholars have attempted to describe how these ancient large estates looked and worked.[3] The Parable of the Tenants (Mark 12:1-12, Luke 20:9-19, Matt 21:33-46), received special treatment from Martin Hengel. This parable refers to a vineyard with tenant farmers, a landlord, and several "slaves" who are sent to collect the rent. Hengel, following leads by earlier scholars,[4] sought to illustrate how this parabolic estate must have been understood by reference to the third century BCE Zenon papyri. The estate of Apollonius in Beth Anath (in Galilee?) was said to have had 80,000

---

3. Hengel, "Gleichnis"; Alt, *Kleine Schriften*, 2:384-95; Klein, "Notes on Large Estates," 1.3; Klein, "Notes on Large Estates," 3.4; Derrett, "Fresh Light"; Krauss, *Antoninus und Rabbi*, 18; Applebaum, "Economic Life in Palestine" esp. 658; Kippenberg, *Religion und Klassenbildung*,118; Freyne, *Galilee*, 164-65; Charlesworth, *Jesus within Judaism*, 39-48; Horsley, *Galilee*, 210-14; Jeremias, *Jerusalem*, 96; Hanson and Oakman, *Palestine*,116-19; Stegemann and Stegemann, *Jesus Movement*, 111.

4. Herz, "Grossgrundbesitz"; Alt, *Kleine Schriften*, 2:384-95; Tcherikover, "Palestine under the Ptolemies."

vines plus fig trees and probably grain fields. Hengel surmised that 80,000 vines required 40 acres and could support 25 workers and their families. He thought that this size was about right for the hypothetical estate of Mark 12/Luke 20/Matt 21. Thus, Hengel thought he had demonstrated the plausibility of the parable of Mark 12, and with it an important feature of the late Second Temple Galilean economy, in finding in an actual estate many of the same elements as in the Parable of the Wicked Tenants.[5]

Ramat ha-Nadiv

How can we visualize what Jesus was picturing in his parables? There are no ruins of such estates in Galilee today. At least, so far, none have been found. There are, however, ruins of such estates farther south. The estate at Ḥorvat Eleq on the Ramat ha-Nadiv ridge three miles from Caesarea Maritima controlled 2,500 acres and was occupied from the Iron Age to the Byzantine period, according to Yizhar Hirschfeld.[6] Hirschfeld had concluded that the most impressive ruins—the mansion, the baths, and the swimming pool—originated from the era that stretches from Herod the Great to the Great Revolt (37 BCE–66 CE). Hirschfeld even speculated that the estate during that period belonged to a member of the Herodian family.

More recent excavations by Orit Peleg-Barkat and Yotam Tepper, however, have reached different conclusions. They conclude that the "zenith of the settlement was during the Persian and Hellenistic periods." They maintain that during the ER period this site was a farm built over the Hellenistic ruins.[7] At any rate, there was a large estate there, whenever it flourished (either in Hell or ER).

Yizhar Hirschfeld believed the estate consisted of two complexes of buildings: the eastern complex (Ḥorvat 'Eleq), with the luxurious living quarters, and the western complex (Ḥorvat Aqav), where the agricultural center was located. Although the dating of some of the constructions on Ḥorvat 'Eleq is now disputed (as noted above), still we may describe the ruins, cautiously following Hirschfeld, as a guide.

The "mansion" on the eastern complex had 150 rooms. One set of around thirty rooms (in the middle of the mansion, see Figure 8.1, below)

---

5. Hengel, "Gleichnis."

6. More recent excavations conclude that the occupation continued through the Ottoman period. See Peleg-Barkat and Tepper, "Between Phoenicia and Judaea."

7. Peleg-Barkat and Tepper, "Between Phoenicia and Judaea," 73: "In our opinion, during the Early Roman period the site was a village or farm, built on the ruins of the earlier Hellenistic site."

produced small finds of a domestic nature: grindstones, jars, cooking pots, and spindle whorls. Hirschfeld believed that these rooms were for the "servants and staff" of the estate.

Another set of rooms, on the south of the palatial complex, contained marble tables and floors, gold jewelry, imported vessels, and stoneware like that found among the Jewish upper class in Jerusalem. This would have been the residence of the wealthy family. The mansion also featured a high tower on one end of it, which may have reached five stories. Hirschfeld surmised that the tower was for defense against irate agricultural workers and, perhaps, bandits. The residents were Jewish at some level since there was an absence of pig bones and the presence of both stoneware vessels and a *mikveh*.[8]

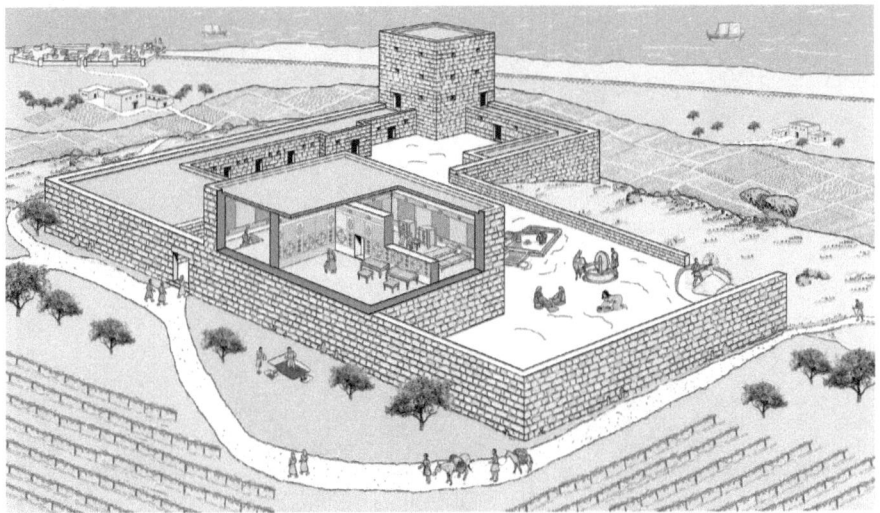

Figure 8.1: Artist's reconstruction of the palatial mansion at Ramat ha-Nadiv (Ḥorvat Eleq), looking northwest[9]

---

8. Hirschfeld, "Ramat ha-Nadiv"; Hirschfeld, "Early Roman Bath"; Hirschfeld, *Ramat Hanadiv Excavations*; and Hirschfeld and Feinberg-Vamosh, "Country Gentleman's Estate."

9. Artist's reconstruction from https://www.ritmeyer.com/. See Hirschfeld, "Ramat ha-Nadiv" *NEAEHL* 5:2004 for details.

Figure 8.2: Ruins of the mansion, Ramat ha-Nadiv (looking west)

Figure 8.3: Hypocaust of the Roman-style bath south of the manor house Ramat ha-Nadiv

Figure 8.4: Ancient swimming pool on the grounds of Ḥorvat ʿEleq, Ramat ha-Nadiv

On the other side of the ridge (at Ḥorvat Aqav) there was another ruin connected to the first one by an ancient road. This was a more modest construction which Hirschfeld concluded was the agricultural center of the estate. Probably the estate overseer (called an *oikonomos* in the New Testament) lived there. One finds there an oil press, two wine presses, a *mikveh*, a threshing floor, and a tower. The agricultural workers might also have lived in the complex, perhaps as enslaved laborers, or traveled there each day to work as day laborers.[10]

---

10. Hirschfeld, "Ramat ha-Nadiv," in *NEAEHL* 4:1257–60; Hirschfeld, *Ramat Hanadiv Excavations*; Murphy-O'Connor, *Holy Land*, 441–42.

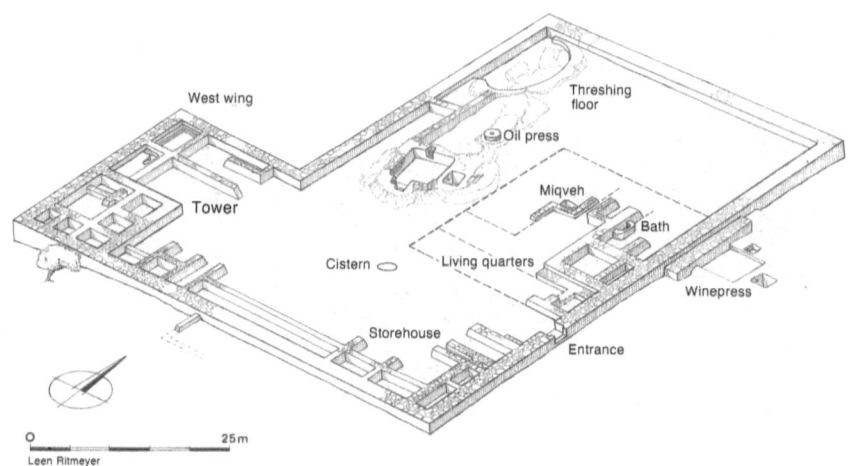

Figure 8.5: Plan of Ḥorvat Aqav, the agricultural center of the estate[11]

Figure 8.6: *Mikveh* at agricultural center, Ramat ha-Nadiv

11. Plan purchased from https://www.ritmeyer.com/. For the details, see Hirschfeld, *Ramat Hanadiv Excavations*.

Figure 8.7: Ḥorvat Aqav. Olive crusher in center; to the upper right, the threshing floor.

The estate at Ramat ha-Nadiv illustrates—regardless of when it flourished, whether Hell I-II or ER—what Jesus had in mind when he told the numerous parables alluding to large landowners. They would have had a mansion—perhaps a bit larger or smaller than this one—and other luxuries in the house and on the grounds. The estate would require an agricultural center where the estate overseer would manage the workers and check on the produce. Although no such ruins have yet surfaced in Galilee, these estates were known to the common people, whether from seeing them in person or hearing about them from travelers. The ruins of estates like the one near Caesarea Maritima give us in the modern world a picture of what Jesus was alluding to.

THE PARABLE OF THE WASTEFUL SON

A man had two sons. The younger one said to his father, "Father, give me the part of the estate that's coming to me." And he distributed to them his property. A short time later, the younger son got everything together and went to a faraway country. There he squandered his wealth by living wastefully. (Luke 15:11–13)

Thus begins the famous parable found only in Luke and often named the Parable of the Prodigal Son. How would Jesus' contemporaries have imagined the story? In the first place, the story begins on a large estate. The father has evidently a considerable *ousia* (financial substance, v. 12), day laborers (vv. 17 and 19), and slaves (v. 22, 26). He awards the wayward son, upon his return, a robe and a ring (v. 22), and he has a stall-fed calf ready at hand for butchering (vv. 23, 30). He has the resources to give a rather substantial banquet (v. 25; see Chapter 11). The father, then, was the owner of a significant estate—perhaps a thousand acres—and he divided up[12] the estate according to the Torah's commands: two-thirds went to the older brother and one-third to the younger.[13] The value of even three hundred acres would have made the younger brother a rich man. He probably could have lived comfortably from the land—without any of his own labor—for life.[14]

How old is the younger brother? Since there is no mention of a wife, we are probably to imagine him in his teenage years (see Chapter 1); fathers married children very young at this time. Presumably, but not necessarily, the wayward son would not have abandoned a wife and child(ren) to run to the faraway country. The audience would have envisioned a boy around fourteen to sixteen years old.

So much for the opening scene of the story, including the estate and the bad son. But what was the faraway country?[15] How would a Jewish audience in Galilee have understood this reference? The "country" need not have been actually far in miles. The detail was a usual one in describing wayward children as in this rabbinic parable which has similarities to Jesus' story:

A king had a son who had gone astray from his father *a journey of a hundred days*; his friends said to him, "Return to your father"; he said, "I cannot." Then his father sent to say, "Return as far as you can, and I will come to you the rest of the way."[16]

12. Other Jewish texts referring to dividing up inheritance before the death of the father are Tobit 8:21 (who settled one-half of his estate on his son); Sir 33:20–24 (who advises against predeath property distribution); m. B. Batra. 8:7. See Nolland, *Luke* 2:782.

13. Deut 21:17; Philo, *Spec. Leg.* 2.133; Josephus, *Ant.* 4.249–50; m. B. Batra 8:4–5.

14. See White, *Roman Farming*, 385–87, for the categories of medium and large estates in antiquity. Large estates were farms with over 300 acres; medium estates were 50–300 acres.

15. Cf. Luke 19:12 where a nobleman journeys to a "faraway country" to seek his kingdom, evidently a veiled reference to Archelaus's journey to Rome.

16. Pesiq. Rab. 184b–185a. Translation in Montefiore and Loewe, *Rabbinic*

The journey of one hundred days is, probably, simply a literary symbol of the son's social and moral distance from his father. So, the faraway country in our parable need not be taken too literally.[17]

To imagine the story, we need a place for the younger brother to flee which afforded him wild living (v. 13), pigs (v. 15), and prostitutes (v. 30), a place where there would be many opportunities to squander a fortune. Where could we find such a place?

It would have been almost certainly in a city. Why would someone from a large landed estate flee to a village to sow his wild oats? The Roman poet Horace (65–8 BCE) lived in ancient Rome and wrote about its attractions. He said (*Epistle* 1.14.15–21) that in the city one found games (i.e., gladiatorial and sports contests), baths, brothels, and greasy restaurants (*popinae*), all considered appealing to those coming in from the countryside. Cities, then, were centers of pleasure even to a wealthy youth who had grown up with all the comforts of his age.

For example, people were drawn to Corinth mainly for two reasons: to visit the temple of Asclepius and to attend the Isthmian games in nearby Isthmia, which took place in the spring every two years. They came to Ephesus not only for the temple of Artemis—one of the wonders of the Greco-Roman world—but to attend the Ephesia, the athletic games and, later, to view the gladiatorial combats. The cities offered pleasures that the village and countryside could never match. We should, then, imagine a city, to which the younger brother betook himself, but which city? How might the village audience have thought about it?

We should not think of one of the cities of Galilee (Sepphoris or Tiberias). Thirty years ago, some interpreters stressed the Greco-Roman nature of the cities of Lower Galilee in the time of Jesus and Antipas. James F. Strange had written of Rome's imposing "a distinctive urban overlay" on a Jewish base in Sepphoris.[18] This measured statement may have been exaggerated in subsequent works by other authors. Thus, one historian called Sepphoris a "Greco-Roman-style city."[19] Another maintained that Galilee was "semi-pagan";[20] another speculated that Jesus might have read the works of Cynic philosophers alongside his reading of the Torah: "Galilee was in fact an

---

Anthology, 321. The emphasis is mine.

17. Cf. m. Yebam. 2:9, 4:6, 10:1, etc. where the expression *medinat hayam*, "land (beyond) the sea," means, according to Danby, "any place beyond the borders of the land of Israel," (*Mishnah*, 221).

18. Strange, "Some Implications of Archaeology," 31.

19. Kee, "Early Christianity in the Galilee," 15.

20. Funk, *Honest to Jesus*, 58.

epitome of Hellenistic culture on the eve of the Roman era."[21] Someone imagining Sepphoris and Tiberias in that way might think the younger brother simply fled a few short miles away to one of the Galilean cities.

But this view of Galilee and its cities is now challenged by archaeologists. Their response has been to cite the material remains as evidence that throughout Galilee, even in Sepphoris and Tiberias, the Jewish residents were Torah observant and were not assimilating as much Greco-Roman culture as one might think.

- Numerous stoneware vessels have been found in many Galilean villages and in both cities (see Chapter 9).
- Many villages have ritual baths. Even Sepphoris had around thirty stepped-pool installations that were probably used for ritual bathing. Both stone vessels and ritual baths have to do with maintaining ritual purity (see Table 6.3 and Chapter 9). Jews meticulous about ritual purity have clearly not given up their Jewishness in favor of Hellenism.
- There is a paucity of pig bones (Lev 11:7). They did turn up in the excavations of the village of Yodefat[22] and the city of Sepphoris.[23] Still, the amount of pig bones was small, and in most other sites the appearance of pig bones is so slight as to be statistically nonexistent.
- None of the coins minted in the reign of Antipas, the tetrarch of Galilee, had images of humans, pagan gods, or animals.[24]

Externals (the "distinctive urban overlay") can be deceiving. One can be a very conservative Jew and still dress like a Greek, speak the Greek language,[25] and live in a Greek-styled house. But at Sepphoris the core values of Judaism seem to be clearly expressed by the above four items.

These clear Jewish markers contrast sharply with what was not in Sepphoris, for example: There were no hippodromes (for chariot racing), no amphitheaters (for gladiatorial combats), no pagan temples, and no

---

21. Mack, *Myth of Innocence*, 64, 66.

22. Aviam, "Socio-Economic," 34, 2 percent pig bones.

23. Grantham, "Faunal Remains," about 4 percent pig bones. Grantham comments: "We must also consider that just because animal remains are found on a site doesn't necessarily mean the people there ate those animals. Some theorize that even Jewish towns kept free ranging pigs around to basically eat the garbage" (private correspondence).

24. See Sidebar 6.1 and Reed, *Archaeology*, 49–51; Chancey and E. M. Meyers, "How Jewish Was Sepphoris"; E. M. Meyers, "Jesus and His World," 191–95; Chancey, *Myth of a Gentile Galilee*, 79–90.

25. But see Chancey, *Greco-Roman Culture*, 124 who challenges even the claim that Galileans spoke Gk. in large numbers.

gymnasia.²⁶ Most of these things, however, can be found in Greek cities in the Decapolis region that we will list below. These were the truly Greco-Roman cities, not Sepphoris and, evidently, not Tiberias.²⁷

So, we should picture the younger brother as fleeing to a thoroughly gentile city, which means probably one of the Decapolis cities. The Decapolis (literally "ten cities") was an informal designation for the mostly pagan, Greek cities in the region of Palestine/Israel. There actually were probably more than ten cities included under this designation, and they did not form any sort of political alliance, strictly speaking. They were individual, semi-autonomous city-states subject to the Roman governor of Syria. These cities included, according to Pliny the Elder (*N.H.* 5.74), Damascus, Philadelphia (modern Amman, Jordan), Raphana, Scythopolis (Beth-She'an of the Hebrew Bible), Gadara, Hippos (Susita in Aram.), Dion, Pella, Gerasa (Jerash in Jordan), and Canatha.²⁸ All of these cities except Scythopolis were east of the Jordan River.

These were true *poleis*, "cities" in the Greco-Roman sense. They shared many architectural features (see the Pausanius reference in Chapter 6), including colonnaded streets, theaters, and baths. Two of them, Scythopolis and Gadara, had hippodromes (in the second century). Their urban features were an eclectic blend of Greek, Roman, and Middle Eastern forms.²⁹

We learn of the Jewish view of Greco-Roman-style cities from various sources. Josephus notes the Jewish reaction to Herod's introduction of "foreign practices" into Jerusalem when he built a theater, an amphitheater, and a hippodrome in 28-27 BCE (*Ant.* 15.267-68, 17.255). Josephus considered these constructions and the associated activities a corruption of Jewish customs.³⁰

The rabbis of the second century CE also discussed the features of the Greco-Roman city:

> R. Judah commenced [the discussion] by observing, "How fine are the works of this people! They have made streets, they have built bridges, they have erected baths" . . . R. Simeon b. Yoḥai answered and said, "All what they made they made for themselves;

---

26. Actually, a gymnasium may have been found at Hamat Tiberias just south of ancient Tiberias and dating from the first century. See Dothan, *Hamat Tiberias*, 16.

27. I say "evidently" because not enough of Tiberias has been excavated to get a clear picture of what the city was like in the first century CE.

28. For lists, see Rey-Coquais, "Decapolis"; Finegan, *Archaeology*, 117; Segal, "Decapolis"; Parker, "Decapolis"; *Encyclopedia Britannica*, s.v. "Decapolis." See Map 1 p. 2 for some of them. Another (somewhat different) list of the cities is in *Ant.* 14.76.

29. See Segal, "Decapolis."

30. On these constructions, see Lichtenberger, "Jesus and the Theater."

they built market-places, to set harlots in them; baths, to rejuvenate themselves; bridges, to levy tolls for them."[31]

He who goes to a stadium or to a camp to see the performances of sorcerers and enchanters or of various kinds of clowns, mimics, buffoons, and the like—lo, this is the seat of scoffers . . . He who sits in an amphitheater (where gladiators are fighting), lo, this one is guilty of bloodshed.[32]

To observant Jews, many of the architectural features of the Greco-Roman city which we admire so much today were an offense. A teenager's head could quickly be turned by seeing such things.

There are three references to the Decapolis in the Gospels: Matt 4:25 says, as Jesus went about Galilee preaching, many from Galilee, the Decapolis, Jerusalem, Judea, and Perea followed him. If people from the Decapolis followed him, he must have been in some of those cities at one time. Mark 5:20, in the context of the exorcism of the demoniac, says that the cleansed man spread the word throughout the Decapolis. Obviously, Jesus was in the region of a Decapolis city when he exorcised the demoniac. In Mark 7:31, it says Jesus left Tyre and Sidon and came to the Sea of Galilee through the Decapolis. Jesus was clearly at times in at least the territory of Decapolis cities if not actually in the cities themselves. The ordinary Galilean villager, however, had probably only heard about these gentile, urban centers.

Let us take a brief look at one of the Decapolis cities, Scythopolis, which lay approximately twenty miles from the Nazareth (see Map 1 p. 2), not "far" exactly but far enough. Scythopolis was, according to Josephus (*War* 3.446), the largest of the Decapolis cities. It was enriched by the lush farmland of the Valley of Jezreel and by controlling the trade route through the valley.[33] Evidently there was some cultural-religious resentment on the part of their Jewish neighbors since during the Jewish War, Justus of Tiberias led raids against the villages surrounding Scythopolis (*Life* 341–42, 410).[34]

Scythopolis, or Old Testament Beth-She'an (see 1 Sam 31:10, 12), was occupied from the Neolithic through the Arab periods. Its time of greatest prosperity, however, was the Roman period (stratum III). At that time, the occupation moved down from the mound (Figure 8.10) to the south. The main features of first-century Roman Scythopolis are:

31. B. Shabb. 33b. Translation in Epstein et al., *Babylonian Talmud*.

32. T. Abod. Zar. 2:5. Translation in Neusner, *Tosefta*. Cf. Weiss, "Theaters," 635: "The theatrical performances, they believed, were arenas of rowdiness, vulgarity, lewdness, and pornography."

33. Jones, *Greek City*, 40; Fiensy, *Social History*, 28–31.

34. See Parker, "Decapolis."

- a theater (seating for 7,000), restored in the second century
- an agora
- a Roman basilica
- gridded streets
- the usual Greco-Roman items of architecture: temples, and baths
- residential areas (along the southwest slope of the mound)[35]

Figure 8.8: A model of Scythopolis in the Roman period (looking northwest) at Beth She'an National Park, Israel. To the left in the photo is the theater (second century restoration of a first-century construction) for dramas, mimes, and pantomimes. Slanting northeast from the theater is the colonnaded Palladius street. To the right of the theater (east) lies the agora. East of that is the first-century CE bath. Just south of the bath were two pagan temples. The mound north of the Hellenistic-Roman city is Tell Beth She'an.

The colonnaded street of Scythopolis seen now (figures 8.9 and 8.10) is second century but covers a first-century street. It extends 590 feet from the theater to the base of the mound and is around 25 feet wide. Our fictional runaway boy might have walked along the first-century version of this street

35. Foerster, "Beth-Shean"; Seligman, "Beth-Shean"; Mazor, "Beth-Shean"; and Murphy-O'Connor, *Holy Land*, 221–26.

from the theater to the base of the mound. As he walked, the runaway could have watched small merchants hawking wares and heard street preachers of philosophy, magic, astrology, and oriental religions selling their ideas. There would also have been purveyors of pleasures of every kind standing around hoping to entice visitors to their dens of entertainment.

Had the fictional runaway boy turned to the right, he would have entered the agora (marketplace) where there was even more intense commercial activity. At the end of the street (Palladius Street), he would find a series of shops. Turning back south along the street bisecting the agora and the baths, he would pass on his left the huge eastern baths measuring 394 X 305 feet. There he could have refreshed himself daily with a soak in the water. But there also might have been invitations in the baths to participate in sexual activity. As he walked around the city, doubtless he would have been exposed to the pagan temples such as those east of the theater, one of which was dedicated to Demeter and Kore. Our fictional boy would have witnessed ceremonies honoring the city's patron deities, Dionysus and Tyche-Nysa.[36]

Figure 8.9: Aerial photo of Scythopolis city center (looking southwest). The colonnaded street (Palladius Street) intersects the photograph. The theater is at the upper left of the photograph with the first-century agora to the left of the street. (Photograph by Avraham Graicer)[37]

36. Foerster, "Beth-Shean"; Seligman, "Beth-Shean"; Mazor, "Beth-Shean"; and Murphy-O'Connor, *Holy Land*, 221–26.

37. Wikimedia Commons: https://commons.wikimedia.org/wiki/File:ANCIENT_BEIT_SHE%27AN_AERIAL.jpg/.

They might have used the theater in the first century not only for dramas, mimes, and pantomimes but also for gladiatorial combats—they often did that throughout the empire—until they built their amphitheater in the second century CE. Later, they also built a hippodrome. The chariot drivers and the gladiators were greatly admired by the common people even though they were considered unrespectable by the elites. They were like the athletic stars of today. A naïve teenager, just in from the farm, could lose a lot of money betting on the gladiatorial contests.

Figure 8.10: The colonnaded street (Palladius Street) running from the theater to the mound of Old Testament Beth-She'an (looking north)

Thus, we imagine the arrogant teenager running to a city like Scythopolis. It was pagan to the core and offered plenty of opportunities for him to squander his money. This could have been his "faraway country." The prodigal left his rather easy life on the large estate of his wealthy father, traveled to the pagan city, and learned a life lesson. How many Jewish boys—even those of more modest means—had done the same in Jesus' day?

Figure 8.11: The second-century theater restored from the first-century construction.

> After he had wasted it all, a severe famine occurred in that country and he began to lack. So, he went out and joined up with one of the citizens of that region and he sent him to a farm to feed swine. He wanted to fill up with the carob pods[38] he was feeding the hogs but nobody gave them to him. (Luke 15:14–16)

After the arrogant boy had blown his small fortune, a famine arose. During famines, the price of food skyrockets. He could no longer afford to live the life of the leisured gentleman in the gentile city so full of pleasures for a young man. That he now hires himself out to tend hogs clearly shows he is not in a predominantly Jewish region.

How could a person in a city find work tending pigs? Interestingly, from 2006 to 2009, excavations were done on a farmstead or small estate, called Tel Zahara, lying around three miles west of Scythopolis. The occupation of the site (with a few gaps) stretches from the Early Bronze Age to the early twentieth century CE. The Hellenistic stratum dates late third–late second BCE. The Roman stratum (stratum II) dates early second–early third CE. Even though the farmstead was vacant during the time of Jesus, it

---

38. On feeding animals carobs, compare m. Ma'as. 3:4 and m. Shabb. 24:2.

can illustrate how a person trapped in a Greco-Roman city during a famine could make his way to its outskirts to find work.[39]

Tel Zahara was a small estate but not a poor one. The buildings were well constructed around a courtyard, and the interior of the residence was decorated with frescos. The ceramics and glassware, however, though abundant, were "basic."[40] The farmstead prospered, but it was not the estate of an extremely wealthy family like the one from which our young man had run away.

This farmstead was a major provider of meat to the city of Scythopolis in the Roman period. Faunal remains recovered from stratum IIA consisted of

- 43 percent sheep/goats,
- 11 percent cattle,
- and 23 percent pigs.[41]

The excavators observe that in the Roman period in Israel, there was an increase in domestic swine production. On this farm, "pork production was a primary activity."[42]

During the Roman period, Tel Zahara was one of many small estates and farmsteads on the environs of Scythopolis that provided the city with food, especially meat. Thus, we can imagine our fictional runaway boy—poor, hungry, and desperate—leaving his enchanted city life of pleasure and trudging three miles to the west to seek any means to stay alive. He must have heard about these estates ringing the city where a person might find work—a thing he had, heretofore, never done. What he found just outside the city would have been a farm, like Tel Zahara, providing the city with meat. Although the farm also raised sheep and goats and cattle, his job was caring for the hogs, perhaps not especially repulsive to our entitled, arrogant boy, but certainly offensive to the Jewish audience hearing the parable.[43]

---

39. Cohen and Więckowski, Introduction.

40. Cohen, "Tel Zahara."

41. The rest of the faunal remains were dog, gazelle, bird, deer, donkey, and freshwater crab.

42. Horwitz, "Faunal Remains"; Cohen, "Tel Zahara."

43. See b. B. Qama 82b: "Cursed be the man who would breed swine"; m. B. Qama 7:7: "None [i.e., no Israelite] may rear swine anywhere"; b. Ned. 49b: "A *Min* (heretic) said to R. Judah, 'Your face is like that of a moneylender or pig breeder.' He replied, 'Both are forbidden to Jews.'" Translations in Epstein, *Talmud*; and Danby, *Mishnah*.

9

Two Controversies

THOSE WHO MET JESUS held varying opinions of him. The religious authorities, though often sympathetic, were the greatest opposition to his ministry. Most of the debates were over *halakhah*, that is, proper application of legal regulations such as Sabbath observance (Luke 6:1–5, 6–11; 13:10–14; 14:1–6) and ritual purity. In addition, there were disagreements about authority. Below are two of the controversies that archaeology helps us understand more clearly.

RITUAL PURITY

> While he was speaking, a Pharisee asked him to dine with him. So, he went in and reclined. But the Pharisee was amazed that he did not first take a (ritual) bath.[1] The Lord said to him, "Now you Pharisees cleanse the outside of the cup and platter but inside is full of greed and evil." (Luke 11:37–39)

A Pharisee invited Jesus for a meal but was shocked that Jesus did not take a (ritual) bath before eating. Jesus then responded by rebuking the Pharisee for his meticulous application of the biblical laws of clean-unclean while neglecting moral purity. This little episode tells us two things: First, Pharisees, who were very particular about with whom they ate a meal, considered

---

1. Gk.: *baptizō*, "to dip in water, immerse," Danker, *Lexicon*. Understanding this as mere handwashing (as in Mark 7:2), is probably inaccurate, *pace* Marshall, *Luke*, 494; Green, *Luke*, 470; and Fitzmyer, *Luke*, 2:947. Nolland, *Luke*, 2:663 offers that some Pharisees practiced total immersion before meals as Booth (*Jesus*, 193) maintained.

Jesus a reputable dining companion. Second, the Pharisee fully expected that Jesus observed the ritual purity laws as assiduously as he.

The Hebrew Bible speaks often about a subject called *tum'ah*. We translate this usually "ritual impurity." It is a kind of impurity distinct from both moral impurity and hygienic dirt. The laws of purity—distinguishing clean and unclean persons, animals, and objects—are found mainly in Lev 11–17 and Num 19. They detail the steps to take if one acquires *tum'ah*. How can you get rid of the impurity and be once again in a state of ritual purity (*tohar*)? The laws of the Hebrew Bible refer mostly to those intending to enter the temple. But something happened in the first century BCE in Palestine. "Purity broke out" or spread out as one rabbinic work stated it (t. Shab. 1:14). In other words, everyone, not just temple officials and those worshipers preparing to enter the temple, wanted to be in a state of ritual purity all or most of the time. They wanted to go beyond the requirements of the Torah. Recently, archaeology has shown us how important the laws of purity and impurity became to the Jews living in Palestine during the time of Jesus.

Ritual Purity in the Torah

A good way to summarize the laws in the Hebrew Bible is to identify the three main causes of uncleanness:

- Leprosy (of humans, clothes, and of buildings)
- Discharge from the sexual organs (a menstruating woman, a man or woman with a diseased flux, a seminal emission, and a woman after childbirth)
- Dead bodies (of animals or humans)[2]

To become unclean meant primarily that one was excluded from the temple until the process of purification could be completed. But there were some consequences of uncleanness that went beyond temple nonparticipation. First, in the case of leprosy,[3] the "unclean" leper or one suspected of having leprosy was shut away from the community until a decision could be reached about the leprosy, and if it was concluded that the unclean person had leprosy, the victim was excluded from the community and had to live outside the village. Second, a man was forbidden to have sexual relations with his wife during her days of menstruation. Third, food that became

---

2. See Roth et al., "Purity and Impurity," 1405.

3. For leprosy, see Chapter 10, below. This was not actually Hansen's disease but various skin conditions.

unclean due to the corpse of a "creeping thing" (*sherets*, i.e., insects, mice, lizards, and so forth) had to be discarded. Thus, even in the First Temple Period (or the period of the Hebrew Bible) uncleanness affected not only one's admissibility into the temple but also had broader implications for daily life.

The book of Leviticus gives several different procedures for purification but they basically included bathing, sometimes washing one's clothes, and waiting until sunset (or longer for some impurities). Corpse uncleanness (that uncleanness contracted through contact with a human corpse) required seven days' wait, sprinkling twice with the water mixed with the ashes of a red heifer, and bathing. Uncleanness after childbirth required seven or fourteen days' wait, depending on whether the child was a boy or girl. Purification from leprosy required bringing two birds to the priest—one of which was killed and the other released—waiting seven days, shaving all hair from one's body, washing the clothes, bathing, and offering three lambs.

Not only could people become unclean, but utensils, clothes, food, and drink as well. The book of Leviticus gives instructions for cleansing some of these objects, but not for the purification of food and drink. Presumably unclean food simply could not be used for temple worship, but food made unclean by the corpse of a creeping thing was probably thrown away (Lev 11:20, 23, 29–30, 41–43). Even houses could be declared unclean from "leprosy." In these cases, the houses were destroyed. The following table summarizes the sources of uncleanness, the means of removing the uncleanness, and where these issues are addressed in the four Gospels:

Impurity	Means of Purification	References in Luke	References in other Gospels
1. corpse uncleanness	Wait 7 days, sacrifice a red heifer, undergo sprinkling with ashes.	10:31–32	
2. childbirth	Wait 7 to 14 days, then wait 33 to 66 days.	2:22	
3. menstruation	Wait 7 days.		
4. diseased discharge from the sexual organ (male) (female)	Wait 7 days, bathe, wash clothes, make sacrifices. Wait 7 days, make sacrifices.	8:43–48	Mark 5:25–34// Matt 9:20–22
5. semen	Bathe, wait until sunset to rejoin group.		

Impurity	Means of Purification	References in Luke	References in other Gospels
6. contact with what one who has a diseased discharge sits, lies, or leans on	Bathe, wash clothes, wait until sunset to rejoin group.		
7. contact with what a menstruating woman sits, lies, or leans on	Bathe, wash clothes, wait until sunset to rejoin group.		
8. vessels which become unclean	Break if fired clay, wash if wooden. (Stone vessels, animal-dung vessels, and unfired clay vessels cannot become unclean.)	11:39	Mark 7:4; Matt 23:25; John 2:6
9. carcass of an unclean animal	People must bathe, wash clothes, and wait until sunset to rejoin group. Vessels must be broken or washed. Wet food must not be used.		
10. leprosy in people, garments, and houses	This is a long and complicated procedure.	4:27, 5:12–14, 7:22, 17:12	Matt 8:2, 26:6; Mark 1:40, 14:3

Table 9.1: Sources of Impurity[4]

These laws run through all four Gospels, popping up in several places, especially in the Gospel of Luke. In the past, commentators have all but ignored the background of ritual purity. Increasingly, they are recognizing how important a concept this was in the ministry of Jesus.

What is striking in this list is how often an unclean person is required to bathe. Impurities 4, 5, 6, 7, 9, and 10 necessitated taking the ritual bath. Not surprisingly we find references in the Gospels to washing, especially fully immersing oneself in water (Gk. *baptizō*): Luke 11:38, Mark 7:4. According to the Mishnaic tractate called *Mikva'ot* ("Baths") one had to immerse oneself entirely under water.[5] If people are conscientious about these laws, they

4. This table is adapted and simplified from that given in Sanders, *Jewish Law*, 151. A helpful series of tables of purification procedures and effects is also given in Milgrom, *Leviticus*, 986–91.

5. By contrast, washing the hands before a meal, according to the Mishnaic tractate Yadaim, was done by pouring (twice) over the hands.

will identify some sort of uncleanness regularly. That means a lot of baths (self-dunking). In a semiarid land, there are not many pools and streams available for such activity. Thus, ritual bathing installations had to be created by digging out pits or tubs and lining them with plaster.

Figure 9.1: Ritual bath in Yodefat (Galilee). Notice the plaster on the walls of the pit.

Archaeological evidence of purity

The material remains of Palestine from the late Second Temple period show that many people were concerned with ritual purity even when not preparing to enter the temple. Two kinds of material remains are important for this topic:

1. Ritual baths
2. Stoneware vessels

First, archaeologists have discovered many ritual bath installations throughout Israel. These baths must be distinguished from the Roman-style hygienic baths—consisting of a hot tank, a warm tank, and a cold tank—in which one soaked for hours. The ritual baths were for a quick self-dunking in only one (cold) tank.

In recent years, over a thousand installations[6] identified as ritual baths (i.e., carved in bedrock, with steps, sometimes with a divider on the steps, with volume enough to immerse a person, and a few with extra water tanks) have been found in Israel. These installations are in Jerusalem (300 baths[7]) as well as in other locations: Jericho, Masada, Herodium, Cypros, Qumran, Gezer, Gamla, Nazareth, Yodefat, Magdala, Sepphoris (30 baths[8]), Qiryat Sefer, En-Gedi, and elsewhere in rural areas near oil and wine presses (430 baths in Judea and 100 baths in Galilee).[9] Since similar installations are absent in gentile areas, these are surely Jewish.

The ritual baths or *mikva'ot* (Figures 7.4, 8.6, 9:1, 9.2, and 12.5) were placed especially in four types of locations:

1. In private houses
2. In public places, especially, in Jerusalem near the Temple
3. Near agricultural installations (wine presses and olive presses)[10]
4. Near tombs[11]

The baths begin appearing in the second century BCE and start disappearing suddenly after 135 CE. This window of time attests to the growing importance of ritual purity in the late Second Temple period.[12] The baths in

---

6. Adler, "Archaeology of Purity," counted 850 installations in his 2011 dissertation. But in private correspondence, he calculated that the number must by now be well over one thousand.

7. According to Charlesworth, "Temple, Purity," 411 who informs that in 2008 two archaeologists gave him that figure.

8. The final publication on the western domestic quarter of Sepphoris lists 30 *mikva'ot*. See Meyers et al., "Chronological Summary"; E. M. Meyers and Gordon, "Ritual Baths"; Galor and E. M. Meyers, "Stepped Water Installations"; and Miller, "New Directions."

9. Adler, "Archaeology of Purity"; Jensen, "Purity and Politics," 17; and Gurevich, "Water Pools." Gurevich affirms that of the nine late Second Temple large pools in Jerusalem, only two were for ritual immersion. Most *mikva'ot* were small. For a list of villages with *mikva'ot*, see Table 6.3.

10. See especially, Adler, "Second Temple Period Ritual Baths."

11. Zissu and Amit, "Common Judaism."

12. See Reich, "They *Are* Ritual Baths"; Reich, "Ritual Baths"; Reich, "Great Mikveh Debate"; Reich, "*Miqwa'ot* (Jewish Ritual Immersion Baths)"; Meyers et al., *Sepphoris*, 28; Deines, *Jüdische Steingefässe*, 4–5; Levine, "Archaeology and the Religious Ethos"; Crossan and Reed, *Excavating Jesus*, 36, 168; Reed, "Galileans, 'Israelite Village Communities.'" See especially the maps in Reich, *Miqwa'ot*. The identification of some of these installations as ritual baths has been challenged in recent years. See Wright, "Jewish Ritual Baths," and especially the discussion in *BAR*: Eshel, "They Are Not Ritual Baths"; and E. M. Meyers, "Yes, They Are." See also E. M. Meyers, "Aspects of Everyday

the Upper City of Jerusalem would probably have been used by Sadducees or the aristocratic priesthood. The baths at Jericho, Herodium, and Cypros are in Herodian or Hasmonean palaces. But the rest were evidently used by ordinary people, far away from the Temple, who wanted to be ritually pure for harvest, for meals, or possibly for prayer in the synagogue.[13]

Figure 9.2: Jerusalem, Pool of Siloam (John 9:7). A huge *mikveh*.[14]

Second, among the material remains are the stoneware (or chalk) objects. Vessels made of stone, animal dung, or unfired clay could not become unclean according to the Mishnah (m. Kel. 4:4, 10:1, m. Ohol. 5:5, m. Parah 5:5, m. Yad. 1:2) based on the rabbinic interpretation of Num 19:14–15.[15] While one would be required to break a fired clay pot if it became unclean (see Table 9.1), and this could be costly if one were really scrupulous about ritual purity, one would be exempt from that worry if the vessel was made of stone.

Life," esp. 211–15.

13. Coussens, "(Mis)Reading Proximity," has challenged that synagogue visitors took a ritual bath.

14. See Area Q in Figure 12.3(p. 205) for another large, public *mikveh* in Jerusalem from the time of Jesus.

15. But, as Stewart Miller reminds us, not every Jewish group agreed. The Qumran sectarians, at least in the early stages of their history, believed stone could become unclean. See 11QTa 49:14; CD 12:15–16; and Miller, "New Directions."

Stone vessels—cups, pots, bowls, and jars—have been found at more than 250 sites[16] in Palestine, especially in and around Jerusalem (concentrated in the City of David and Upper City),[17] in Galilee, and on the Golan, but also in the Jordan Valley, on the Coastal Plain, and in Perea. At Capernaum, each house from the first century contained stone vessel fragments.[18] In the city of Sepphoris, in Galilee, over one hundred fragments of stone vessels were recovered in excavations.[19] In the "land of Benjamin" area of Judea every Jewish site from the late Second Temple period had stoneware vessels in its ruins (and also *mikva'ot*).[20] Mordechai Aviam has recently published a map identifying the locations in Galilee and the Golan where stoneware vessels have been recovered in excavations. He lists twenty-five sites where the stone items were found.[21] A recent survey of the Golan found 212 stone vessel fragments at twelve sites dating from the Hell II to the MR period.[22] There were several stone or chalk vessel workshops in Jerusalem and its environs as well as in Galilean villages (one newly discovered near Nazareth) and in the Golan.[23]

A recent analysis of one thousand fragments of stoneware in a first-century CE garbage dump in Jerusalem showed that the majority of the vessels were hand-carved cups and small pitchers, with a close second place to lathe-turned bowls.[24] But also made were stone tables and large jars (like those in John 2:6; see Figure 9.3, below). Clearly the Jerusalem residents were using stone vessels freely.

Chalk vessels (vessels made from soft limestone) began to be popular in the first century BCE, continued to be commonly used in the first century CE, and on into the second century CE until the end of the Bar Kokhba War (135 CE).[25] Thus, their popularity coincides with the building of ritual baths in Palestine.

16. Adler, "Archaeology of Purity"; and Jensen, "Purity and Politics," 13. Again, this is an old count. The total must be many more at this date.

17. Magen, "Stone Vessel Industry," 23.

18. Crossan and Reed, *Excavating Jesus*, 167.

19. Reed, "Stone-Vessel Assemblage."

20. Magen, "Land of Benjamin," 22.

21. Aviam, "Distribution Maps," 119.

22. Fridman, "Chalk-Stone Vessels."

23. See the survey of stone vessel remains in Deines, *Jüdische Steingefässe*, 71–165 (map on p. 165); Magen, "Jerusalem as a Center"; Magen, "Ancient Israel's Stone Age" (also with map); Magen, *Stone Vessel Industry*, map for Galilee on p. 161; Reed, *Archaeology*, 44; Jensen, "Purity and Politics," 13; Berlin, "Jewish Life," 430; Fridman, "Chalk-Stone Vessels"; and Ngo, "Jewish Purification."

24. Adler, "Quantitative Analysis."

25. Adler, "Archaeology of Purity."

Sidebar 9.1

The Mishnah

The word *Mishnah* means "repetition." This definition is a key to its method and its content. The rabbis of the Mishnah (and their Pharisaic forebears) conceived of it as being the distillation of centuries of oral law. The conception was that on Mount Sinai Moses received both written law and oral law. This oral law was passed on by word of mouth by being taught to other tradents throughout several generations (m. Avot chapters 1–4; m. Ḥag. 2:2; t. Ḥag. 2:8). The Pharisees, the forerunners and associates of the scholars listed in the Mishnah, were well known for their adherence to oral law or "traditions" (*Ant.* 13.297; Mark 7:3; Gal 1:14).

E. E. Urbach[26] considered the sources of the Mishnah to be mainly three: (1) priestly circles (temple regulations), (2) the courts (about civil law), and (3) expositions of the Bible.

All of these laws were memorized by repetition and taught to others by the same method until the end of the second century CE. Then the Mishnah began to be written down. Its final form is attributed to Rabbi Judah ha-Nasi who compiled it in Sepphoris in Galilee.

The use of stone vessels also coincides with the decline of the ESA ceramic ware.[27] This imported pottery—made in gentile cities—was coated with a red glossy substance and was very popular until around the late-first century BCE. It continued to be used in gentile cities such as Tel Anafa, Dor, Ashdod, Ashkelon, and the predominantly gentile Caesarea. But in the first century CE it is almost completely absent from Judea and Galilee. It is not found, for example, in Et-Tell (in the Golan), in Capernaum, or in Yodefat (Galilee).[28] In general, the attractive ceramic ware declines in Jewish villages in our time period even though it continues in gentile settlements.[29] Why did Jews start avoiding this type of gentile pottery? Was it pure economics (the cost of transporting it)? Were there religious reasons (the vessels might be impure since they were manufactured by gentiles)?

---

26. Urbach, "Mishnah."
27. Root, *Galilee*, 101. This type of pottery is also abbreviated ETS.
28. Berlin, "Jewish Life," 433; Adler, "Purity in the Roman Period," 247.
29. Excavators found some of this pottery in the houses of the wealthy in the Upper City of Jerusalem, however.

Yonatan Adler opines that gentiles in this period were considered to have inherent impurity, and so any vessel made by them must also be impure.[30] At any rate, the decline of the imported pottery and the rise of the stone vessels seem not to be a coincidence.[31]

The stone vessels seem not to have been merely a fashion but to have been used for religious reasons. This conclusion is supported by the fact that stone vessels have rarely been found in non-Jewish settlements. Thus, they were not a phenomenon of the gentiles. Further, many of them have been found in houses with ritual baths in Jerusalem, in Sepphoris, in rural villages, and on farms. Finally, they were used by rich and poor alike, by the aristocracy and the humble.[32] The widespread use of stoneware, evidently to avoid ritual impurity—both of the vessels and the contents of the vessels—testifies that the desire to maintain ritual purity, even in ordinary meals, was widespread. Small wonder, then, that the topic shows up in the Gospels.

Figure 9.3: Replica stoneware vessels (large jar, cup, bowl), Jerusalem, the Burnt House.

---

30. Adler, "Purity in the Roman Period," 247. Adler cites Josephus, *War* 1.229, 2.150, and Acts 10:28.

31. For differing viewpoints, see Adler, "Archaeology of Purity"; and Magness, *Stone and Dung*, 55. See Berlin, "Jewish Life," 445 who writes that the disappearance of the ESA ware at Jewish sites looks like "deliberate rejection."

32. See Jensen, "Purity and Politics," 15.

Levels of Ritual Purity

The tendency of most contemporary readers is to think that the first Jesus-followers cared nothing at all about the Torah or ritual purity because most Jesus-followers today do not. But that conclusion is unwarranted. These regulations are in the Torah, the Bible; one did not just ignore them. Jesus instructed lepers to follow Torah in seeking cleansing (Luke 8:4 and par.), and he wore tassels or fringes as the Torah required.[33] The impression the Synoptic Gospels give is that Jesus and his disciples kept the ritual purity laws though perhaps not in the way some of the other groups did.

STRICTEST LEVEL	1. Priests
	2. Essenes
	3. Special sects within the Pharisees (e.g., *Haverim*, pietists)
	4. Most Pharisees
	5. Ordinary People (including Jesus and disciples)
	6. Am ha-Aretz "People of the Land" (known for hedging on purity observances and on tithing)
LEAST STRICT	7. Unobservant Jews

Table 9.2: Levels of ritual purity strictness in Late Second Temple Judaism[34]

How high on the grade of ritual purity were Jesus and his disciples? They certainly were not as scrupulous as the priests, nor were they required to be. We also have no evidence that Jesus and his disciples attempted to be as meticulous as the Essenes, Pharisees, and other pietists. The incident of Luke 11:37–39 argues they were not. On the other hand, there is no reason to doubt that Jesus kept purity laws and taught his disciples to do the same.[35] There was a growing concern among the ordinary people to become and remain ritually clean (to purge themselves from *tum'ah*) in the first century CE as evidenced by the hundreds of *mikva'ot* and the stone vessels. A reasonable conclusion is that Jesus was below the Pharisees in purity strictness, but above the nonobservant Jews and *am ha-aretz* (Table 9.2).[36] It is

---

33. Num 14:38–39; Deut. 22:12. See Luke 8:44; Matt 9:20, 14:36, 23:5; and Mark 6:56. See also Magness, *Stone and Dung*, 117–18.

34. Based on Sanders, *Jewish Law*, 205–7. See m. Hag. 2:7; Fiensy, *Jesus the Galilean*, 176, 180.

35. For the evidence, see Fiensy, *Jesus the Galilean*, 177–80.

36. Cf. Charlesworth, "Temple, Purity," 425: "The Jewish Jesus observed some purity customs." Also, Kazen, "Perhaps Less Halakic Jesus," 11: "If Jesus addressed issues of purity—and cult—rhetorically, from the perspective of an eschatological prophet, he

also possible, since he dined with Pharisees, that he maintained a somewhat higher level of purity than the ordinary peasant.

Jesus would have taken a ritual bath before entering the temple, and he would have purified himself from corpse uncleanness with the ashes of the red heifer. He probably would have taken a ritual bath after having contact with a leper or a woman with a flux. Possibly, he went through purification before prayer and before entering a synagogue. He also may have maintained ritual purity in general for its own sake, without reference to any special preparation. He did not accept Pharisaic and pietistic teaching concerning the washing of the hands and concerning bathing before meals.

THE RULER OF THE SYNAGOGUE

There was also the controversy over authority:

> He was teaching in one of the synagogues on the sabbath. A woman was there who had a spirit of infirmity for eighteen years. She was doubled over and unable to stand up fully. When Jesus saw her, he said, "Woman, be loosed from your infirmity!" He laid hands on her and she immediately stood straight and glorified God. But the *archisynagōgos* became indignant because Jesus healed on the sabbath. (Luke 13:10–14a)

This synagogue official, the *archisynagōgos*, was the "leader or president" of the synagogue.[37] He or she was in charge of the synagogue functions. Sometimes this official may have been the teacher or preacher, but it appears that this person mostly administrated the activities rather than served as the expositor of the scripture.

Occasionally, the position seems to have been inherited and might have been awarded because a family had built the synagogue building or part of the building. There are several references in the Lukan literature (and a few in the Gospel of Mark) to the position of synagogue leader, as well as over thirty Greek and Latin inscriptions that refer to this synagogal official.[38] At least three of them were women. We offer a representative list of the mentions of this person followed by inscriptions that help clarify his/her role:

---

would have aimed at abolishing neither."

37. Danker, *Lexicon*. Danker suggests the Heb. equivalent for this term was *rōsh ha-knesset*. See m. Yoma 7:1 and b. Pes. 49b. The latter source ranks the leader of the synagogue third in honor after scholars and "great men of the generation" (translation in Epstein et al., *Babylonian Talmud*).

38. According to Brooten, *Women Leaders*, 23.

Inscription #	Location	Date	Name of the *archisynagōgos/ archisynagōgissa*	Gender of the synagogue leader	Source of reference
	Galilee	1st CE	Jairus	M	Luke 8:49; Mark 5:35 (22, 36,38)
	Galilee	1st CE	— —	M[39]	Luke 13:14
	Antioch of Pisidia (Asia Minor)	1st CE	— —	M[40]	Acts 13:15
	Corinth (Greece)	1st CE	Crispus	M	Acts 18:8
	Corinth (Greece)	1st CE	Sosthenes	M	Acts 18:17
1	Jerusalem (Judea)	1st CE	Theodotus	M	Jerusalem Inscription
2	Acmonia (Asia Minor)	1st CE	Lucius	M	Building inscription
3	Ostia (Italy)	1st CE	Plotius Fortunatus	M	Monument in necropolis
4	Smyrna (Asia Minor)	2nd CE	Rufina	F	Marble plaque
5	Crete	4th–5th CE	Sophia	F	Sepulchral plaque
6	Caria (Asia Minor)	4th–5th CE	Theopempte	F	Donative inscription
7	Chorazin (Galilee)	4th CE	Judah ben Ishmael	M	Inscription on the "Seat of Moses"
8	Apamea (Syria)	391 CE	Eusebios, Nemios, and Phineos	M	Floor mosaic

Table 9.3: References to the *archisynagōgos/archisynagōgissa* in the New Testament and other sources

With the help of inscriptions and a few artifacts, we can sketch a brief narrative of the synagogue leader called in Greek *archisynagōgos* (feminine: either *archisynagōgos* or *archisynagōgissa*). In the Gospel of Luke, we first meet with Jairus (8:41), the synagogue leader who implores Jesus to

39. Based on the gender of the participle.
40. Based on the gender of the article.

heal his daughter. Then we encounter another synagogue leader in 13:14 who rebukes Jesus for healing on the Sabbath. He seems to be in charge of synagogue activities and to be designated as the preserver of Torah regulations. In the book of Acts, the *archisynagōgoi* in one place invited Paul and Barnabas to speak to the congregation (13:15), demonstrating that they had the authority to oversee who taught/preached there. At Corinth there were two *archisynagōgoi*, one of whom became a member of the Jesus-movement (18:8), while the other, who accused Paul and Barnabas before the proconsul Gallio, was beaten by a Greek mob (18:17). Some of these officials, then, were supportive of the movement while others opposed it. The New Testament references demonstrate that this official was not necessarily hostile to Jesus and his movement.

How do the inscriptions compare with these texts? We will offer a selection of eight of them (seven in Gk., one in Lat.) as representative of the total. These should give us an idea of the function of this important office featured in the Lukan literature.

First is the Theodotus text. This inscription was discovered in 1913 on the slope of the Ophel in Jerusalem:

> Theodotos, son of Vettenus, priest and *archisynagōgos*, son of an *archisynagōgos*, built the synagogue for the reading of the law and the teaching of the commandments, and also the guest chamber and the upper rooms and the ritual pools of water for accommodating those needing them from abroad, which his fathers, the elders and Simonides founded.[41]

---

41. Translation in Runesson et al., *Ancient Synagogue*, 53.

Figure 9.4: The Theodotus synagogue inscription from Jerusalem.[42] (Photograph by Andrey Zeigarnik)

The consensus today is that this inscription dates to before 70 CE. It is clear that Theodotus has inherited the title and function *archisynagōgos* and that he has done so, at least in part, because he and his father paid for the structure. The striking thing is that Theodotus and his father are also priests. Further, the name Vettenus—his father's name—is a Latin name, showing that he had once lived outside Palestine/Israel; this is a diaspora family.[43] Vettenus evidently returned to Israel, where he took up his priestly duties once more, and, out of his own resources, built a synagogue for use especially for Jewish pilgrims also from the diaspora.

Note that the synagogue functioned mainly for teaching the Torah but, also, secondarily, as a refuge for religious pilgrims coming to Jerusalem. It offered guest housing (*kataluma*; cf. Luke 2:7 and 22:11//Mark 14:14) and a place for a ritual bath. Nearby the place where the inscription was found, south of the temple, excavators found several *mikva'ot*.[44]

A second inscription was recovered from the diaspora (outside the land of Israel), in the town of Acmonia in Asia Minor, and dates from the second half of the first century CE:

> This building was erected by Julia Severa; Publius Tyrronios Clados, *archisynagōgos* for life, and Lucius, son of Lucius,

---

42. Wikimedia Commons: https://commons.wikimedia.org/wiki/File:8V2A3067_(47715698331).jpg/.

43. Runesson et al., *Ancient Synagogue*, 54.

44. Runesson et al., *Ancient Synagogue*, 54.

archisynagōgos, and Popilios Zoticos, the *archōn* ("ruler"), restored it with their own funds and with money which had been contributed . . .[45]

Anders Runesson et al. observe that we have three functionaries mentioned in this inscription. One is *archisynagōgos* for life (perhaps meaning he is emeritus) and the second is the functioning *archisynagōgos*. How they differ from the third man, who is merely *archōn*, is not clear.[46] Possibly, the last man oversaw the physical building and the first two concerned themselves with the religious leadership, opine Runesson et al. The three men have used their own funds to restore the synagogue building along with a gentile woman, Julia Severa, who had originally built the structure (like the centurion of Luke 7:4-5).[47] Again, we notice that these leaders made a financial contribution to the synagogue building.

A third inscription (in Lat.) comes from Ostia, Italy, and dates from the first-second century CE:

> For Plotius Fortunatus, *archisynagōgos*. Plotius Ampliatus, Secundinus and Secunda built it (for our father?), and Ofilia Basilia for her well-deserving husband.[48]

This was an inscription on a monument where an ancient necropolis once was located. Photius Fortunatus was probably the head of the synagogue of Ostia.

A fourth inscription comes from Smyrna in Asia Minor in the second century and gives us some unexpected information. This inscription seems to indicate that the synagogue leader was a woman:

> Rufina, a Jewess, *archisynagōgos*,[49] built this tomb for her freed slaves and the slaves raised in her house.[50]

It is probable that the inscription is identifying Rufina—definitely a feminine name—as holding the office of synagogue ruler. Some tried

---

45. Runesson et al., *Ancient Synagogue*, 134.

46. Luke and Matt at times interchange the *archōn* of the synagogue with the term *archisynagōgos*. See Matt 9:18 and Luke 8:41 in comparison with Mark 5:22.

47. Runesson et al., *Ancient Synagogue*, 135. The authors inform us that Julia Severa served as high priestess of the imperial cult in Acmonia during the reign of Nero (54-68 CE). Hence, she was not Jewish.

48. Runesson et al., *Ancient Synagogue*, 224.

49. The noun *archisynagōgos* can be either masculine or feminine. Cf. the word *diakonos* (Rom. 16:1), which can also be either.

50. Translation in Brooten, *Women Leaders*, 5.

initially to insist that it was her husband's title or was merely an honorary title,[51] but it appears that this woman was actually the synagogue head. She was a woman of means who had slaves and maintained freedpersons for whom she was providing a burial. She fits the profile elsewhere for the synagogue rulers as being well-to-do.

Fifth, is a fourth–fifth-century CE inscription from Crete which, again, references a female synagogue leader:

> Sophia of Gortyn, elder and *archisynagōgissa* of Kisamos (lies) here. The memory of the righteous one forever. Amen.[52]

Some dated this inscription to the first century CE; Brooten, however, inclines toward the later date.[53] This woman is celebrated in a sepulchral plaque as a leader of the local synagogue.

Sixth, is another female synagogue leader from a fourth–fifth-century inscription in Caria in Asia Minor:

> [From Th]eopempte, *archisynagōgos*, and her son Eusebios.[54]

This inscription seems to indicate that Theopempte and her son have made a donation to the synagogue. Again, this was a common, though not universal, feature in the *archisynagōgos*. They were mostly persons of means who made significant donations to the synagogue.

Seventh, is the "seat of Moses" found in the Chorazin (fourth century CE) synagogue (see Figure 7.1, above p. 115). Jack Finegan opined that this was the seat of the *archisynagōgos*. It might have been occupied on a given Sabbath by a visiting teacher such as a scribe or notable Pharisee. Ordinarily, however, (so, Finegan) the leader of the synagogue sat in it. On the front of the seat at Chorazin was a decorative rosette and the inscription:

> Remembered be for good Judah ben Ishmael who made this stoa and its staircase. As his reward may he have a share with the righteous.[55]

Finegan believed that the "stoa" was the platform on which the seat was placed and that the "staircase" was the steps up to the chair. The inscription, then, honors the donation of part of the synagogue. Perhaps Judah ben Ishmael was himself the *archisynagōgos* of the Chorazin synagogue. At least, the chair seems to have been for that person.

51. See the discussion in Brooten, *Women Leaders*, 6–7.
52. Translation in Brooten, *Women Leaders*, 11.
53. Brooten, *Women Leaders*, 12.
54. Translation in Brooten, *Women Leaders*, 13.
55. Translation in Finegan, *Archaeology*, 97.

Eighth, there is an inscription from Apamea (Syria) celebrating a donation to the synagogue on the part of Ilasios, the synagogue ruler:

> At the time of the most illustrious *archisynagōgoi*, Eusebios, Nemios and Phineos, and under the gerusiarch Theodoros, and the most illustrious elders Eisakios and Saulos and the others, Ilasios, *archisynagōgos* of the Antiochenes, made the entrance of the mosaic, 150 feet, in the year 703 (= 391 CE), in the seventh month of Audyneos. Blessing on all.[56]

In the inscription, the current *archisynagōgos*, Ilasios, has made a large donation—paying for a mosaic floor—which is honored in this inscription. There are several others mentioned, including "illustrious" leaders (emeritus leaders?) of the synagogue, the gerusiarch and the elders. Thus, there could be several officers in the synagogue.

Inscriptions 1, 2, 6, 7, and 8 show that the *archisynagōgos* had often made a donation to the construction or restoration of the synagogue building. Brooten,[57] however, cautions us. Others are reported as having made contributions as well and they were not installed as *archisynagōgoi*. Still, it does seem that many of them must have taken the lead in support of the building from their finances. That might suggest that only persons of wealth would be candidates for this office.

The functions of the *archisynagōgos* were evidently the following:

- overseeing the teaching of the Law (as we see in Luke 13:14 and Acts 13:15),
- collecting donations, and
- building and restoring buildings from their own resources when necessary.[58]

Therefore, it is no surprise that in the Gospels (and Acts) this synagogue official was on occasion in conflict with Jesus and the early Jesus-movement. The surprise is that there are not more conflicts narrated in the New Testament. The leader's authority in the synagogue might be seen as challenged by the new teaching. Those following the "Way" might siphon off funds needed for the synagogue. As the overseer of all functions of the congregation, both spiritual and financial, the *archisynagōgos* would naturally respond with alarm at anyone challenging its order.

---

56. Translation in Brooten, *Women Leaders*, 26.
57. Brooten, *Women Leaders*, 23–24.
58. See Brooten, *Women Leaders*, 28–29.

10

Disease and Death

THE STUDY OF MORBIDITY and mortality is not pleasant. Yet, the *realia* speak to us. Nothing so clearly reveals a society's well-being, or ill-being, than information about common, chronic illnesses and average life spans, especially of children. This information furnishes us with important background for the Jesus-movement and forces us from our assumed and inaccurate understanding of the world in which Jesus and his movement existed.

The non-elites wrote nothing, but they did leave behind something of themselves for us to study today: their bodily remains. These persons are speaking to us from the grave if we will listen. A careful analysis of their remains (bones, personal ornamentation, and even human waste) can tell us a great deal about their story. Such an investigation may be, as recognized over a century ago, neither "attractive nor cheerful . . . but it may not be labor altogether useless."[1] By placing these finds in the context of what we already know from both literary sources and other archaeological discoveries, we will construct an account of community health in Israel in the first century CE.

DISEASES

Luke 7:21–22 offers a review of afflictions: "diseases, torments, evil spirits, many blind persons, crippled people, lepers, deaf people . . ." That is quite a list confirmed by other ancient literary sources.[2] But what diseases do we

---

1. Merrins, "Deaths," 562.
2. See Fiensy, *Archaeology of Daily Life*, 200–201.

have explicit evidence for archaeologically? Here there are a few surprises. One disease we expect to encounter in the skeletal remains—because of references in the literature—is almost totally absent. Two others, which most commentators had not expected—because one is almost totally absent from the New Testament and the other only hinted at—do appear.

Leprosy (and Tuberculosis)

First, we need to report what archaeology does *not* find in the skeletal remains. Surprisingly, leprosy was rare in ancient Israel. Although leprosy was certainly present in the rest of the ancient world,[3] it seldom, if ever, afflicted Jews during the time of Jesus. Here, we ask two questions: First, how can a person know that leprosy was rare in Palestine in the time of Jesus? Second, why are there so many references to leprosy in both the Old and New Testaments if this disease seldom or never afflicted people?

We can answer the first question by appealing, once again, to the field of osteoarchaeology. Chronic illnesses often leave evidence in the bones. Medical experts have observed that often tuberculosis and leprosy are found together in the same patients. Yet, both were absent, or nearly so, in late Second Temple Israel.

One of the foremost Israeli anthropologists, Joseph Zias, has examined the remains of hundreds of individuals from our time period. Zias notes[4] that he has found only two cases of tuberculosis in the skeletal remains of Jews in antiquity and suggests that they had an "inherited immunity." More recently, Shimon Gibson[5] reports on four persons (two were infants) in a Jerusalem tomb dating to the first century CE who had tuberculosis.

Rosemary Luff points to studies from Britain which show low incidence of tuberculosis (which would be evidenced by bone lesions in skeletons) but a high incidence reported from documentary evidence of the "late and post-medieval" periods. She believes that some types of tuberculosis do not show up in the bones and, therefore, the Jews in Jesus' day might have suffered a much higher incidence of this disease than Zias maintains.[6] This caution is important; we should always allow that the evidence is incomplete and that the final assessment of the conditions might be changed. But barring such

---

3. See Grmek, *Diseases*; Živanović, *Diseases*, 220; Preuss, *Preuss' Biblical and Talmudic Medicine*.
4. See Zias, "Arnona," 119; and Zias, "Death and Disease," 152–53.
5. Gibson, *Final Days*, 139–47.
6. Luff, *Impact of Jesus*, 119–20.

evidence, one must follow Zias and conclude that although some Jews in our time period may have contracted tuberculosis, it was, evidently, rare.

Zias makes a similar observation about leprosy. He has not found *any cases* from his examination of the skeletal remains in tombs in Israel dating from the time of Jesus. Interestingly, however, a case of genuine leprosy (Hansen's disease) has now been found. The sufferer was one of the individuals from the tomb just referred to—one of the four individuals with tuberculosis—whose Jerusalem tomb was discovered in the year 2000.[7] This tomb is famous because much of the material for this man's burial shroud was intact, leading to the archaeologists naming him the Shrouded Man. He was clearly suffering from leprosy, or Hansen's disease as it is called today. So, there may be at least one case of real leprosy from the time of Jesus. Again, Luff points to the one clear case of Hansen's disease as proof that real leprosy existed among the Jews of Jesus' day.[8] It seems a question of a half-full or half-empty glass. Luff points to the one clear case; Zias maintains that there is only one.

However, the case of the Shrouded Man may not be clear. Some archaeologists argue that the individuals in this tomb were not natives but repatriate Jews (who could have intermarried with gentiles in the diaspora). Some even maintain that they were not necessarily Jews at all. The doubt arises from the weave in the shroud. It is not a local weave but imported, thus making it possible that the entire family immigrated.[9] At any rate, finding one case of Hansen's disease should not alter the correctness of Zias's observation, even if this is a real case of Jewish infection.[10]

But what about all those references to leprosy in the Bible?[11] Why did people talk about it so much if hardly anyone—or no one—had it? It is now commonly concluded that the Hebrew term ṣaraʾat (the term used throughout Leviticus) and the Greek *lepra* did not refer to Hansen's disease.[12] There were certainly skin conditions which the ancients called by

---

7. Gibson, *Final Days*, 146; Hebrew University of Jerusalem, "DNA of Jesus-Era Shrouded Man."

8. Luff, *Impact of Jesus*, 115–19.

9. See Taylor, *What Did Jesus Look Like?*, 166; and Avni and Greenhut, "Resting Place," 41.

10. Cf. the conclusion of Roberts and Manchester, *Archaeology of Disease*, 201. After reporting on four skulls found in Ptolemaic Egypt (c. 250 BCE), they hypothesize that leprosy entered the Mediterranean area with Alexander the Great and his army (evidently, after returning from India).

11. See e.g., Lev 13–14; 2 Kgs 5; 2 Chr 26. For New Testament, see Matt 8:2, 10:9, 11:5, Mark 1:40, 42, 14:3; Luke 4:27, 5:12–13, 7:22, 17:12.

12. See Hamel, *Poverty*, 53; Feder, "Polemic Regarding Skin Disease"; Kiuchi, "Paradox of the Skin Disease"; Zias, "Death and Disease," 149–50; and Mull and Mull,

those names, but they were not what we today refer to as leprosy. Therefore, we should not imagine those Jesus healed were afflicted with the disease we now call by that name.

Do we know to what disease these terms were referring? There was a brief time in which scholars thought these Hebrew and Greek words described psoriasis. Today that hypothesis seems to be abandoned.[13] We do not know precisely what this ailment was. We do know that it was widespread in the ancient world, especially in Palestine/Israel.

Parasites

Just as modern health workers routinely monitor wastewater to keep their finger on the pulse of community pathology,[14] so archaeologists increasingly study the remains of ancient latrines. Examination of dozens of latrines throughout the former Roman Empire—in Italy, Great Britain, France, Germany, Austria, Greece, Turkey, and Egypt—has resulted consistently in evidence of intestinal parasitic infection in the general population as proven by the prevalence of parasite eggs in the latrine soil.[15] The residents of the empire were commonly infected with worms. As one palaeopathologist has concluded, in the Roman Empire, "intestinal parasites were endemic."[16] This disease was a surprise, hardly suspected from the literature. Was it also true of Israel?

"Biblical Leprosy," for the Hebrew Bible. For the Greco-Roman medical texts, see Touwaide, "Disease," 547. He explains that *lepra* was not leprosy in the modern sense but another (unknown?) skin disease.

13. Krauss, "Kritische Bemerkung," challenges the common conclusion that *ṣaraʿat* was psoriasis.

14. Huang and Rizzo, "Tracking Health Threats."

15. See Mitchell, "Human Parasites," 51; Le Bailly and Bouchet, "*Diphyllobothrium*"; Anastasiou et al., "Infectious Disease"; Williams et al., "Intestinal Parasites"; Nezamabadi et al., "Paleoparasitological Analysis"; Searcey et al., "Parasitism of the Zweeloo Woman." The reader should also bear in mind the many studies of mummies from Egypt (more than 8,000) which show parasite infections. See Jackson, *Doctors and Diseases*, 15 who lists five species of intestinal parasites; and Živanović, *Ancient Diseases*, 220.

16. Jackson, *Doctors and Diseases*, 37.

Archaeologists[17] now commonly analyze remains from ancient latrines, cesspits, coprolites, fecal soil, and pelvic soil from burials.[18] The eggs from helminth worms survive for thousands of years and are quite evident in microscopic examination.[19] Seven archaeological sites in Israel, four of them from near our period, have indicated widespread infection. The four are

1. Early Roman period Qumran (soil samples from fecal area[20])
2. Early Roman period Jerusalem (pelvic soil from a tomb)
3. Middle–Late Roman period Scythopolis (from a latrine)
4. Roman period[21] Caesarea Maritima (from a latrine)

The remains were full of intestinal parasites, whipworms mostly but also tapeworms and roundworms. At the Qumran site, archaeologists found evidence of whipworm, tapeworm, pinworm, and roundworm.[22] Likewise, pelvic soil from a Herodian tomb in Jerusalem yielded the discovery of "two hollow, pebble-like artifacts" found in the abdominal cavity of an individual. The two objects turned out to be cysts of intestinal parasites.[23] Excavators found fish tapeworm in latrines dating from the middle to late Roman period at Scythopolis and at Caesarea Maritima.[24] The presence of parasite eggs in the fecal remains of humans indicates a very poor hygienic environment as well as undercooked meat and population crowding.[25]

---

17. Harter et al., "Toilet Practices"; Mitchell and Tepper, "Intestinal Parasitic Worm Eggs"; Neufeld, "Hygiene Conditions"; Zias, "Death and Disease"; Cahill et al., "It Had to Happen"; Reinhard and Araújo, "Archaeoparasitology"; Geggel, "Medieval Parasite"; University of Cambridge Research, "Human Parasites."

18. See Mitchell, "Human Parasites," 49.

19. Reinhard and Araújo, "Archaeoparasitology," 495.

20. The Qumran samples were not actually from a latrine or cesspit but from an area evidently used by the residents to defecate in shallow holes which were then immediately covered.

21. Le Bailly and Bouchet, "*Diphyllobothrium* in the Past" do not give dates for these samples, but one assumes this era from the context.

22. Harter et al., "Toilet Practices"; Zias et al., "Toilets at Qumran"; University of North Carolina at Charlotte, "Ancient Parasites." This is the first archaeologically attested evidence of pinworm in the ancient near east.

23. Zias, "Death and Disease."

24. Le Bailly and Bouchet, "*Diphyllobothrium* in the Past." See also Cahill et al., "It Had To Happen"; Mitchell and Tepper, "Intestinal Parasitic Worm Eggs"; Yeh et al., "Human Intestinal Parasites," 75; Geggel, "Medieval Parasite"; and University of Cambridge Research, "Human Parasites."

25. Reinhard and Araújo, "Archaeoparasitology," 498. Harter et al., "Toilet Practices," surmise that the residents of Qumran also contracted the parasites by ritually bathing after an infected person (582).

Parasites pose several health challenges. They compete with their host for food. They might in times of plenty have caused only mild anemia in children or a feeling of weariness or weakness in an otherwise healthy adult.[26] But when a person's diet was challenged, the parasites caused many complications. Children would be especially vulnerable, for their growth would be stunted and their mental capacities and speech development reduced due to "vitamin deficiencies and impaired growth."[27] They would be underweight and under height. The parasites could even cause anorexia. Chronic malnutrition would usually lead to deteriorating immune systems and therefore to susceptibility to other diseases. Therefore, the parasites often led *indirectly* to death.[28]

But in times of famine, a real crisis arises. Now the host competes with the infestation for less and less food. Those so infected will feel the effects of starvation the quickest. Mitchell and Tepper observe grimly, "Those with the most parasites in their intestines . . . die from starvation first."[29] Therefore, the indirect consequences of intestinal parasites range from anemia (under prosperous conditions) to starvation in times of famine.

But there can also be more *directly* lethal consequences of intestinal parasites. Extreme cases of infection could lead to diarrhea, bowl blockages, malabsorption of food, and hence to death with extreme abdominal pain.[30] Although a minority of victims dies in this way directly from the infection, such cases are well known. They happen today and certainly happened in antiquity.

As said above, the literary evidence would probably not lead us to think of this horrible affliction as common in Second Temple Israel, but there are a few suggestive texts:

---

26. Cruz-Cruz et al., "Stunting," note that sometimes the infection is a-symptomatic but usually announces itself with some sort of discomfort such as fever, lung inflammation, abdominal pain, or diarrhea.

27. Mitchell and Tepper, "Intestinal Parasitic Worm Eggs," 93–94. See also Mitchell quoted in University of Cambridge Research, "Human Parasites." Cruz-Cruz et al., "Stunting," record the stunting problem in southern Mexico today in which one-third of the children are infected with parasites leading to "cognitive development failure," furthering the cycle of poverty.

28. See in this regard, especially Gutiérrez-Jiménez et al., "Malnutrition and Intestinal Parasites"; and Tyoalumun et al., "Prevalence." In Nigeria, one study found that 37% of children were stunted, 29% were underweight, and 18% were "wasting" due to intestinal parasites (Tyoalumun et al., "Prevalence," 147).

29. Mitchell and Tepper, "Intestinal Parasitic Worm Eggs," 94.

30. Mitchell and Tepper, "Intestinal Parasitic Worm Eggs," 94.

- Antiochus Epiphanes IV was allegedly killed by (or partially killed by) such an infection (2 Macc 9:5–10).
- Herod the Great also died with this affliction (*War* 1.656).
- Agrippa I was reportedly "eaten by worms" at his death (Acts 12:23).

These are details that we previously passed over as embellishments but now might take more seriously. One physician who practiced in the Levant in the early 20th century and who was quite familiar with this disease was confident that these three cases in the literature were actual parasite infections.[31] At any rate, many of the children and adults of Galilee who listened to Jesus teach probably suffered from this disease.

Malaria

The New Testament Gospels refer to fever in two passages. One Synoptic passage narrates the healing of Peter's mother-in-law, who was in bed with a fever (Gk., *puretos*; Mark 1:30–31; Matt 8:14–15; Luke 4:38–39). Luke describes the woman's illness as a "high fever," perhaps wanting the reader to think of the disease we now call malaria. The second story (Matt 8:5–13; Luke 7:1–10; John 4:46–54) tells of the healing of an official's son/slave who was also afflicted with fever (according to John 4:52). Both stories are set in Capernaum, which is on the north shore of the Sea of Galilee.

Like parasitic infection, malaria was endemic in the Mediterranean region at this time and persisted until the early 20th century. Its symptoms and effects can be debilitating to entire communities. It is a mosquito-borne illness caused by a microscopic parasite.[32]

None of the sources from the literature in the Greco-Roman world use a term that translates as "malaria."[33] Indeed, there was no such word. Instead, the common people called the disease the "fever" (*puretos*[34]), the "great fever," or the "fevers," the last term evidently alluding to their intermittent symptoms. There are several types of malaria, of which only three

---

31. Merrins, "Deaths."

32. Živanović, *Ancient Diseases*, 219: "A mosquito bites an infected individual and draws out blood together with the parasites. When it bites another individual the parasites are transmitted to a fresh victim."

33. The word *malaria* is Italian for "bad air." It was first used, according to Sallares, in the fifteenth century (*Malaria and Rome*, 7).

34. This Gk. word came to mean malarial fever and not fever in general according to Grmek, *Diseases*, 280. The plural of the term evidently indicates intermittent fever with chills, the symptoms of malaria. See Keener, "Fever."

were endemic in the Mediterranean area. The Greco-Roman physicians called the three varieties of the disease "tertian fever," "semi-tertian fever," and "quartan fever,"[35] based on how often the fever returned. Those fevers that returned in two days were the tertian, those that returned in three days were the quartan, and those fevers that recurred in one and one-half days were the deadly semitertian.[36]

Of course, fever can arise from other causes, but in an area near water where people were known to get sick with fevers, one suspects malaria borne by mosquitoes as the illness. Further, the "periodicity of intense fever" that characterizes malaria makes the diagnosis as reported in the ancient texts certain.[37]

Archaeological evidence of malaria comes to us in the form of metal-foil amulets discovered mostly in tombs in Israel and dating from the fourth to the seventh centuries CE. These amulets were inscribed with magical prayers intending to ward off the "fever," probably the fever of malaria. So far, six have been found:[38]

- a bronze amulet from Sepphoris in Galilee[39]
- a copper amulet from Western Galilee near 'Evron[40]
- two copper amulets from the village of Ḥorvat Kanaf (northeast of the Sea of Galilee)[41]
- a silver amulet from Tiberias[42]

---

35. Grmek, *Diseases*, 280; Sallares, *Malaria and Rome*, 133, 222.

36. For descriptions of the three fevers in antiquity, see Plato, *Timaeus* 86a; Hippocrates, *Epidemics*, books 1–3 (with several case studies); Celsus, *De Medicina* 3.7–13; and Galen, *On Critical Days*, books 1 and 2. Masterman, a medical doctor who practiced for twenty years in Palestine, noted in 1918 that malaria presented in those same three forms ("Hygiene and Disease," 62).

37. Sallares, *Malaria and Rome*, 10.

38. In addition to the six named here, Naveh and Shaked, *Amulets*, 55–62, 83–84, 102–4, and 224–29; and Naveh and Shaked, *Magic Spells*, 142–43, 80–82, describe one from Aleppo, two from Egypt (one from the Cairo Geniza and one from Oxyrhynchus), one from Mesopotamia (an incantation bowl), and two from an unknown provenance—all of which seek to protect the wearer from malaria. A recently discovered amulet, from Khirbet Wadi Ḥamam (near the Sea of Galilee), is illegible but could plausibly have been a protection against malaria. See Leiman and Leibner. "Amulet."

39. See McCollough and Glazier-McDonald, "Magic and Medicine."

40. See Kotansky, "Inscribed Copper Amulet."

41. See Reed, "Instability"; Naveh and Shaked, *Amulets*, 45, 51; and Center for Online Judaic Studies, "Horvat Kanaf Amulet."

42. Naveh and Shaked, *Magic Spells*, 50–53.

- a bronze amulet from Ḥorvat Kannah (on the north side of the Bet Netofah valley in Galilee)[43]

The metal-foil amulets were rolled up, attached to a string, and worn about the neck. They invoked secret, magical formulae to protect persons from the fever:

- "amulet against fever *protracted* that burns and *does not cease*" (Sepphoris);[44]
- "let the fever be extinguished from (Casius) both the *great* (fever) and the slight (fever)" (Evron);[45]
- "Yahu, Yahu, Yahu, Yahu, Yahu, exorcise the *fever and the chills*" (Ḥorvat Kanaf);[46]
- "the angels that are [appointed] over *fever and shivering*, cure Ele[azar]" (Ḥorvat Kanaf);[47]
- "eradicate from the body of Ina daughter of Ze'irti all *hectic fever* and illness and sickness in the name of yhwh . . ." (Tiberias);[48]
- ". . . to expel the great fever and the *tertian fever* and the *chronic fever* and the *semi-tertian fever* . . . from the body of Simon, son of Kattia." (Ḥorvat Kannah).[49]

In the amulets, in addition to praying for relief from fever, there are—to us—nonsensical syllables and sounds which evidently were taken to have magical power. The invocations inscribed on the amulets inform us of the great fear that people had of contracting them and dying from fever. The amulet prayers describe the fevers as chronic ("protracted . . . does not cease"), severe ("great [fever]"), and intermittent ("fever and chills"; "fever and shivering"; "hectic fever")—all characteristic of malaria. The sixth amulet even uses the Greek medical terms for tertian and semitertian fever, even though the amulets are in the Aramaic language. Such descriptions, in regions near the Bet Netofa valley in Galilee and near the lake, lead one strongly to suspect malaria was a major problem.

---

43. Naveh and Shaked, *Magic Spells*, 60–63.
44. McCollough and Glazier-McDonald, "Magic and Medicine," 146 (italics added).
45. Kotansky, "Inscribed Copper Amulet," 82 (italics added).
46. Naveh and Shaked, *Amulets*, 45 (italics added).
47. Naveh and Shaked, *Amulets*, 51 (italics added).
48. Naveh and Shaked, *Magic Spells*, 50–53 (italics added).
49. Naveh and Shaked, *Magic Spells*, 60–63 (italics added).

Sidebar 10.1

The Amulet: This amulet, from Sepphoris, prays for a cure from "fever *protracted* that burns and *does not cease*."

The transcription of the bronze foil amulet pictured to the right

The unrolled, bronze-foil amulet found at Sepphoris

Images courtesy of C. Thomas McCollough.

The presence of amulets[50] specifically for fever suggests that malaria was a danger for many persons in the region of Galilee. Although the amulets date centuries after the late Second Temple period, the time of Jesus and Antipas, they, nevertheless, attest to the nature of the region, which

---

50. Pliny the Elder (*N.H.* 28.11.46) refers to another bizarre amulet many pagans used: hanging a nail or rope used in a crucifixion about one's neck to ward off malarial fevers. See Evans, *Jesus and the Remains*, 140.

would not have changed until modern efforts to kill mosquitoes and control standing water.

The literary sources from our time—though infrequently referring to this problem—confirm the archaeological remains. Josephus described the "air" around the Sea of Galilee as "pestilential" (*nosōdē*; *War* 4.457). He wrote that the Jordan rift valley was hot and dry in the summer and thus the air became conducive to sickness. Those living in the Mediterranean region thought until the early twentieth century that malaria was spread by breathing bad air. Thus, in the first century CE, the residents of the Jordan rift valley knew that those living there would become sick at certain times of the year, namely summer. The "air" during this season was pestilential, however, because that was when mosquitoes emerged from their pupate state.

The premodern yet recent informants offer even more illuminating evidence. E. W. G. Masterman, a physician who practiced in Palestine in the early twentieth century, offers a rare glimpse of the problem at that time. He reported in 1918 that the most important disease in Palestine was malaria. He observed that it occurred in all parts of Palestine, even in Jerusalem where the open cisterns bred the mosquito larvae. He wrote, "Most of the Jordan Valley is quite unfit for European families. It is intensely malarious."[51] All three forms of malaria showed up in his hospital. In one survey he did, he found that 25.5% had the tertian malaria, 27.4% the quartan, and a shocking 47.1% had the deadly semitertian (or as he termed it, "tropical"). Many were infected by two forms of the disease at the same time; some had all three varieties.[52] Even in those cases of the less dangerous varieties of malaria, the anemia they caused left the sufferers "open to infection by various other diseases on account of their reduced constitutional resistance."[53]

Thus, the *realia* offer three surprises. First, leprosy as we think of it was extremely rare, perhaps nonexistent in late Second Temple Israel. Second, intestinal parasitic infections were endemic throughout the Mediterranean world. Third, malaria was the bane of the Roman Empire, including Israel.

DEATH

How did these diseases, confirmed by archaeological remains, affect the population, especially the children? Children were the most vulnerable to the parasitic and malarial afflictions. What were the other hazards to life in this age beyond disease about which archaeology can inform?

51. Masterman, "Hygiene and Disease," 61.
52. Masterman, "Hygiene and Disease," 63.
53. Masterman, "Hygiene and Disease," 63.

Child Mortality

Our question, simply put, is, if you and your spouse brought ten children into the world, how many would live to biological adulthood? How many would die within the first year of life?

We again will look at osteoarchaeology to determine child mortality by analyzing skeletal remains from tombs giving data for the following categories:

1. Biological non-adults (0–19 years): based on nineteen tomb complexes or cemeteries
2. Children (0–5 years): based on seventeen tomb complexes
3. Infants (0–1 year): based on eight cemeteries[54]

We will look at data from the broadest category (0–19 years old) to the smallest, the infants. Our total database consists of 1,724 individuals. One of the tomb complexes is in Upper Galilee (Meiron); one is in Perea (Tel Hesban); a few are in southern Samaria (see "8 tombs in Judea and Samaria"); but most are found in Judea, especially near Jerusalem.

Cohort	Sample size	Percent mortality
Pre-adults (0–19 years)[55]	1,724	44 %
0–5 years old[56]	1,477	33%

54. "Tomb complexes and cemeteries" because a number of these sites consist of multiple tombs in a close geographical association.

55. Compiled from data in Arieli, "Human Remains"; Arensburg and Smith, "Anthropological Tables"; Smith and Zias, "French Hill"; Arensburg and Rak, "French Hill"; Hachlili and Smith, "Genealogy"; Haas, "Anthropological Observations," (Giv'at, ha-Mivtar); Smith et al., "Skeletal Remains" (Meiron); Nagar and Torgeé, "Biological Characteristics" (8 tombs); Zias, "Caiaphas' Tomb"; Haas, "Giv'at ha-Mivtar"; Zias, "Arnona"; Zias, "Mount Scopus"; Zias, "Anthropological Analysis (Akeldama)"; Nathan, "Naḥal Ḥever"; Smith, "Abba Cave"; Arensburg and Belfer-Cohen, "En-Gedi"; Hadas, "En-Gedi"; Kahana, "Wadi-Ḥalaf." Steckoll, "Preliminary Excavation Report"; Broshi and Eshel, "Whose Bones?" Röhrer-Ertl, "Facts and Results"; Tendler et al., "Typical and Atypical Burial," (5 tombs); and Grauer and Armelagos, "Skeletal Biology" (Tel Hesban).

56. This result is produced by combined evidence in: Nathan, "Naḥal Ḥever"; Arieli, "Human Remains"; Hachlili and Smith, "Genealogy"; Arensburg and Rak, "French Hill"; Smith and Zias, "French Hill"; Haas, "Anthropological Observations" (Giv'at, ha-Mivtar); Nagar and Torgeé, "Biological Characteristics" (8 tombs); Smith et al., "Skeletal Remains" (Meiron); Zias, "Caiaphas' Tomb"; Zias, "Mount Scopus"; Zias, "Anthropological Analysis" (Akeldama); Zias, "Armona"; Nathan, "Naḥal Ḥever"; Arensburg and Belfer-Cohen, "En-Gedi"; Smith, "Abba Cave"; Hadas, "En-Gedi"; Kahana,

Cohort	Sample size	Percent mortality
0–1 year[57]	632	19%

Table 10.1: Child mortality in three cohorts in ancient Israel (Hell II through ER II periods)

To place these figures into an understandable context, one can compare the largest cohort with those from other regions in the Roman imperial period:

Location	Youth mortality percentage
Rome[58]	54%
Carthage[59]	50%
Italian countryside[60]	42%
Eastern Mediterranean[61]	47%

Table 10.2: Youth mortality in the Greco-Roman world

Overall, the cemeteries of Hell II, ER I, and ER II from Israel exhibit a youth mortality rate that is 10% lower than that in the city of Rome, but slightly higher than that evidenced from other sites in Italy. How one explains this difference (the ritual washing of Judaism, simply better DNA, better nutrition, or the lack of sanitation in the cities) remains unclear. At any rate, one had a slightly better chance of growing to adulthood in Israel (and in the Italian countryside) than in cities like Rome.[62]

Child mortality (0–5 years old) is usually lower than 1 percent in wealthy countries today, but in premodern times it ranged from 30 percent

---

"Wadi-Ḥalaf"; and Tendler et al., "Typical and Atypical Burial"; Grauer and Armelagos, "Skeletal Biology."

57. This result is produced by combined evidence in: Arieli, "Human Remains"; Hachlili and Smith, "Genealogy"; Haas, "Anthropological Observations," (Giv'at, ha-Mivtar); Smith, et al., "Skeletal Remains" (Meiron); Zias, "Caiaphas' Tomb"; Zias, "Armona"; Nathan, "Naḥal Ḥever"; Grauer and Armelagos, "Skeletal Biology," (Tel Hesban).

58. Hopkins, "Age Structure." Hopkins's figure for Rome was based on 8,065 inscriptions; his figure for the Italian countryside was based on 5,343 inscriptions.

59. Humphrey, *Circus*, 218–20.

60. Hopkins, "Age Structure."

61. Angel, "Ecology," 94.

62. See Bar-Ilan, "Infant Mortality," for his calculations of child mortality based on Talmudic evidence. He arrives at a figure similar to mine.

to 50 percent. In 1800 the global average was 43 percent; now it is 3.4 percent. Thus, this child mortality rate for ancient Palestine/Israel is not high by premodern standards. It was toward the lower end of the range.[63]

Based on the calculations above—and confirmed by those of others from elsewhere in the empire—the conclusions are, if a couple gave birth to ten children,[64] two of them would die before the first birthday, one more before age five, and one or two more before age nineteen. Of the remaining five or six children, two or three more would die before their midthirties (see Chapter 1, Life Expectancy). Only two or three of the ten could expect to live past age forty. Further, shortly after the birth of the tenth child, one of the parents would die, leaving the surviving parent with five or six children to rear alone.

Thus, there was mourning in every household over dead children. Such high child mortality must have meant that death, mourning, and sadness were a reality for every family almost constantly. They did not lose just one child but several. This reality is presented to us in the New Testament Gospels where families are frequently mourning a dead child (Mark 5:35; Luke 7:12, 8:49; John 11:14) or showing anxiety over the illness of a child (Mark 9:17-18; Luke 8:42; 9:42; John 4:49). Indeed, the only dead persons we encounter in the four Gospels—except for Jesus—are children and teenagers.

We begin to ponder familiar scenes in a different way when we bear in mind the childhood mortality in the ancient world. When we read that parents brought their children to Jesus so that he might "touch them" and bless them (Mark 10:13//Matt 19:13//Luke 18:15), we must imagine, in light of the above evidence, a different picture than we usually do. Probably those parents had already lost children. The scene, then, was not a happy one but a desperate one.

Evidence of Violence

> "But bring here my enemies who did not want me to be king over them and slaughter them in front of me." (Luke 19:27)

> And Herod said, "I decapitated John; who is this about whom I hear such things?" And he sought to see him. (Luke 9:9)

---

63. See Roser, "Child Mortality."

64. Giving birth to ten live children would not have been usual, but I use this calculation for illustrative purposes.

"The master of that slave will come on a day he does not expect and in an hour he does not know and he will cut him in two.[65]" (Luke 12:46)

"And they will fall by the edge of the sword and be taken captive into all the nations." (Luke 21:24)

These horrible references describe a violent society in which a would-be king (reminiscent of Archelaus, one of Herod's heirs[66]) takes revenge on his subjects and has them slaughtered in front of him (cf. 1 Sam 15:33; *Ant.* 13.380). The second text alludes to Antipas's beheading of John the Baptist. The third text narrates a parable in which the master returns to find his head servant misbehaving and punishes him by dismembering his body (after death or before?). Finally, Jesus predicts the coming Roman slaughter in which many will die from the sword.

One should exercise caution in overly dramatizing these texts and others like them. Was life in the Roman Empire more violent than life today in the "civilized" countries? Invasions, war crimes, and mass shootings lead to great hesitation, and humility, in affirming that it was so. Yet, that violence of this sort did exist is confirmed not only by texts but also, now, by archaeology. Once again, we turn to the osteological evidence. There are at least ten cases[67] of violence indicated in the skeletal remains:

1. Attacks with a sword

    a. In a Mount Scopus tomb (north of Jerusalem) were the remains of a woman (aged 50–60) whose arm, the "distal end of the right humerus," had been sheared off with a sharp instrument.[68]

    b. Also in a Mount Scopus tomb were the bones of a man (aged 18–25) who had been hacked to death with a "sharp weapon." There were blows to the upper arms (one of which was severed), to the head, and to the pelvis. Zias concluded, based on the type and severity of the blows, that the event was an execution.[69]

---

65. The verb describes an action, depicted elsewhere with sometimes different language, of dismemberment of a condemned person (Danker, *Lexicon*). Other (nonbiblical) texts say, "cut in two by the sword," "cut them in the middle," or "taking a large sword and sawing in the middle" (Danker, *Lexicon*). Cf. Heb 11:37.

66. *War* 2.80–92; *Ant.* 17.208–22, 299–314. See Sidebar 2.6.

67. I will leave the one incontrovertible case of crucifixion until Chapter 14.

68. Zias, "Anthropological Evidence of Interpersonal Violence."

69. Zias, "Death and Disease."

2. Attacks with a blunt object

   a. In Mount Scopus tomb D was an individual (male, 25–30) whose cranium had a depression fracture in the right frontal. The fracture had healed.[70]

   b. At Qumran was excavated the remains of a 65-year-old man who had received a severe head wound which had healed before his death but only after a long time of suffering. The man suffered from "nasal haemmorrhagies [sic], violent headaches." The wound was probably from a slingstone.[71]

   c. In the Giv'at ha-Mivtar cemetery (north of Jerusalem) was a woman (50–60) whose head was smashed with a mace resulting in her death.[72]

   d. Also, in Giv'at ha-Mivtar was a man (aged 50–60) who had died from a spike to the skull.[73]

3. Death by burning

   a. In the Giv'at ha-Mivtar cemetery were found the skeletal remains of a young man (16–17) who had died from burning on a rack.[74]

   b. In the same cemetery were a woman's (aged 24) remains indicating that she had died from burning.[75]

4. Decapitation

   a. In a Mount Scopus tomb archaeologists found the bones of a man (aged 50) who had been beheaded. The decapitation had required two blows to complete.[76]

   b. In the Abba Cave were the remains of two adults, one a young man, and the other an "older" woman. The woman had been

---

70. Zias, "Anthropological Evidence of Interpersonal Violence."
71. Haas and Nathan, "Anthropological Survey." See in this volume Table 5.4, number 14.
72. Haas, "Anthropological Observations." See in this volume Table 5.4, number 5.
73. Haas, "Anthropological Observations."
74. Haas, "Anthropological Observations."
75. Haas, "Anthropological Observations."
76. Zias, "Anthropological Evidence of Interpersonal Violence." Zias suggested that the two blows mean the death was an act of violence, not an execution. But Luff, *Impact of Jesus*, 135 argues otherwise.

decapitated, also by two blows. The cuts came from the side and sheared off most of the face.[77]

One question we have with respect to these events is who perpetrated them? Were they done by the Romans in war or by Jewish executioners, or were they domestic violence? Luff inclines toward execution for many of these attacks; Tal Ilan hypothesizes that domestic violence may account for the women's deaths.[78] There may have been multiple reasons for the attacks. Certainly one thinks immediately of the Romans either in war or in punitive acts, but the other two causes may also have played a role. It is very difficult from our position to reach a definitive conclusion.

A second question is, do these ten cases indicate that there was overwhelming and rampant violence in this society, or since there are only ten, a lack of violence? Again, we are faced with the historian's decision about what to make of the evidence. If the violence were rampant, might we expect more osteological evidence? The question is like that about crucifixion (see Chapter 14). So far, they have found the skeletal remains of only one incontrovertibly crucified person in Palestine and one in Briton even though literary sources indicate thousands were crucified.

But these osteological data should lead to a clear conclusion. Violence was at least as common then as in modern societies. Although these people had no weapons of mass destruction, they were brutal and cruel with what they did have.

---

77. Smith, "Abba Cave." Smith offered that either the woman was moving during the attack or the executioner was "inept."

78. Luff, *Impact of Jesus*, 135; Ilan, *Integrating Women*, 210.

11

Jericho

ACCORDING TO THE SYNOPTIC Gospels, Jesus made his journey to Jerusalem (Luke 9:51, 18:31–33) by passing through the village of Jericho. Jericho is famous because it is both the lowest city on the planet—846 feet below sea level—and allegedly the oldest.[1] So far, the excavations of New Testament Jericho have focused on the lavish palaces of the Hasmoneans and the Herods, with their huge *triclinia*, swimming pools, baths, gardens, and hippodromes.[2] These remains, of course, do not tell us much about the life of the ordinary people, like the blind man who sat beside the road and begged. Even the wealthy tax collector, Zaccheus, probably never visited the Herodian palaces, owned during Jesus' ministry by the Roman emperor, Tiberius.

THE LARGE ESTATE

> When he came near to Jericho there was a blind man sitting by the road begging. (Luke 18:35).

The agricultural region around Jericho—which included En-Gedi, Phasaelis, and Archelais (see Map 1 p. 2) west of the Jordan River and Livias east of the river—was world famous for its two crops: balsam oil and dates. Balsam trees grew only here in Palestine and in Egypt and were very valuable because the oil derived from the trees was believed to have extraordinary

---

1. Murphy-O'Connor, *Holy Land*, 327.
2. Netzer, "Jericho: Exploration since 1973"; Netzer, "Jericho: Tell es-Samarat"; Bar-Nathan and Gärtner, "Pottery."

healing powers. The dates from this region were regarded as some of the finest in the world (Pliny, *N.H.* 13.9.44; Pausanias, *Descr.* 9.19.8) due, perhaps, to the soil. The date plantation alone was eleven miles long (Strabo 16.2.41); the balsam plantation covered 128 acres.[3]

Figure 11.1: The mouth of Wadi Qelt and the Jericho plain

The Persians first developed the lucrative region, followed by Alexander the Great's successors.[4] The Hasmoneans inherited the plantation and not only developed the two main crops but built winter palaces at the mouth of the Wadi Qelt (Figure 11.1). Herod the Great built his own winter palaces (three of them[5]) as well in roughly the same area. He also profited enormously from the valuable yields of balsam and dates. After Herod died in one of these palaces (*War* 1.666), it was subsequently burned down by one of his agricultural slaves, named Simon (*Ant.* 17.274). His son, Archelaus, inherited the estate, rebuilt the palace (*Ant.* 17.340), and expanded the landholding. When Archelaus was banished in 6 CE, Augustus evidently took over the lands as his private property and then deeded them to his heir, Tiberius (reigned 14–37 CE).[6]

---

3. Hengel, *Judaism and Hellenism*, 45; Fiensy, *Social History*, 25.
4. See Fiensy, *Social History*, 25–28.
5. For the Hasmonean and Herodian winter palaces, see Netzer, "Jericho: Exploration since 1973."
6. Finegan, *Archaeology*, 147–50; Stern, "Province of Judaea," 334.

Figure 11.2: Herod's winter palace, Jericho. The "Great Hall" *triclinium* (see Figure 11.7 p. 198) is at the bottom of the photo. Just above the Great Hall or *triclinium* is the peristyle court; above it and to the left were the baths.[7]

East of the Hasmonean and Herodian palaces, on the fringe of the royal estate, was a building much more modest than the palatial residences. This construction perhaps housed "administrative staff," according to the excavator Ehud Netzer.[8] Every large estate needed a bailiff or steward (called an *oikonomos* in Jesus' parables; Luke 12:42, 16:1). This building was evidently for the estate overseer and his family.

Can we identify a plausible family of the *oikonomos*? Excavators (and local looters) have found near Jericho 103 tombs on eight hills. All tombs date from the first century BCE to the first century CE. Archaeologists did not excavate every tomb, but in those they excavated, they found a total of 185 individuals.[9] The Goliath family tomb (on hill H; see Table 5.4), was more elaborate than the others. The three-generational tomb (spanning c. 10–70 CE) featured a "large size . . . delicate frescoes on the walls of the upper chamber, and a high proportion of inscribed ossuaries." The frescoes

---

7. Purchased from www.BibleLandPictures.com/. For the identification of the rooms of the palace, see Netzer, "Jericho: Exploration since 1973," 688.

8. Netzer, "Roman Jericho."

9. Hachlili and Killebrew, *Jericho*, 5, 192–94.

depicted vines with grapes and birds perched on them. These characteristics indicate, according to Rachel Hachlili and Patricia Smith, the "high status of its owners."[10]

One individual in this tomb, Theodotos/Nathanel, had been the slave of Queen Agrippina (Emperor Claudius' wife and Emperor Nero's mother[11]), had been manumitted (c. 51–55 CE[12]), and had returned home. Being a freedman of Agrippina would have been a high-status position. Rachel Hachlili suggests that Theodotus "was in charge of Roman interests or property of the empress in Jericho itself or in some other neighboring area."[13] It is, therefore, reasonable, but certainly not provable, that this family worked as estate overseers. That would mean they were a level above the others in the village in the resources they enjoyed.

We have, then, the elites (the Herodian family and, later, the imperial family), more than adequately represented in the ruins of the winter palaces. We also have an architectural, and possibly a burial, footprint of the bailiffs, the estate overseers. But where do we find the workers?

Archaeologists found evidence of farming activity near the winter palaces. The Hasmoneans had constructed two aqueducts originating in Wadi Qelt and flowing to the farmland (110 acres) just north of the palaces. Later, a third aqueduct was added, watering not only the crops but also the winter palaces (their swimming pools and baths). Nearby, excavators discovered two large presses, perhaps used for date wine production or for pressing date honey. They also discovered two workshops in which there are paved floors, pools, and stoves. They crushed the balsam branches on the paved floors, soaked them in the pools (Figure 11.4), and then used the stoves to distill the liquid produced in the pools. There were also several *mikva'ot* in the workshops, evidently indicating that the workers wanted to produce liquids in a ritually pure state. The liquid-storage buildings nearby held the precious balsam oil and date wine until the workers were ready to ship it. On the edge of this farm stood a combined watchtower/columbarium (dovecote). The Herodian owners of the region had continued using the Hasmonean farming installations.[14]

---

10. Hachlili and Smith, "Genealogy," 70; and Hachlili, "Goliath Family," 31. Cf. Luff, *Impact of Jesus*, 132.
11. Tacitus, *Ann*. 12.1–8. Claudius reigned 41–54 CE; Nero 54–68 CE.
12. According to Hachlili, "Goliath Family," 34.
13. Hachlili, "Goliath Family," 34.
14. Netzer, "Jericho: Exploration since 1973"; Netzer, "Roman Jericho."

Figure 11.3: Date palms at Jericho

Figure 11.4: Balsam-pressing installation, Jericho (www.HolyLandPhotos.org)

An estate of this size, located near a village, usually meant that the villagers worked for the estate owner. There would have been very little land available for the average person to own and farm. Instead, most of them—except the overseers (the *oikonomoi*) and the utterly destitute like the blind man—would have been tenant farmers, day laborers, or slaves. They may have tended the trees and picked the fruit in season. Others would have worked in processing the fruit in the workshop.

We know of one of those laborers from the writings of Josephus. The enslaved worker, the aforementioned Simon, belonged to Herod the Great and was said to be an unusually large man with great bodily strength. After Herod's death, Simon led a revolt in which he proclaimed himself king. He and his men set fire to Herod's palace at Jericho and carried off some of its treasures. Simon was soon killed in battle by the Herodian army.[15]

Thus, we do not find the people of Jericho with whom Jesus interacted in the ruins of what people today call "New Testament Jericho." Those ruins are the Herodian palaces. We find some trace of the non-elite persons in the workshop where they worked to produce the master's precious balsam oil and date products. We could also surmise that some of the agricultural workers were buried in the 130 tombs near the winter palaces.[16]

While ordinary persons might have lived very modestly in Jericho, the elites who owned the lands around it profited greatly. At the time Jesus passed through the village, Tiberius (Augustus's heir) owned the estate and the winter palaces and, of course, he had no knowledge of (and probably no interest in) the people who lived in the village and produced a fortune for him in precious agricultural products.

AVERAGE STATURE IN THE TIME OF JESUS

The elites, or highest class, of Palestine were the Herodian family, the chief priests, and other wealthy families. These persons were the leisured class. They did not labor either manually or mentally. Between the elites and the working class (from the poorest day laborer to the fairly comfortable skilled-craft families) were the "retainers."[17] Retainers mediated between the workers and the leisured class. They supervised those workers that the leisured class controlled in one way or another. Examples of retainers would

---

15. See Josephus, *Ant.* 17.273–76.

16. But almost certainly not all. The number of tombs would not have been enough. Most of the workers were put in the ground in trench graves, undoubtedly. See Chapter 15.

17. The term was coined in Lenski, *Power and Privilege*, 243–48.

be farm managers of large estates (the *oikonomoi* mentioned above), judicial magistrates, and officials of the Herodian government like Chuza, Joanna's husband (Luke 8:3). One of the most hated of the retainers, however, was the tax collector. These might be tax farmers, who collected the main source of revenue, or toll collectors at the borders of tetrarchies.[18]

> He entered and passed through Jericho. There was a man there named Zacchaeus who was one of the chief tax collectors and was rich. He was trying to see Jesus but could not because of the crowd, for he was small of stature. (Luke 19:2–3)[19]

In Luke's narrative of Jesus' travel to Jerusalem, he includes the story of his meeting with Zacchaeus the tax collector. In the story, the tax collector wants to catch a glimpse of the great Galilean holy man and prophet but cannot because he is small of stature. That brings up the question, how tall were men and women in Palestine/Israel in those days? How tall should we imagine Zacchaeus to have been? For that matter, how tall would Jesus probably have been? How can we answer these questions?

How Tall Were They?

Once again, we return to the study of osteoarchaeology, that is, the examination of human skeletal remains. Physical anthropologists can by measuring certain bones—especially the femur—calculate the stature, on average, of people. They sometimes give these data in their reports and at other times—owing to time constraints and perhaps other considerations—omit it. But we will take the data out there and offer a reasoned average stature for males and females for this region and time.

To find an average, we will simply note the average stature of individuals from various tombs and then average these together. Our database is difficult to assess (300–500+). The reason for the difficulty is some reports give an average stature only for the entire tomb complex or complexes and note that many of the individuals' remains were not measurable. Thus, the number of individuals used to calculate some averages is unknown. Nevertheless, one can gain some perspective on this question by looking at the averages submitted by these anthropologists. The table below has the results:

---

18. See Herrenbrück, "Zölner?"; and Udoh, "Taxation," 380. For an example of a wealthy tax collector see *War* 2.287.

19. Green's suggestion (*Luke*, 669) that Zacchaeus was not small of stature but young in age is unconvincing due to the context.

Number of Sites/tombs	Male Average Height	Female Average Height
7	165.5 (5'5")	150 (4'11")

Table 11.1: Stature in the Hell II through ER II periods in Israel[20]

The average adult man stood five feet five inches and the average adult woman stood four feet eleven inches. This figure agrees essentially with Zias, who affirms that the average height of Jewish males from the Hellenistic to the Roman-Byzantine periods was 166 cm (5'5") and of females was 148 cm (4'10"). Joan Taylor maintains, based on her study of skeletal remains, that Jesus would have been between 164 and 168 cm (5'4" to 5'6").[21] My results based on an average of the averages of stature calculated from skeletal remains is consistent with two other studies.

The men and women of Palestine/Israel were a bit smaller than those attested for Greece in the Classical and Hellenistic periods:

	Males	Females
Greece Classical period	169.8 cm	156.3 cm
Greece Hellenistic period	171.8 cm	156.6 cm

Table 11.2: Average stature in Greece[22]

Missing from these calculations, however, are the outlying data from two tombs. A family buried in Tomb H in Jericho, sometimes called the "Goliath Family Tomb," had one member of unusual stature. We told something of this individual and his tomb in Table 5.4, above. As the name indicates, some of these persons were unusually tall in comparison with the others from their period. While we do not know exactly which ossuary belonged to the man nicknamed Goliath, the anthropologists surmised that one man in the three-generational family tomb measuring 188.5 cm (6'2"), was the one given this moniker.[23]

Likewise, in the Meiron tombs, although the average stature of the men was 165.5 cm (5'5"), there were two men somewhat taller, one measuring 175

---

20. The table is composed from information in Zias, "Mount Scopus" (Meiron, En-Gedi, and Mount Scopus); Haas, "Anthropological Observations" (Giv'at ha-Mivtar); Nagar and Torgeé, "Biological Characteristics" (8 tombs in Judea); Nathan, "Naḥal Ḥever"; and Arensburg and Rak, "French Hill."

21. Zias, "Appendix A," 125; Taylor, *What Did Jesus Look Like?*, 159.

22. Grmek, *Diseases*, 109. Gallant, *Risk*, 69.

23. Hachlili and Smith, "Genealogy," 68.

cm (5'9") and the other 177 cm (5'10").[24] Thus, there were men well over five feet five inches tall (even over six feet tall at rare times) in the ancient Mediterranean and Middle Eastern world. But these were the exceptions.[25]

We would suggest, along with others, that Jesus and his disciples—the Twelve—were somewhere near five feet five inches tall but that some might have been a few inches taller or shorter. Joan Taylor notes, for example, that the male skeletons found in the caves of Naḥal Ḥever ranged from 5'2" to 5'8" and in the Giv'at ha-Mivtar tomb in Jerusalem from 4'11" to 5'11".[26] But a person like the man nicknamed Goliath was considered a giant.

Likewise, Jesus' mother, Mary, was probably 4'11" tall, tiny by most contemporary societies' standards. Of the three women featured in Table 5.4 above one was exactly that height but the two others were a bit smaller.[27]

But how tall, then, was Zacchaeus? Excavators found, in the Giv'at ha-Mivtar tomb, the remains of a young man named Saul. This man had died—actually, had been executed[28]—at age sixteen. Presumably he had most, if not all, of his growth by that time. He was four feet eleven inches tall. This is the size one can imagine Zacchaeus to have been.

Weight and Facial Type

We have a good idea about the stature of the average man and woman, but what about the average weight? Zias has speculated in one publication on this issue. He opines, based again on skeletal remains, that the average male weighed between 62 and 67 kilograms (137 to 148 pounds). He further reasons that since Galilee had more food sources (agricultural plus the fish from the Sea of Galilee), the males there would tend toward the upper weight. The other regions such as Judea would have tended toward the lower. Those living in the desert, such as the Essenes at Qumran, would have been perhaps a little lower than the 137 pounds.[29]

---

24. Smith et al., "Skeletal Remains" (Meiron).

25. Cf. the man 6'7" found just north of Rome in a grave dating to the third century CE. Minozzi et al., "Roman Giant"; and Dell'Amore, "Roman Giant." The anthropologists surmised that he suffered from an endocrine disorder.

26. Taylor, *What Did Jesus Look Like?*, 158–59 gives other examples.

27. Again, looking only at the Givat ha-Mivtar tomb: one female was 4'8" and another 4'9". See Haas, "Anthropological Observations"; and Table 5.4 above, individuals 5 and 6.

28. The anthropologist determined that he had been burned to death while on a rack. See Haas, "Anthropological Observations."

29. Zias, "Appendix A."

Joan Taylor finds hints in Jesus' teachings that he was often hungry. This information plus the indication that he was an artisan—a *tektōn*—means, to her, that Jesus was very slim with the "physique of someone who did manual craft."[30]

After examining the archaeological evidence from the skeletal remains of Jewish men, comparing first-century Jews with east Mediterranean people today, and looking at ancient depictions of Jews (on late synagogue walls, on coins, and in literature), Taylor summarizes her picture of Jesus' appearance:

- 5'5" tall
- slim
- "reasonably muscular"
- olive-brown skin
- brown eyes
- dark brown or black hair
- short beard
- short hair[31]

These features seem about right for most Jewish men from our period of time. Her idea that Jesus was unusually "slim" because he was frequently hungry, however, disagrees with Zias's view that the Galileans consumed more calories than elsewhere in Palestine.

A final issue regarding physique of the ancient Jewish people can be cleared up from the skeletal remains. What were their facial features? H. Nathan lays out the usual conclusion

> The original Jewish people is generally considered to belong to the basic Mediterranean dolichocephalic stock, much the same as their present Arab neighbors . . . Sephardini and oriental Jews have retained this original Mediterranean type.[32]

In other words, Jesus and his followers looked much like the Arabs of Palestine (and the Sephardic Jews) do today. They *probably* had brown

---

30. Taylor, *What Did Jesus Look Like?*, 167. But the references to being hungry are dubious. Jesus blessed the poor and hungry, to be sure, but does that mean that he was often without food himself?

31. Taylor, *What Did Jesus Look Like?*, 168.

32. Nathan, "Naḥal Ḥever," 173.

skin—as Taylor maintained—and long-looking faces.[33] The Galilean men stood around 5'5" tall and weighed around 140 pounds. John the Baptist, however, was probably more in the 130-pound category since he had lived in the desert. The females from Galilee (Jesus' mother, Mary Magdalene, and so forth) stood, on average, 4'11".

BANQUETS

Banqueting was a major event in this culture, and it plays a rather significant role in the background to many of the scenes of the Gospels, especially in Luke's telling of the story. Jesus often attended banquets; he also told several parables with banquets as the background scenery. At Jericho, he was invited by Zacchaeus to dine, after which the tax collector—evidently after hearing the table talk—repented of his predatory ways (Luke 19:1–10).

> And everybody, when they saw this, complained, "He's gone inside to be the (banqueting) guest of a sinner!" (Luke 19:7)

Banqueting culture in the Israel in Jesus' day derived from the Greeks[34] often filtered through the Romans. Banquets were events of "leisure and luxury" even if celebrated in a modest setting.[35] Invitations, whether oral or written (cf. Luke 14:17), would be sent out by slaves[36] ahead of the event (a day or two before; sometimes on the same day). We actually have some written invitations to banquets preserved for us in the papyri of Egypt. The first written invitation quoted below, sent by a woman, invites guests to a *klinē* (Gk.: couch; see Figure 11.5, below) at three o'clock in the afternoon in a dining room of the temple of Sarapis. Since the hostess is a woman, we might presume that she and other women were present at the banquet:

> Herais asks you to dine in the (banquet) room of the Sarapeion at a kline (*eis klinēn*) of the Lord Sarapis tomorrow, which is the 11th at the 9th hour.[37]

---

33. Yet, surprisingly, Nathan finds in the seventeen skulls from Naḥal Ḥever that they are more similar to the Ashkenazi Jews, assumed to have changed their look due to intermarriage with eastern Europeans in the diaspora. See Nathan, "Naḥal Ḥever," 174. Nathan further speculates that there were actually two populations—one dolichocephalic and the other brachycephalic—making up the ancient Jews. Thus, one cannot be definite about the facial features of Jesus and his disciples.

34. The Greeks borrowed the custom of reclining at table during their "orientalizing period" in the seventh century BCE. See Mols, *Wooden Furniture*, 127.

35. Smith, "Greco-Roman Banquet."

36. Binder, "Banquet: Rome."

37. Translation in Standhartinger, "Women in Early Christian," 90. The text is from

Another invitation, very similar, was sent by a man:

> Chaeremon requests you to dine at the banquet (*klinē*) of the Lord Sarapis in the Sarapeion tomorrow, the 15th, at the 9th hour.[38]

The guests would clean up and take special care with their clothing (cf. Matt 22:11–13). They would then enter the "men's room," the banqueting room which was only for men (and their female entertainment). An enslaved person would wash their feet and get them ready for the evening. The Greek banquet was in two phases: the meal (*deipnon*) and the drinking party (*symposion*). During the second phase, the entertainment was brought in: music—especially the flute girls—games, dancing girls, and the *hetaerae*[39]). The invited guests might try to sneak in a few *parasitoi* (Gk.: parasites) or *umbrae* (Lat.: shadows) to crash the party.[40]

The Romans did make a slight change in the type of guests at the banquet. Increasingly, women (wives and even children) were allowed to dine with the men. In Roman culture the banquet began in midafternoon (as in the invitations quoted above).[41]

The Greeks dined reclining on the left elbow on couches, and the Romans, who had originally eaten seated around their hearth, imitated them.[42] If the couches were made of stone, they often have left traces in the remains of houses. Carolyn Osiek has described a large building complex with three dining rooms where the couches are still visible.[43] Most *klinai*, however, were made of wood (or, more expensively, of bronze) and were movable. Mattresses and blankets were placed over the couches to add to their comfort. In Greece, usually there were one or two places per couch. In Rome the arrangement of three places and three couches became the standard. From this, the name *triclinium*, "triple couch," came about. The term was later transferred to the room which accommodated the three couches.[44]

Hanson, *Collectanea Papyrologica*, 1:52.

38. Translation in Smith, *From Symposium to Eucharist*, 23. The papyrus is P.Oxy. 110 (second century CE).
39. The word *hetaera* means "courtesan."
40. Schmitt Pantel, "Banquet: Greece"; and Binder, "Banquet: Rome."
41. Schmitt Pantel, "Banquet: Greece"; and Binder, "Banquet: Rome."
42. Badian, "Triclinium"; Schmitt Pantel, "Triclinium."
43. Osiek, "What Kinds of Meals."
44. Schmitt Pantel, "Triclinium"; Badian, "Triclinium."

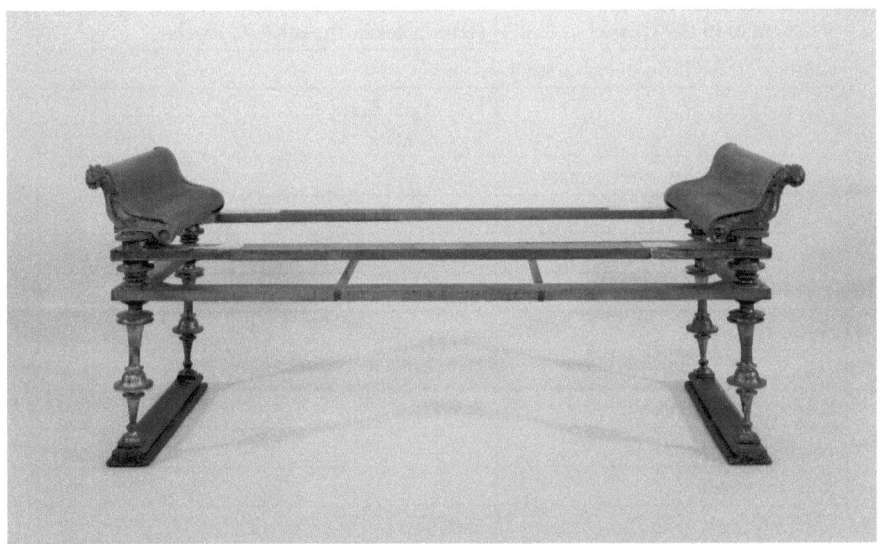

Figure 11.5: An actual Roman bed/couch (Gk., *klinē*; Lat., *lectus*) from first century BCE, made of bronze.[45]

But hosts also gave banquets with the guests reclining on the floor. A text in Eccl. R. (3.9.1) reflects the various means of sitting and reclining. In the story, a king has invited guests to a banquet and instructs them to bring whatever they want to sit or recline on, whether rugs, mats, mattresses, chairs, logs, or stones. This window into the past offers us a glimpse of a poor person's banquet (even though in the story a king is the host). The couches were not necessary to have a banquet. People loved banqueting and did not need a Greek- or Roman-style *triclinium* to host one. Nor did they need to serve lavish dishes, or even very much of any food. There are papyri from Egypt from our time period that describe banquets consisting of only wine and bread and, even, at times, of only a cup of wine and no food.[46] No matter the extent of the feasting, people loved banqueting. We should probably imagine that some of the banquets Jesus attended were of the poorer sort.

The casual reader of the Gospels usually misses the numerous references to Greek-style dining:

---

45. Available at Wikimedia Commons: https://commons.wikimedia.org/wiki/File:Roman_-_Banquet_Couch_-_Walters_542365.jpg/. For other images, see Andrianou, "Evidence for Furnished Interiors"; and Richter, *Ancient Furniture*.

46. Last and Harland, *Group Survival*, 28–29.

References in the Gospel of Luke	References in the other Gospels
deipnon "feast, dinner, elaborate meal"	
14:12, 17, 24, 20:46	Matt 23:6, Mark 6:21, 12:39, John 12:2, 13:2,4, 21:20
ariston "breakfast, noon meal"	
11:38, 14:12	Matt 22:4
Aristaō "to dine"	
11:37	John 21:12, 15
Dochē "banquet"	
5:29, 14:13	
Dining too lavishly	
12:19, 45, 16:19, 21:34	
The *symposion*	
Luke 7:31–35, 22:20	Matt 11:16–19; 1 Cor 11:25
Washing feet prior to reclining	
7:44	John 13:3–5
anaklinō "to recline at meal"	
12:37, 13:29	Matt 8:11
anakeimai "to recline at table, dine"	
22:27	Matt 9:10, 22:10–11, 26:7, 20, Mark 6:26, 14:18, 16:14, John 12:2, 13:23, 28,
synanakeimai "to recline at table with (someone) for the purpose of eating"	
7:49, 14:10, 15	Matt 9:10, 14:9, Mark 2:15, 6:22
anapiptō "recline on a couch to eat"	
Luke 11:37, 17:7, 22:14	John 13:12
kataklinō "recline at dinner"	
7:36, 14:8, 24:30	
katakeimai "recline (on a couch) for the purpose of dining"	
5:29, 7:37	Mark 14:3
prōtoklisia "reclining place of honor at dinner"	
Luke 14:7–8, 20:46	Matt 23:6; Mark 12:39

Table 11.3: Dining terminology in Luke[47]

By Jesus' time, the well-to-do in Palestine/Israel had adopted the Greco-Roman style of dining. The first meal and the noon meal were more a snack than a meal and often skipped entirely. It was the evening meal where

47. The definitions of the terms are from Danker, *Lexicon*.

people nourished themselves. These meals would be modest offerings for poor families, more elaborate dining for the affluent, and could be extravagant affairs for banquets. The typical evening meal for a Roman consisted of three courses: the hors d'oeuvres, the main course, and the dessert, with wine being served throughout.[48] A lavish banquet, however, might have several more courses.[49]

Dennis Smith[50] argued that the Greek model of banqueting dominates in the New Testament. After the dessert, in the Greek custom, came the drinking party (*symposion*), which could last until the early hours of the next day. The banqueters drank wine mixed with water so the drinking would not inebriate them. This was the time for entertainment or, in Greek philosophical circles, for intellectual conversation. Smith finds references to the Greek custom in 1 Cor 11:23–25, Paul's account of the Last Supper, at which Jesus took the "cup after dining" (v. 25). The same wording occurs in Luke 22:20.

Possibly the Greek type of dining predominated over the Roman in Palestine/Israel in the late Second Temple period, as Smith maintained, but it seems more reasonable to assume that the practice was mixed. The banqueting host might choose to follow either one or the other depending on the occasion and the preferences of the host. He/she might serve wine throughout the meal (the Roman custom) or wait until after the dinner and serve it as a *symposion*.

The Greeks reclined in rooms which could accommodate from seven to eleven guests per room.[51] As mentioned above, the Romans refined this custom to an arrangement of three couches; each couch was shared by three diners, making a total of nine (see Figure 11.6, below). The banquet halls of monarchs or other great leaders, however, though retaining the name *triclinia*, might have held scores if not hundreds of diners.

By the time of Jesus, everyone in Palestine/Israel knew you reclined at a banquet:

> A householder who was reclining at table and eating ... (t. Ber. 4:20).[52]

> What is the order for reclining [when several eat together]? When there are two couches, the greatest [in importance] among them

---

48. Binder, "Banquet: Rome."
49. See Carcopino, *Daily Life*, 263–64; Casson, *Everyday Life*, 18–19.
50. Smith, "Greco-Roman Banquet."
51. See Smith, "Dinner with Jesus & Paul."
52. Translation from Neusner, *Tosefta*.

reclines at the head of the first, the second [in importance] to him reclines below him. When there are three couches, the greatest [in importance] reclines at the head of the middle [couch], the second [in importance] to him [reclines] above him, and the third [in importance] below him (t. Ber. 5:5).[53]

Even at the Passover, everyone had to recline:

Even the poorest man in Israel must not eat (on Passover night) without reclining[54] (m. Pes. 10:1).

Passover was a banquet, a celebration, and by the time the Mishnah was written down (second century CE), but surely also before, the Jewish custom had identified the Greek practice of reclining with banqueting.

Figure 11.6: Reconstruction of a *triclinium*[55] (Creator and photographer: Mattes)

Archaeologists have discovered several large houses in Palestine/Israel from the time of Jesus with rooms identified as *triclinia*. One was discovered just west of the Western Wall in Jerusalem. The building comprises two halls

53. Translation in Neusner, *The Tosefta*.
54. Translation from Jastrow, *Dictionary*.
55. Wikimedia Commons: https://commons.wikimedia.org/wiki/File:Roman_Triclinium_or_Dining_Room.jpg/.

and a fountain room in between, evidently, two *triclinia* separated by the fountain. The walls were decorated with pilasters and Corinthian capitals. Its function as a double dining hall or double *triclinium* can be seen in the marks left on the stone walls by the couches in both rooms. Wealthy families would often have several *triclinia* in their large mansions.[56] The architectural style suggested to the excavators that it had been built by Herod the Great. The dining hall was in use for about sixty years and went out of use in about 33 CE when it was partially destroyed by an earthquake.[57]

Sidebar 11.1

Artist's reconstruction of diners in a *triclinium*[58]

The Herodian constructions are always grander than anything others could do. But they do illustrate—if we can imagine a more modest version of them—how people ate at leisurely banquets. Another *triclinium*, this one truly of colossal size, is in Herod the Great's palace at Jericho. The "great hall" of the palace measured 92 X 62 feet and would actually accommodate "hundreds of guests," according to the excavator, Ehud Netzer.[59] Obviously, they did not merely recline on three couches at these affairs but on many.

56. Badian, "Triclinium."
57. Patrich and Weksler-Bdolah, "Old, New Banquet Hall."
58. Source Wikimedia Commons: http://www.gutenberg.org/etext/12254/.
59. Netzer, "Jericho: Exploration since 1973," 687.

Still, the name *triclinium* was used to refer to these dining halls. The hall was surrounded on three sides by colonnades and paved with colorful stones in a pattern called *opus sectile*. The great hall was the palace's main *triclinium*, designed for huge banquets (Figure 11.7).[60] Most likely, Jesus did not dine at a facility like this one. His dinners were probably more like the standard Roman three-couch and nine-person events and, on occasion, merely reclining on the floor on a mat.

Figure 11.7: The great hall (*triclinium*) of Herod the Great's third winter palace at Jericho. One can still see the indentations on the floor from the *opus sectile* flooring[61]

At the Greek banquets, there might be an atmosphere of a "stag party" according to Dennis Smith. When respectable women did attend Greek banquets, they usually did not recline on couches like the men. Among the Greeks, women, children, and enslaved persons did not recline when they ate, only freeborn males.[62] Well-to-do Romans, however, both men and women, would recline at the evening meal (the *cena*, Lat. equivalent to Gk. *deipnon*). But children, slaves, village rustics, and travelers staying in inns ate sitting.[63]

60. Netzer, "Jericho: Exploration since 1973"; Singer, "Winter Palaces."
61. Photo purchased from www.BibleLandPictures.com/.
62. Smith, "Dinner with Jesus & Paul."
63. Carcopino, *Daily Life*, 265; and Badian, "Triclinium."

Roman aristocrats complained when women reclined alongside men at these dinners: "Women would dine, sitting, with their men reclining," griped Valerius Maximus (first century CE).[64] Thus, women might have attended the banquets sitting upright while men reclined. In the Gospels, we have, according to Dennis Smith, a clear case of women sitting as opposed to reclining. In the story of Luke 10:38–42, where Jesus eats with and instructs Mary and Martha, Mary is said to "sit" (*parakathizō*; 10:39) at Jesus' feet (probably on the floor on a mat) as opposed to reclining on a couch with the other diners. Thus, Mary is a respectable woman as opposed to the reclining women of questionable character at Greek and Roman dinners.[65]

Jody Magness[66] suggests that Jewish villagers in Galilee usually ate while sitting on the floor, citing the following text: "But couches and the seats and earthenware vessels having a tightly stopped-up cover remain clean"[67] (m. Tohor. 7:5). Thus, reclining was for the wealthy, perhaps every day, and for others when in a banqueting situation. The fact that we see Jesus so often reclining means that he was frequently at banquets.

One other group ate sitting instead of reclining: the sectarians at Qumran. The Temple Scroll (11QT 37:8–9) refers to chairs instead of couches for eating: "Inside the [in]ner cou[rt] you are to design a qu[ar]ter with s[e]ats for the priests, with tables placed before the seats."[68] It appears that the sectarians did not approve of the assimilated Greco-Roman custom of reclining at meals.[69] They wanted to maintain the old-fashioned practice of sitting upright, whether on a chair (a luxury) or on the floor.

Dennis Smith suggests that dogs were often present at these dinner parties. Thus, Jesus could refer to the "dogs" in his dialogue with the Syro-Phoenician woman (Mark 7:24–30; Matt 15:21–28). Jesus says in that text he should not take food from the children (Israel) and give it to dogs (gentiles). The woman answers that the dogs eat the crumbs thrown from the table. Smith's comment also helps picture the parable of the Rich Man and Lazarus. Lazarus, like the dogs, ate the scraps thrown from the table (Luke 16:19–31).[70]

---

64. Valerius Maximus, *Memorable Doings and Sayings* 2.1.2. Lat. text in *Facta et dicta memorabilia*: https://penelope.uchicago.edu/Thayer/L/Roman/Texts/Valerius_Maximus/2*.html/ (my translation).
65. Smith, "Dinner with Jesus & Paul."
66. Magness, *Stone and Dung*, 81.
67. Translation in Danby, *Mishnah*.
68. Translation in Wise et al., *Dead Sea Scrolls*.
69. See Magness, *Stone and Dung*, 81.
70. Smith, "Dinner with Jesus & Paul."

There was always entertainment at banquets ranging from the frivolous (games) to the light (music or storytelling) to the heavy (philosophical or theological discussions).[71] It appears that often Jesus himself was the entertainment. He tells parables (Luke 14:7-11, 14:16-24) and engages in theological table talk (Luke 19:8) as one can surmise from the result of the banquet at Zacchaeus's house in Jericho.

---

71. Casson, *Everyday Life*, 21.

12

The Upper City, Eleona, and Gethsemane

THE UPPER CITY

> On one of the days while he was teaching the people in the temple and evangelizing, the chief priests and scribes along with the elders appeared, . . . and the scribes and chief priests sought to apprehend him at that very hour, but they were afraid of the people. (Luke 20:1, 19)

Luke	Summary	Other Texts
9:22	Jesus predicts his death at the hands of the chief priests.	Matt 16:21, Mark 8:31
19:47	The chief priests want to kill Jesus.	
20:1	The chief priests challenge the authority of Jesus.	Matt 21:23, Mark 11:27
20:19	The chief priests want to arrest Jesus.	Matt 21:45–46, Mark 12:12
22:2	The chief priests explore ways to kill Jesus.	Matt 26:3, Mark 14:1, John 11:49
22:4	Judas agrees to assist the chief priests.	Matt 26:14, Mark 14:10
22:52	Jesus speaks to the chief priests and others.	

22:66	The chief priests and others meet to try Jesus.	Matt 26:59, Mark 14:55
23:4, 13	Pilate speaks to the chief priests.	
23:10	The chief priests accuse Jesus.	Matt 27:12, Mark 15:3
24:20	The chief priests condemned Jesus.	
Acts	Summary	
4:1	The chief priests and Sadducees arrest Peter and John.	
4:6	Relatives of the high priest interrogate Peter and John.	
5:17	Peter and John report to the church what the chief priests told them.	
9:1, 14, 21, 22:5, 26:10, 12	The chief priests give Saul authority to persecute the church.	
22:30	The chief priests try Paul.	
23:14	Assassins report to the chief priests their plot to kill Paul.	
24:1, 25:2, 15	The chief priests accuse Paul.	

Table 12.1: The chief priests in the Lukan narratives

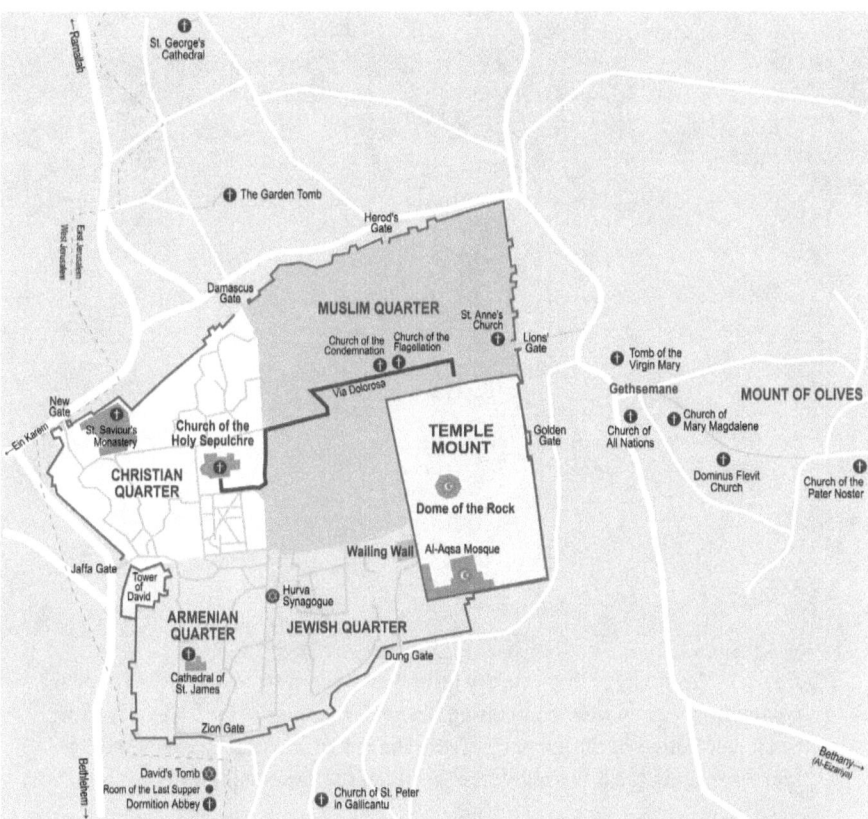

Figure 12.1: Plan of the Old City of Jerusalem as it is today. Note in the south the Cenacle (David's Tomb) and the Church of Saint Peter in Gallicantu. In the north, note the Garden Tomb. To the east is Gethsemane. Inside the walls of Old Jerusalem are the four sections (Quarters) making up the city. (Plan by Obendorf[1])

1. Wikimedia Commons: https://commons.wikimedia.org/wiki/File:Map_of_the_Old_City_and_surroundings_of_Jerusalem.svg/.

Figure 12.2: The model of first-century Jerusalem (according to Michael Avi-Yonah), looking from east to west, contrasting the modest houses of the lower city with the upscale houses of the upper city (with the red-tiled roofs). The hypothetical hippodrome is in the foreground; the theater in the upper middle of the photo.[2]

Jerusalem's upper class, whose members were the temple nobility and the lay nobility, lived mainly in the upper city (Figure 15.1). Ananias, the high priest when the revolt began in 66 CE, had a house there, evidently, near the palace of Agrippa II and Berenice. These houses, including the public archives which held records of debts, were at that time set on fire by the rebels, necessitating the escape, through the sewer drains under the streets, of the high priest, the other chief priests, and the powerful nonpriestly families (*War* 2.426-29). The upper city, then, was the neighborhood of choice for the wealthy and the target of ire for others.

Most of the residents of the upper city, even the wealthy priests, were probably owners of large estates, though some may have been wealthy

---

2. Cabaret, *Topography*, 75 believes, however, the hippodrome and theater of Jerusalem were north of the temple. Lichtenberger, "Jesus and the Theater," argues for a wooden theater, amphitheater, and hippodrome erected by Herod the Great (*Ant.* 15.167-76) but no longer standing in the days of Jesus. For other suggestions as to the location of the theater, amphitheater, and hippodrome, see Cabaret, *Topography*.

merchants. Literary and archaeological sources[3] have identified many medium-to-large estates[4] in Judea and even around Jerusalem itself. Since large landowners tended in antiquity to live in the city as absentee landlords and to leave the administration of their estates to bailiffs, these landholdings may well have belonged to the members of the Jerusalem upper class. Probably the most significant class of wealthy landowners was the aristocratic priests, especially the high priestly families.[5]

Figure 12.3: Excavations in the Jewish Quarter (cf. Figure 12.1, above). Key: P=Palatial Mansion; M=Atrium House; F=Spacious Dwellings; E=Herodian House; B=Burnt House; A=Where the depiction of the temple menorah was found; Q=Large Public *Mikveh*[6] (Image courtesy Israel Exploration Society, Jerusalem[7])

The aristocratic neighborhood of Jerusalem developed toward the end of Herod the Great's reign. The excavation team of Nahman Avigad[8] discovered in the upper city large mansions owned obviously by very rich

---

3. See Applebaum, "Problem of the Roman Villa"; Applebaum, *Judaea*; Applebaum, "Judaea as a Roman Province." See also Fiensy, *Social History*, 21–73.

4. For estate sizes in antiquity, see Chapter 8.

5. Stern, "Aspects of Jewish Society," 586–87.

6. Key from Gutfeld, Introduction, 3.

7. Plan from Avigad, "Upper City: Herodian Period," 730.

8. Avigad, *Discovering Jerusalem*, 83–137; and Avigad, "How the Wealthy Lived"; Geva, "Stratigraphy and Architecture (Herodian House)."

people. The "Herodian house" (area E on Figure 12.3, above) both went up and came down in the first century BCE when it covered c. 1,400 square feet. The multiroom house with white plastered walls included a *mikveh* and a stone basin near its entrance, evidently for washing the feet. The wealth of the family can be seen by their imported vessels and other goods. They used imported, fine ceramic ware (ESA) and drank fine wines brought from Italy.[9] Yet toward the end of Herod the Great's reign this house and others like it in Areas E and J were paved over to create an east-west street running through the sector. These residents, evidently, had to move out to make room for the even more elaborate architecture.[10]

In Area A excavators discovered in the stratum of a large public building dating from the first century CE many fragments of decorated plaster and on two plaster fragments a depiction of the temple menorah. The depiction, incised on white plaster, measures c. 8 X 5 inches. There are possibly portions of other temple vessels (the altar of incense and the table of showbread) remaining on the right side of the depiction.[11] That a picture of temple vessels was engraved on one's wall probably meant that the engraver had actually seen them. Thus, the excavators conclude that the residents of this area were priestly.

---

9. See Avigad, "Upper City"; Avigad, *Discovering Jerusalem*, 84-88.

10. Geva, "Stratigraphy and Architecture (Herodian House)."

11. Geva, "Summary and Discussion," 534; Habas, "Incised Depiction." Reich ("Area A," 101) believes this area was offered for rental to religious pilgrims. The buildings were very small and plain. The colored fresco fragments found in this area were probably brought from nearby areas and used as fill. Thus, the menorah graffito probably did not hang on a wall in this district.

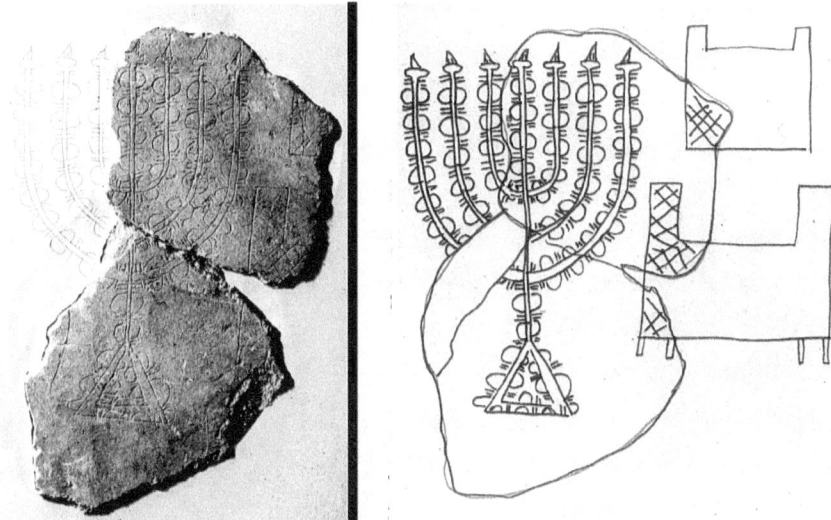

Figure 12.4: Incised temple menorah found in two fragments in Area A, with possible other temple vessels indicated.[12]

An entire length of houses, running 423 feet long, was excavated in this neighborhood (areas F, M, and P). This area covered 29,000 square feet (2,700 m²) and enclosed the remains of "six or seven" houses from the Herodian period. Most impressive was the so-called Palatial Mansion (area P). It stretched to c. 6,500 square feet but had a basement—hence c. 13,000 square feet. The living quarters, however, were only on the ground floor, the basement being used for water installations.[13] The house had been burned at some point, probably in 70 CE when the Romans destroyed the city. Soot was everywhere and the floors were covered with ash. Coins on the floors enabled the excavators to date the fire to the First Jewish Revolt (66–73 CE).[14]

---

12. Image purchased from www.BibleLandPictures.com/.

13. The house possibly had a second story, or perhaps the stairway led only to the roof. See Avigad, *Discovering Jerusalem*, 97–120.

14. Avigad, *Discovering Jerusalem*, 97.

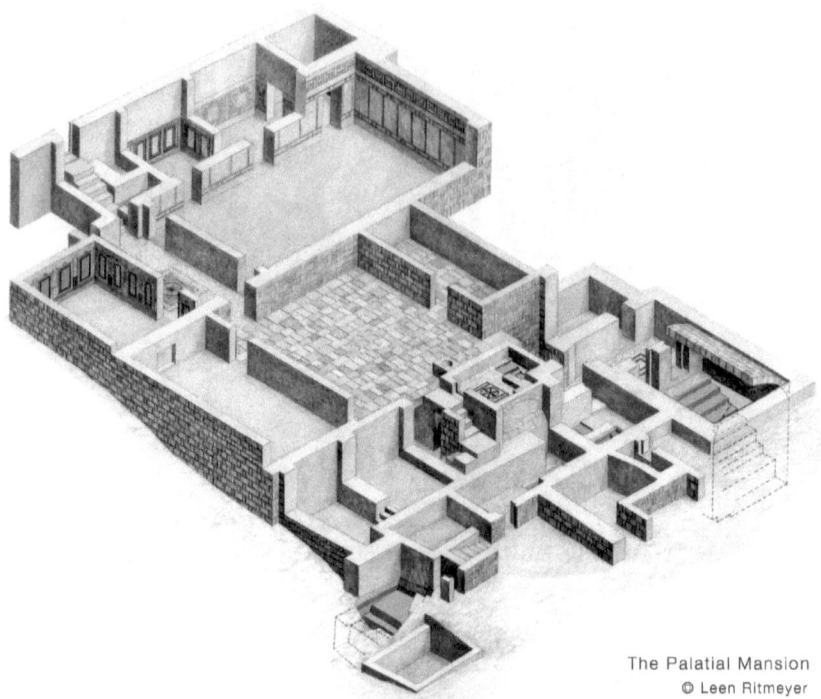

The Palatial Mansion
© Leen Ritmeyer

Figure 12.5: Isometric of the Palatial Mansion.[15] The reception hall is near the top and center of the plan. The flagstone courtyard is in the middle. The large, stepped *mikveh* is in the lower right-hand corner.

The mansion was built around a courtyard paved with stone. West of the courtyard was a large "reception hall" 21 X 36 feet (see Figure 12.6, below) plastered with stucco. East of the courtyard were a bathroom with tub and mosaic floor. The frescoed walls, decorated ceilings, and mosaic floors imitated those found in Pompeii and Herculaneum (Figure 12.7). Some of the walls were finished in a style mastered in Greece. The large house had at least three *mikva'ot*, one of which was quite large (11 X 13 feet).[16]

---

15. Image purchased from https://www.ritmeyer.com/. For explanation of the house, see Avigad, *Discovering Jerusalem*, 11.

16. Avigad, *Discovering Jerusalem*, 99–106.

Figure 12.6: The reception hall[17]

Also, inside this large "villa-like" house were stone tables, stone vessels (Figure 12.8), attesting to care in ritual purity, and floor mosaics with geometric (not animal or human) figures, indicating adherence to the commandment against graven images (Exod 20:4). The ritual baths and the abundance of stone vessels and tables demonstrate that these were not only wealthy Jews but strictly observant ones. The building was constructed during the reign of Herod the Great.[18]

Sidebar 12.1[19]

Caliph Hakim (985–1021)

He was caliph in Egypt from 996 to 1021. He was only eleven years old when he came to power. At age fifteen, he killed his teacher and regent. From then, he became what many regard as a fanatic. In 1008, he seized the property of the church in Jerusalem and forbade Palm Sunday processions. In 1009, he ordered the Church of the Holy Sepulcher completely destroyed and all traces of it removed. Constantine's church was at that time demolished.

---

17. Image purchased from https://www.ritmeyer.com/.
18. See Avigad, "Upper City."
19. Wilkinson, *Jerusalem Pilgrims*, 13–14.

Figure 12.7: Frescoed walls, "Palatial Mansion," Jerusalem.

Nahman Avigad asks, why a house looking like something from Italy in its furnishings would have so many *mikva'ot*, and one of them be much larger than needed for one-person use. No family needs that many ritual baths and certainly not one that large. He concluded that this house belonged to a priestly family meticulous about ritual purity and wondered if perhaps the house were not the dwelling of the high priest. Avigad seemed to suggest that whoever the high priest was at the time gained access to this domicile. He assumed that the high priest would make accommodation for many other priests to immerse themselves before their temple duties.[20]

---

20. Avigad, *Discovering Jerusalem*, 120.

Figure 12.8: Stone tables and stone jar stand in front of frescoed wall in the Palatial Mansion.

This area of Jerusalem is also where the "Burnt House" (area B) was found by Nahman Avigad's archaeological team. The excavated rooms covered around 600 square feet, but the rooms were probably "part of a larger dwelling."[21] Only the basement or ground floor is left to examine; either nothing of the residential floor remains, or the family resided in a wing not excavated.[22] The excavated remains include a small courtyard, four rooms, a kitchen, and a small *mikveh*. Inground ovens in most of the rooms told the excavators that this part of the house was not residential. From an inscription on a stone weight, which read [*d'*]*bar qatros* ("[of the] son of Qathros," Figure 12.9, below), Avigad concluded that the house belonged to a scion of the priestly house of Qathros. The Qathros family was one of the four main high-priestly families of the Herodian period. They are today famous because of the two rabbinic laments which denounced the families ("houses") of Boethus, Elḥanan (i.e., Annas[23]), Qadros (i.e., Qathros or Kathros), and Phiabi for their corruption:

---

21. Geva, "Stratigraphy (Burnt House)," 33.

22. The excavators could only determine the limits of the structure on the south and west; the house probably extended farther to the north and east. See Geva, "Stratigraphy (Burnt House)" 33–34.

23. See Sidebar 12.2 for the family-dynasty of Annas (Elḥanan or Ḥannan/Hanin).

t. Men. 13:21	b. Pes. 57a
Woe is me because of the house of Boethus. Woe is me because of their staves.	Woe is me because of the house of Boethus, woe is me because of their staves!
Woe is me because of the house of Qadros. Woe is me because of their pen.	Woe is me because of the house of Hanin, woe is me because of their whisperings!
Woe is me because of the house of Elḥanan. Woe is me because of their whispering.	Woe is me because of the house of Kathros, woe is me because of their pens!
Woe is me because of the house of Ishmail the son of Phiabi.[24]	Woe is me because of the house of Ishmail the son of Phabi, woe is me because of their fists.[25]

Table 12.2: The four priestly houses (families) according to the rabbinic sources

The Burnt House was also destroyed in 70 CE (*War* 6.8–10). In the building was evidence of violence, including black soot on the walls, a spear, and in the kitchen the arm and hand bones of a twenty-five-year-old woman.[26] This house, like the Palatial Mansion and virtually every other house in this neighborhood, had been razed by the Romans in the revolt.

Figure 12.9: Stone weight with Aramaic inscription "*[d'] bar qathros.*"[27]

24. Translation in Neusner, *Tosefta*.
25. Translation in Epstein et al., *Babylonian Talmud*.
26. Arensburg, "Analysis of Human Forearm Bones." He estimated the woman's stature, based on the length of her forearm, at between 5'5" and 5'7", unusually tall for this region and time. See Chapter 11.
27. Image purchased from https://www.ritmeyer.com/.

Other items were also found in the basement of this house, including many stone vessels (Figure 9.3), glass perfume bottles, cooking pots, mortars, measuring cups, and weights. The main excavator asked why there should be so many of these items, much more than a single family would need. He concluded that the basement was a workshop of the priestly family Qathros. He speculated that this family manufactured products for the temple, including "probably spices, incense, or the like."[28] Others have maintained that the family measured agricultural produce given to priests in Jerusalem or perhaps were the *agoranomoi* (marketplace supervisors).[29] At any rate, the family, based on the inscription on the stone weight, on the other stone weights, and on the many ovens in this wing of the house, seems to have been important.

The Burnt House is in the same general area of the city as the Palatial Mansion and other large and luxurious houses that were standing on the eve of the revolt.[30] Based on what can be discerned from the basement or working wing, the dwelling was much smaller than the Palatial Mansion, even if we double the size of the area excavated. Although no luxury items, frescoed walls, or mosaic floors were found in the excavation of this floor (or wing) of the house, Hillel Geva speculates that fine ceramics and other luxuries might lie beneath unexcavated parts of the house, perhaps under those parts extending to the north or east.[31]

There are further discoveries south of the Jewish Quarter excavations. In this same neighborhood is located the traditional site of the house of Caiaphas, now in the Monastery of Saint Savior in the Armenian Quarter of the Old City of Jerusalem (Figure 12.1). Chapter 13 will consider this site more fully. Further southeast of the house of Caiaphas is the Church of Saint Peter in Gallicantu (Figure 13.4) where excavators uncovered a mansion of some 1,600 square feet (more in Chapter 13).

The upper city, then, from the citadel (i.e., Herod the Great's palace) in the northwest (Chapter 14) to the present Church of Saint Peter in Gallicantu in the southeast, was populated by wealthy families who, for the most part, lived in luxurious houses. This is where the chief priests, who interacted with Jesus and later with the Jesus-followers, lived.

---

28. Avigad, *Discovering Jerusalem*, 131.

29. See Geva, "Stratigraphy (Burnt House)," 64; Schwartz, "Bar Qatros." On marketplace supervisors in Jerusalem, see t. B. Metzia 1:14.

30. See Avigad, "Burnt House"; Avigad, *Discovering Jerusalem*, 66–72.

31. Geva, "Stratigraphy (Burnt House)," 34, 64.

THE ELEONA CHURCH

> And when some people talked about the temple and that it had been decorated with beautiful stones and offerings, he (Jesus) said, "These things which you see—the days will come in which there will not be left one stone on another which has not been destroyed." (Luke 21:5-6)

The four Gospels indicate that Jesus and his disciples were often on the Mount of Olives (the hill east of Jerusalem) perhaps because of the prediction in Zech 14:4 that "his [Adonay's] feet will stand on the mount of Olives." It was from this hill that Jesus made his entrance into the holy city just before Passover (Matt 21:1; Mark 11:1; Luke 19:29, 37). The Gospel of John states (18:1-2) that Jesus usually lodged somewhere on the hill when visiting Jerusalem. Luke also affirms that somewhere on this hill Jesus and his disciples found shelter during their final Passover together (Luke 21:37; 22:39). Finally, it was somewhere on the hill that Jesus went to pray in agony[32] a "stone's throw" from a place called Gethsemane.[33] Thus, there were two locations on the Mount of Olives remembered for the night of the arrest: the place of prayer (a stone's throw away) and the place where the disciples stayed (see below).

But the pre-Constantinian church also remembered at least one other site on the Mount of Olives: the place where Jesus was accustomed to gather with his disciples to teach them. The ancient church was intrigued by Jesus' teaching about the destruction of the temple and the cosmic signs of the end (Luke 21:7-36//Matt 24:3-42//Mark 13:3-37). Although Luke does not narrate it, Matthew (24:3) and Mark (13:3) wrote that Jesus gave the mysterious teaching while seated with his disciples on the Mount of Olives. Later, the apocryphal Acts of John 97 (second or third century CE) said Jesus taught his disciples on this mountain while sitting in a cave.

Subsequently, Constantine's mother, Helena Augusta (Sidebar 15.3), built a church over the cave to commemorate the place of Jesus' mysterious teaching.

> Once more, his imperial mother raised a stately structure on the Mount of Olives also, in memory of His ascent to heaven who

---

32. Luke 22:44, a disputed verse. For its textual authenticity, see Metzger, *Textual Commentary*, 177. The committee, at the time he was writing, decided that the verse was not a part of Luke's original text but a very ancient witness. Thus, they included the verse with a C rating. But in the fourth edition of the UBS text, the editors gave the verses an A rating.

33. See Mark 14:32, Matt 26:36 for Gethsemane; Luke 22:41 for "a stone's throw."

is the Saviour of Mankind, erecting a sacred church or temple on the very summit of the mount. And indeed authentic history informs us that in a cave on this very spot the Saviour imparted mysterious and secret revelations to his disciples.[34]

This church, called the Eleona ("olive") church, was built on one of the four holy places in Palestine that Constantine and his mother honored with churches.[35] Eusebius seems to have been convinced that the tradition connecting this cave with Jesus was sound, although he identified the place of secret teaching with the spot of the ascension while other witnesses speak of two different locations.[36]

The Bordeaux Pilgrim saw the church in 333 CE and declared that it was where "the Lord taught the disciples."[37] Aetheria (traveled 381–86) described it as the "Eleona, on the Mount of Olives where is the cave in which the Lord was wont to teach."[38]

Excavations in 1910 revealed the crypt-cave. From the ruins archaeologists could sketch out the plan of the original church. It was much like the Church of the Nativity at Bethlehem, with the cave under the eastern end of the apse. The church measured 230 X 72 feet and the grotto was 21 X 10 feet.[39] The original church was destroyed in 614 by the Persians, rebuilt (Arculf saw a new church there in 670), but then destroyed again by Calif Hakim in 1010 (Sidebar 12.1).[40]

We cannot be convinced about the accuracy of this location for events in the life of Jesus. The ancient church certainly believed in its location, but there is no accompanying archaeological evidence either to confirm it or at least to make it plausible. We know by archaeological ruins that a fourth-century church was located here. That proves the ancient church venerated this spot. It is possible that somewhere in the vicinity of the Eleona Church Jesus and the disciples often gathered for teaching.

---

34. Eusebius, *Vit. Const.* 3.43.

35. Wilkinson, *Jerusalem*, 120 wrote about only three churches, the other two being the Church of the Nativity in Bethlehem and the Church of the Holy Sepulcher in Jerusalem. Finegan, however (*Archaeology*, 30), notes that Eusebius in the *Life of Constantine* 3.26–29, 43, 51, reports that Constantine also built a church at Mamre (Gen. 18:1) to commemorate the pre-existent Christ's appearance.

36. Aetheria consistently (later in the fourth century CE) separated the Eleona and the "Imbomon" (place of the ascension) churches. See e.g., *Pilgrimage* 5.2.

37. Translation in Finegan, *Archaeology*, 166.

38. Translation in McClure and Feltoe, *Etheria*, 65. Aetheria repeatedly refers to the Eleona in this way (pp. 71, 82, 87).

39. Finegan, *Archaeology*, 166; Wilkinson, *Jerusalem*, 121; Bloedhorn, "Eleona."

40. Hoade, *Guide*, 265.

GETHSEMANE

> During the days he was in the temple teaching but during the night he went out and found lodging on the mountain called Olives. (Luke 21:37)

> He went out and came, as was his custom, into the Mount of Olives and the disciples followed him. (Luke 22:39)

We get the impression from several scriptural references that when Jesus and his disciples were in Jerusalem, they often spent the night on the Mount of Olives. Luke tells that he and his disciples spent the night at the Mount of Olives (Luke 21:37) "as was his custom" (Luke 22:39). The Gospel of John seems to indicate the same thing. In the story of the adulteress—which may not belong in the Gospel of John where most English translations place it[41]—Jesus went at night to the Mount of Olives (John 8:1). During Jesus' last Passover, the Gospel of John is explicit. Jesus was in the habit of staying the night somewhere on the Mount of Olives:

> After he said these things, Jesus went out with his disciples beyond the Wadi Kedron where there was a garden into which he and his disciples entered. Judas his betrayer knew the place because many times Jesus gathered there with his disciples. (John 18:1–2)

The Wadi Kedron is a winter stream that separates Jerusalem from the Mount of Olives to the east. Thus, if he and his disciples left the upper room and crossed the wadi, they came to the Mount of Olives. The Gospel of John alleges that Jesus and his disciples went there "many times." Like Luke, John wants us to think of the Mount of Olives as the usual place of refuge for Jesus and his disciples when he was in Jerusalem.

The Gospels of Mark and Matthew also talk about Jesus and his disciples walking from the upper room to the Mount of Olives (Mark 14:26; Matt 26:30) and specifically that "they came into a place the name of which was Gethsemani" (Mark 14:32; Matt 26:36). So, Jesus and his disciples spent the night not only on the Mount of Olives but at a place called Gethsemane, which means "press of olives."[42]

---

41. The section about the adulteress (John 7:53—8:11) has multiple textual difficulties. See Metzger, *Textual Commentary*, 219–23.

42. Heb. *gat shemanim* "vat of oils." See Danker, *Lexicon*; and Taylor, "Garden of Gethsemane." The words do not work out precisely since the Heb. word *gat* usually means "winepress." See Holliday, *Lexicon*. Yet, the word can also mean a vat in general. See Jastrow, *Dictionary*.

Can we identify today the location where Jesus gathered with his disciples during his visits to Jerusalem? Many archaeologists and geographers think we can. They identify it with the cave near the Church of All Nations.

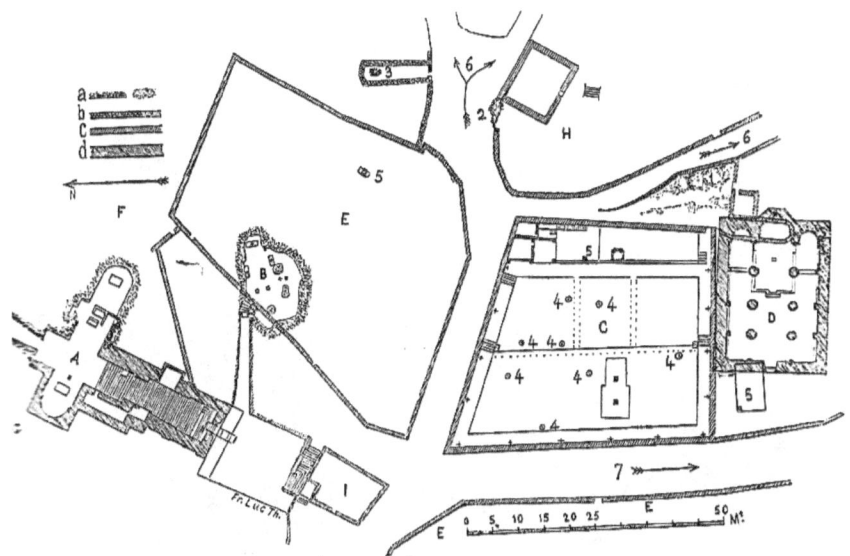

Figure 12.10: Plan of Gethsemane area (from 1909): B on the plan is the cave of Gethsemane; C is the garden; D is the Church of Saint Savior, rebuilt in 1924 as the Church of All Nations[43] (Image courtesy Studium Biblicum Franciscanum, Jerusalem)

Eusebius wrote (330 CE) that up against the Mount of Olives one can still visit the spot where Jesus prayed before his crucifixion.[44] Consequently, a church was built (before 380 CE) called the Church of the Agony, on the spot where pre-Constantinian Christians believed Jesus had prayed during that night. This building evidently featured a rock on which the ancients surmised Jesus had knelt to pray (see Figure 12.12, below). The first visitor we know of to the church was Aetheria. She called this building a "graceful church." Aetheria observed that the church honored two locations: one spot where Jesus prayed and one where he was betrayed and arrested. The place of the arrest was Gethsemane. In the sixth century, Arculf visited the site and reported that near Gethsemane, in a "field," there was a rock on which

---

43. Plan is in Corbo, *Ricerche archeologiche*, 85, and was drawn by Luc Thönessen, who excavated the church in 1909. The structure labeled A is the tomb of the Virgin Mary.

44. Eusebius, *Onomasticon*. See Finegan, *Archaeology*, 175.

Jesus knelt to pray. This church was destroyed in 614 by the Persians. The Crusaders built a new church in 1170, slightly off line from the original. In 1924 a new church was built over the foundations of the old, and called the Church of All Nations.[45]

Figure 12.11: Olive trees near Gethsemane

The olive trees in the garden adjacent to the church, although old, are certainly not from the days of Jesus. In the first place, the Romans, during the First Jewish War cut down all the trees in the Jerusalem area (*War* 5.264). In the second place, these trees do not live two thousand years. Nor is it likely that the church remembered the exact rock where Jesus knelt and prayed, if indeed he actually knelt on a rock. Thus, the rock featured inside the Church of All Nations can scarcely be a reliable location. On the other hand, somewhere in this vicinity ("a stone's throw" away), according to Luke 22:41, Jesus went off to pray on the night of his arrest.

---

45. See Finegan, *Archaeology*, 181–82; Wilkinson, *Jerusalem*, 130; Murphy-O'Connor, *Holy Land*, 147.

Figure 12.12: The "Rock of Agony" inside the Church of All Nations

The cave (see Figure 12.13, below) has much more archaeological confirmation than the other spots in this area. We are looking for a location that could conceivably be named "vat of (olive) oils" as the Gospels of Matthew, Mark, and John call it. None of the Gospels mentions a cave associated with the night of Jesus' arrest. The Gospel of John calls the area a "garden" or "orchard" (*kēpos*; 18:1, 26) while the other Gospels call it simply a "place" (*chōrion*; Mark 14:32//Matt 26:36). Nor did early pilgrims to Jerusalem mention that the traditional site of Gethsemane ("vat of oils") was in a cave.

But beginning in the sixth century these reports increasingly link the oil press with the cave near the Church of the Agony/All Nations. The Piacenza Pilgrim (sixth century) visited the cave and reported there were three "couches" on which Jesus reclined at the Last Supper. Theodosius (sixth century) writes that

> Four couches are there in the place where my Lord reclined in the midst of the apostles, and each couch holds three men . . . and this place is a cave.[46]

In the seventh century, Arculf described the Gethsemane cave:

---

46. Translation in Wilkinson, *Jerusalem Pilgrims*, 66.

On the Mount of Olives there is a cave which faces the Valley of Jehoshaphat. In it are two very deep wells . . . This cave also contains four rock tables.⁴⁷

Arculf, like other pilgrims before him, assumed the stone ledges were couches or tables. Later, in the 12th century, another pilgrim, named Saewulf, described the interior of the cave as having "beds."⁴⁸ The consistent witness of pilgrims visiting the cave near the Church of the Agony then was that inside the cave were some sort of rock ledges, which they assumed were couches for dining or beds for sleeping.

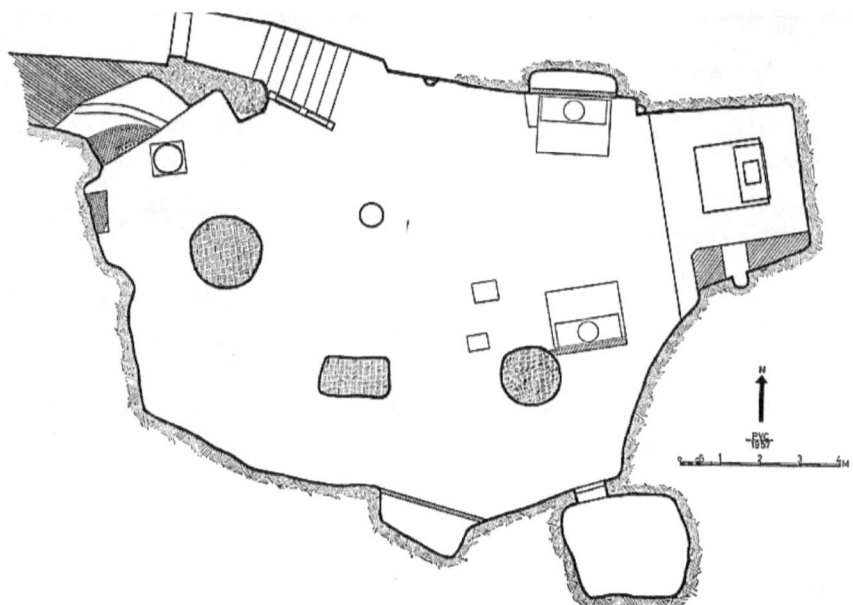

Figure 12.13: Plan of Gethsemane Cave⁴⁹ (Image courtesy Studium Biblicum Franciscanum, Jerusalem)

According to Joan E. Taylor,⁵⁰ the archaeological evidence in the cave supports these pilgrim accounts. Many oil presses at this time were in caves.⁵¹ The cave measures 60 X 36 feet, and its roof is supported by

---

47. Translation in Wilkinson, *Jerusalem Pilgrims*, 99.
48. Taylor, "Garden of Gethsemane."
49. Plan from Corbo, *Ricerche archeologiche*.
50. Taylor, "Garden of Gethsemane." See also Grey, "Olive Processing and Ritual Purity."
51. See Grey, "Olive Processing and Ritual Purity"; Aviam, "Yodefat-Jotapata," 113; and Peterson and Stripling, "Kh. el-Maqatir."

four rock pillars. There is a square, artificial extension in the eastern wall of the cave. This was where an oil press once stood. The evidence for this identification is a niche cut into the south wall of the artificial recess, a hole which once held a beam used to press out oil from baskets of olives. First, olives were crushed (Figure 8.7). Next, they were put into baskets and pressed for oil (Figure 12.14). The beam held stone weights which would weight the basket, squeezing out the oil. This is the technique found in several other oil-pressing installations from the first century in Palestine/Israel. The couches or beds, as the pilgrims named them, were actually—so Taylor surmises—cut into recesses for the olive baskets and the collecting vat. Over the years, these ledges have disappeared.[52] Arculf's description also refers to two "wells." The cave has two cisterns which would have been necessary for the olive processing, according to Taylor.

To these finds Matthew Grey adds the reference to a "cellar" in Virgilio Corbo's excavation account. This feature, on the southeast part of the cave, is considered by Taylor to be a Byzantine or medieval storage room. But Grey dates the storage room, filled with jars of oil during the pressing season, to the first century. The olive oil would have been ladled out from the vats into the jars and then brought into this room for storage.[53]

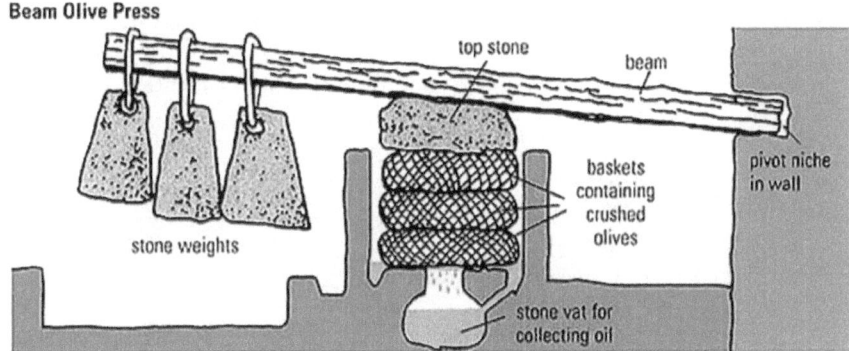

Figure 12.14: Olive press in first-century Palestine/Israel (Image courtesy *BAR*)

There may be, therefore, three archaeological features that argue that this was an oil-pressing cave:

1. a niche for the pressing beam

---

52. I see no reason to doubt that these ledges were dining couches. There are many *triclinia* with stone couches—over which they placed mattresses—left in Greco-Roman ruins. If the cave doubled in the feast season as an inn (see below), why would couches be unlikely? See Osiek, "What Kinds of Meals" for stone couches in *triclinia*.

53. Grey, "Olive Processing and Ritual Purity."

2. a room for oil-vessel storage,
3. water installations.

Since there is no archaeological evidence of oil pressing anywhere else in this vicinity, this cave is quite likely the cave of Gethsemane ("vat of oils"), the place where Jesus was arrested.

Sidebar 12.2

The High Priestly Dynasty of the House of Annas

Luke, in his two references to Caiaphas (Luke 3:2; Acts 4:6), lists his father-in-law, Annas, alongside him. He implies that both were high priest at the same time. The Gospel of John more carefully distinguishes them but still gives Annas prominence. It is likely that Annas, as the founder of the high priestly dynasty, maintained control of the temple. Thus, he was the de facto high priest still. Annas (Heb.: Ḥannan) began a dynasty of the high priesthood that lasted for decades. Several of his sons, his son-in-law, Caiaphas, and one grandson ascended to the high priesthood before, during, and after the ministry of Jesus. The list below gives the names and the years of their high priesthood:[54]

Name of priest	Years as high priest	Reference
Annas	6–15 CE	*Ant.* 18.26
Eleazar ben Annas	16–17 CE	*Ant.* 18.34
Joseph Caiaphas	18–37 CE	*Ant.* 18.35
Jonathan ben Annas	37 CE	*Ant.* 18.95
Theophilus ben Annas	37–41 CE	*Ant.* 18.123
Matthias ben Annas	41–44 CE	*Ant.* 19.313–16
Ananus ben Annas	62 CE	*Ant.* 20.197
Matthias ben Theophilus	65–67 CE	*Ant.* 20.223

Joan E. Taylor[55] surmises that the cave would have been used for pressing only in the fall and winter harvests. In the spring, during the religious festivals of Passover and Pentecost, the owner of the press would have rented out the cave as shelter for pilgrims. During these feasts, hundreds

---

54. See Smallwood, "High Priests"; Stern, "Aspects of Jewish Society."
55. Taylor, "Garden of Gethsemane."

of thousands would have arrived seeking shelter. The spacious cave would have been an excellent temporary dwelling for them.

This plausible hypothesis leads us to ask if there might have been others camping in the cave along with Jesus and the Twelve. A space of over two thousand square feet would accommodate quite a few sleeping on the floor. The intriguing story of the young man sleeping with only a linen cloth who witnessed Jesus' arrest (Mark 14:51–52) might be best explained by other persons in the cave in addition to the Twelve. Chapter 13 will suggest that women (and children) were present at the Last Supper. Were they also sleeping in the cave with Jesus' other disciples? Jesus, according to the Synoptic narratives, went off to pray and three times returned to find the disciples asleep (Matt 26:40, 43, 45; Mark 14:37, 40, 41; Luke 22:45). Were they just lying in the open or were they on their sleeping mats for the night?

Most likely, pilgrims, traveling with rolled-up reed mats on their backs, rented a sleeping space in the cave for a small fee and reclined on the cave floor at night with their *himation* ("cloak") as their cover. It is often chilly at night (cf. John 18:18) in the spring and there can be a heavy dew. Such an accommodation out of the weather would be necessary. Thus, there might have been a rather large crowd—although half asleep—to witness Jesus' arrest.[56]

Matthew Grey[57] accepts that the cave is likely the original Gethsemane (oil vat). He, however, challenges that the two "wells," as Arculf called them, were cisterns. One of the water installations had steps, meaning that it probably was a *mikveh*. Indeed, near the cave two other *mikva'ot* were recently discovered. Grey, therefore, surmises that this area at the foot of the Mount of Olives was a "ritual purity zone" in which pilgrims came to bathe and prepare themselves for entry into the temple. He is doubtless correct about the ritual bath in the cave. *Mikva'ot* were often placed near the processing of liquids in villages and at farms.[58] That this area was a major ritual purification center, however, is, though possible, speculative.[59] Most likely, the ritual bath installations serviced the olive workers.

Thus, it looks like we know the spot where Jesus and his disciples overnighted while in Jerusalem and, therefore, the location of his arrest: the Gethsemane cave. Several scholars have reached this conclusion.[60] The other

---

56. Cf. Taylor, "Garden of Gethsemane."

57. Grey, "Olive Processing and Ritual Purity."

58. See Chapter 9 of this volume and Aviam, "Yodefat-Jotapata," 113.

59. The area south of the temple was replete with ritual bathing installations, and the Pool of Siloam was a very large *mikveh*. Two or three small baths would probably not constitute a ritual purification center.

60. See Finegan, *Archaeology*, 175–81; Murphy-O'Connor, "What Really Happened at Gethsemane?"; Taylor, "Garden of Gethsemane"; Grey, "Olive Processing and Ritual

sites on the Mount of Olives, however, such as the Eleona Church and the Church of All Nations, while possible as places of events in the life of Jesus, are not archaeologically confirmed and cannot command credence.

Sidebar 12.3

Annas the High Priest

- He served as high priest from 6 to 15 CE
- References to him in the New Testament are Luke 3:2; Acts 4:6; John 18:13, 24
- His tomb may have been found. Josephus's description puts the high priest's tomb in the vicinity of Akeldama (south of Jerusalem; *War* 5.505–6).
- A tomb was found in this vicinity decorated with rosettes similar to those gracing the temple area.
- Some think a certain *loculus* or niche in the tomb can be identified as that of Annas because it is decorated with an Attic-style doorway.[61]
- See Figure 15.3 (p. 272) for an interior view of the alleged tomb of Annas.

Purity."

61. Ritmeyer and Ritmeyer, "Potter's Field or High Priest's Tomb?"

13

The Last Supper and the Arrest

Figure 13.1: Madaba Map (east is at the top). The elliptical figure is walled Jerusalem in the sixth century. The basilica on the lower right of the ellipse is the Holy Sion Church. The smaller building to the right of it is, according to some, the Jewish-Christian synagogue or small church built over the ruins of the original upper room.[1]

1. The Constantinian Church of the Holy Sepulcher is in the middle bottom of the ellipse. Photo courtesy Wikimedia Commons (https://commons.wikimedia.org/wiki/File:Madaba_map.jpg)

THE UPPER ROOM

> The day of unleavening[2] came in which they were supposed to eat the Passover (meal). And he sent Peter and John, saying, "Go and prepare for us to eat the Passover." And they said to him, "Where do you want us to prepare it?" He said to them, "As you go into the city, a man carrying a clay jar of water will meet you. Follow him into the house he enters. Say to the householder, "The teacher says, 'Where is the guest room where I can eat the Passover with my disciples?'" He will show you a large, furnished room upstairs." And they went and found it just as he had said to them and prepared the Passover. (Luke 22:7–13)

As Jesus sees the Passover approaching, he instructs Peter and John to find them a place for the meal. The place will be an "upper room." The flat roofs in this period, when the walls were strong enough to support it, often held an upper room, either the full size of the room below or, more often, only as a partial second story.[3] There are numerous references to these second stories, called *'aliyyah* in the Hebrew Bible: Judg 3:20; 1 Kgs 17:19; 2 Kgs 1:2; 4:10.[4]

The Greek equivalents to *'aliyyah* were the words *anagaion* (Luke 22:12, Mark 14:15), "room upstairs";[5] *hyperōon* (Acts 1:13), "upper room"; and *kataluma* (Luke 22:11), "guest room," which can also mean "dining room."[6] In the text above, Luke uses *anagaion* and *kataluma*, both of which Jerome, in his fourth-century CE Latin translation, rendered *cenaculum*. From the Latin term we get the name commonly used today for this building in Jerusalem: the Cenacle.

Traditional village dwellers in Palestine use the upper room of their houses for resting in private, for summer sleeping, and for hosting guests and leaders of the clan.[7] The upper story is cooler in summer and in the winter helps the residents escape some of the barn odors emanating from

---

2. Passover week was not the time to refrain only from leavened bread but from *ḥamētz* (Heb.: "that which has fermented"; Gk.: *zumē*), of any sort, whether food or not. See m. Pes. 3:1.

3. See Safrai and Brunner, "Home and Family" 730; Krauss, *Talmudische Archäologie*, 1:29; and Jdt 8:5, Mark 14:15, Acts 1:3, 20:8, m. Shabb. 1:4, m. B. Batra 2:2–3, m. Ned. 7:4. For an example of a flat roof, see Meyers et al., *Excavations at Ancient Meiron*, 40.

4. See Stager, "Archaeology," 16.

5. Danker, *Lexicon*.

6. Luke 2:7, 22:11, Mark 14:14. See Danker, *Lexicon*.

7. See Dalman, *Haus*, 58–59.

below when the livestock are stalled there. The second story is especially used as a "wedding house" or "honeymoon room" for a son and his wife. They would live there as long as their family size allowed. The upper room could also be reserved for a widowed relative.[8]

In addition, the flat roofs serve as extensions of the courtyard. One can use the roof for eating, praying, drying food, storing items, and sleeping. It is a place apart from the noise of the rest of the household.[9] This was the use of the guest room in Jerusalem that Jesus and his disciples borrowed for the Passover meal.

Many important events in the life of the Jesus-movement happened in an upper room (presumably but not assuredly in the same one): the Last Supper (Mark 14:15//Luke 22:12), some of the resurrection appearances (Luke 24:36–43; John 20:19–29), the pre-Pentecost gatherings (Acts 1:13), the Pentecost outpouring of the Holy Spirit (Acts 2:1–4), and several special meetings of early church leaders (Acts 4:23, 31; 11:2; 12:12; 15:6; 21:17). Some in the ancient church also believed that Mary, Jesus' mother, had died in this same upper room.[10] It would only be natural that the Jerusalem Jesus-followers would want to remember the location of this house and perhaps even to convert the house with its upper room into a house-church. Since this is the location of so many important events, it "may be the oldest place of Christian worship in the world"[11] and was deserving of the epithet, given by the ancient church, "the mother of all churches."[12]

The precise location of the upper room is now impossible to ascertain. We know that a fourth-century church—the Holy Sion Basilica—commemorated the upper room. Did the Holy Sion Church enclose the Cenacle, or was it near the current building called the Cenacle? Archaeology *may* be able to help, but we must be discerning.[13] It is possible that we can at least identify the general area in Jerusalem where the upper room once stood but not necessarily the exact locus which was "the oldest place of Christian worship in the world" and "the mother of all churches." It probably stood on the hill known today as Mount Zion (Sion to the Gk.- and Lat.-speaking

8. Killebrew and Fine, "Qatzrin," 46.

9. Hirschfeld, *Palestinian Dwelling*, 246–47.

10. Arculf, who drew a sketch (rectangular) of the floor plan of the Holy Sion basilica (670 CE), placed on the plan the place where the last supper was eaten, where the Holy Spirit had descended, where Jesus had been flogged, and where Mary had died. See Finegan, *Archaeology*, 235.

11. Wilkinson, *Jerusalem*, 169–70.

12. Said by the Liturgy of Saint James (fifth century CE) and Theodosius (sixth century CE), among others.

13. To date, the most important work on this subject is Clausen, *Upper Room*.

residents), just outside the Zion Gate in the current walls around the Old City of Jerusalem (see Figures 12.1 p. 203 and 15.1 p. 267).

In searching for the original upper room, we need to introduce ourselves to several locations in Jerusalem, both contemporary and ancient (and to the confusing and confused ancient witnesses):

- The Tomb of David is the name of a dubious site that in the Middle Ages came to be identified as King David's burial place. Over this rectangular building—its second story—is the so-called Cenacle, supposedly the spot—not the actual building—where the original upper room was.

- A small "church of God" in existence in the second century CE, is mentioned by Epiphanius of Salamis (315–403 CE), who maintained that when Emperor Hadrian came to Jerusalem (c. 130), he saw a "church of God, which was small, where the disciples . . . went to the upper room."[14] This small church was on the hill of Jerusalem called at that time Mount Sion (but called the upper city in Jesus' time). Some have surmised that three of the walls of what today is called the Tomb of David (the northern, eastern, and southern walls) might have been the walls of this late first- or early second-century church building.[15]

- Alternatively, those same walls of the Tomb of David might be remnants of a first- or fourth-century synagogue. Some Christian pilgrims referred to "seven synagogues" which once stood on Mount Sion, one of which was still standing in the second century.[16] There is in the north wall of the Tomb of David a niche similar to Torah niches in other Jewish synagogues.[17] Bargil Pixner, though, argued for its being not a Jewish synagogue but a Jewish-Christian synagogue.[18] David

14. Epiphanius of Salamis, *Weights and Measures* 14. Translation in Finegan, *Archaeology*, 233. Eusebius, *Dem. ev.* 3.5 also referred to this second-century church. See Clausen, *Upper Room*, 23. See Murphy-O'Connor, "Cenacle" for the description and possible location of this church.

15. See Pixner, "Church of the Apostles"; Finegan, *Archaeology*, 233; Wilkinson, *Jerusalem*, 164. Finegan surmised that the original house with the upper room used by Jesus and the disciples had been turned into a church like the House of Peter at Capernaum. Wilkinson suggested that this small church was destroyed in 303 under the persecution of Emperor Diocletian.

16. Epiphanius of Salamis refers to the seven synagogues along with the little church of God. The Bordeaux Pilgrim (333 CE) recorded that when he visited Jerusalem, only one synagogue (the "little church of God?") was still standing.

17. Hirschberg, "Remains of an Ancient Synagogue." See also the conclusion of Jacob Pinkerfeld (summarized in Clausen, *Upper Room*, 167).

18. Pixner, "Church of the Apostles."

Christian Clausen, however, has effectively refuted any claim that this construction (the ancient walls of the Tomb of David) had ever been a synagogue.[19]

- The Holy Sion Basilica was built in the fourth century CE[20] and destroyed by the Persians in the seventh century. Although the walls of the Tomb of David *might* be a remnant of part of this basilica,[21] most scholars today argue that the Holy Sion Church stood adjacent to the Cenacle (Figure 13.1) and did not enclose it.

Sidebar 13.1

The Size of the Holy Sion Church

Archaeologists can only estimate the size of the fourth-century basilica based on scant remains and comparison with other churches.[22]

Heinrich Renard (1868–1928)	197 X 131 feet
Louis Hugues Vincent (1872–1960)	197 X 203 feet
Mauritius Gisler (1855–1940)	180 X 130 feet

Can archaeology identify the actual house with the upper room where Jesus and his disciples gathered? It cannot. It *may* be able to find slight traces of the ancient church which was built either *over* the ruins of the ancient upper room or *adjacent* to the fourth-century Cenacle. The masonry in the Tomb of David (beneath the building currently labeled the Cenacle or the upper room) is clearly ancient. It could be either Herodian or Byzantine. But one must also ask when the ashlar stone blocks in the Tomb of David were used. Were they originally cut for this building or taken later from a ruin and reused? Archaeological investigation has lately proven that they were reused. Thus, there is no argument that part of the wall of the Tomb of

---

19. Clausen, *Upper Room*, 168–75. He observes that the building had neither stone benches around the interior walls nor columns, features almost universally attested in other synagogues (observations also made by Pixner, "Church of the Apostles").

20. Cyril (313–386), bishop of Jerusalem, spoke in his catechetical lectures of the "upper church" where the Holy Spirit had descended (Wilkinson, *Jerusalem*, 164).

21. Wilkinson, *Jerusalem*, 169–70.

22. For these calculations, see Clausen, *Upper Room*, 139–49.

David is a remnant of the original upper room.[23] Even if the ancient ashlar stones of part of the Tomb of David were cut in the Herodian period, they were reused later, probably in the Byzantine period. At best, this building attests to the fourth-century Christian presence in Jerusalem.

We can offer four conclusions, then, about the location of the upper room, the "mother of all churches": First, in the Byzantine age, they often built churches on sacred sites.[24] Thus, the Holy Sion Church was probably not placed on Mount Zion by accident. This was where (or near where) the ancient church thought the upper room had been located.

Second, church tradition clearly places the upper room on Mount Zion. Aetheria (visited 381–86 CE) wrote in the account of her pilgrimage:

> All the people escort the bishop with hymns to Sion . . . and that passage from the gospel is read where the Lord on the same day and in the same place where the church now is in Sion came in to His disciples when the doors were shut [John 20:19–25] . . . [and] the Acts of the Apostles [Acts 2:1–4] is read where the Spirit came down . . . because that is the place in Sion.[25]

Third, the archaeological evidence points to a fourth-century date for both the Cenacle and the Holy Sion Church. Jacob Pinkerfeld's excavation (in 1951) discerned three strata beneath the floor of the present Tomb of David. In digging test pits in the lowest stratum, two later archaeologists recovered a coin and sherd both dated to the fourth century CE. In 2012 another two probed pits in the courtyard behind the south wall of the Cenacle turned up a fourth-century coin in the mortar between the stones and sherds and produced roof tiles dated second–fourth century CE.[26] To date, nothing from the first century has been recovered from the foundations of the Tomb of David (also known as the Cenacle) on Mount Zion.[27]

Fourth, most archaeologists today agree that the Cenacle was not originally a part of the Holy Sion Basilica. It was built separately, perhaps adjacently, to the basilica, as the Madaba Map may depict it.[28] It appears that

---

23. See Clausen, "Upper Room and Tomb of David."
24. See Clausen, *Upper Room*, 33 and the other churches discussed in this volume.
25. Translation in McClure and Feltoe, *Etheria*, 82–83, 86.
26. See Clausen, *Upper Room*, 151 and 165. Murphy-O'Connor ("Cenacle") makes a similar argument as far as the archaeological evidence.
27. Bargil Pixner's suggestion ("Mount Zion, Jesus, and Archaeology") that the Cenacle was built soon after 74 CE has no archaeological support.
28. Avi-Yonah's conclusion, cited in Clausen, *Upper Room*, 151.

the Cenacle was constructed in the early fourth century and the Holy Sion Church adjacent to it later in the same century.[29]

We may never know the exact location of the upper room since nothing of it remains (as far as we know at present). There is, however, agreement that the Holy Sion Church—and the original upper room—were in this general area, that is, in the region called the upper city of first-century Jerusalem and presently just south of the Zion Gate of the Old City (Figure 12.1). This area is not far from those excavations in the Jewish Quarter of old Jerusalem where so many Herodian-period luxurious houses were found. These results *could* mean that a wealthy family,[30] even a priestly family, owned this house.

> And when the time came, he reclined and the apostles with him.
> (Luke 22:14)

We can now apply some of the insights archaeology and ancient texts have given us in previous chapters. In the Western Hemisphere, we get the impression that the Last Supper was like that in the famous Leonardo da Vinci painting: thirteen men sat upright at a long table. The reality was otherwise. In the first place, the men reclined (see Chapter 11). The Greek word in Luke 22:14 makes clear that they did not sit. The banqueting custom involved reclining, and the Mishnah makes reclining, along with four cups of wine, mandatory at Passover (m. Pes. 10:1).

But, second, there were probably more than just the twelve male disciples present with Jesus at this Passover supper. Passover was a family event. Men, women, and children were supposed to celebrate. At some point, a child must ask the four questions (including, i.e., Why is this night different from other nights? [m. Pes. 10:4]). Passover meal was not a males-only club meeting.

In the book of Exodus, the Passover meal was clearly a family affair. Moses delivered YHWH's instructions to the "whole congregation" (Exod 12:3). Each head of household was supposed to take a lamb to be eaten by the entire family. If the family was too small to eat the entire lamb in one night, they would combine with other households (Exod 12:3b–4). The Torah's instruction, then, was for the entire family to participate.

---

29. Bargil Pixner's suggestion ("Mount Zion, Jesus, and Archaeology") that the Holy Sion Church was constructed in 415 CE is untenable since Aetheria visited it during her late fourth-century pilgrimage.

30. Yet, Pixner ("Mount Zion, Jesus, and Archaeology," 316–17) reported a recent excavation on the southern part of Mt. Zion (near the wealthy section of the city) in which several poorly built houses from the first century were discovered. Thus, the owner of the upper room need not have been wealthy.

Further, the sources from the late Second Temple and Mishnaic periods report that women took part. Philo said all of the Jewish people in Alexandria, Egypt, in the first century CE celebrated the Passover (*Spec. Leg.* 2.145–49). The Mishnah (Pes. 8:1) refers to women and children eating the Passover (lamb). The Babylonian Talmud also mentions the presence of women: "All are bound to (drink) the four cups [of wine], men, women, and children"[31] (b. Pes. 108b). Further, if the son is too young to be tutored by the father in asking the four questions, he must be tutored by the mother (b. Pes. 116a). The Passover was a family event in Judaism.

We should presume, then, that not only the Twelve were present at the meal but many of the Galilean women who followed Jesus as well (see Chapter 5). Even if the meal was not an actual Passover meal—as some contend[32]—it is reasonable that the women were present. Why would Jesus and the disciples exclude those ministering women from this meal? Later, women are present in the upper room (Acts 1:14). Why not this time? Luke mentions only the apostles because only they reclined and because his telling of the story focuses on the men. Although the men reclined along with Jesus as the Mishnah—and custom—demanded, the women and children sat, probably on the floor on mats or rugs. Therefore, our mental picture of this event should be of Jesus and the Twelve reclining on four or five couches, women sitting upright, and children running about, not at all the scene da Vinci dreamed up.

CAIAPHAS

> After arresting (Jesus), they led him away and brought him to the high priest. (Luke 22:54)

Jesus was apprehended at Gethsemane cave and brought first to the high priest's house. The high priest at that time would have been Caiaphas, whose name is given in several references in the New Testament (Matt 26:3, 57; Luke 3:2; John 11:49; 18:13, 14, 24, 28; Acts 4:6). It is interesting that neither Mark nor Luke names the high priest who presided over Jesus' trial (or informal hearing). Luke gives his name as a chronological marker in 3:2 (and later in Acts 4:6) but not during the trial scene itself. Mark never mentions the name of either Caiaphas or his father-in-law, Annas.

31. Translation in Epstein et al., *Babylonian Talmud*. See Standhartinger, "Women in Early Christian," 96.

32. The debate as to whether this meal was truly Passover continues. See Marcus, "Passover and Last Supper"; and Klawans, "Was Jesus' Last Supper a Seder?" for the two views.

The high priest, Caiaphas, also appears in Josephus where he is called Joseph Caiaphas. The first reference to Caiaphas in Josephus states simply that he was appointed high priest: "Josepus the Caiaphas was the successor (to Simon)" (*Ant.* 18.35). The second reference seems to imply that the name Caiaphas was a nickname: "Vitellius released the high priest Josepus called Caiaphas from the high priesthood and instituted Jonathan" (*Ant.* 18.95). The name Caiaphas, meaning "basket" or, possibly, "carrier," seems to have attached itself to the family as a nickname. One epigrapher suggests that somewhere in the family's past this nickname described the type of work the family did.[33]

Further, there are others in Jewish literature with this unusual nickname: There was a man named Elio'eynai son of Qayaf[34] mentioned in the Mishnah (m. Para 3:5). Some opine that this man was the son of Joseph Caiaphas, others that the two were brothers.[35] There was a family called Qifa (t. Yeb. 1:10), referred to in the Tosephta, and a man named Jonathan Qaifa (j. Ma'as. 52a).[36] We also have two ossuaries (below) that name a son and granddaughter of Caiaphas. An extended family, then, bore this nickname throughout the first century CE.

It is now likely that the tomb of some members of this family and perhaps of the high priest himself has been found.[37] South of Jerusalem a *loculus* tomb was discovered[38] with four niches. In it were twelve ossuaries, five of which bore inscriptions. The ossuaries were decorated with typical motifs: rosettes, date palms, and geometric designs. The tomb was for a small family but was in use for a long time as evidenced by the number of ossuaries. Two of the ossuaries had the name Qafa and/or Qayafa. On the first ossuary, on the long side was inscribed *Yehosef bar Qayafa* ("Joseph son of Caiaphas"), and on the narrow side, *Yehosef bar Qafa*, using a variant spelling for Caiaphas. Gathered in this ossuary were the bones of six individuals: two infants, a child aged two to five, a boy aged thirteen to eighteen, an adult woman, and a man aged sixty years. This ossuary was more highly decorated than any of the others (see Figure 13.2, below).

The other ossuary in this tomb with the name Qafa had five individuals of about the same ages as those in the first ossuary, but no adult male. The

---

33. See Reich, "Caiaphas Name"; Josephus, LCL 9:376, footnote a.

34. Was he identical with Elio'eynai son of Cantheras (or, as in some manuscripts, Kithairus or Kithaius) in *Ant.* 19.342 and 20.16? See Josephus, LCL 9:376, footnote a.

35. See Reich, "Ossuary Inscriptions."

36. Reich, "Ossuary Inscriptions." Since Jonathan's father was called Maxima, the additional name, "Qaifa," must be his nickname, observes Reich.

37. Greenhut, "Burial Cave"; Reich, "Caiaphas Name."

38. For *loculus* tombs, see Chapter 15.

inscription on it simply read *Qafa*: i.e., "Caiaphas."[39] Naturally, historians ask, could the bones of the sixty-year-old man in the first ossuary have been those of the high priest who presided as Jesus' trial? Most have accepted that this tomb was for the family of the high priest, but there can be no certainty that this particular ossuary contained his bones.

Helen Bond lists the four common objections to this tomb and this ossuary belonging to Caiaphas, the high priest who presided at Jesus' trial, and his family:

1. If it were the tomb of the high priest, why did it not indicate it somewhere?
2. This is not a very ornate or grand tomb, unlikely for a high priest.
3. One individual in the tomb was buried with a coin in the mouth (they found it in the skull), a pagan custom. Would the high priest's family have done such a thing?
4. Most significantly, the different spellings of the nickname (Qayafa and Qafa) are troublesome. Only the first spelling matches the name given in the Gospels and Josephus.

Bond assesses these arguments and finds them unconvincing,[40] concluding that "the bones of the sixty-year-old male may well have been our one tangible link with a man who played a crucial part in the history of humankind: Joseph Caiaphas."[41] Therefore, some archaeologists may have looked briefly (before reburial) at the skeletal remains of the high priest who presided at Jesus' Sanhedrin trial/hearing. At any rate, those individuals deposited in this tomb probably were related to the high priest since (at least) two of them bore the unusual name Caiaphas.

---

39. The other three ossuaries in the tomb that had inscriptions read: "Mary daughter of Simon," "Salome," and one that simply read "Shm," a puzzle to the epigraphers.

40. Bond, *Caiaphas*, 7–8. Bond answers: Specific references to religious offices on ossuaries are rare. Second, we might expect Caiaphas's father-in-law, Annas (John 18:13), founder of a dynasty of high priests (see Sidebars 12.2 and 12.3) to have an ornate tomb but not necessarily Caiaphas himself. Third, even if Jews borrowed a pagan custom, the borrowing itself does not necessarily mean the custom had the same content for Jews. Finally, the double spelling of the nickname may only mean that the inscriber was a careless one. "None of the objections raised against the tomb, then, is conclusive" (Bond, *Caiaphas*, 8).

41. Bond, *Caiaphas*, 8. Evans, "Excavating Caiaphas" doubts that this is the high priest's tomb. Rousseau and Arav, *Jesus and His World*, 139–42 affirm that it is. Both Reich ("Caiaphas Name") and Greenhut ("Burial Cave") seem inclined to believe that this was the high priest's tomb.

Figure 13.2: Highly decorated ossuary with the name *Yehoseph bar Qayafa* (or Qafa) twice inscribed on it. Inside the ossuary were the remains of six people: two infants, a child between the ages of two and five, a youth aged 13 to 18, an adult female and a man about 60 years old. Was this man the high priest who presided over Jesus' trial before the Sanhedrin?[42] (Photograph by B. R. Burton)

Since this discovery, however, another ossuary has come into light. This was acquired by the Israel Antiquities Authority as an unprovenanced item. It allegedly came from a tomb in the Elah Valley in Judea. The ossuary bears an inscription which reads: "Mariah daughter of Yeshua son of Caiaphas (Qayafa'), priests of Ma'aziah from Beth 'Imri." The ossuary is decorated with two large rosettes but otherwise not distinctive. Scientists from the antiquities authority examined the patina of the ossuary and of the inscription and determined that both were genuine.[43] This conclusion seems to have held.[44] If so, we know something further about the Caiaphas family: They were in the priestly division of Ma'aziah (1 Chr 24:18) and lived in or around a village called Beth 'Imri, possibly in the vicinity of Hebron.[45] The

---

42. Wikimedia Commons: https://commons.wikimedia.org/wiki/File:Kayafa%27s_Ossuary_2.JPG/.

43. Examination showed a "complex process that occurred over a prolonged sequence of time, which is seemingly extremely difficult—if not impossible—to replicate in laboratory conditions." (Zissu and Goren, "Ossuary," 91–92).

44. E.g., Jacobson, "Mariam," accepts it.

45. Zissu and Goren, "Ossuary."

named woman, Mariah, may have been the granddaughter of the high priest who presided at Jesus' Sanhedrin trial.

> After arresting him, they led him away and brought him to the high priest's house. (Luke 22:54).

Finding Caiaphas's house has been a quest for many years. There are two competing locations. One is near the Holy Sion Church (see above), the approximate location—probably—of the upper room used by Jesus for the Last Supper and by the disciples on Pentecost. This location for the house of Caiaphas is in the present courtyard of the Monastery of Saint Savior in the Armenian Quarter. The other site is down the hill from the currently named Mount Zion (Figures 12.1 and 15.1).

As related in Chapter 12, a later high priest named Ananias had a house in the upper city evidently near the royal palace of Agrippa II and Bernice. Since Ananias's house was in that vicinity, historians have assumed that Caiaphas and all the other high priests had houses there as well. Some even speculate that living in or owning a luxurious house was part of the privilege of serving as high priest and that Ananias as well as past and future high priests were granted temporary use of the house while in office.[46] If so, the house Ananias lived in was also the house Caiaphas and his family inhabited for a while. This suggestion is a possibility, but there is no evidence for it. More likely, each high priest had his own house, probably in the upper city (the Armenian and Jewish Quarters of the current Old City) where the well-to-do lived.

Once again, we will appeal to ancient witnesses—both Christian pilgrims and Jerusalem residents—and archaeology to attempt to locate Caiaphas's house. In the fourth century, the house was known but had been destroyed. The Bordeau Pilgrim (333 CE) during his visit to Jerusalem saw the place where the house of Caiaphas "was," implying that it was no longer there but only a ruin. Cyril of Jerusalem (c. 313–386) referred to the house as a ruin.[47]

Theodosius (530 CE) reported that the house of Caiaphas was near the Holy Sion Church. He wrote that the house had been converted into a church named after Peter: "From Holy Sion to the house of Caiaphas, now the church of St. Peter, it is 50 paces more or less."[48] Jerome Murphy-O'Connor calculated the 50 paces at 75 meters (246 feet) and measured this as almost exactly the distance from the Cenacle to the Saint Savior Monastery.[49]

46. See Finegan, *Archaeology*, 242.
47. Cyril, *Catechetical Lectures* 13.38.
48. Translation in Finegan, *Archaeology*, 243.
49. Murphy-O'Connor, "Cenacle."

The Armenian Monastery of Saint Savior lies north of the tomb of David. The monastery was built in the fifteenth century over the ruins of a sixth-century church. This may have been the so-called Church of Saint Peter referred to by the Christian pilgrims.[50] In the courtyard of the Armenian monastery excavators found several luxurious Herodian-period houses.

Magen Broshi, one of the excavators of this area, reported that the houses were Herodian (first century BCE to first century CE) and rose to heights of two or three stories. There were many water installations, including *mikva'ot* and cisterns with vaulted ceilings. He lists some of the small finds: a sword (evidence of the battle in the city in 70 CE), fresco fragments (decorated with birds, flowers, and wreaths), and pottery. There was evidence of wealth in the excavations. Broshi did not indicate how many houses were represented in the excavations, but he accepted the church tradition that placed Caiaphas's house in this area.[51]

Thus, archaeological finds might confirm church tradition that remembered the location of Caiaphas's house. Based on this information, we could compose a narrative in which the house of Caiaphas went to ruin, having been destroyed during the Jewish War like the house of Ananias. Christian pilgrims were shown the ruins over the next few centuries. In the sixth century, they built a church over the ruins to commemorate Peter's denial of Jesus (Luke 23:54–62 and parallels).

But there is a second church, the Church of Saint Peter in Gallicantu ("the rooster's crowing"), that vies today for identification with Caiaphas's house. It is down the hill from the Holy Sion Church (the Cenacle or the Tomb of David; Figures 12.1 p. 203 and 15.1 p. 267). Epiphanius of Salamis (313–403) wrote that the Holy Sion was the upper room and that the house of Caiaphas was nearby, but that there was also another church farther away where Peter wept bitterly.[52] Saewulf (1102) said that a bowshot south of the Holy Sion Church was the Church of Saint Peter in Gallicantu. Daniel (1106) spoke of a deep cave thirty-two steps down a hill where Peter fled to weep after denying Jesus. An anonymous pilgrim (1145) reported that beyond Mount Zion is a church where Peter fled at the rooster-crowing.[53] Thus, the pilgrims reported two locations associated with Peter: where he denied Jesus and the place to which he fled to weep.

50. Finegan, *Archaeology*, 243.
51. Broshi, "Excavations in the House of Caiaphas."
52. Finegan, *Archaeology*, 244.
53. Finegan, *Archaeology*, 244.

Figure 13.3: The Church of Saint Peter in Gallicantu. Does this church sit on the foundations of Caiaphas's first-century CE house?

Archaeologists identified this location and began excavating in 1888, returning in 1911 and 1914. In 1931 a new church was built here (Figure 13.3). Excavations determined that there had been a fifth-century church on this site. That was probably the Church of Saint Peter in Gallicantu, the place traditionally identified where Peter went to weep and repent his denial of Jesus.

Yet, some have maintained since these excavations that this was the house of Caiaphas and that the rock-cut structures under the church—"cellars, cisterns, stables"[54]—preserve the prison where Jesus was held overnight awaiting his trial.[55] But other archaeologists conclude today that these structures were more likely just ancient cisterns or even tombs (see Sidebar 13.2).[56]

Excavations near the church carried out in this vicinity from 1992 to 2000 uncovered several ruins from the late Second Temple period. One excavation area in particular[57] revealed the remains of a mansion from the

54. Murphy-O'Connor, *Holy Land*, 119.

55. See Foreman, "From the Upper Room," 487, who notes this view and rejects it.

56. See Finegan, *Archaeology*, 244; Wilkinson, *Jerusalem*, 133; Hoade, *Guide*, 294.

57. This excavation area is labeled area G on the site plan of Hillel Geva, "Church of St. Peter."

first century. The mansion had several rooms surrounding a courtyard. The rooms had plastered floors and painted, stuccoed walls. Although the report did not indicate the size of the dwelling, from the site plan it looks like it was around 1,600 square feet. The pottery and other finds gave evidence that the house, like the others in the upper city, was destroyed in 70 CE.[58] Such a mansion could also have been a residence of a high priest such as Caiaphas.[59] Thus, there is archaeological evidence that this location is possible for the house of Caiaphas. Yet the Christian traditional witnesses seem to favor the northern location.

Sidebar 13.2

Where Was Caiaphas's House?

Six archaeologists weigh in:[60]

In the current Monastery of Saint Savior	At the Church of Saint Peter in Gallicantu
Jerome Murphy-O'Connor	Bargil Pixner
Jack Finegan	Rainer Riesner
John Wilkinson	Denys Pringle

Figure 13.4: Left: under the church of Saint Peter in Gallicantu in the cistern (or tomb?). Right: wall under the church, which some have alleged was used to hold prisoners waiting for trial by Sanhedrin. Note the highlighted hole in the wall where prisoners were allegedly chained

---

58. Geva, "Church of St. Peter."
59. Geva, "Church of St. Peter."
60. See Clausen, *Upper Room*, 227, n. 17.

14

The Crucifixion

SOME INTERPRETERS BELIEVE THE trial—or one of the trials[1]—before Caiaphas[2] was an official trial and was held in the Chamber of Hewn Stone, a side room of the temple. This room was said in the Talmud (m. Sanh. 11:2; b. Sanh. 88b) to have been the official meeting place of the seventy-one-member great Sanhedrin (as opposed to the smaller bodies of twenty-three members). The room was in the shape of a basilica (b. Yoma 25a) and constructed of "squared stones" (Heb. *gazît*). Samuel Safrai[3] located the Chamber on the south side of the temple (m. Mid. 5:4).[4] If so, this was the sequence of events:

1. Jesus was arrested at or near Gethsemane cave,
2. taken to the house of Caiaphas,
3. taken from there to the Chamber of Hewn Stone in the Temple,
4. taken to the Praetorium,
5. and, finally, to Golgotha.

---

1. Bock, *Luke*, 2:1793, e.g., suggests an inquiry before Annas, an evening meeting with Caiaphas (at his house?), and an official trial with the Sanhedrin on the next morning.
2. Mark 14:53–65; Matt 26:57–68; Luke 22:54–71; John 18:13–24.
3. Safrai, "Temple."
4. Yet b. Shabb. 15a states that forty years before the temple was destroyed (in 70 CE) the Sanhedrin "went into exile" and moved its meeting place somewhere else. Thus, it may no longer have been meeting in the Chamber of Hewn Stone during Jesus' trial, if, indeed, it was an official trial.

Figure 14.1: Model of the Praetorium with courtyard
(according to Michael Avi-Yonah)

PONTIUS PILATE

And the entire crowd rose up and led him to Pilate. (Luke 23:1)

In the past, commentators have assumed that Pilate's seat of governance—the Praetorium[5]—was set up in the Fortress of Antonia (Figure 15.1). The *Via Dolorosa*, the street from the location of this military tower to the Church of the Holy Sepulcher (Figure 12.1), is a favorite walk for Christian pilgrims to Jerusalem. It is not likely, however, that Jesus took that route from the headquarters of Pilate to the place of execution. The Fortress of Antonia was merely an observation tower (to watch over the temple activities) and too small to accommodate the visiting procurator and troops.[6]

Most now conclude that the Jerusalem quarters of the procurator or prefect of Judea were in one of the Herodian palaces. Herod the Great had at

---

5. *Praetorium* is the Lat. term used for the governor's residence and/or a government building in the provinces. See Mark 15:16, Matt 27:27, and John 18:28, 33, 19:9. Luke only used the term in Acts 23:35 of the residence in Caesarea.

6. Gibson, *Final Days*, 91 measured the foundations (all that remains of the tower of Antonia) at 90 X 40 meters (295 X 131 feet).

his disposal the old Hasmonean palace lower down the hill from the upper city. But to this he added his own construction to the west and up the hill along with three towers (Phasael, Hippicus, and Mariamme, *Ant.* 15.318; *War* 5.176-81) and gardens to the south.[7] Josephus presents a summary description of its grandeur, writing that the palace included

1. high walls and three towers,
2. banqueting halls,
3. many bedchambers,
4. colored, imported stones for decoration,
5. wooden beams,
6. a variety of designs,
7. porticoes,
8. large gardens,
9. water pools, and
10. columbaria.[8]

It is probable that the Roman procurators who later administered Judea and who lived for the most part in Caesarea (Maritima) resided in one of these palaces when in Jerusalem. They would come to the city in times of stress such as for the pilgrim feasts to oversee the events. During those times, the huge crowds would have been more likely to start something violent. Jack Finegan[9] leans toward the conclusion that Jesus was tried before Pilate in the lower palace (the old Hasmonean palace) of Herod. Most[10] prefer the upper or western palace. At any rate, few name the Fortress of Antonia—in the northwest corner of the temple—as the place of Jesus' trial.[11]

The western palace, second only to the Temple in Jerusalem for its grandeur, has left behind few ruins. What excavators have uncovered, however, can help us imagine the massive construction. Excavators have located some of the retaining walls "with massive earth fills between them which

---

7. Finegan, *Archaeology*, 249 calculates that Herod built his luxury palace around 24–23 BCE.

8. Summary in Peleg-Barkat, "Herod's Western Palace," 60.

9. Finegan, *Archaeology*, 249. Finegan observes that the Christian tradition, from pilgrims, points to the lower palace.

10. Gibson (*Final Days*, 91 and "Trial of Jesus," 108) observes that there is a consensus that the trial took place in the upper palace constructed by Herod the Great himself. Wilkinson, *Jerusalem*, 138–41 agrees.

11. Gibson, "Trial of Jesus," 108.

formed a raised platform (podium) for Herod's palace." A massive sewer drain (twenty-one feet from floor to ceiling) was uncovered, doubtless the sewage system for the famous Bethso.[12]

But the more recent finds of monumental ionic columns (bases, drums and fragments of capitals) indicate the beauty of this palace.[13] The foundations, visible here and there, afford a rough idea of its size. The palace was, according to one estimate, a square of approximately 460 feet (212,000 square feet).[14] The palace stretched from the citadel in the north through the Armenian Gardens in the south in the current Old City of Jerusalem (Figure 12.1). It was apparently torn down completely in the sixth century CE. In Jerusalem's Old City today visitors to the citadel find walls and foundations from the Hasmonean and Herodian periods along with Byzantine and Early Islamic remains.[15]

Shimon Gibson has speculated that the so-called Essene Gate mentioned by Josephus (*War* 5.145) was actually the gate into the middle of this massive palace on the west. He further opines that Jesus' trial at the *lithostrōtos*[16] (John 19:13) "stone pavement," was in the courtyard separating the inner gate from the outer Essene gate. He believes that Pilate would have governed in the middle of the gate to protect observant Jews from impurity (by entering his unclean residence).[17]

Therefore, one must visualize Jesus' trial and subsequent walk to the cross, his *via Dolorosa*, as taking place at one the palaces of Herod (probably the upper palace or the citadel). The walk from the upper palace would have been a shorter distance than the route from the Fortress of Antonia.

Herod built in Caesarea (Maritima) a Roman-style theater (with a spectator capacity of five thousand) for producing Greek and Roman dramas.[18] More important to New Testament students than the entertainment value of the theater is the inscription found in one of the stones used to

---

12. Broshi and Gibson, "Excavations," 152–53. The Bethso (Heb.: *bet ṣo'a*, "place of sewers") is mentioned by Josephus (*War* 5.145).

13. Peleg-Barkat, "Herod's Western Palace," 58, 63. See also Peleg-Barkat and Haim, "Monumental Ionic Columns." In Area Q (see Figure 12.3 p. 205) excavators found more ionic columns which may have come from Herod's palace.

14. According to Gibson, *Final Days*, 92; Gibson, "Trial of Jesus," 110. For varied estimates of its size, see Peleg-Barkat, "Herod's Western Palace."

15. Murphy-O'Connor, *Holy Land*, 25–28.

16. Called in Aram. *gabbatha* "hill" (John 19:13). See Jastrow, *Dictionary*.

17. Gibson, "Trial of Jesus," 112–17.

18. Porath, "Vegas"; Patrich, "Caesarea," 153. But see Bull, "Caesarea," 113, who writes that the theater only held 4,000 persons.

repair its steps. A stone had been moved from its original place and reused in a late repair of the theater. The stone contained a Latin inscription:

> Pontius Pilate, the Prefect of Judea, has dedicated to the people of Caesarea a temple in honor of Tiberius.[19] (see Sidebar 14.1)

It had been, then, a dedicatory inscription for a structure, a temple or edifice "associated with the imperial cult,"[20] in honor of Emperor Tiberius (reigned 14–37 CE). Later, when the theater needed repairs, the workers pulled up the stone and moved it to the steps of the theater. The Judean governor who sentenced Jesus to death is named in this inscription.

Sidebar 14.1

The Pilate Inscriptions

- Dimensions: 80 X 68 X 20 centimeters
- Medium: hard limestone[21]
- Date: sometime between 26–36 CE (Pilate's prefecture)
- Language: Latin
- Historical significance: A character described in the four Gospels is archaeologically named.
- Pilate is also mentioned by the Roman historian Tacitus and by Jewish authors Philo and Josephus.[22]
- Below, photograph and sketch of the ring with Pilate's name inscribed.

(Photograph by B. R. Burton)[23]

19. Translation in Bull, "Caesarea," 113. See also Rousseau and Arav. *Jesus and His World*, 225–27.

20. Gibson, *Last Days*, 87.

21. Dimensions given by the Israel Museum: https://www.imj.org.il/en/collections/395572/.

22. See Josephus, *War* 2.169–77; *Ant.* 18.55–64, 85–89; Philo, *Legat.* 299–305; Tacitus, *Ann.* 15.44.

23. Wikimedia Commons: https://commons.wikimedia.org/wiki/

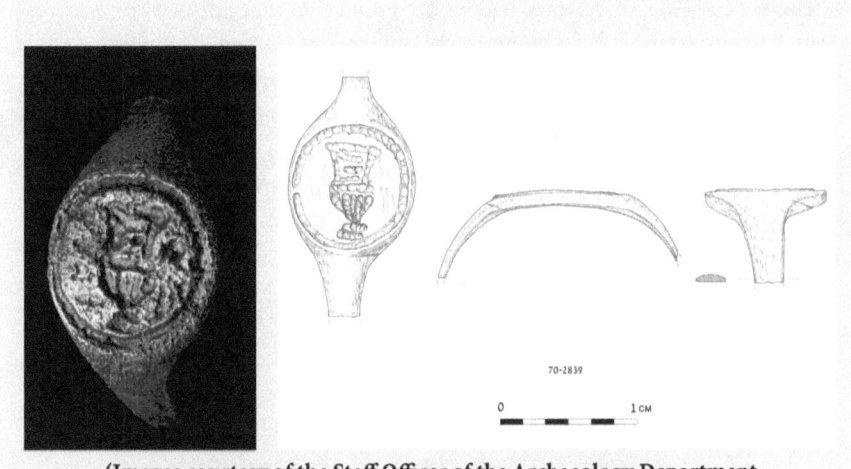

(Images courtesy of the Staff Officer of the Archaeology Department
of the Civil Administration in Judea and Samaria and the IAA
Photographic Department. Drawing: J. Rodman; Photo: C. Amit)

There now may be a second inscription referring to Pontius Pilate. Excavations of Herodium (Figure 2.6) in 1968–69 unearthed a cheap copper finger-ring (signet ring). The inscription on the ring was difficult to read, but using RTI photography,[24] the excavators deciphered it as: *Pilato[u]*; "of Pilate."[25] Some excavators doubted that this ring belonged to Pilate himself, since it was not made of gold and had no jewels encrusted in it. More likely, they maintained, it was the ring of a slave or freedman of Pilate, a member of Pilate's government, or a member of Pilate's family.[26] Other scholars suggested that Pilate himself wore it as his everyday ring (signet ring) as opposed to an ornate one he reserved for formal occasions.[27] The date of the ring (first century BCE–early first century CE)[28] matches the time Pontius

---

File:Pontius_Pilate_Inscription.JPG/.

24. I.e., Reflectance Transformation Imaging.

25. Literally "*Pilato*," using Gk. characters. In Gk. this ending means nothing. It is possibly a Lat. word (dative case, "belonging to Pilate," see Graves, "Pilate's Ring") using the Gk. alphabet or, alternatively, as a genuine Gk. spelling, a final upsilon is missing (*Pilato[u]*, "of Pilate," see Amorai-Stark et al., "Finger Ring").

26. Amorai-Stark et al., "Finger Ring"; Graves, "Pilate's Ring"; Jarus, "Ring"; and Cargill, "Pilate's Ring." Cargill's suggestion: The ring was worn by "some papyrus-pusher working for Pilate."

27. "Ring of Pontius Pilate."

28. The ring was discovered in fill along with pottery, glass, and other metal objects from this period although Amorai-Stark et al. ("Finger Ring," 216, 218) also concede

Pilate was in Palestine/Israel. The name Pilate was rare, argued the excavators, making it unlikely to be just a coincidence of names.

But recently two other historians have challenged the previous interpretation of the ring.[29] These scholars argue that the krater depicted on the ring (see figures within Sidebar 14.1, above) was a Jewish symbol, not the symbol of a Roman prefect. This fact plus finding the ring at Herodium argues, they maintain, that it was a Jewish ring. They suggest reading the inscription on the ring as abbreviations for two words or names: *Pi . . . lato[mos];* or "Pi the stonecutter."[30]

The debate over the inscription of the ring will likely be on-going for some time, and there can be no prediction as to where the consensus will land. We *may* have a second archaeological reference to Pontius Pilate, or it may amount to nothing at all that is relevant to the life of Jesus.

BEARING THE CROSS

> As they led him, they laid hold of Simon, a certain Cyrenian,
> who was just then coming from the countryside. (Luke 23:26a)

This family may be known to us today through eleven ossuaries found in Jerusalem (Sidebar 14.2). Mark 15:21 gives not only the name Simon, but the names of his two sons, Alexander and Rufus. The author of Mark may have given the names of the sons because one or both them were known to his Christian community (see Rom 16:13 for Rufus).

The tomb in which the eleven ossuaries were deposited is located south of the current Silwan village, southeast of the Old City. Ossuary 9 of this tomb was inscribed on several sides to identify the bones. The deceased was named "Alexander QRNYT," possibly meaning from the city of Cyrene, and he was the "(son) of Simon." Ossuary 5 in the tomb was inscribed with: "(ossuary) of Sarah the daughter of Simon of Ptolemais." Since both Cyrene and Ptolemais are cities in the Roman province of Cyrenaica (northern Africa), some have concluded that this is the tomb of a family from that location. The two identifiers (Simon's son's name, Alexander, and his place of origin) make it plausible that this is Simon's son's ossuary and that we therefore have the bearer of Jesus' cross named archaeologically.

---

the ring could be dated as late as 71 CE.

29. Eck and Ecker, "Signet Ring."

30. Eck and Ecker, "Signet Ring," 94. The name "Pi" would be an abbreviation of Pikos, Pittakion, or the like.

There is a third indicator that this may be the tomb of the family of the bearer of Jesus' cross. The epigrapher who interpreted the inscriptions on the ossuaries noted repeatedly that many of the names etched on them were common for the province of Cyrenaica but rare in Israel at this time. It seems probable that this extended family originated from the diaspora, specifically from the province of Cyrenaica (in which the city of Cyrene was located).[31] The family later became important members in the Jesus-movement and, therefore, was remembered by Mark (15:21).[32]

Sidebar 14.2
Simon of Cyrene mentioned on an ossuary?

- The tomb is in the Kidron Valley, south of the Silwan village
- The pottery found in the tomb indicates the burials took place in the first century CE.
- Of the eleven ossuaries in the tomb, nine were inscribed with names and identifiers.
- Ossuary number 9 (see photo below) contained the bones of Alexander, who is further identified as the son of Simon in Greek and "Alexander QRNYT" in Hebrew. The epithet QRNYT could mean he was a Cyrenian.[33]
- Ossuary 5, containing the bones of "Sarah, daughter of Simon" evidently informs us of another member of Simon's immediate family.
- Cyrene was a city on the coast of northern Africa in the province of Cyrenaica.
- Several names in this tomb were common in Cyrenaica but rare in Israel at this time.
- Most of the inscriptions are in Greek but one (number 9) is bilingual.

---

31. Avigad, "Depository."

32. See Finegan, *Archaeology*, 361–63; Evans, *Jesus and the Remains*, 63–64.

33. Avigad, "Depository," offered another interpretation: a plant (thus this may be a nickname denoting Simon's trade). He seemed to lack confidence in this understanding, however. He also suggested that the inscriber miswrote a final tav for a hey. Thus, QRNYT should be QRNYH, *qoraniah*, or Cyrene.

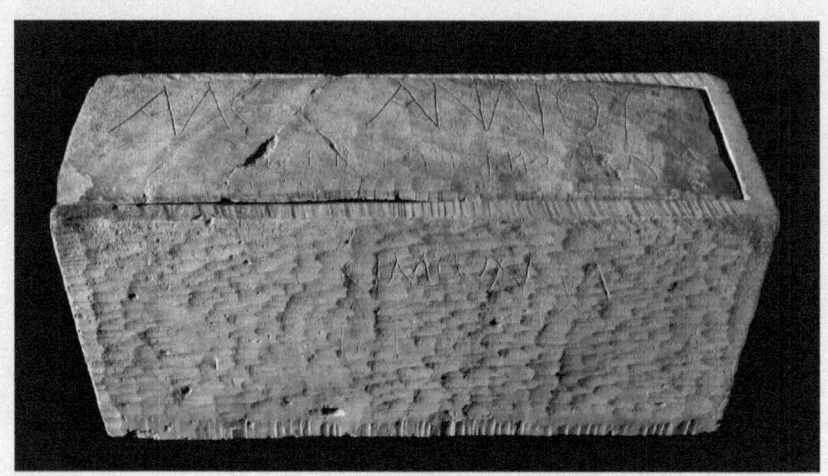

On the lid, top line: ΑΛΕΞΑΝΔΡΟΥ

On the lid, bottom line: אלכסנדרוסקרנית

(Image courtesy of the Institute of Archaeology, the Hebrew University of Jerusalem. Photo by Gabi Laron)[34]

> They put on him (i.e., Simon) the cross to carry following Jesus. (Luke 23:26b)

The victim did not carry the entire cross but was often compelled to carry his crossbeam (Lat.: *patibulum*) to the place of crucifixion. The following selections demonstrate this practice:

> I believe that you will soon go out the gate in that direction led with hands spread out on the *patibulum* which you will have.[35]

> They (convicted criminals) are bound to the *patibula*. They are bound and led around and fixed to the cross.[36]

---

34. Ossuary, Inventory No. HUJI 1965.
35. Plautus, *Mil. glor.* 359; translation in Cook, "Envisioning," 267.
36. Clodius, *History*; text in Cook, "Envisioning," 267.

> He carries the *patibulum* through the city and then is fastened to the cross.[37]

> When you become old, you will stretch out your hands and someone will bind you and carry you where you do not want (to go).[38]

In the last quote, Jesus is describing Peter's manner of death and specifically his being bound to the crossbeam and led to crucifixion. Consider also Jesus' admonition to his followers to "take up their cross" and follow him (Matt 16:24; Mark 8:34; Luke 9:23). Finally, we have the statement from the Gospel of John which describes Jesus as "carrying his own cross" to the place of execution (19:17) while the Synoptic Gospels state that the executioners compelled Simon of Cyrene, at some point, to carry Jesus' crossbeam (Matt 27:32; Mark 15:21; Luke 23:26). The condemned person carried the crossbeam, to which their hands or arms were nailed and/or tied, and then the crossbeam was attached to the upright stake (a pole or a tree).[39]

SKULL

> And when they came to the place called "Skull," . . ." (Luke 23:33a)

The other three Gospels give the Aramaic name of the place of crucifixion: *Golgotha* (Matt 27:33; Mark 15:22; John 19:17). The Latin equivalent is *calvarius*, hence the name Calvary. Why it was called Skull is not known. Some suggest the place itself looked like a human skull;[40] others that the entire topographical region had the appearance of a human skeleton with a hill as the head; and others that the closely parallel Hebrew term in the Mishnah, *bet gilgol* "place of hills and depressions" (m. Toh. 6:6), accurately describes a quarry, which is what the area had become (see below).[41] Perhaps the best

---

37. Plautus, *Carbonaria*, Fragment 2. Text in Chapman and Schnabel, *Trial*, 284.

38. John 21:18.

39. For other texts on the victim carrying his/her crossbeam, see Chapman and Schnabel, *Trial*, 282–92; and van Wingerden, "Carrying a *stauros*."

40. Bock, *Luke*, 2:1849 and see Gordon's *Calvary*, Figure 15.9, below (p. 286). Foreman ("Locating Jesus' Crucifixion," 506) observes that some envision the back of the skull, thus a knob or hill, and others the front of a skull, thus two caves resembling eye sockets.

41. See the survey of views in Kelley, *Holy Sepulchre*, 72.

hypothesis is simply that crucifixions and other executions took place there.[42] We should point out that nowhere in the Gospels is Golgotha described as a hill; it is called everywhere simply a "place" (*topos*).[43]

Figure 14.2: Jerusalem model (after Avi-Yonah) showing the quarry west of the second wall with the rock monolith that now stands in the Holy Sepulcher Church surrounded by houses that were built later. The quarry area in the model is too small. See Figure 14.3, below p. 252.

We have clues from various New Testament references as to the location of Skull. They say the place of execution was

- outside the gates (Heb 13:12),
- near the city (John 19:20),
- near a road or path (Mark 15:12) since Simon of Cyrene, who was walking by, could be commandeered to carry Jesus' cross.[44]

Today, visitors to Jerusalem see a rock monolith inside the Church of the Holy Sepulcher and not far from the alleged tomb of Jesus. Marcel Serr and Dieter Vieweger present three arguments that this monolith "could well be authentic," marking the actual spot of Jesus' crucifixion:

42. As Finegan, *Archaeology*, 261; Gibson and Taylor, *Holy Sepulchre*, 59; and Foreman, "Locating Jesus' Crucifixion," 506 offered.

43. Matt 27:33, Mark 15:22, Luke 23:33, John 19:17.

44. See Corbo, *Sepolcro* 1:28.

1. It is true that they would not have crucified anyone inside the walls of Jerusalem (where the Church of the Holy Sepulcher now stands). The vast stone quarry found underneath the church, however (see below), indicates that this area was outside the city wall in Jesus' time. The Second Wall must be somewhere east of today's Church of the Redeemer (Figure 15.7).

2. The Gospels tell us that the place of Jesus' crucifixion was surrounded by gardens or fields (Mark 15:21; Luke 23:26; John 19:41, 20:15). Corbo's excavations showed that the stratum above the quarry had traces of gardens or fields and can be dated to the first century A.D.

3. Golgotha was probably at a high elevation that was greatly visible as mentioned in Mark 15:40, Matthew 27:55 and Luke 23:49. The difference in height between the "garden" stratum and Golgotha in the Holy Sepulcher is considerable.[45]

That the rock outcropping in the church is the actual Golgotha, however, is contested by Shimon Gibson and Joan E. Taylor. The shape of the monolith itself argues against it. It is both too small on its peak and too high. The top of the rocky crag measures 5 ½ feet from east to west and 12 feet from north to south. That space seems too tight for the three crucifixions the Gospels narrate. It also stands 41 feet on the east above the surrounding rock, 29 feet above the surroundings on the north, and 16 feet above rock to the west. It is, according to Gibson and Taylor, too high and steep for crucifixions.[46]

---

45. Serr and Vieweger, "Golgotha," 29.
46. Gibson and Taylor, *Holy Sepulchre*, 57–59.

Figure 14.3: The rock (center of photo) inside the Church of the Holy Sepulcher alleged to be Golgotha. Could it support three crosses? (Image inspired by the work of Guy Couturier)[47]

On the other hand, Corbo maintains that the rock monolith measured by Gibson and Taylor was originally larger. It was cut back by Constantine when he built his basilica in the early fourth century. Thus, the hill of Golgotha would have been able originally to accommodate three crosses.[48] Corbo's plan of the alleged Golgotha inside the Church of the Holy Sepulcher is as follows:

---

47. Wikimedia Commons, https://commons.wikimedia.org/wiki/File:Golgotha_et_sa_chapelle_HEB.jpg/.

48. Corbo, *Sepolcro*, 2:67.

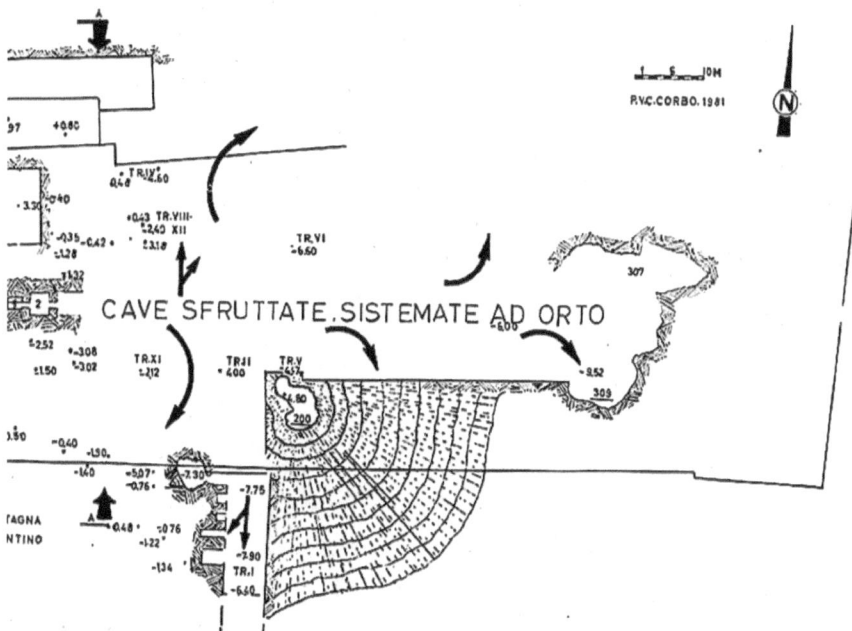

Figure 14.4: The original condition of Calvary/Golgotha (#200) according to Corbo. The rock rose gradually to a height of 16 feet but was cut away, isolating the exact spot of the crucifixion when Constantine erected the Church of the Holy Sepulcher, according to Corbo.[49] (Image courtesy Studium Biblicum Franciscanum, Jerusalem)

So, which view is correct? One inclines toward Gibson's and Taylor's view. Even if the monolith was larger before Constantine's construction, the placement of three crosses here seems problematic. Would Constantine's stone masons have cut down the original hill into the shape this monolith is now? One would expect a symmetrically cut monolith not the very irregular outcropping that is there now. Gibson and Taylor suggest that the odd shape of the monolith was made because the stone in this vein was unsuitable for building and thus was merely left by the quarriers.

The context for the monolith is also problematic. It is only c. 130 feet from the tomb of Jesus and even closer to another first-century tomb found under the south atrium of the crusader reconstruction of the Holy Sepulcher.[50] The area seems to have been a cemetery, not a place of execution (see Chapter 15). One might expect a common place of execution to have been near a pauper's mass grave site not in the middle of rather nicely cut rock tombs.

49. Corbo, *Sepolcro*, 2:67. The caption in the center of the plan reads: "Quarry systematically exploited for a garden." The tomb of Jesus is #1 on the plan.

50. See Corbo, *Sepolcro*, 2:67; 3.4–5.

Third, the site had been since the Iron Age a stone quarry—later also a cemetery—measuring 980 feet north to south and 492 feet east to west. The Church of the Holy Sepulcher sits about in the middle of the old quarry.[51] That locus would be rather far away for passersby entering the Gennath Gate into the city (Figure 14.5) to observe the execution. Yet, the Gospels indicate that people came out to watch (Mark 15:29; Matt 27:30; Luke 23:35).

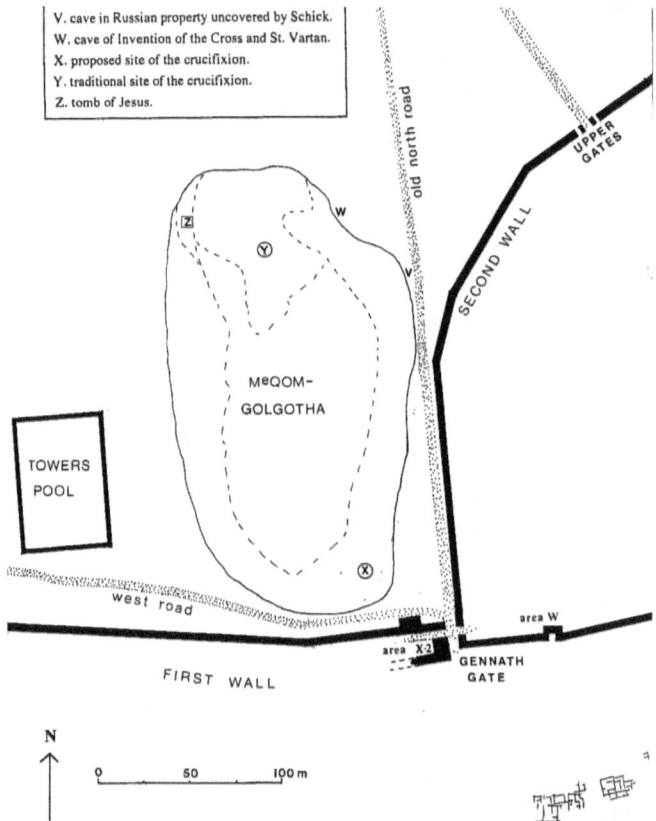

Figure 14.5: The suggested location of the crucifixion (X) compared with the traditional site (Y), according to Taylor.[52] (Figure courtesy Joan Taylor)

Gibson and Taylor inform that in the city of Rome there was a spot commonly used for executions (just outside the Esquiline Gate; Tacitus, *Ann.* 2.32). They suggest that Jerusalem also had such a place: the entire old quarry area called in Aramaic Golgotha. Although the outcropping in

---

51. Corbo, *Sepolcro*, 1:29 and 2:67; Cabaret, *Topography*, 12–14.
52. Map from Taylor, "Golgotha," 185.

the Church of the Holy Sepulcher would be c. 295 feet west of the supposed north wall or second wall of Jerusalem (thus outside the city), thus making it theoretically possible for the crucifixion site, we should probably conclude that the execution was somewhere in the southern part of the old quarry.[53]

CRUCIFIXION

> They crucified him and the criminals, one on his right and the other on his left. (Luke 23:33b)

Estimates are that the Romans crucified at least thirty thousand persons from the Second Punic War to the time of Constantine, of which we know the names of around twenty.[54] It was the terrorist weapon of choice.[55] We have known texts about crucifixion for centuries, some with only vague hints about how it was done, and, sometimes, others with more explicit descriptions. Now, with the help of archaeology—both inscriptions (from crude graffiti to artistically depicted scenes) and excavations of crucified persons—we can expand on our knowledge of this gruesome and barbaric form of execution. John Granger Cook, who has written one of the definitive works on the subject, has summarized his results:

1. Crucifixion was the punishment of slaves and severe criminals.
2. Crucifixion was done by "a public executioner or a military authority."
3. Various tortures could precede crucifixion.
4. The victims often walked in chains to the place of the "stake."
5. The victims might be "patibulated," i.e., forced to carry the crossbeam (not the whole cross).
6. The victims would be stripped though not always completely naked.
7. Ropes or nails (sometimes both) fastened the victim to the crossbeam and stake.
8. Victims were crucified in various positions.

---

53. See Gibson and Taylor, *Holy Sepulchre*, 57–59; and Kelley, *Holy Sepulchre*, 72. Gibson and Taylor suggest a spot near the Gennath Gate as the place of execution (Figure 14.5). For the layout of the Constantinian Church of the Holy Sepulcher, see Figure 15.10 (p. 291).
54. Cook, "Roman Crucifixions"; Cook, *Crucifixion*, 160.
55. Tombs, "Crucifixion"; Adams, "Crucifixion."

9. A magistrate read from a placard the charge against the victim and this placard could be placed on the cross.
10. The bodies of crucifixion victims might be either left on the cross to decompose or given to families for burial.[56]

This summary is about right, although one may add or subtract here and there. What follows here, then, will essentially agree with these ten summary statements. First, we give a selection of texts; next we present ancient depictions of crucifixions; finally, we offer the example of two crucified victims known to us through archaeology.

Texts

Some of the texts that are useful in determining how the Romans crucified are as follows:

> Punished on their tortured (bodies), they see the stake (i.e., cross) as their fate. In the bitterest of torment, they have been fastened with nails, (to become) evil banquets for birds and terrible scraps for dogs.[57]

This brief yet thorough description tells us that crucified persons were in a state of torture, that they were attached to their crossbeam and perhaps the wooden post or tree by nails, and that their corpse often was left to scavenger animals.

A picture of torture both before and during crucifixion comes from statements by Seneca:

> [Pre-crucifixion] . . . racks, the hook, men thrust through the middle until the stake emerges from the mouth, bodily limbs torn apart by chariots going in opposite directions, the tunic smeared with flammable substances . . .[58]

> [During crucifixion] I see crosses not only of one sort but made in various ways. Some [executioners] hang [their victims] upside

---

56. The list is compiled in Harley, "Crucifixion," 317 summarizing Cook, *Crucifixion*, 423–30. Cf. on most of these items Chapman and Schnabel, *Trial*, 284–85, 487, 665–71.

57. Ps-Mantheo 4.198–99. Gk. text in Hengel, *Crucifixion*, 9.

58. Seneca, *Ep.* 14.5. Lat. text in Seneca, LCL; translation by Gummere in Seneca, LCL.

down; others drive stakes through the genitals (of the victims); still others extend (the victims') arms on the *patibulum*.⁵⁹

These texts leave the reader with the impression that crucifixion could be accompanied by many other tortures. They also might involve sexual humiliation and assault.⁶⁰ As a rule, the more the victim was tortured before crucifixion, the less time he took to die on the cross. This might mean that Jesus, since he was on the cross for only about six hours, according to the Synoptic Gospels (Mark 15:25, 34; Luke 23:44), was tortured significantly before the actual crucifixion.⁶¹

The victims were often executed without clothing, though not always totally naked. This evidently was both to make them more susceptible to blows and to increase their shame.⁶² Melito, second-century CE bishop of Sardis, wrote in his sermon on the passion of Christ: "The Sovereign has been made unrecognizable by his naked body, and is not even allowed a garment to keep him from view."⁶³ Thus, Melito knew, because people of his day had witnessed crucifixions, that the victims were often executed without clothing. The reader should also consider the Seneca quote above informing that the genitals of the victim were sometimes impaled and also the gemstone depiction of Jesus' crucifixion (below), which presents him totally unclothed. The Synoptic Gospels indicate that Jesus was stripped of his clothes (Matt 27:35; Mark 15:24; Luke 23:34). Yet, that victims were always completely naked is debatable. The Jewish sources (m. Sanh. 6:4–6; Sifre on Deut 21:22, par. 221) demanded a piece of cloth to cover the genitals of execution victims.⁶⁴ In the graffito from the Palatine in Rome (below), the crucifixion victim wore a tunic. Thus, it is not certain that Jesus was crucified completely unclothed.

Ancient Depictions

One of the depictions of crucifixion that has survived from the ancient world is a graffito evidently mocking Christians, discovered in 1856 on the Palatine hill in Rome. Under the crude drawing are the words "Alexamenos worships god."

59. Seneca, *Dial.* 6.20.3. Lat. text in Hengel, *Crucifixion*, 25.

60. Tombs, "Crucifixion"; Adams, "Crucifixion," 117–18. See Seneca, *De Ira* 3.3.6 for other precrucifixion tortures.

61. See Adams, "Crucifixion."

62. Artemidorus, *Onirocriticon* 2.53; Dionysius of Halicarnassus, *Ant. rom.* 7.69

63. Melito, *Passion* 97; translation in Hall, *Melito*, 55.

64. See Chapman and Schnabel, *Trial*, 674.

Figure 14.6: Alexamenos worships god.⁶⁵

This drawing's date is uncertain (probably sometime between the first and third centuries CE).⁶⁶ The figure on the cross has the head of a donkey (in mockery), but the drawing may depict some accurate details about crucifixion. First the arms are stretched out to the sides, evidently attached to the crossbeam (*patibulum*). Second, the figure is raised a bit off the ground. In this drawing, however, the figure seems to have a platform to stand on. There are no such platforms attested in the literature.⁶⁷ Also as Cook notes, the crucified figure is wearing a short tunic, in contrast to the literary sources that sometimes indicate that the victims were crucified

---

65. Courtesy Wikimedia Commons: https://commons.wikimedia.org/wiki/File:Alexorig.jpg/.

66. Adams, "Crucifixion," 113 affirms a date of 225 CE.

67. Schneider, "*stauros, stauroō*," 573.

naked.[68] Finally, the victim's feet seem to straddle the stake, a position attested in other depictions and in the inferred evidence from skeletal remains, but do not appear to be nailed to the stake.

There are even attested cases of women being crucified. Cook[69] has noted one such case. Josephus reports a story of a freed woman who was crucified for helping in the seduction of a noble Roman lady (*Ant.* 18.66–80). Further, Tacitus (*Ann.* 14.42, 45) reports the execution of every slave in the household of one Pedianus Secundus after he was murdered by one of them. He makes it clear that those of both sexes were among the number executed. Since the slave's form of execution was always crucifixion, it would mean that some women were crucified on that occasion. Further, Joseph Zias[70] notes that the rabbinic tractate Sem. 2.11 refers to women being crucified ("A man whose wife has been crucified in the same city..."[71]). The Mishnah (Sanh. 6:5) refers to eighty witches being crucified. But the references to the crucifixion of women seem to indicate that it was rare.

Yet, there is a remarkable depiction of a female crucifixion found in Puteoli, Italy, among the excavations of eight *tabernae*. The graffito is a crude drawing of a figure on a cross with the name "*Alkimila*" etched near it.[72] Since the name is feminine, one assumes that the figure is supposed to represent a woman. Note, the figure seems fully clothed in a long tunic:

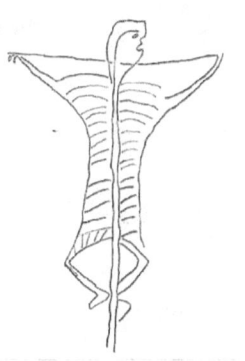

Figure 14.7: Sketch of the crucifixion of Alkimila. Note that the feet straddle the stake.[73]

---

68. Cook, "Envisioning," 283–85.
69. Cook, "Envisioning," 278.
70. Zias, "Crucifixion."
71. Zlotnick, *Semahot*, 36.
72. Cook, "Spectacle," 95; Cook, *Crucifixion*, 203.
73. Sketch by the author from the photograph of G. Camodeca, *Puteoli*, 207. The graffito was found on the wall of a *taberna*. It is 40 cm (15 inches) high.

A third depiction comes from the second–third century CE, probably from Turkey, Syria, or somewhere in the eastern Mediterranean. The magical amulet is a "bloodstone intaglio" and is the earliest depiction of Jesus (as the inscription shows) crucified. The gem pictures Jesus as bearded, with long hair, and nude (as the literary references above indicate might have happened). Jesus' arms are stretched out beneath the *patibulum* of the cross and attached to it by two ropes; his hands are not nailed in this depiction. His feet seem too far from the stake to have been nailed to it. The depiction is comparable to the crucified figure in the Palatine graffito, "which must be roughly contemporary with this amulet."[74] We get a better idea of how crucifixion was done from all these sources than from our usual medieval and Renaissance art.

Figure 14.8: Magical gem; intaglio; green-brown jasper; oval; beveled edge; chipped on all sides; engraved on obverse: nude, crucified man with head to left; inscribed on both sides.[75]

74. Kotansky, "Crucifixion Gem."
75. Permission purchased from the British Museum.

All the above depictions have the victim upright with legs straddling the stake. But victims could be placed on the cross (or more precisely on the wooden post or tree) in several different ways. Recall the quote from Seneca above. Likewise, Josephus noted that when the Romans crucified large numbers of Jewish rebels in the Jewish War (66–73 CE) they used a variety of positions: "The soldiers out of rage and hatred amused themselves by nailing their prisoners in different postures."[76]

Evidently, nails were often (but not always) used in crucifixions. The literature frequently refers to nails. For example, Seneca (*Dial.* 7.19.3) writes of the criminals having driven their own nails into the crosses (by their behavior).[77] The criminal Piso was charged with nailing to crosses some soldiers, and even a Roman citizen, without a trial. Those practicing the magical arts were known to covet the nails of crucifixion victims since they were believed to have great power.[78] Recall also the statement of Josephus, quoted above, that the Roman soldiers "nailed" their victims to crosses. Thus, nails were a common—though not necessarily a required—feature in crucifixion.

Archaeology

Also important in this consideration are the archaeological discoveries of the bones of six men:

1. One was buried in the Giv'at ha-Mivtar tomb north of Jerusalem in the first century CE.[79]

2. One was buried in the "Abba" tomb in Jerusalem in the first century BCE.[80]

3. One was buried in the Caiaphas tomb in Jerusalem in the first century CE.[81]

4. A fourth was found in England and dated to the second or third century CE.[82]

---

76. *War* 5.51; translation by Thackery, in Josephus, LCL.

77. See Cook, "Envisioning," 272.

78. Apuleius, *Metam.* 3.17; Pliny the Elder, *Nat. Hist.* 28.46. See Cook "Envisioning" 271–73,

79. Zias, "Crucifixion"; Tzaferis, "Jewish Tombs"; Strange, "Crucifixion"; Haas, "Anthropological Observations"; Zias and Sekeles, "Crucified Man."

80. Smith, "Abba Cave"; Tzaferis, "Abba Burial."

81. Zias, "Caiaphas Tomb"; Greenhut, "Burial Cave"; Reich, "Ossuary Inscriptions."

82. For the crucifixion victim in England, see Steinmeyer, "Rare Evidence"; "Roman Crucifixion in Britain." Some date the grave to the second century. David Ingham of

5. A fifth was found in northern Italy (the Po Valley) dating to the "Roman period."[83];

6. The sixth was found in Egypt in the Nile Delta and dated 0 CE (+ or—100 years).[84]

Only numbers 1 and 4 are certainly crucifixions. The others, while possible, are disputed.

In a tomb near Giv'at ha-Mivtar, was found an ossuary containing the bones of a man who had an iron nail measuring 4.5 inches (11.5 centimeters) driven through his heel (Sidebar 14.3). These are to date the only certain remains of a crucified person to be found in Israel. Joseph Zias,[85] based on an examination of the remains, postulated that the crucified victim would have been placed on the cross with arms slung over the crossbeam and tied and with ankles nailed to the sides of the stake.

The second and third possibilities focus on nails found in these two tombs. Were the nails used to crucify the deceased? Evans argues that the presence of "human calcium" on some of the nails in these two tombs suggests they were used in crucifixion.[86] Cook, however, doubts the conclusion. In the case of the Abba Cave, two nails were "in association" with the phalanges of a skeleton. A third nail was present, but no bones were touching it. There were no grooves or scratch marks on the phalanges that might suggest the nails were driven through the hands.[87] Likewise, Cook concludes that there is no evidence the nails in the Caiaphas tomb were used for crucifixion. Rather, they were used to scratch inscriptions on the ossuaries.[88] One assumes, then, that the calcium from human bones found adhering to the nails was there because the nails were interred in the ossuaries alongside the bones. Therefore, although the nails in the two tombs could *possibly* have come from crucifixion victims, there is no clear evidence they did.

The crucifixion victim from England had a nail (still lodged in place) driven into his heel bone similar to case number 1, the man from the Giv'at

---

Albion Archaeology prefers a third-century date and offers the evidence: "It's probably a 3rd-century crucifixion victim rather than 2nd-century, by the way—the radiocarbon date came out as 210–340 CE at 68% probability," (private correspondence).

83. For the victim in Italy, see Gualdi-Russo et al., "Multidisciplinary Study."
84. Aufderheide, and Rodríguez-Martín, *Cambridge Encyclopedia*, 38–39.
85. Zias, "Crucifixion."
86. Evans, *Jesus and the Remains*, 142.
87. Cook, *Crucifixion*, 464.
88. Cook, *Crucifixion*, 471.

ha-Mivtar tomb. We can accept this one as almost certainly a crucifixion victim (Sidebar 14.3).

The skeletal remains from Italy and Egypt, although they had perforations—one in the heel and the other in the distal end of the femur—which, in the estimation of the anthropologists examining it, were made by nails,[89] have been interpreted variously. In addition, our case number 6, from Egypt, exhibited, along with a possible nail hole, long bone fractures possibly indicating *crurifragium* (like John 19:31–33). Yet, Cook concluded that the individuals from Italy and Egypt presented not nail holes in the heel/leg bones but holes caused by tree roots growing through the skeletal remains over many centuries.[90]

Thus of the archaeological evidence of six possible crucifixion victims, two are almost certain, but the other four only possible. Still, the skeletal remains of the two victims from widely separated geographical regions (Israel and Briton) seem to indicate that persons executed by crucifixion often had nails driven into their heel bones on each side of the stake. It is plausible to conclude that Jesus was treated in similar fashion.

Sidebar 14.3: Heel Bones of Two Crucifixion Victims

Two victims of crucifixion, on the left from Israel in the first century and on the right from Briton in the third century. The nails are still piercing the heel bones. This is most likely the way Jesus was crucified.

Replica of nail in heel of Jerusalem victim (first century CE)[1]

Nail in heel of victim in England (third century CE) (Photo courtesy of Albion Archaeology)

89. Gualdi-Russo et al., "Multidisciplinary Study" for Italy; Aufderheide and Rodríguez-Martín, *Cambridge Encyclopedia*, 38 for Egypt.

90. Cook, *Crucifixion*, 471–74.

1. Photo purchased from www.BibleLandPictures.com/.

The one being executed by crucifixion was usually raised a bit from the ground so he could not support his weight by standing. Apparently, the condemned was not lifted up very high. Schneider[2] suggested that the criminal was elevated just above his own height or, if he was to be displayed to persons from afar, a little higher. But several texts suggest that the victim was kept low enough to the ground that dogs and other wild beasts could gnaw on his/her legs.[3]

The condemned were usually crucified beside well-traveled roads: "Whenever we crucify criminals, the most frequented roads are chosen."[4] Crassus the Roman triumvir and general, crucified the slaves of the Spartacus rebellion (six thousand of them) along the Appian Way (Appian, *Bell. Civ.* 1.120). Jews were crucified within view of the walls of Jerusalem during the Jewish rebellion (*War* 5.449-51).

Perhaps the cruelest practice was abusing or even executing the victim's family members as he hung on the cross. The Athenians crucified Artayctes by nailing him to a wooden plank and while he was thus fastened, they stoned his son in front of him (Herodotus 9.120; see also 4.202). Alexander Jannaeus, the Jewish high priest and prince, crucified eight hundred Pharisees and had their wives and children slaughtered in front of them as they hung from the crosses (*Ant.* 13.380-83).[5] We have no indications that Jesus' family, e.g., his mother and brothers, were abused in this way. Yet, his mother was at the cross (John 19:25-27). Was she there by choice?

---

2. Schneider, "*stauros, stauroō*," 573.
3. Philo, *Flacc.* 2.84-85; Ps-Manetho 4.198-99; Horace, *Ep.* 1.16.46-48.
4. Quintilian, *Decl.* 274; Lat. text in Hengel, *Crucifixion*, 50.
5. See also *Diodorus of Sicily* 18.16.3; translation in Diodorus of Sicily, LCL; cf. b. Abod. Zar. 18a.

Sidebar 14.4
Jesus' crucifixion reported in other sources

b. Sanh. 43a[1]	"On the eve of Passover, Yeshu [the Nazarean[2]] was hanged."
Tacitus, *Ann.* 15.44[3]	"Christus, from whom the name [Christians] had its origin, suffered the extreme penalty during the reign of Tiberius at the hands of one of our procurators, Pontius Pilatus ..."
Josephus, *Ant.* 18.63–64[4]	"When Pilate, upon hearing [Jesus] accused by men of the highest standing amongst us, had condemned him to be crucified, those who had in the first place come to love him did not give up their affection for him."

1. Translation in Epstein et al., *Babylonian Talmud*. The Heb. way of describing crucifixion was the verb "hanged," *talah* (though they also used the verb *tsalav* "impale" Jastrow, *Dictionary*). See Betz, "Jesus and the Temple Scroll," 84; Zias and Charlesworth, "Crucifixion," 277–78; Brown, *Death*, 1:377; Acts 5:30 and 10:39; 4QpNah 3–4; and 11QT 64:8–12. The word does not mean hanged by the neck but fastened to a wooden pole or tree.

2. One manuscript adds the words in brackets. See Epstein et al., *Babylonian Talmud*.

3. Translation in Church and Brodribb, *Tacitus*, 380.

4. Translation by Feldman in Josephus, LCL.

15

Jewish Burials and the Tomb of Jesus

BURIALS IN JUDAISM AND JESUS' BURIAL

The duty to bury the dead was felt especially strongly in Judaism. To leave one's relatives unburied was a grievous offense (*Apion* 2.211). Even to ignore the burial of a stranger was considered a violation of taboo. On the other hand, to bury the poor and strangers was a distinctly virtuous act.[1]

The Procedure for Burial

As soon as a person died, the family would tear their garments (Sem. 9.1–7, m. Mo'ed Qat. 3:7), at least three fingers width, and then would light lamps at the head and feet of the corpse (m. Ber. 8:6).[2] They would wash the corpse, then wrap it in a body shroud and a head shroud.[3] They might add spices to the shroud and sprinkle spices on the bier as it was being carried to the tomb.[4]

---

1. See Hengel, *Charismatic Leader*, 8–9 and Tobit 1:17–20; 4 Ezra 2:23–24; m. Sanh. 6:5; Sem. 4.16, 18, 19, 11.1. j. Ber. 3.1.

2. Safrai and Brunner, "Home and Family," 774.

3. Safrai and Brunner, "Home and Family," 776; Gibson, *Final Days*, 137–47. See m. Shabb. 23:4–5; John 11:44, 20:6–7; Acts 9:37; Matt 27:59.

4. Safrai and Brunner, "Home and Family," 776. See John 19:39–40; Mark 16:1; Luke 24:1; *Ant.* 17.199//*War* 1.673; m. Ber. 8:6)

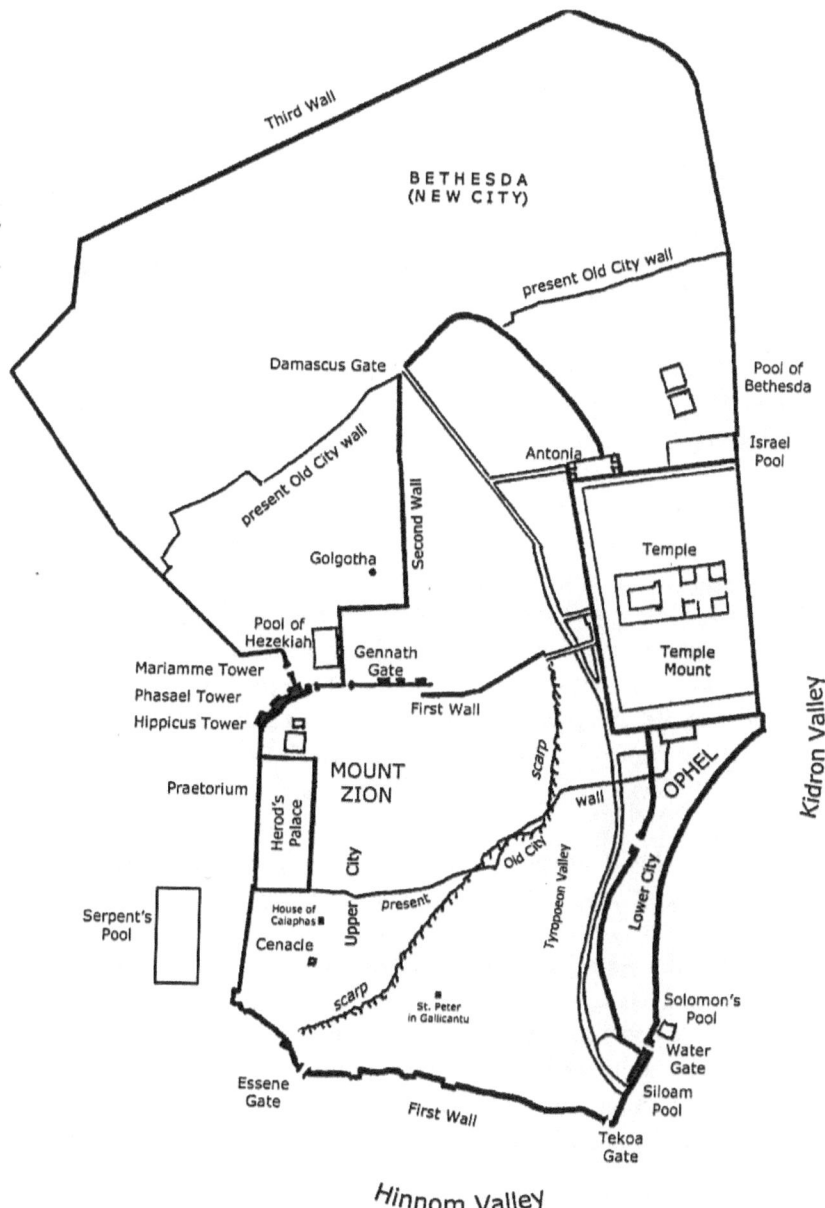

Figure 15.1: Jerusalem in the first century CE including Golgotha, the Praetorium, the Gennath Gate, the Cenacle, the House of Caiaphas, and the Church of Saint Peter in Gallicantu. (Image courtesy mcfarlandbooks.com[5])

5. Image from *The Upper Room and Tomb of David: The History, Art and Archaeology of the Cenacle on Mount Zion* © 2016 David Christian Clausen by permission of

In the Jewish and New Testament literature there are numerous references to the burial shroud.[6] In general, there was evidently a tendency to spend a lot of money on the shroud, perhaps due to the belief that the clothes one wore in burial would be the clothes one would also wear in the age to come (Sem. 9.23). The Testament of Judah 26:3[7] advises not to spend too much on the shroud; one rabbi allegedly exhorted his heirs to bury him in cheap flax (b. Ket. 8b).

We know something about the burial shrouds from archaeological finds. In the Jewish burials of Judea discovered so far, with only one exception, the shrouds are made of linen. Linen shrouds have been discovered in burials at both Jericho and En Gedi, with the best-preserved shrouds (Hell II-ER periods) coming from the latter village. They were found in eight Jewish tombs on the southern bank of Naḥal 'Arugot and in one tomb on the northern bank of Naḥal David.[8]

The "one exception" mentioned above of a nonlinen shroud is an imported woolen cloth. It was found in a tomb near Jerusalem, a tomb evidently belonging to a wealthy family. The shroud was made of "good quality" sheep's or goat's wool. It was not one piece of cloth but four separate wrappings. Because of the type of weave, experts concluded that the body shroud was imported from Syria, Anatolia, Greece, or even Italy. This was not a simple, cheap burial shroud. The radiocarbon dating confirmed that the cloth was from the early first century CE. In addition to the body shroud, there was a linen facial shroud reminiscent of one mentioned in John 11:44.[9]

The reference to Joseph of Arimathea's burying Jesus in a linen shroud (Gk.: *sindōn*—Matt 27:59; Mark 15:46; Luke 23:53; *othion*—John 19:40) was not a sign of Joseph's wealth. The words used in the Gospels do not equal the word *byssos*, "fine linen," used of the garment worn by the Rich Man (as opposed to Lazarus) in Luke 16:19. Joseph of Arimathea was simply adhering to the common Jewish practice, in Judea at least, of shrouding the dead in linen.

After shrouding the body, mourners would proceed to the tomb. They hired wailing persons and flute players for the funeral procession.[10] In the rabbinic literature of the second century CE and later, it appears that the

---

McFarland and Company, Inc., Box 611, Jefferson, NC, 28640. www.mcfarlandbooks.com/.

6. M. Kil. 9:4; m. Ma'as. S. 5:10; Sem. 12.10; John 19:40, 11:44; Acts 5:6.

7. Kee, "Testaments of the Twelve," 802.

8. Shamir, "Mixed Wool and Linen."

9. Gibson, *Final Days*, 144–46. The shroud was wrapped around the man referred to in Chapter 10 who had died of leprosy and tuberculosis.

10. Mark 5:38; Matt 9:23; m. Ket. 4:4; m. Shabb. 23:4; t. Ned. 2:7; Sem. 14.7.

professional wailers were always women,[11] but men may also have been for hire at such events in the first century (see *War* 3.437; Matt 9:23[12]). The wailing involved screaming words of woe which communicated in their culture utter distress.[13]

The burial would usually be the same day as the death (John 11; Acts 5:6, 10; m. Sanh. 6:5; Sem. 11.1), or, barring that, as soon as possible.[14] The funeral procession would begin at the house of the deceased and move to the tomb with the family and friends in tow. The family accompanied the corpse "with tears."[15] Some walked before the bier, others after it (Luke 7:12; Sem. 9.21–22, 10.5).

In the story in Luke 7:11–16, the dead son—evidently an unmarried teenager since he is called a "youth" (v. 14) and there is no mention of a wife and children—is being carried on a bier (v. 14) to the tomb or shaft grave outside the village of Nain. The mother is in the procession weeping (v. 13), and she and her son are accompanied evidently by the entire village (v. 12). This description fits perfectly with the information in *Semahot*.[16]

The procession might halt a few times along the way to allow for added mourning (m. Meg. 4:3; m. B. Batra 6:7; m. Ohol. 18:4) as the procession halted in the story in Luke 7:11–16 (v. 14).[17] The wailers and flute players made what must have been a loud racket on the way (Mark 5:38). They not only wailed and screamed, but sang dirges, clapped their hands,[18] and hit themselves in the chest (Matt 11:17, 24:30, Luke 8:52, 18:13, 23:27, Rev 1:7, 18:9; *Ant.* 7.252).[19] Anyone who encountered a procession to a cemetery was obligated to join in and accompany the mourners (*Apion* 2.205; b. Ber. 18a).

---

11. m. Mo'ed Qat. 3:9; t. Yebam. 14:7; t. Ned. 2:7; m. Ket. 4:4; and cf. Luke 23:27. See Ilan, *Jewish Women*, 189–90. This was one of the two acceptable occupations women could hold (along with the occupation of midwife). The Greeks also used women exclusively as wailers. See Lucian, *Luct.* 12.

12. As Safrai and Brunner, "Home and Family," 776 observed, the Gk. terms in these texts are masculine plural.

13. See b. Mo'ed Qat. 28b for funeral dirges.

14. McCane, *Roll Back the Stone*, 31.

15. Syr. Men. 465. Baarda, "Sentences," 606.

16. This rabbinic text (the name means "joys") describes burials, funerals, and mourning. Although many scholars date the final editing of the text to the eighth century CE, Zlotnick ("Semahot") suggests a third-century date.

17. McCane, *Roll Back the Stone*, 32.

18. M. Mo'ed Qat. 3:8;

19. For the Gk. term *koptō* meaning "beat oneself in the chest" (i.e., in mourning), see Danker, *Lexicon*; and Stählin, "*typtō*," 262n18. For beating the chest in mourning (along with rolling on the ground, beating one's head on the floor, tearing out the hair, and scratching one's cheeks bloody), see also Lucian, *Luct.* 12.

Newborn infants who had died were carried to the tomb wrapped in a cloth; those infants who died between thirty days old and twelve months old were borne in a small casket resting in one person's arms; and a dead child twelve months to three years old was laid in a casket resting on the shoulders and in procession. Children who died after three years old were carried on a bier[20] like adults (Sem. 3.1-3; Luke 7:11-16).

At the tomb, after the family had placed the body inside, there would be a funeral oration/eulogy and prayers (Sem. 8.13; m. Mo'ed Qat. 3:7). The courtyards of some tombs had benches on which an orator would sit to preach.[21] One had to be at least three years old if a poor child or four years old if a wealthy child (Sem. 3.4) to receive a funeral oration. After the funeral oration, the grieving family would stand, and friends and fellow villagers would form a line which filed past to offer comfort (Sem. 10.8, 11.3, m. Mo'ed Qat. 3:7; b. Sanh. 19a; b. Ber. 16b).

The Time of Mourning

After a funeral, a period of mourning was observed — the time varied in accordance with the age of the deceased and the relationship of the survivors to the deceased — during which certain activities and the wearing of certain kinds of clothing were halted.[22]

There are some persons listed in *Semaḥot* who should not be mourned: a fetus, a stillborn baby, a pagan slave, a suicide, and one executed by a Jewish court (Sem. 1.8,10, 2.1, 6). Interestingly, a person executed by a gentile court (the "state") may be fully mourned. That person may have been considered guilty of no real crime but a victim of oppressive occupiers. Thus, Jesus' disciples would have been allowed to mourn his death according to Jewish regulations. Although the Gospels seem to indicate some sort of condemnation by the Sanhedrin or some members of that body, the official decree to execute came from Pontius Pilate, the Roman official.

After the initial seven days of mourning, *Semaḥot* prescribes an additional thirty days during which time one may work but may not cut the hair or nails, may not wear pressed clothing, may not engage in trade, and may not attend a banquet (Sem. 7.8, 10, 11, 9.14, 15). During the thirty-day mourning, they might return to the tomb to check on the corpse (John

---

20. For a royal funeral procession with gem-encrusted bier, see Josephus's description of Herod the Great's funeral (*War* 1.671-73).

21. McCane, *Roll Back the Stone*, 37.

22. See McCane, *Roll Back the Stone*, 38; Fiensy, *Archaeology of Daily Life*, 252-54. The rabbinic text Lam. R. 1.1 lists the things mourners typically did.

11:31, 20:1; Matt 28:1; Mark 16:1–2; Luke 24:1; Sem. 8.1). This extended period was a time of less withdrawal from society but still a special honor paid to the dead.

For mourning the death of a parent, the prohibitions of the thirty days lasted a full year (Sem. 9.10, 15). Further, while one had to rend the garments to mourn for the dead and later mend them, tears in the garment for one's father and mother should never be mended (Sem. 9.19). This one-year extended time of mourning seems to have applied, however, only for one's father and mother. At the end of the year, ossilegium was practiced in Judea (see Chapter 5), the transferring of the bones of the deceased into a bone box usually made of stone but also sometimes of clay or wood.

Tombs

Figure 15.2: Monumental tombs: the tomb of Benei Hezir and the tomb of Zechariah, east of Jerusalem (Photograph by Oren Rozen)[23]

Families buried their dead in four types of tombs/graves (with variations).[24] The type of one's tomb would depend on one's family's finances and social

23. Wikimedia Commons: https://commons.wikimedia.org/wiki/File:Kidron_tombs_Jerusalem_200509.JPG/.

24. Berlin, "Jewish Life," 454; Hachlili, *Jewish Funerary Customs*, 30; Magness, *Stone*

standing. But, also, the burial type depended on changing social and religious conventions.

Monumental Tombs

Families rarely used monumental or "display" tombs. These have only been found so far in Jerusalem (less than forty are known). Those that are visible today indicate that they were characterized by ashlar construction, columns, carved moldings, and decorated features (pyramidal or conical shapes, domes, and so forth). They were monuments to the wealthy and powerful. The New Testament may refer to some of these tombs in Matt 23:29: "they adorn monuments (*mnēmeia*)[25] to the prophets and the righteous persons." Josephus seems to have disapproved of such displays of grandeur in one's burial when he wrote that the Torah does not provide for the dead to put up costly monuments (*Apion* 2.205). Several are clearly visible today east of the Old City of Jerusalem.[26]

Figure 15.3: Loculus tomb: Interior of the alleged tomb of Annas the high priest. See Sidebar 12.3. (www.HolyLandPhotos.org)

---

and Dung, 157; Tendler et al., "Typical and Atypical."

25. The Gk. term can mean both "monument" and "tomb." See Danker, *Lexicon*.

26. Berlin, "Jewish Life," 457; Evans, *Jesus and the Ossuaries*, 18–19. See photos of Jason's tomb, the tomb of Zachariah, the cave of Jehoshaphat, and the Absalom monument in Raḥmani, "Ossuaries and *Ossilegium*"; and Fine, "Death," 444–45.

Loculus Tombs

Second were the rock-cut tombs with niches (Lat.: *loculi;* Aram.: *kokhim*) for the bodies and later to receive the ossuaries. The *loculus* was "a long, narrow slot carved deep into the wall of the tomb" perpendicular to the wall.[27] Over one thousand *loculus* tombs have been found in the vicinity of Jerusalem with hundreds more located in Judea and Galilee.[28] These human-made caves are characterized not only by the niches but also by a central chamber with benches for mourners. The entrance to the tomb was "sealed" with a stone, either circular or, more likely, square (Figure 15.5).[29] In most of the loculus tombs in Judea there is evidence of secondary burial, that is, of ossuaries. But not all families—especially not those living outside the city—practiced secondary burial, even in Judea. Some (living in the Shephelah and on the coast) still buried more like Israelites did in the Iron Age.[30]

Figure 15.4: *Arcosolium* in the tomb of Helena of Adiabene, north of Jerusalem (www.HolyLandPhotos.org)

---

27. McCane, "Death and Burial," 263.

28. Gibson, *Final Days*, 156 for the count of rock-cut tombs.

29. Matt 27:6//Mark 15:46; Mark 16:3; Luke 24:2//John 20:1; John 11:38; m. 'Erub. 1:7; m. Sheq. 1:1; m. Mo'ed Qat. 1:2.

30. Tendler et al., "Typical and Atypical"; and Fischer and Taxel, "Ancient Yavneh."

Arcosolium Tombs

Third were the *arcosolium* tombs: These were also hand-cut caves but without niches. They consisted of "a wide, shallow, arch-shaped" bench carved into the wall of the tomb.[31] Since these tombs could only accommodate three or four persons, they tended to belong to the wealthy families while the *loculus* tombs were used more frequently by the working classes. The corpse was then laid on a ledge under the arch or in a sarcophagus (stone coffin) on the ledge. According to Rachel Hachlili, the *arcosolium* tombs came into fashion toward the end of the late Second Temple period.[32] So far, only about one hundred such tombs have been found.[33] A variation of this type tomb was the bench-tomb in which the deceased were simply laid on stone benches in the tomb and the bones later collected into a pit.[34] It appears that Jesus was placed on a bench in an *arcosolium* tomb since visitors could peer into the tomb to see the empty place where he had been laid (Luke 24:12; John 20:3–8) and the text can speak of "angels . . . one at the head and one at the feet" of where Jesus had lain (John 20:12). If so, Jesus lay on a stone bench under an arch in the rather expensive tomb excavated for Joseph of Arimathea.

Trench Graves

Finally, there were trench graves, those dug into the ground as most modern people do. This was clearly the burial method of choice at Qumran, as the over 1,200 graves near the site of the ruin testify. Trench graves have also been found at En El-Ghuweir (just south of Qumran), East Talpiyot (south of Jerusalem), Beit Safafa (south of Jerusalem), and Ḥorvat Egog (in the Judean hills).[35] In many of the graves near Ḥorvat Ashun (near Modi'in) people were buried in standing-pit graves. At Lod during this period, the majority of burials were graves dug into the sand.[36] At Yavneh (Jamnia)

---

31. McCane, "Death and Burial," 263.

32. Hachlili, "Burials, Ancient Jewish," 790. See also Evans, *Jesus and the Ossuaries*, 12; McCane, "Death and Burial," 264.

33. Rousseau and Arav, *Jesus and His World*, 167.

34. Tendler et al., "Typical and Atypical."

35. See Berlin, "Jewish Life," 463. There were 17 shaft graves at En el-Ghuweir; 2 shaft graves at east Talpiyot; 53 cyst graves at Beit Safafa; and 7 shaft graves at Horbat Egog. Amos Kloner reported that he had discovered 83 "shaft and field burials," dating to the Second Temple period, in his survey of Jerusalem. See Magness, "Disposing of the Dead," 121–22.

36. Tendler et al., "Typical and Atypical."

several tombs were rock-cut but with trench or "trough" graves dug into the floor of the cave.[37] Thus, there is a growing list of burials that were not in caves, whether natural or handmade.[38]

The Blocking Stone

They found the stone rolled back from the tomb. (Luke 24:2)

Figure 15.5: Late Second Temple tomb with square blocking stone.[39]

Figure 15.5 illustrates a stone blocking the entrance of a tomb. The Greek verb in Luke 24:2 (cf. Mark 16:4) seems to imply a round stone that could be rolled. But most tombs were sealed not with circular but with square stones.[40] Kelley reports that of the 900-plus tombs discovered in the Jerusalem area, only four blocked their entrance with a round stone. According

---

37. Fischer and Taxel, "Ancient Yavneh."
38. Jodi Magness maintains that rock-cut caves were expensive and that only the wealthy could have been buried in them. Magness, *Stone and Dung*, 157; Magness, "Disposing of the Dead," 125. Cf. Gudme, "Mortuary Rituals," 359 who agrees with Magness.
39. Photo purchased from A. D. Riddle/BiblePlaces.com/. The tomb is near Nebi Samwil in the land of Benjamin.
40. See Evans, *Jesus and the Ossuaries*, 12; von Wahlde, "Rolling Stone"; Kelley, *Holy Sepulchre*, 75–76.

to one historian, "The more common form of closure for a rock-cut tomb was something like a mushroom cap or a champagne cork on its side."[41] Further, pilgrims to the tomb in Constantine's church—before Caliph Hakim destroyed it—reported seeing a square blocking stone nearby.[42] Kelley suggests that the expression "rolling stone" (Heb. *gōlel*, see m. Ohol. 2:4) was a technical term for the standard square blocking stone of the first century CE and not actually a round stone.[43]

JESUS' TOMB

> A man named Joseph, a member of the council, who was good and just—he had not been in agreement with the council and their actions—from the village of Arimathea of Judea, who was expecting the Kingdom of God, came to Pilate to ask for the body of Jesus. Then he took it down and wrapped it in linen and put it in a rock-cut tomb where no one had yet lain. (Luke 23:50–53)

What happened to the body after crucifixion? One of three processes would result. First, the body could be left on the cross to decompose and for animals, especially vultures and ravens, to consume. An enslaved man laments in a comedy of Plautus: "I know the cross will be my sepulcher: that is where my forbears are, my father, grandfathers, great grandfathers, and great great grandfathers."[44] In other words, there would be no burial for this man. Cook gives an inscription from Caria which details the murder of a master by his slave. The slave was: "hung while yet living for the wild animals and birds."[45] Crucifixion victims were often referred to as food for ravens or vultures (Petronius, *Satyricon* 58.2; Juvenal, *Satires* 14.77–78).

Second, the corpse might be taken from the cross, dragged through the streets, and then thrown into a mass grave for criminals.[46] John Dominic Crossan[47] has insisted that Jesus' body was treated in this fashion. He believes that the Gospels' accounts of the burial of Jesus are fictional.

41. Von Wahlde, "Rolling Stone"; Kelley, *Holy Sepulchre*, 75.
42. Arculf (seventh century CE); Hugeberc (c. 780 CE), *Life of Willibald*; and Photius (886–95 CE), *Letters to Amphilochus, Question 107*.
43. Kelley, *Holy Sepulchre*, 75–76. Cf. Jastrow, *Dictionary*, who defines the verb *galal* as "to roll," but the noun *gōlēl* as the blocking stone of a burial cave.
44. Plautus, *Mil. glor.* 372–72; text in Cook "Crucifixion and Burial," 206.
45. Text in Cook, "Crucifixion and Burial" 206.
46. Cook, "Envisioning" 280.
47. Crossan, *Who Killed Jesus?*, 160–61; Crossan, *Jesus*, 154–56. On this subject, see

Finally, some condemned persons were handed over to family for burial. Cook quotes the Ulpian *Digest* of Roman law, which states that corpses of condemned criminals are not to be withheld from family members: "The corpses of those who were sentenced to die are not to be withheld from their relatives."[48] Cook presents six examples of crucifixion victims being released for burial.[49] Philo observed that in Alexandria, Egypt, he had known of cases where the bodies of crucified persons were given to their relatives, especially on holiday evenings (Philo, *Flacc.* 83). Most important are the statements of Josephus (*War* 4.317, *Ant.* 4.202, 265; see Sidebar 15.1) that inform us that crucified persons in Judea were regularly given to families for burial. The example of the crucified man described in Chapter 14, whose bones were found in a tomb near Jerusalem, demonstrates that crucifixion victims were sometimes buried. Perhaps, given the Jewish sensitivity about burial, the Romans normally allowed them to bury even condemned criminals.

Sidebar 15.1[50]

Four reasons one should conclude Jesus was buried:

1. The burial is narrated in all four Gospels as well as in Paul (1 Cor 15:4).
2. The person performing the righteous act of burial was Joseph of Arimathea, an unknown up to then, and not one of Jesus' devoted disciples. The criterion of embarrassment argues that the story is not fabricated. A heretofore complete stranger does the pious act of burial while Jesus' disciples, even the future leader, Peter, cower in fear.
3. Jewish ethos demanded burial. It was a pious act to bury the dead and a defilement to ignore it.

    a. Deut 21:23 (cf. 11QT 64): "His corpse will not hang all night on the tree. You will surely bury him."

    b. Josephus: "Jews show concern for burials so that they even take down those crucified and bury them before sunset"[51] (*War* 4.317; cf. *Ant.* 4.202, 265).

McCane, *Roll Back the Stone*, 90, 105; Brown, *Death*, 2:1207–11; and Magness, "Jesus' Tomb."

48. Cook, "Envisioning" 279; Cook, "Crucifixion and Burial," 195.
49. Cook, "Crucifixion and Burial," 210–12.
50. See, among others, Cook, *Crucifixion*, 461–62; Cook, "Crucifixion and Burial."
51. Text in Cook, "Crucifixion and Burial," 212.

> c. Semaḥot 2.9 states that Jews allow the burial of people executed by the Romans.
>
> d. Bones of Yoḥanan: He had been crucified but was buried. See Chapter 14.
>
> e. Other executed Jews were allowed burial.[52]
>
> 4. The Romans in other parts of the empire would release the body of a crucifixion victim to the family for burial:
>
>> a. Ulpian's *Digest* (a compendia of Roman laws compiled by Emperor Justinian in the sixth century but based on earlier rulings) refers to the release of bodies of executed criminals to families.
>>
>> b. The example of the victim from England (see Chapter 14) shows that the Jewish burial of a crucifixion victim was not an anomaly.

> On the first day of the week, very early, the women came to the tomb bringing the spices they had prepared. They found the stone rolled back from the tomb. When they went in, they did not find the body of the Lord Jesus. (Luke 24:1–3)

We can, through biblical references, Christian tradition, and archaeology, be reasonably sure about the *general* location and the nature of Jesus' tomb. First, we have a few biblical clues; the tomb was

- in or near a garden (John 19:41),
- a rock-cut tomb (Matt 27:60; Luke 23:53),
- An *arcosolium* tomb (see above), and
- near the place of crucifixion (John 19:41).

The tomb was in a garden, wrote the author of the Fourth Gospel. The gate in north Jerusalem, the Gennath Gate, attests to the presence of a "garden" (*War* 5.146).[53] The archaeological evidence also supports the area near the Church of the Holy Sepulcher as a garden. Virgilio C. Corbo surmised that the old quarry in which the church was constructed (see Chapter 14)

---

52. See Evans, "Family Buried Together," who presents "three or four" cases of individuals evidently killed by execution whose bones were placed in an ossuary. See also the section of Chapter 11 of this volume called "Evidence of Violence."

53. *Gantha/ganna* is Aram. for "garden" (Jennings and Gantillon, *Lexicon*; Jastrow, *Dictionary*). See Figure 15.1, above.

was still in use until the first century BCE when it was filled in with soil and stone chips and became a garden or orchard growing vines, figs, carobs, and olives.[54] Further, Cyril of Jerusalem (*Catechesis* 14.5) in the fourth century noted that the area "formerly was a garden, and the signs and the remnants of this remain."[55] The topography near the current Church of the Holy Sepulcher, therefore, matches the reference in John 19:41.

Second, many historians today agree that at the time of Constantine the place of Jesus' entombment was correctly identified.[56] These historians presume that the early church would have remembered the (general) location of Jesus' execution and burial. Raymond Brown surmised that since James, Jesus' brother, was a major figure in the Jerusalem church (Gal 2:9; 1 Cor 15:7; *Ant.* 20.200), the church would have remembered where Jesus' tomb was. Further, offered Brown, the Jewish people at this time venerated the tombs of martyrs, prophets, and holy men.[57]

Many maintain that emperor Hadrian (see Sidebar 1.4), as he may have done at Jesus' birthplace and at the birthplace of John the Baptist (see Chapter 1), decided to create replacement monuments for three sacred places in Jerusalem: the temple, the place of Jesus' crucifixion, and the tomb of Jesus. At the ruins of the Jewish Temple he put up a temple to (or statue of) Jupiter.[58] Dio Cassius (150–235) wrote that "At Jerusalem he founded a city in place of the one which had been razed to the ground, naming it Aelia Capitolina, and on the site of the temple of the god he raised a new temple to Jupiter" (69.12).[59] Jerome (342/347–420), in his *Commentary on Isaiah* (1.2.9), also reported on the replacement of the Jewish Temple: "Where there once were the temple and the religion of God, there a statue of Hadrian and an idol of Jupiter are set up together."[60] In addition, Hadrian built a temple

54. Corbo, *Sepolcro* 1:29. Excavators found an olive press under the church (Corbo, *Sepolcro* 3:124, 125, and 126. See also Brown, *Death*, 2:1269–70; Gibson, *Last Days*, 119; Cabaret, *Topography*, 12; and Bahat, "Does the Holy Sepulchre Church." Remains of the Gennath Gate have been found. See Avigad, *Discovering Jerusalem*, 69.

55. Böer, *Lectures*, 479. For the garden, see also Gospel of Peter 6.24.

56. See Gibson, *Last Days*, 121; Finegan, *Archaeology*, 261; Wilkinson, *Jerusalem*, 147–48; Murphy-O'Connor, *Holy Land*, 49; Barkay, "Garden Tomb"; Bahat, "Does the Holy Sepulchre Church"; Charlesworth, "Jesus Research," 35; Meyers and Chancey, *From Alexander to Constantine*, 181. Yet there has been pushback from some: White, "Garden Tomb Association"; Chadwick, "In Defense of the Garden Tomb."

57. Brown, *Death*, 2:1281. Jesus' later generation of kin also lived in Jerusalem. See Eusebius, *H.E.* 3.19–20.

58. See Dio Cassius, *Hist. rom.* (229 CE) 69.12 and Jerome, *Comm. Isa.* 1.2.9. Dio says Hadrian built a new temple; Jerome mentions only an "idol of Jupiter."

59. Translation in E. Cary, LCL online: https://penelope.uchicago.edu/Thayer/e/roman/texts/cassius_dio/69*.html/.

60. Translation in Finegan, *Archaeology*, 199.

of Jupiter on Mount Gerizim, the holy mountain of the Samaritans where they had once had their own temple.[61] The emperor, it seems, wanted to obliterate any devotion to Israelite religion (both Jewish and Samaritan) in the Middle East.[62]

Figure 15.6: Current entrance into the Church of the Holy Sepulcher (Photograph by Jorge Lascar[63])

According to fourth-century Christian authors, Hadrian took the same measures to replace Christian sacred sites. He knew where they were (because Jewish Christians were venerating them) and tried to obliterate any devotion to them by erecting his own pagan shrines, as he had done with the Israelite and Samaritan temples. Jerome reported that from the time of Hadrian until the reign of Constantine there was on the rock where Jesus' cross had allegedly stood a marble statue of Venus, and a figure of Jupiter over the tomb of Jesus (*Letter 58 to Paulinus*). To replace two Christian sacred places, Hadrian had covered over the alleged hill of crucifixion and the tomb of Jesus with earth and a stone pavement and on the pavement erected the Capitoline Temple.[64] Over the loci of the crucifixion and the

61. As evidenced by coins minted in Neapolis beginning in the reign of Antoninus Pius (138–61) and minted for a century. See Finegan, *Archaeology*, 67.

62. These actions precipitated the Second Jewish Revolt against Rome, 132–35 CE, led by Simeon bar Kosiba (aka Bar Kokhba).

63. Photo at Wikimedia Commons: https://commons.wikimedia.org/wiki/File:The_Church_of_the_Holy_Sepulchre-Jerusalem.JPG/.

64. Eusebius, *Vit. Const.*, 3.26.

tomb, he erected the statues of Venus and of Jupiter, respectively.[65] If this is true, Hadrian must have hoped that the church would forget about the two sacred places and, instead, focus on his new shrines. But, actually, he "had permanently marked the site(s)."[66]

In 326—nearly two hundred years after Hadrian—the first archaeological excavation took place. Constantine wanted to remove the Roman earthworks over the "hill" of Golgotha (Eusebius, *Vit. Const.* 3.26). To everyone's surprise, when the pavement was removed and the earth was excavated away, the tomb and rock/monolith of crucifixion were preserved under the fill. Eusebius described the scene:

> But as soon as the original surface of the ground, beneath the covering of earth, appeared, immediately, and contrary to all expectation, the venerable and hallowed monument of our Saviour's resurrection was discovered.[67]

This discovery prompted Constantine to plan his own monument, which became the Church of the Holy Sepulcher. Work began on Constantine's church (a basilica to enclose both the supposed rock monolith of crucifixion and the tomb), a building following the orientation of Hadrian's Capitoline Temple; it was consecrated in 335.[68] Constantine removed all bedrock except that enclosing the tomb, according to a report from Cyril of Jerusalem between c. 340 and 350: "For now [the tomb's vestibule] is not to be seen, since the outer cave was cut away at that time for the sake of the present adornment."[69]

Meanwhile, while the church was under construction, pilgrims could view the tomb and the supposed rock of Golgotha as they had been two hundred years prior. The Bordeaux Pilgrim in 333 CE visited Jerusalem and wrote about these sites:

> On the left hand is the little hill of Golgotha where the Lord was crucified. About a stone's throw from these is a crypt where his body was laid and the third day was raised.[70]

---

65. Jerome, *Letter 58 to Paulinus.*

66. As Hoade, *Guide,* 105 remarked.

67. Eusebius, *Vit. Const.,* 3.28. Translation in Eusebius, *Life of the Blessed Emperor,* 96.

68. See Finegan, *Archaeology,* 262; Hoade, *Guide,* 105; Wilkinson, *Jerusalem,* 147–49; Cabaret, *Topography,* 283–92. Constantine's church "more or less re-occup[ied] (the Capitoline Temple's) whole footprint," (Cabaret, *Topography,* 294).

69. Cyril, *Catecheses,* 14.9. Translation in Böer, *Lectures,* 481. See Hoade, *Guide,* 106; Murphy-O'Connor, *Holy Land,* 51.

70. Translation in Finegan, *Archaeology,* 262–63.

Third, archaeological excavations offer support to the church's identification of this site as the place of Jesus' burial. The wall of the first-century city of Jerusalem was clearly east of this tomb. Although the Holy Sepulcher Church is now inside the Turkish walls of the Old City of Jerusalem, it was not inside the first-century walls. If Jerusalem's second wall (or north wall; Figure 15.1, above) had enclosed what later became the Church of the Holy Sepulcher, it could not be the authentic location of Jesus' tomb since Jewish regulations prohibited tombs inside cities and villages (m. B. Batra 2:9). Both the New Testament and basic knowledge of the Jewish customs argue that crucifixions and burials did not take place inside the holy city. These considerations would mean that the tomb must have been located outside both the first wall and the second wall but not necessarily where the third wall was built some years after Jesus' lifetime (nor outside the present Turkish wall). The archaeological results confirm that the Holy Sepulcher Church is outside what the boundaries of the city were in the first century.

Excavations have taken place off and on in areas beneath the Church of the Holy Sepulcher and vicinity from the 1960s through 1990s (and have recently begun again[71]). These excavations have shown that the area around Jesus' tomb was since the ninth century BCE a quarry (see Sidebar 15.2 p. 287 and Figure 14.5, above p. 254). Later the area was also used as a cemetery. Many other tombs near the Church of the Holy Sepulcher have been identified.[72] Thus, it is plausible that Joseph of Arimathea could have had a garden tomb in this vicinity as the Gospel of John indicates.

---

71. As of this writing (in 2022), the Church of the Holy Sepulcher is currently undergoing restoration, which will enable further excavation beneath some of its floors. See "Restoring the Church of the Holy Sepulchre"; Steinmeyer, "Restoration of the Church of the Holy Sepulchre."

72. Bahat, "Does the Holy Sepulchre Church"; Bahat, "Jerusalem"; Brown, *Death*, 2:1279; Kelley, *Holy Sepulchre*, 41; Cabaret, *Topography*, 4; and Avni and Seligman, "New Excavations." Gibson and Taylor, *Holy Sepulchre*, 63 give a rather extensive list of tombs discovered in the area dating from the Iron Age through the ER period. The Hasmonean prince John Hycanus had a tomb in this area (*War* 5.259, 304, 356; 6.169).

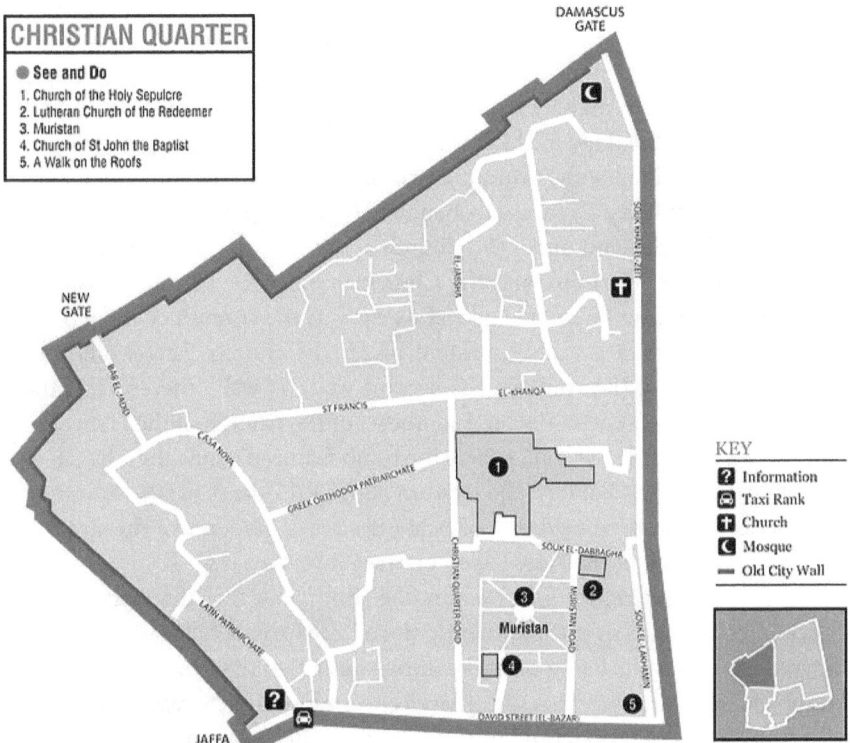

Figure 15.7: Christian Quarter in Old Jerusalem: The Church of the Holy Sepulcher (1), the Church of the Redeemer (2), Muristan area (3), and the Church of Saint John Prodromos (4) (Figure by Bjorgen)[73]

Excavations of nearby locations, namely, north of the Church of the Holy Sepulcher (under the Coptic Patriarchate) and south of the church in the Muristan area and under the Church of Saint John Prodromos, revealed the same as under the Church of the Holy Sepulcher. The area had been a quarry since the Iron Age and remained "vacant and deserted until the town-planning operations of Aelia Capitolina" (second century CE).[74] The quarry was probably continually used over the subsequent centuries especially as the Hasmonean leaders and, later, Herod the Great expanded Jerusalem building.[75] Since this area lies directly north and directly south of

73. Wikimedia Commons: https://commons.wikimedia.org/wiki/File:Jerusalem_Christian_Quarter.jpg/.

74. Kenyon, *Jerusalem*, 153; Avni and Seligman, "New Excavations." See also Kelley, *Holy Sepulchre*, 40–42.

75. As Kelley (*Holy Sepulchre*, 67) suggests.

the Church of the Holy Sepulcher and was obviously outside the city (stone was not quarried inside the congested Middle Eastern cities), obviously the Holy Sepulcher Church was as well.

More recently, archaeological excavations by the German Protestant Institute of Archaeology at the Lutheran Church of the Redeemer (Figure 15.7) have provided some additional confirmation to the Holy Sepulcher Church's authenticity. Excavations beneath the Church of the Redeemer revealed that like the land under the Church of the Holy Sepulcher, the Coptic Patriarchate, the Muristan, and the Church of Saint John Prodromos, this area too was originally a stone quarry as early as the seventh century BCE. Further, no trace of a wall was found under the church. That would put it outside the city (i.e., outside the second wall) as well. Therefore, if the Church of the Redeemer—located southeast of the Church of the Holy Sepulcher—was outside the wall, so was the tomb featured inside the Church of the Holy Sepulcher. Further, the stratum above the quarry at the Church of the Redeemer showed evidence of being used as a garden like the stratum above the Church of the Holy Sepulcher (see John 19:41).[76]

This archaeological information does not prove that the Holy Sepulcher Church stands over the authentic site of Jesus' tomb, but it removes any argument against its being so and demonstrates that the description of the tomb's location fits with this site. There is no archaeological reason to doubt the testimony of Eusebius and others regarding this location.

As to the size of the tomb celebrated in the church, we can learn something from pilgrims who visited Constantine's basilica (before Caliph Hakim destroyed the tomb; Sidebar 12.1). Shimon Gibson and Joan E. Taylor have assessed the evidence from Arculf, Photius, and Daniel and concluded that the tomb—not counting the forecourt—must have been quite small. Their figures would equal a square area of roughly 5 ½ feet on each side. It is further the consensus, they maintain, that the tomb into which Jesus was placed was of the *arcosolium* type.[77]

Constantine's church (Figure 15.10) was partially destroyed in 614 then restored using a smaller plan. In 1009 that version was itself destroyed under Caliph Hakim. This time the destruction was complete and included not just the church but also the tomb. The atrium and the basilica of the church were never returned to the complex. The current church, basically

---

76. Serr and Vieweger. "Golgatha"; Spathi, "Small Finds," 26; Kelley, *Holy Sepulchre*, 41–42; Cabaret, *Topography*, 13–14.

77. Gibson and Taylor, *Holy Sepulchre*, 62–63.

the Crusader (12th century) restoration, is, therefore, smaller than the Constantinian church.⁷⁸

Figure 15.8: Inside the Church of the Holy Sepulcher, Easter 1941: The tomb was destroyed under Caliph Hakim. The Edicule stands on the spot where it was.⁷⁹

The only modern competitors for identification of Golgotha and the tomb were those suggested in the nineteenth century by several scholars and administrators: the so-called Garden Tomb (Figure 12.1) and "Gordon's Calvary" (Figure 15.9). Gordon followed the view of earlier explorers and excavators (Otto Thenius in 1842, Conrad Schick in 1867, and Charles Conder in 1881) that a rocky craig just north of the present Damascus Gate with two small caves looked like a skull. Not far from this hill was located an ancient tomb which was then named the Garden Tomb and alleged to have been Jesus' tomb. Many visitors to Jerusalem today conclude that these are Golgotha and the tomb of Jesus. The Garden Tomb administrators still argue for its validity.⁸⁰ Yet, there are problems. The main issue is that the Garden

78. Hoade, *Guide*, 106–15; Wikipedia, s.v. "Church of the Holy Sepulchre"; Kelley, "Holy Sepulchre."

79. Photograph courtesy Wikimedia Commons: https://commons.wikimedia.org/wiki/File:Calendar_of_religious_ceremonies_in_Jer._(i.e.,_Jerusalem)_Easter_period,_1941._Looking_down_from_dome_on_to_processions_going_round_the_Edicule_(Church_of_the_Holy_Sepulchre)_LOC_matpc.04412.jpg/.

80. White, "Garden Tomb Association"; Chadwick, "In Defense of the Garden Tomb."

Tomb was probably an Iron Age tomb (eighth to seventh centuries BCE) and, therefore, was not in use in the time of Jesus.[81] Further, we need not think that the place (not called a hill in the Gospels) necessarily looked like a skull. It may have received the name Skull for other reasons (see Chapter 14).

Figure 15.9: Gordon's Calvary from the north wall of the Old City, Jerusalem, as it appeared in the 1930s. In the middle of the photograph are two small caves that look like the eye sockets of a skull.[82]

A more recent challenge to the Church of the Holy Sepulcher as the site of Jesus' tomb has come from Joan Taylor's 1993 monograph. Taylor's overall thesis is that there was no ongoing Jewish Christian veneration of sites in Israel sacred to the story of the Jesus-movement, and that, therefore, we should give almost no credence to the authenticity of these places

---

81. See Finegan, *Archaeology*, 282–83; Meyers and Chancey, *From Alexander to Constantine*, 184; Foreman, "Locating Jesus' Crucifixion" 507–8. See also Wilkinson, *Jerusalem*, who gives in an appendix (198–200) the letter of General Gordon detailing his rationale for selecting his spot for Golgotha and the tomb. Wilkinson finds the argument unconvincing.

82. Photo from Wikimedia Commons: https://commons.wikimedia.org/wiki/File:Gordon%27s_Calvary_LOC_matpc.03428.jpg/. Cropped to highlight the two "eye sockets."

(including the Church of the Nativity in Bethlehem). She rejects Jerome's claim that Hadrian tried to replace Christian venerated sites. Christians, she argues further, would not have visited Jesus' tomb—unlike other tombs in Israel—since the tomb was empty. Further, there were several tombs in the vicinity of what became the Church of the Holy Sepulcher. How was the correct one assuredly identified?[83]

Sidebar 15.2

Timeline of the Church of the Holy Sepulcher and Vicinity[84]

9th–8th BCE	The area is used as quarry.
7th–6th BCE	Some Iron II tombs are in the area.
5th BCE	The area is cultivated and quarried and continued to be used as cemetery.
c. 140 BCE	A Jerusalem fortification project adds a second wall on the north which excludes the ancient quarry.
Late 30s–early 40s CE	Tombs in area are emptied to add the Third North Wall.
135 CE	Hadrian constructs a forum covering much of the vicinity. On the podium he erects a temple dedicated to Venus.
326 CE	Emperor Constantine, after tearing down Hadrian's temple, commissions a basilica over the tomb of Jesus and the nearby rock believed to be Golgotha.
1009 CE	Caliph Hakim orders destruction of the basilica.
1145 CE	The Crusader Church of the Holy Sepulcher consecrated.
1808 CE	The Edicule (rotunda over the tomb) is rebuilt.
1960–1980s CE	Repairs and reconstruction begin, affording opportunity for archaeological excavations.
1997	Excavations take place under the Coptic Patriarchate (just north of the church).
2022 CE	Repairs to certain sections of the church allow further excavation.

These are certainly important questions to consider. It is quite possible that we have no idea where Jesus' tomb was. Yet, one can offer an analysis of these arguments. First, there is evidence that Hadrian sought to replace

83. Taylor, *Christians and the Holy Places*, 1–5, 136–37, 139, 141–42.

84. Adapted from Kelley, *Holy Sepulchre*, 9–12; Avni and Seligman, "New Excavations"; and Gibson and Taylor, *Holy Sepulchre*, xix.

venerated sites since the pagan author Dio Cassius as well as Jerome describe his building a pagan temple on the spot where the Jewish Temple had been, and since archaeology has proven a pagan temple's construction on Mount Gerizim (see above). Because Hadrian made those replacements, it is plausible he would have also tried to replace Christian sites.

Second, it is speculation to affirm Christians cared nothing about Jesus' tomb because unlike other Jewish venerated tombs, it was empty. Jews today venerate the alleged Tomb of David (see Figure 12.1, p. 203) even though it contains a cenotaph. Further, in Christian belief a great miracle occurred at that site. It would seem contrary to human nature that the site would not be important to the Christian community.

However, Taylor's third point (that it is impossible to identify Jesus' tomb with several in the same area)[85] does seem a valid caution. One might be a bit hesitant to conclude that Constantine found the correct tomb after three hundred years. It would mean that Hadrian—based on Christian memory—knew the tomb. This is a plausible conclusion but not provable. Thus, the identification of the tomb in the Church of the Holy Sepulcher with Jesus' tomb is a good possibility, but one must not insist on it.

---

85. Taylor also observes that the alleged tomb of Jesus was an *arcosolium* tomb, a type she supposed, incorrectly (see above), to have been in existence for hundreds of years before the time of Jesus. Also, Taylor notices that the Church of the Holy Sepulcher is not perfectly aligned with the tomb. See Taylor, *Christians and the Holy Places*, 138.

Sidebar 15.3[86]

Emperor Constantine (272/274–337)

The Roman emperor who presided (with his mother, Helena) over building four churches in Palestine in the fourth century:

1. The Church of the Holy Sepulcher (Jerusalem)
2. The Church of the Nativity (Bethlehem)
3. The Eleona Church (Jerusalem)
4. The church at Mamre (Hebron)

His life was celebrated in Eusebius's biography *The Life of Constantine*. After defeating his rival, Maxentius, in 312, he became a champion of Christianity, later accepting baptism. He began the close association of Christianity to the government, presiding himself over the Nicaean Council (325 CE) to settle the Arian dispute.

Constantine's Head at Capitoline (Photograph by Allan T. Kohl)[87]

---

86. Cross and Livingstone, "Constantine the Great."

87. Wikimedia Commons: https://commons.wikimedia.org/wiki/File:Emperor_Constantine,_head_and_fragments_from_a_colossal_statue_(11970811516).jpg. Photo cropped to fit the table/.

Sidebar 15.4[88]

Helena (c. 255–c. 330), mother of Constantine

She came from humble origins in the province of Bithynia (northern Asia Minor). She married Emperor Constantius Chlorus, by whom she had a son, Constantine. She was later abandoned by her husband, who entered into a more advantageous marriage. After Constantine became emperor, he elevated Helena to a prominent position. In 326, she visited Palestine where she was influential in founding the Church of Nativity (in Bethlehem) and the Eleona Church (in Jerusalem, on the Mount of Olives).

Figure 15.10 (on the next page): Plan of the Constantinian Church of the Holy Sepulcher according to V. Corbo.[89]

1. At the top of the plan (west) is the Anastasis with the tomb of Jesus (#1) under the dome and another tomb (#28) west of the dome.

2. Below it (east) is the Triportico with the alleged rock of Calvary (#200) in its lower left-hand corner (south-east).

3. Below that (yet farther east) is the Martyrium (measuring 147 X 85 feet) where the liturgy was performed. Note the stone quarry indicated under this part of the church.

4. At the very bottom is the east atrium.

Later, in the Crusader period, another atrium was built, south of the Triportico. In this area excavators discovered another first century tomb. Some of the walls and foundations of this church are still visible in the current construction. Constantine's church followed the "footprint" of Hadrian's Capitoline Temple.[90] (Image courtesy Studium Biblicum Franciscanum, Jerusalem)

---

88. Cross and Livingstone, "Helena, St."

89. Corbo, *Sepolcro* 2.3.

90. Murphy-O'Connor, *Holy Land*, 55, 56–58; Wilkinson, *Jerusalem*, 180–94; Cabaret, *Topography*, 294.

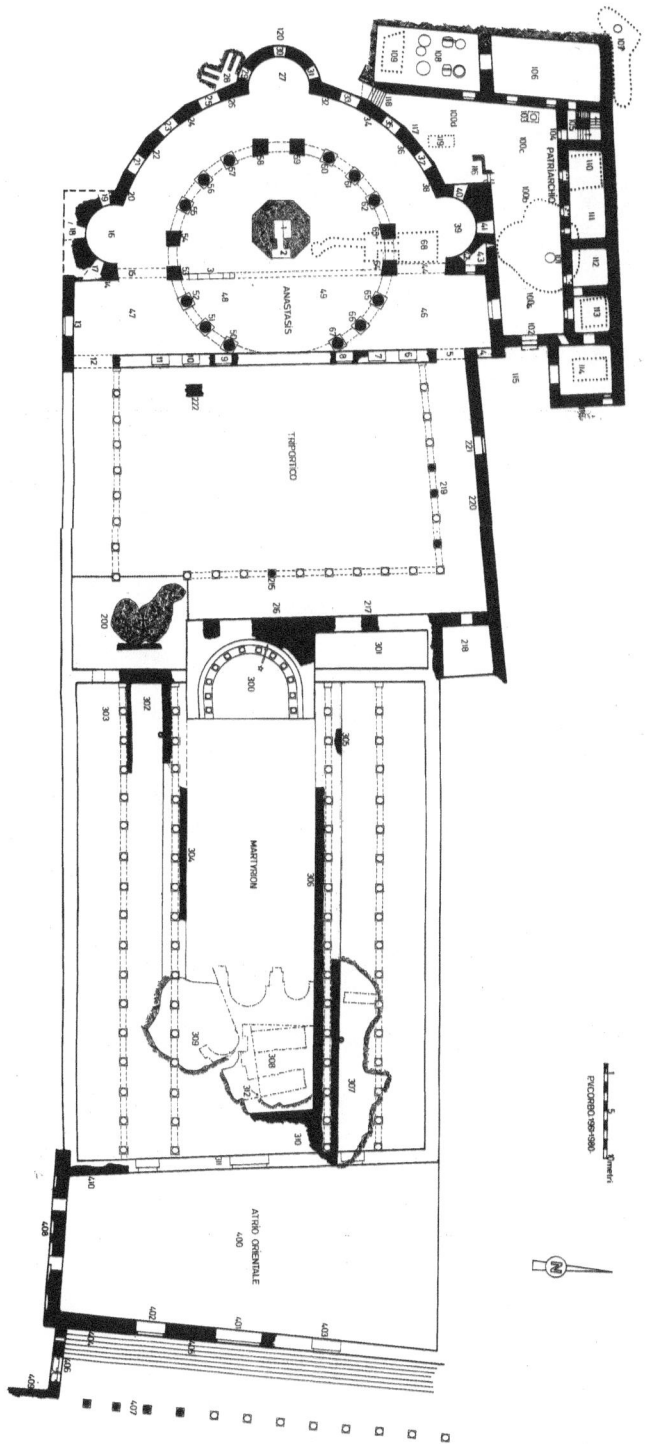

Appendix A

Archaeological Periods of Palestine[1]

Archaeological Period	Abbreviation	Dates
Iron IA		1200–1150 BCE
Iron IB		1150–1000 BCE
Iron IIA		1000–925 BCE
Iron IIB		925–720 BCE
Iron IIC		720–586 BCE
Persian		586–333 BCE
Hellenistic I	Hell I	333–152 BCE
Hellenistic II	Hell II	152–37 BCE
(Hasmonean 125–63 BCE)[2]		
Early Roman I	ER I	37 BCE–70 CE
Early Roman II	ER II	70–135 CE[3]
Middle Roman	MR	135–250 CE
Late Roman	LR	250–363 CE
Byzantine I	Byz 1	363–451 CE
Byzantine II	Byz 2	451–640 CE
Early Arab		640–1099 CE
Crusader and Ayyubid		1099–1291 CE

1. From Mazar, *Archaeology*, 30; Fiensy and Strange, "Archaeological Chronology" in *GLSTMP* 1:ix; and Levy, preface in *Archaeology of Society*, xvi.

2. Following Root, *Galilee*, 7 in further delineating the Hellenistic II period.

3. Again, following Root, *Galilee*, 7.

APPENDIX A

Archaeological Period	Abbreviation	Dates
Late Arab		1291–1516
Ottoman		1516–1917

Appendix B

Glossary[4]

Adyton: The part of the Greek temple not to be entered; the innermost sanctuary.

Antae: A quadrangular pilaster at each end of a wall.

Arcosolium tomb: An arched recess carved into rock.

Ashlar: large stone block with smoothly finished sides

Cardo: The "Hinge," i.e., the main north-south street of any city laid out in the Hippodamian grid (which see).

Cella: The place in a temple where the image of the god(dess) stood.

Columbarium: Dovecote.

Decapolis: a loose confederation of ten Hellenized, gentile cities, all but one of which (Scythopolis) lay east of the Jordan River.

Decumanus: One of the main streets (running east-west) in a Roman city plan.

ESA: Eastern Terra Sigillata A (ceramic ware). It had a glossy, red color.

Ethnography: The study of a people group or village by qualified academic personnel and using current sociological methods.

Hippodamian grid: The checkerboard arrangement of streets which became the standard for a *polis* in the New Testament era.

Insula: Lat. "island." It refers to a block of buildings on a grid pattern.

---

4. For these definitions, see LSJM; Stern, "Glossary," 1535–40; and Fiensy and Strange, "Glossary," in *GLSTMP* 2:443–48.

Kokhim (singular: *kokh,* Heb.) tomb: A tomb with niches to receive corpses and/or ossuaries. Also called by the Lat. term *loculus* tomb.

Loculus: The Lat. term for niche within a tomb.

Mikveh (plural: *mikva'ot*): a "collection" of water, either naturally in a stream or river or artificially in a stepped pool, for ritual immersion.

Naḥal: Heb. for dried stream bed (= Arabic "wadi").

opus sectile: Inlaid floor of colored stone or marble.

Ossilegium: the process of secondary burial as practiced in Judea in the New Testament/Second Temple period.

Ossuary: a box for the deposit of human bones. Most were made of stone, but some of wood or clay.

Osteoarchaeology: The excavation and investigation of bones.

Ostracon (plural: ostraca): a potsherd with writing on it

Palaeopathology: The study of diseases of the ancient world.

Pronaos: The front hall of a temple

Pseudepigrapha: literally "false writings," the noncanonical Jewish writings, roughly from the time of Jesus, which are also not included in the Apocrypha (the deuterocanonical books in some Bibles)

Triclinium: a room equipped with three couches on which diners reclined

Via maris: "road of the sea," the highway running along the Mediterranean Sea in Israel, which then turned eastward through the Jezreel Valley until it reached the Sea of Galilee where it turned north, passing near Capernaum.

Wadi: Arabic for dried stream bed

Bibliography

Abegg, Martin, Jr., et al., trans. *The Dead Sea Scrolls Bible*. New York: HarperCollins, 1999.
Adams, Sean A. "Crucifixion in the Ancient World: A Response to L. L. Welborn." In *Paul's World*, edited by Stanley E. Porter, 111–29. Pauline Studies 4. Leiden: Brill, 2008.
Adan-Bayewitz, David, and Mordechai Aviam. "Iotapa, Josephus, and the Siege of 67: Preliminary Report on the 1992–1994 Seasons." *JRA* 10 (1997) 131–65.
Adler, Yonatan. "The Archaeology of Purity: Archaeological Evidence for the Observance of Ritual Purity in Erez-Israel from the Hasmonean Period until the End of the Talmudic Era (164 BCE—400 CE)." PhD diss., Bar Ilan University, 2011.
———. "Purity in the Roman Period." In *OEBA* 2:240–49.
———. "Second Temple Period Ritual Baths Adjacent to Agricultural Installations: The Archaeological Evidence in Light of the Halakhic Sources." *JJS* 59 (2008) 62–72.
———. "A Quantitative Analysis of Jewish Chalk Vessel Frequencies in Early Roman Jerusalem: A View from the City's Garbage Dump." *IEJ* 66 (2016) 202–19.
Aharoni, Yohanan. *The Land of the Bible: A Historical Geography*. Translated from the Hebrew and edited by A. F. Rainey. 2nd ed., rev. and enl. Philadelphia: Westminster, 1979.
Alexandre, Yardenna. "Karm er-Ras Near Kafr Kanna." In *GLSTMP* 2:146–57.
Alföldy, Géza. "Pontius Pilatus und das Tiberieum von Caesarea Maritima." *Scripta Classica Israelitica* 18 (1999) 85–108.
Alt, Albrecht. *Kleine Schriften*. 3 vols. Munich: Beck, 1959.
Amiry, Suad, and Vera Tamari. *The Palestinian Village Home*. London: British Museum Publications, 1989.
Amorai-Stark, Shua, et al. "An Inscribed Copper-Alloy Finger Ring from Herodium Depicting a Krater." *IEJ* 68 (2018) 208–20.
Anastasiou, Evilena, et al. "Infectious Disease in the Ancient Aegean: Intestinal Parasitic Worms in the Neolithic to Roman Period Inhabitants of Kea, Greece." *Journal of Archaeological Science* 17 (2018) 860–64.
Andrianou, Dimitra. "Evidence for Furnished Interiors in Hellenist Greece." *Hesperia* 75 (2006) 219–66.
Angel, J. Lawrence. "Ecology and Population in the Eastern Mediterranean." *World Archaeology* 4 (1972) 88–105.

———. "The Length of Life in Ancient Greece." *Journal of Gerontology* 2.1 (1947) 18–24.
Applebaum, Shimʻon. "Economic Life in Palestine." In *JPFC* I.2:631–700.
———. "Judea as a Roman Province: The Countryside as a Political and Economic Factor." *ANRW* II.8 (1978) 355–96.
———. *Judaea in Hellenistic and Roman Times*. SJLA 40. Leiden: Brill, 1989.
———. "The Problem of the Roman Villa in Eretz Israel." *Eretz Israel* 19 (1987) 1–5.
———. "The Zealots: The Case for Reevaluation." *JRS* 61 (1971) 155–70.
Arav, Rami. "Bethsaida Excavations: Preliminary Report, 1978–1993." In *Bethsaida* 1:3–63.
———. "Bethsaida Excavations: Preliminary Report, 1994–1996." In *Bethsaida* 2:3–113.
———. "Bethsaida—A Response to Steven Notley." *NEA* 74.2 (2011) 92–100.
———. "Final Report on Area A, Stratum V: The City Gate." In *Bethsaida* 4:1–122.
Arav, Rami and Carl E. Savage. "Bethsaida." In *GLSTMP* 2:258–79.
Arensburg, Baruch. "Analysis of Human Forearm Bone." In *JQE* 4:288–89.
Arensburg, Baruch, and Anna Belfer-Cohen. "Preliminary Report on the Skeletal Remains from the 'En Gedi Tombs." *Atiqot* 24.12 (1994)12–14.
Arensburg, Baruch, and Yoel Rak. "Skeletal Remains of an Ancient Jewish Population from French Hill, Jerusalem." *BASOR* 219 (1975) 69–71.
Arensburg, Baruch, and Patricia Smith. "Anthropological Tables." In *Jericho: The Jewish Cemetery of the Second Temple Period*, edited by Rachel Hachlili and Ann E. Killebrew, 192–94. IAA Reports 7. Jerusalem: IAA, 1999.
———. "Appendix: The Jewish Population of Jericho 100 BC–70 AD." *PEQ* 115 (1983) 133–39.
Arieli, Rotem. "Human Remains from the Har Haẓofim Observatory Tombs (Mt. Scopus, Jerusalem)." *Atiqot* 35 (1998) 37–42.
Aufderheide, Arthur C., and Conrado Rodríguez-Martín. *The Cambridge Encyclopedia of Human Paleopathology*. Cambridge: Cambridge University Press, 1998.
Aviam, Mordechai. "Distribution Maps of Archaeological Data from the Galilee: An Attempt to Establish Zones Indicative of Ethnicity and Religious Affiliation." In *Religion, Ethnicity, and Identity in Ancient Galilee: A Region in Transition*, edited by Jürgen Zangenberg et al., 115–32. WUNT 210. Tübigen: Mohr Siebeck, 2007.
———. "Galilee: The Hellenistic to Byzantine Periods." In *NEAEHL* 2:453–58.
———. "Socio-Economic Hierarchy and its Economic Foundations in First Century Galilee: The Evidence from Yodefat and Gamla." In *Flavius Josephus: Interpretation and History*, edited by Jack Pastor et al., 29–38. JSJSup 146. Leiden: Brill, 2011.
———. "The Synagogue." In *MOG*, 127–34.
———. "Yodefat-Jotapata." In *GLSTMP* 2:109–26.
Aviam, Mordechai, and R. Steven Notley. "In Search of the City of the Apostles." *NovT* 63.2 (2021) 143–58.
Avigad, Nahman. "A Depository of Inscribed Ossuaries in the Kidron Valley." *IEJ* 12.1 (1962) 1–12.
———. *Discovering Jerusalem*. Oxford: Blackwell, 1984.
———. "How the Wealthy Lived in Herodian Jerusalem." *BAR* 2.4 (1976) 22–35.
———. "Jerusalem in Flames—The Burnt House Captures a Moment in Time." *BAR* 9.6 (1983) 66–72.
———. "Samaria (City)." In *NEAEHL* 4:1300–1310.
———. "Upper City: Herodian Period." In *NEAEHL* 2:729–35.

Avi-Yonah, Michael. "Bethlehem." In *NEAEHL* 1:203–8.
———. "Caesarea." In *NEAEHL* 1:278–79.
———. *The Holy Land*. Grand Rapids: Baker, 1966.
———. "A List of Priestly Courses from Caesarea." *IEJ* 12 (1962) 137–39.
———. *The Madaba Mosaic Map*. Jerusalem: Israel Exploration Society, 1954.
Avni, Gideon, and Tania Coen-Uzzielli. *The Akeldama Tombs: Three Burial Caves in the Kidron Valley, Jerusalem*. IAA Reports 1. Jerusalem: IAA, 1996.
Avni, Gideon, and Zvi Greenhut. "Resting Place of the Rich and Famous." *BAR* 20.6 (1994) 36–46.
Avni, Gideon, and Jon Seligman. "New Excavations at the Church of the Holy Sepulchre Compound." In *One Land, Many Cultures*, edited by G. Claudio Bottini, et al., 153–62. SBFCMa 41. Jerusalem: Franciscan, 2003.
Baarda, Tjitze. "The Sentences of the Syriac Menander." In *OTP* 2:583–606.
Bacci, Michele. *The Mystic Cave: A History of the Nativity Church in Bethlehem*. Convivia 1. Brno, Czek Republic: Masaryk University, 2017.
Badian, E. "Triclinium." In *OCD*, 1093–94.
Bagati, B. "Nazareth, Excavations." In *NEAEHL* 3:1103–5.
Bagnall, Roger S. and Bruce W. Frier. *The Demography of Roman Egypt*. Cambridge: Cambridge Studies in Population, Economy, and Society in Past Time. Cambridge University Press, 1994.
Bahat, Dan. "Does the Holy Sepulchre Church Mark the Burial of Jesus?" *BAR* 12.3 (1986) 26–45.
———. "Jerusalem: Church of the Holy Sepulcher." *NEAEHL* 5:1821.
Bailey, Kenneth E. *Jesus through Middle Eastern Eyes*. Downers Grove, IL: IVP Academic, 2008.
———. *Through Peasant Eyes*. Grand Rapids: Eerdmans, 1980.
Balentine, Jerry R. "Malaria." Edited by Charles Patrick Davis. *MedicineNet.com* (website). https://www.medicinenet.com/malaria_facts/article.htm/.
Barkay, Gabriel. "The Garden Tomb: Was Jesus Buried Here?" *BAR* 12.2 (1986) 40–57.
Bar-Ilan, Meir. "Infant Mortality in the Land of Israel in Late Antiquity." In *The Social Scientific Study of Judaism and Jewish Society*, edited by Simcha Fishbane and Jack N. Lightstone, 3-25. Montreal: Department of Religion, Concordia University, 1990. https://www.academia.edu/92426846/Infant_Mortality_in_The_Land_of_Israel_in_Late_Antiquity/.
Bar-Nathan, Rachel, and Judit Gärtner. "The Pottery from the Hippodrome at Jericho." In *The Hasmonean and Herodian Palaces at Jericho*, edited by Rachel Bar-Nathan and Judit Gärtner, 4:85–99. 5 vols. Jerusalem: Israel Exploration Society, 2013.
Batey, Richard A. "'Is Not This the Carpenter?'" *NTS* 30 (1984) 249–58
———. *Jesus and the Forgotten City*. Grand Rapids: Baker, 1991.
———. "Sepphoris: An Urban Portrait of Jesus." *BAR* 18.3 (1992) 50–62.
Bauckham, Richard. "Additional Note B." In *MOG*, 358–61.
———. *Jesus and the Eyewitnesses: The Gospels as Eyewitness Testimony*. Grand Rapids: Eerdmans, 2006.
———. "Magdala and the Fishing Industry." In *MOG*, 185–267.
———. "Magdala as We Now Know it: An Overview." In *MOG*, 1–67.
———. "Magdala in Rabbinic Traditions." In *MOG*, 307–44.
Becker, Eve-Marie. "Jesus and Capernaum in the Apostolic Age: Balancing Sources and Their Evidence." In *The Mission of Jesus*, edited by Samuel Byrskog and Tobias Hägerland, 113–39. WUNT 2/391. Tübingen: Mohr Siebeck, 2015.

Beebe, H Keith. "Domestic Architecture and the New Testament." *BA* 38.3/4 (1975) 89–104.
Ben-David, Arye. *Talmudische Ökonomie*. Hildesheim: Olms, 1974.
Benoit, Pierre, et al. *Les Grottes des Murabba'at*. 2 vols. DJD 2. Oxford: Clarendon, 1961.
Berlin, Andrea M. "Jewish Life before the Revolt: The Archaeological Evidence." *JSJ* 36 (2005) 417–70.
Betz, Otto. "Jesus and the Temple Scroll." In *Jesus and the Dead Sea Scrolls*, edited by James H. Charlesworth, 75–103. ABRL. New York: Doubleday, 1992.
———. "Was John the Baptist an Essene?" *BR* 6.6 (1990) 18–25.
Binder, Gerhard. "Banquet: Rome." In *BNP* 2:494–97.
Bloedhorn, Hanswulf. "Die Eleona und das Imbomon in Jerusalem: Eine Doppelkirchenanlage auf dem Ölberg?" In *Akten des XII. Internationalen Kongresses für Christliche Archäologie*, edited by Ernst Dassmann and Josef Engemann, 568–71. JAC 20. Studi di antichità cristiana 52. Münster: Aschendorff, 1995.
Blümner, Hugo. *Technologie und Terminologie der Gewerbe und Künste*. 4 vols. in 3 bks. Leipzig: Teubner, 1875–1887.
Bock, Darrell L. *Luke*. 2 vols. BECNT 3. Grand Rapids: Baker, 1994, 1996.
Böer, Paul A., ed. *The Catechetical Lectures of St. Cyril of Jerusalem*. Edmond, OK: Veritatis Splendor, 2014.
Boer, Roland. "Malaria in the Ancient World." *Political Theology Network* (blog), April 17, 2016. http://www.politicaltheology.com/blog/malaria-the-ancient-world/
Bond, Helen K. *Caiaphas: Friend of Rome and Judge of Jesus?* Louisville: Westminster John Knox, 2004.
Bonnie, Rick. "How 'Urban' Was Tiberias in the First Century CE?" In *Essays in Honor of James F. Strange*, edited by James Riley Strange and C. Thomas McCollough. Kinneret, Israel: Ostracon, forthcoming.
Bonnie, Rick, and Julian Richard. "Building D1 at Magdala Revisited in the Light of Public Fountain Architecture in the Late-Hellenistic East." *IEJ* 62 (2012) 71–88.
Booth, Roger P. *Jesus and the Laws of Purity*. JSNTSup 13. Sheffield: JSOT Press, 1986.
Borowski, Oded. *Every Living Thing: Daily Use of Animals in Ancient Israel*. Walnut Creek, CA: AltaMira, 1998.
———. *Daily Life in Biblical Times*. ABS 5. Atlanta: Society of Biblical Literature, 2003.
Branch, Robin Gallaher. "Anna in the Bible: Luke Reveals the Prophetess as a Biblical Model for Aging." *Bible History Daily* (blog), September 23, 2023. https://www.biblicalarchaeology.org/daily/people-cultures-in-the-bible/people-in-the-bible/anna-in-the-bible/
Brewster, Ethel H. *Roman Craftsmen and Tradesmen of the Early Empire*. New York: Franklin, 1917.
Brooten, Bernadette J. *Women Leaders in the Ancient Synagogue: Inscriptional Evidence and Background Issues*. BJS 36. Atlanta: Scholars, 1982.
Broshi, Magen. "Estimating the Population of Ancient Jerusalem." *BAR* 4.2 (1978) 10–15.
———. "Excavations in the House of Caiaphas, Mt. Zion." In *JR* 57–60.
———. "The Population of Western Palestine in the Roman-Byzantine Period" *BASOR* 236 (1979) 1–10.
Broshi, Magen, and Hanan Eshel. "Whose Bones?" *BAR* 29.1 (2003) 26–33, 71.
Broshi, Magen and Shimon Gibson. "Excavations along the Western and Southern Walls of the Old City of Jerusalem." In *AJR* 147–55.

Brown, Raymond E. *The Death of the Messiah.* 2 vols. ABRL. New York: Doubleday, 1994.

———. *The Gospel according to John.* 2 vols. AB 29–29A. New York: Doubleday, 1966, 1970.

———. *An Introduction to the New Testament.* ABRL. New York: Doubleday, 1997.

Brownlee, W. H. "John the Baptist in the New Light of the Ancient Scrolls." *Int* 9.1 (1955) 71–90.

Bull, Robert J. "Caesarea Maritima—The Search for Herod's City." In *Archaeology in the World of Herod, Jesus, and Paul,* edited by Hershel Shanks and Dan P. Cole, 106–23. Archaeology and the Bible 2. Washington, DC: Biblical Archaeology Society, 1990.

Burford, Alison M. *Craftsmen in Greek and Roman Society.* Aspects of Greek and Roman Life. Ithaca: Cornell University Press, 1972.

———. "The Economics of Greek Temple Building." *Proceedings of the Cambridge Philological Society* 191 (1965) 21–34.

Burn, A. R. "Hic Breve Vivitur: A Study of the Expectation of Life in the Roman Empire." *Past and Present* 4 (1953) 2–31.

Cabaret, Dominique-Marie. *The Topography of Ancient Jerusalem.* Translated by David Orton. CahRB 102. Series archaeologica 4. Leuven: Peeters, 2022.

Cahill, Jane M., et al. "It Had To Happen." *BAR* 17.3 (1991) 64–69.

Camodeca, Giuseppe. *Puteoli romana: istituzioni e societa.* Naples: Saggi, 2018.

Canaan, Taufik. *The Palestinian Arab House: Its Architecture and Folklore.* Jerusalem: Syrian Orphanage Press, 1933.

"Capernaum: the town of Jesus." https://travelingisrael.com/capernaum/.

Carcopino, Jérôme. *Daily Life in Ancient Rome.* Edited with bibliography and notes by Henry T. Rowell. Translated from the French by E. O. Lorimer. New Haven: Yale University Press, 1940.

Cargill, Robert R. "Was Pontius Pilate's Ring Discovered at Herodium?" First Person. *BAR* 45.2 (2019) 6.

Case, Shirley Jackson. *Jesus: A New Biography.* Chicago: University of Chicago Press, 1927.

Casson, Lionel. *Everyday Life in Ancient Rome.* Rev. and expanded ed. Baltimore: Johns Hopkins University Press, 1998.

Center for Disease Control and Prevention. "About Malaria." https://www.cdc.gov/malaria/about/disease.html/.

Center for Online Judaic Studies. "Horvat Kanaf Amulet: Incantation against Fever and Pain." http://cojs.org/horvat_kanaf_amulet-_incantation_against_fever_and_pain/.

Chadwick, Jeffrey. "In Defense of the Garden Tomb." Queries & Comments. *BAR* 12.4 (1986) 16–17.

Chancey, Mark A. "The Cultural Milieu of Ancient Sepphoris." *NTS* 47 (2001) 127–45.

———. *Greco-Roman Culture and the Galilee of Jesus.* SNTSMS 134. Cambridge: Cambridge University Press, 2005.

———. *The Myth of a Gentile Galilee.* SNTSMS 118. Cambridge: Cambridge University Press, 2002.

Chancey, Mark, and Eric M. Meyers. "How Jewish Was Sepphoris in Jesus' Time?" *BAR* 26.4 (2000) 18–33, 61.

Chapman, David W., and Eckhard J. Schnabel. *The Trial and Crucifixion of Jesus.* WUNT 344. Tübingen: Mohr Siebeck, 2015.

Charlesworth, James H. "Archaeology, Jesus and Christian Faith." In *What Has Archaeology to Do with Faith?*, edited by James H. Charlesworth and Walter P. Weaver, 1–22. Faith and Scholarship Colloquies. Philadelphia: Trinity, 1992.
———. "Jesus Research and Archaeology: A New Perspective." In *JA* 11–63.
———. *Jesus within Judaism: New Light from Exciting Archaeological Discoveries.* ABRL. New York: Doubleday, 1988.
———. "The Temple, Purity, and the Background to Jesus' Death." *Revista Catalana de Teologa* 33 (2008) 395–442.
Church, Alfred John, and William Jackson Brodribb, trans. *The Complete Works of Tacitus.* The Modern Library of the World's Best Books. New York: Modern Library, 1942.
Clark, K. W. "Sea of Galilee." *IDB* 2:348–50.
Clausen, David Christian. "Mount Zion's Upper Room and Tomb of David." Archaeological Views. *BAR* 43.1 (2017) 24–25, 61.
———. *The Upper Room and Tomb of David: The History, Art and Archaeology of the Cenacle on Mount Zion.* Jefferson, NC: McFarland, 2016.
Cohen, Susan L. "Tel Zahara in the Hellenistic and Roman Periods." In *ETZ*, 147–52.
Cohen, Susan L., with W. Więckowski. Introduction. In *ETZ*, 1–7.
Cook, Edward M. *Solving the Mysteries of the Dead Sea Scrolls.* Grand Rapids: Zondervan, 1994.
Cook, John Granger. "Crucifixion and Burial." *NTS* 57.2 (2011) 193–213.
———. "Crucifixion as Spectacle in Roman Campania." *NovT* 54 (2012) 68–100.
———. *Crucifixion in the Mediterranean World.* WUNT 327. Tübingen: Mohr Siebeck, 2019.
———. "Envisioning Crucifixion: Light from Several Inscriptions and the Palatine Graffito." *NovT* 5.3 (2008) 262–85.
———. "Roman Crucifixions: From the Second Punic War to Constantine." *ZNW* 104.1 (2013) 1–32.
Cooper, Alison Burford. "Crafts, Trade." In *BNP* 3:899–907.
Corbo, Virgilio C. "Capernaum." In *ABD* 1:866–69.
———. *Carfarnao.* Vol. 1. SBF 19. Jerusalem: Franciscan, 1975.
———. *The House of St. Peter at Capharnaum.* Translated by Sylvester Saller. SBFCMi 5. Jerusalem: Franciscan, 1972.
———. *Ricerche archeologiche al Monte degli Ulivi.* SBF 16. Jerusalem: Franciscan, 1965.
———. *Il Santo Sepolcro di Gerusalemme, Aspetti arceologici dalle origini al periodo crociato*, Parts I–III. SBFCMa 29. Jerusalem: Franciscan, 1981–1982.
Cotton, Hannah. "A Cancelled Marriage Contract from the Juadean Desert." *JRS* 84 (1994) 64–86.
Cotton, Hannah M., et al. "Fish Sauces from Herodian Masada." *JRA* 9 (1996) 223–38.
Cotton, Hannah M., and Ada Yardeni, eds. *Aramaic, Hebrew, and Greek Documentary Texts from Naḥal Ḥever and other Sites with an Appendix Containing Alleged Qumran Texts.* The Seiyâl Collection 2. DJD 27. Oxford: Clarendon, 1997.
Coussens Brian A. "(Mis)Reading Proximity as Co-functionality: Re-examining the Relationship between the Miqweh and the Synagogue in the Late Second Temple Period." Paper Presented to the Society of Biblical Literature Annual Meeting, Denver, Colorado, November 2022.
Cox, F. E. G. "History of Human Parasitology." *Clinical Microbiology Reviews* 15.4 (2002) 595–612. https://www.ncbi.nlm.nih.gov/pmc/articles/PMC126866/ .

Cranfield, C. E. B. *The Gospel according to St. Mark.* Cambridge: Cambridge University Press, 1963.
Cross, F. L., and E. A. Livingstone. "Constantine the Great." In *ODCC*.
———. "Cyril, St." In *ODCC*.
———. "Epiphanius, St." In *ODCC*.
———. "Etheria." In *ODCC*.
———. "Eusebius." In *ODCC*.
———. "Helena, St." In *ODCC*.
———. "Jerome, St." *ODCC*.
———. "Justin." *ODCC*.
———. "Origen." *ODCC*.
———. "Paulinus, St." *ODCC*.
Crossan, John Dominic. *Jesus: A Revolutionary Biography.* New York: HarperOne, 1995.
———. *Who Killed Jesus? Exposing the Roots of Anti-Semitism in the Gospel Story of the Death of Jesus.* New York: Harper One, 1996.
Crossan, John Dominic and Jonathan L. Reed. *Excavating Jesus: Beneath the Stones, Behind the Texts.* San Francisco: HarperSanFrancisco, 2001.
Cruz-Cruz, Carolina, et al. "Stunting and Intestinal Parasites in School Children From High Marginalized Localities at the Mexican Southeast." *Journal of Infection in Developing Countries* 12.11 (2018) 1026–33.
Cytryn-Silverman, Katia. "Tiberias, From Its Foundation to the End of the Early Islamic Period." In *GLSTMP* 2:186–210.
Dalman, Gustaf. *Arbeit und Sitte in Palästina.* Bd. 7, *Das Haus, Hühnerzucht, Taubenzucht, Bienenzucht.* Schriften des Deutschen Palästina-Instituts. Gütersloh: Bertelsmann, 1942.
Danby, Herbert, ed. and trans. *The Mishnah.* Oxford: Oxford University Press, 1933.
Danker, Frederick William. *A Greek-English Lexicon of the New Testament and Other Early Christian Literature,* 3rd ed. Chicago: University of Chicago Press, 2000.
Dar, Shimon. *Landscape and Pattern: An Archaeological Survey of Samaria 800 B.C.E.–636 C.E.* With a historical commentary by Shimon Applebaum. BAR International Series 308. Oxford: BAR, 1986.
Dark, Ken. "The Archaeology of Nazareth in the Early First Century." *The Bible and Interpretation* (blog), July 2020. https://bibleinterp.arizona.edu/articles/archaeology-nazareth-early-first-century/.
———. "Early Roman-Period Nazareth and the Sisters of Nazareth Convent." *Antiquaries Journal* 92 (2012) 37–64.
———. "Has Jesus' Nazareth House Been Found?" *BAR* 41.2 (2015) 54–63.
Deines Roland. *Jüdische Steingefässe und Pharisäische Frömmigkeit.* WUNT 2/52. Tübingen: Mohr Siebeck, 1993.
Dell'Amore, Christine. "Ancient Roman Giant Found—Oldest Complete Skeleton With Gigantism." *National Geographic* (blog), November 10, 2012. https://www.nationalgeographic.com/science/article/121102-gigantism-ancient-skeleton-archaeology-history-science-rome/
De Luca, Stefano. "Capernaum." In *OEBA* 1:168–80.
De Luca, Stefano, and Anna Lena. "Magdala, Taricheae." In *GLSTMP* 2:280–342.
Demand, Nancy. *Birth, Death, and Motherhood in Classical Greece.* Ancient Society and History. Baltimore: Johns Hopkins University Press, 1994.
Derrett, J. D. M. "Fresh Light on the Parable of the Wicked Vinedressers." *Revue international des droits de l'antiquité* 10 (1963) 11–41.

Dever, William G. "Archaeology, History and the Bible." In *Harper's Bible Dictionary*, edited by Paul J. Achetemeier, 44. San Francisco: Harper & Row, 1985.

———. *The Lives of Ordinary People in Ancient Israel: Where Archaeology and the Bible Intersect*. Grand Rapids: Eerdmans, 2012.

———. *Recent Archaeological Discoveries and Biblical Research*. The Samuel and Althea Stroum Lectures in Jewish Studies. Seattle: University of Washington Press, 1990.

———. *What Did the Biblical Writers Know and When Did They Know it? What Archaeology Can Tell us about the Reality of Ancient Israel*. Grand Rapids: Eerdmans, 2001.

Donfried, Karl P. "Chronology: New Testament." In *ABD* 1:1011–1022.

Dothan, Moshe. *Hammath Tiberias*. Ancient Synagogues Studies. Jerusalem: Israel Exploration Society, 1983.

———. "Hamath-Tiberias." In *NEAEHL* 2:573–77.

Durand, John D. "Mortality Estimates from Roman Tombstone Inscriptions." *American Journal of Sociology* 65.4 (1960) 365–73.

Eakins, J. Kenneth. "Human Osteology and Archeology." *BA* 43.2 (1980) 89–96.

Eck, Werner, and Avner Ecker. "Not a 'Signet Ring' of Pontius Pilatus." *Atiqot* 110 (2023) 89–96.

Edwards, Douglas R. "Khirbet Qana: From Jewish Village to Christian Pilgrim Site." In *The Roman and Byzantine Near East*, edited by John H. Humphrey, 3:101–32. JRASup 49. Ann Arbor: Journal of Roman Archaeology, 2002.

———. "Identity and Social Location in Roman Galilean Villages." In *Religion, Ethnicity, and Identity in Ancient Galilee*, edited by Jürgen Zangenberg et al., 357–74. WUNT 210. Tübingen: Mohr Siebeck, 2007.

Ehrenberg, V. "Polis." In *OCD*.

Encyclopedia Britannica, s.v. "Decapolis." https://www.britannica.com/place/Decapolis-ancient-cities-Palestine/.

Epstein, Isidore, et al., eds. *The Babylonian Talmud*. 13 vols. London: Soncino, 1938.

Eshel, Hanan. "They're Not Ritual Baths." *BAR* 26.4 (2000) 42–45.

Eshel, Hanan, and Rivka Leiman. "Jewish Amulets Written on Metal Scrolls." *JAJ* 1.2 (2010) 189–99.

Eusebius Pamphilius. *The Life of the Blessed Emperor Constantine*. London: Aeterna, 2014.

Evans, Craig A. "Excavating Caiaphas, Pilate, and Simon of Cyrene: Assessing the Literary and Archaeological Evidence." In *JA* 323–40.

———. "The Family Buried Together Stays Together: On the Burial of the Executed in Family Tombs." In *The World of Jesus and the Early Church: Identity and Interpretation in Early Communities of Faith*, edited by Craig A. Evans, 87–96. Peabody, MA: Hendrickson, 2011.

———. *Jesus and the Ossuaries*. Waco, TX: Baylor University Press, 2003.

———. *Jesus and the Remains of His Day: Studies in Jesus and the Evidence of Material Culture*. Peabody, MA: Hendrickson, 2015.

Feder, Yitzhaq. "The Polemic Regarding Skin Disease in 4QMMT." *DSD* 19.1 (2012) 55–70.

Feldman, Louis H. "Josephus." In *ABD* 3:981–98.

Fiensy, David A. *The Archaeology of Daily Life: Ordinary Persons in Late Second Temple Israel*. Eugene, OR: Cascade Books, 2020.

———. *Christian Origins and the Ancient Economy*. Eugene, OR: Cascade Books, 2014.

———. *Insights from Archaeology. Reading the Bible in the 21st Century*. Minneapolis: Fortress, 2017.

———. *Jesus the Galilean: Soundings in a FirMetzgert Century Life*. Piscataway, NJ: Gorgias, 2007.

———. *The Social History of Palestine in the Herodian Period: The Land Is Mine*. Studies in the Bible and Early Christianity 20. Lewiston, NY: Mellen, 1991.

Fiensy, David A., and James Riley Strange, eds. *Galilee in the Late Second Temple and Mishnaic Periods*. Vol. 1, *Life, Culture, and Society*. Minneapolis: Fortress, 2014.

———, eds. *Galilee in the Late Second Temple and Mishnaic Periods*. Vol. 2, *The Archaeological Record From Cities, Towns, and Villages*. Minneapolis: Fortress, 2015.

———, eds. "Glossary." In *GLSTP* 2:243–48.

Fine, Steven. "Death, Burial, and Afterlife." In *OHJDL*, 440–62.

———. "Did the Synagogue Replace the Temple?" *BR* 12.2 (1996) 18–26, 41

Finegan, Jack. *The Archaeology of the New Testament: The Life of Jesus and the Beginning of the Early Church*. Rev. ed. Princeton Paperbacks. Princeton: Princeton University Press, 1992.

———. *Handbook of Biblical Chronology*. Princeton: Princeton University Press, 1964.

Fischer, Moshe, and Itamar Taxel. "Ancient Yavneh: Its History and Archaeology." *Journal of the Institute of Archaeology of Tel Aviv University* 34.2 (2007) 204–84.

Fitzmyer, Joseph A. *The Dead Sea Scrolls and Christian Origins*. Studies in the Dead Sea Scrolls and Related Literature. Grand Rapids: Eerdmans, 2000.

———. *The Gospel according to Luke*. 2 vols. AB. New York: Doubleday, 1981, 1985.

Fitzmyer, Joseph A., and Daniel J. Harrington. *A Manual of Palestinian Aramaic Texts*. BibOr 34. Rome: Biblical Institute Press, 1978.

The Flavius Josephus Primer Home Page http://www.josephus.org/

Foerster, Gideon. "Beth-Shean at the Foot of the Mount" In *NEAEHL* 1:223–35

———. "Herodium." In *NEAEHL* 2:618–21.

———. "Tiberias: Excavation South of the City." In *NEAEHL* 4:1470–73.

Foreman, Benjamin A. "From the Upper Room to the Judgment Seat." In *Lexham Geographic Commentary on the Gospels*, edited by Barry J. Beitzel and Kristopher A. Lyle, 483–503. Bellingham, WA: Lexham, 2017.

———. "Locating Jesus' Crucifixion and Burial." In *Lexham Geographic Commentary on the Gospels*, edited by Barry J. Beitzel and Kristopher A. Lyle, 504–17. Bellingham, WA: Lexham, 2017.

Fortner, Sandra Ann. "The Fishing Implements and Maritime Activities of Bethsaida-Julias (et-Tell)." *Bethsaida* 2:269–80.

Frankel, Rafael, et al. *Settlement Dynamics and Regional Diversity in Ancient Galilee*. IAA Reports 14. Jeruslaem: IAA, 2001.

Freeman, Philip. *Alexander the Great*. New York: Simon & Schuster, 2011.

Freund, Richard A. "The Incense Shovel of Bethsaida and Synagogue Iconography in Late Antiquity." *Bethsaida* 2:413–59.

———. "The Search for Bethsaida in Rabbinic Literature." *Bethsaida* 1:267–311.

Frey, Jean-Baptiste. *Corpus Inscriptionum Iudaicarum*. 2 vols. Sussidi allo studio delle antichità cristian 1, 3. 1936. Reprint, Rome: Pontificio Instituto di Archeologia Cristiana, 1952.

Freyne, Seán. "Archaeology and the Historical Jesus." In *Archaeology and Biblical Interpretation*, edited by John R. Bartlett, 117–44. London: Routledge, 1997.

———. *Galilee, from Alexander the Great to Hadrian, 323 B.C.E. to 135 C.E.* Judaism and Christianity in Antiquity 5. Wilmington, DE: Glazier, 1980.
Fridman, Sharya. "Chalk-Stone Vessels in the Southern Golan: Archaeological, Historical and Cultural Contexts." *IEJ* 71 (2021) 180–203.
Frier, Bruce. "Roman Life Expectancy: Ulpian's Evidence." *HSCP* 86 (1982) 213–51.
Fuchs, Ron. "The Palestinian Arab House and the Islamic 'Primitive Hut.'" *Muqarnas* 15 (1998) 157–77.
Fuller, Anne H. *Buarij, Portrait of a Lebanese Muslim Village*. Harvard Middle Eastern Monographs 6. Cambridge: distributed for the Harvard University Department of Middle Eastern Studies by Harvard University Press, 1961 (i.e., 1963).
Funk, Robert W. *Honest to Jesus: Jesus for a New Millennium*. San Francisco: HarperSanFrancisco, 1996.
Furfey, Paul Hanly. "Christ as τεκτων." *CBQ* 17 (1955) 324–35.
Gallant, Thomas W. *Risk and Survival in Ancient Greece*. Stanford: Stanford University Press, 1991.
Galor, Katharina. "Qumran's Plastered Pools: A New Perspective." *Academia* https://www.academia.edu/36464210/Qumran_s_Plastered_Pools_A_New_Perspective?email_work_card=view-paper/.
Galor, Katharina, with Eric M. Meyers. "The Stepped Water Installations of the Western Summit." In *ASAWSS* 1:419–44.
Garroway, Kristine Henriksen. *Children in the Ancient Near Eastern Household*. Explorations in Ancient Near Eastern Civilizations. Winona Lake, IN: Eisenbrauns, 2014.
Geggel, Laura. "Medieval Parasite-Filled Poop Found in Jerusalem Latrine." *Yahoo News* (website), March 30, 2015. https://news.yahoo.com/medieval-parasite-filled-poop-found-jerusalem-latrine-114618131.html/.
Geyser, A. S. "The Youth of John the Baptist." Short Notes. *NovT* 1 (1956) 70–75.
Geva, Hillel. "The Church of St. Peter in Gallicantu." In *NEAEHL* 5:1814–15.
———. "Stratigraphy and Architecture (Herodian House)." *JQE* 3:1–78.
———. "Stratigraphy and Architecture (Burnt House)." *JQE* 4:1–82.
———. "Summary and Discussion of Findings from Areas A, W and X-2." *JQE* 2.501–52.
Gibson, Shimon. *The Cave of John the Baptist: The First Archaeological Evidence of the Historical Reality of the Gospel Story*. 1st Image books ed. New York: Image, 2005.
———. *The Final Days of Jesus: The Archaeological Evidence*. New York: Harper Collins, 2009.
———. "On John the Baptist at the Jordan River: Geohistorical and Archaeological Considerations." In *Fountains of Wisdom: In Conversation with James H. Charlesworth*, edited by Gerbern S. Oegema et al., 217–40. London: T. & T. Clark, 2022.
———. "The Trial of Jesus at the Jerusalem Praetorium: New Archaeological Evidence." In *The World of Jesus and the Early Church*, edited by Craig A. Evans, 97–118. Peabody, MA: Hendrickson, 2011.
Gibson, Shimon, and Joan E. Taylor. *Beneath the Church of the Holy Sepulchre Jerusalem: The Archaeology and Early History of Traditional Golgotha*. Palestine Exploration Fund monographs Series Maior 1. London: Palestine Exploration Fund, 1994.
Glancy, Jennifer A. *Slavery in Early Christianity*. Minneapolis: Fortress, 2006.
Glotz, Gustave. *Ancient Greece at Work*. History of Civilization. New York: Barnes & Noble, 1965.

Goldsworthy, Adrian. *Augustus*. New Haven: Yale University Press, 2014.
Goodman, Martin. *State and Society in Roman Galilee*. Totowa, NJ: Rowman and Allenheld, 1983.
Gordon, Benjamin D. "Units Ia, Ib, and Ic: Buildings in the Eastern Part of the Excavated Areas." In *ASAWSS* 1:43–111.
Grantham, Billy J. "The Faunal Remains." In *ASAWSS* 2:871–88.
Grauer, Anne L., and George J. Armelagos. "Skeletal Biology of Hesban: A Biocultural Interpretation." In *The Necropolis of Hesban: A Typology of Tombs*, edited by S. Douglas Waterhouse, 109–31. Hesban 10. Berrien Springs, MI: Andrews University Press, 1998.
Graves, David E. *The Archaeology of the New Testament*. Moncton, NB: Electronic Christian Media, 2021. https://truthandgrace.com/Archaeology_of_the_New_Testament.pdf/.
———. "Pilate's Ring and Roman Religion." *Near East Archaeology Society Bulletin* 64 (2019) 1–20.
Green, Joel B. *The Gospel of Luke*. NICNT. Grand Rapids: Eerdmans, 1997.
Greenhut, Zvi. "Burial Cave of the Caiaphas Family." *BAR* 18.5 (1992) 29–32, 35–36.
Grey, Matthew J. "Olive Processing and Ritual Purity in the 'Place of the Oil Press': Reexamining the 1st Century Features and Functions of Jerusalem's Gethsemane Grotto." In *To Explore the Land of Canaan: Studies in Biblical Archaeology in Honor of Jeffrey R. Chadwick*, edited by Aren M. Maeir and George A. Pierce, 313–52. Archaeology of the Biblical worlds 4. Berlin: De Gruyter, 2021.
Grey, Matthew J., and Chad S. Spigel. "Ḥuqoq in the Late Hallenistic and Early Roman Periods." In *GLSTMP* 2:362–78.
Grmek, Mirko D. *Diseases in the Ancient Greek World*. Translated by Mireille Muellner and Leonard Muellner. Baltimore: Johns Hopkins University Press, 1989.
Groh, Dennis. "The American Field School and the Future of Biblical Archaeology." In *A City Set on a Hill: Essays in Honor of James F. Strange*, edited by Daniel A. Warner and Donald D. Binder, 128–60. Mountain Home, AR: BorderStone, 2014.
Gross, Boaz. "The Other Side of Beth Shemesh." *Bible History Daily* (blog), May 28, 2021. https://www.biblicalarchaeology.org/daily/the-other-side-of-beth-shemesh/.
Gualdi-Russo, Emanuela, et al. "A Multidisciplinary Study of Calcaneal Trauma in Roman Italy: A Possible Case of Crucifixion?" *Archaeological and Anthropological Sciences* 11 (2019) 1783–91.
Gudme, Anne Katrine de Hemmer. "Mortuary Rituals." In *The Oxford Handbook of Early Christian Ritual*, edited by Risto Uro et al., 353–69. Oxford Handbooks. Oxford: Oxford University Press, 2019.
Gurevich, David. "The Water Pools and the Pilgrimage to Jerusalem in the Late Second Temple Period." *PEQ* 149.2 (2017) 103–34.
Gurtner, Daniel M., and Loren T. Stuckenbruck, eds. *T. & T. Clark Encyclopaedia of Second Temple Judaism*. 2 vols. London: T. & T. Clark, 2019.
Gutfeld, Oren. "Hyrcania." In *NEAEHL* 5:1787–88.
———. "Hyrcania's Mysterious Tunnels: Searching for the Treasures of the Copper Scroll." *BAR* 32.5 (2006) 46–51, 54–55, 60–61.
———. Introduction. In *JQE* 5:1–12.
Gutiérrez-Jiménez, Javier, et al. "Malnutrition and Intestinal Parasites: Mexico Perspectives." https://www.academia.edu/34590130/Malnutrition_and_Intestinal_Parasites_Mexico_Perspectives/.
Gutman, Shmaryahu. "Gamala." In *NEAEHL* 2:459–63.

Haas, Nicu. "Anthropological Observations on the Skeletal Remains from Giv'at ha-Mivtar." *IEJ* 20 (1970) 38–59.

Haas, Nicu, and H. Nathan. "Anthropological Survey of Human Skeletal Remains from Qumran" *RevQ* 6.3 (1968) 345–52.

Habas, Li-hi. "An Incised Depiction of the Temple Menorah and Other Cult Objects of the Second Temple Period." In *JQE* 2:329–42.

Haber, Susan. "Common Judaism, Common Synagogue? Purity, Holiness, and Sacred Space at the Turn of the Common Era." In *Common Judaism: Explorations in Second-Temple Judaism*, edited by Wayne O. McCready and Adele Reinharts, 63–77. Minneapolis: Fortress, 2008.

Hachlili, Rachel. *Ancient Synagogues—Archaeology and Art: New Discoveries and Current Research*. Handbook of Oriental Studies. Section 1, The Near and Middle East 105 Leiden: Brill, 2013.

———. "Burials, Ancient Jewish." In *ABD* 2:789–94.

———. "Burial Practices." In *The Eerdmans Dictionary of Early Judaism*, edited by John J. Collins and Daniel C. Harlow, 448–52. Grand Rapids: Eerdmans, 2010.

———. "The Goliath Family in Jericho: Funerary Inscriptions from a First Century A.D. Jewish Monumental Tomb." *BASOR* 235 (1979) 31–66.

———. *Jewish Funerary Customs, Practices and Rites in the Second Temple Period*. JSJSup 94. Leiden: Brill, 2005.

Hachlili, Rachel, and Ann E. Killebrew. *Jericho: The Jewish Cemetery of the Second Temple Period*. IAA Reports 7. Jerusalem: IAA, 1999.

Hachlili, Rachel, and Patricia Smith. "The Genealogy of the Goliath Family." *BASOR* 235 (1979) 67–70.

Hadas, Gideon. "Abstract: Nine Tombs of the Second Temple Period at 'En-Gedi." *Atiqot* 24 (1994) 1–14.

———. "En-Gedi." In *NEAEHL* 2:1723–24.

Hall, Stuart George, ed. *Melito of Sardis on Pascha*. Oxford: Clarendon, 1979.

Hamel, Gildas. *Poverty and Charity in Roman Palestine, First Three Centuries C.E.* University of California Publications. Near Eastern Studies 23. Berkeley: University of California Press, 1990.

Hanson, Ann Ellis, ed. *Collectanea Papyrologica: Texts Published in Honor of H. C. Youtie*. 2 vols. Papyrologische Texte und Abhandlungen 19–20. Bonn: Habelt, 1976.

Hanson, K. C. "Galilean Fishing Economy and the Jesus Tradition." *BTB* 27 (1997) 99–111.

Hanson, K. C., and Douglas E. Oakman. *Palestine in the Time of Jesus: Social Structures and Social Conflicts*. 2nd ed. Minneapolis: Fortress, 2008.

Har-Even, Benyamin. "A Second Temple Period Synagogue at Ḥorvat Diab in Western Benjamin." *Qadmoniot* 151 (2016) 49–53. (Hebrew)

Harley, Felicity. "Crucifixion in Roman Antiquity: The State of the Field." *Journal of Early Christian Studies* 27(2019) 303–23.

Harrison, R. K. "Disease, Bible and Spade." *BA* 16.4 (1953) 88–92.

Harter, Stephanie, et al. "Toilet Practices among Members of the Dead Sea Scroll Sect at Qumran." *RevQ* 21 (2004) 579–84.

Hasegawa, Shuichi, Hisao Kuwabara, and Yitzhak Paz. "Tel Rekhesh-2017." *HA-ESI* 134 (blog) January 27, 2022 https://hadashot-esi.org.il/report_detail_eng.aspx?id=26123&mag_id=134/.

Hebrew University of Jerusalem. "DNA of Jesus-Era Shrouded Man in Jerusalem Reveals Earliest Case of Leprosy." Science News. *Science Daily* (blog), December 16, 2009. https://www.sciencedaily.com/releases/2009/12/091216103558.htm/.
Hengel, Martin. *The Charismatic Leader and His Followers*. Translated by James Greig. New York: Crossroad, 1981.
———. *Crucifixion in the Ancient World and the Folly of the Message of the Cross.* Philadelphia: Fortress, 1977.
———. "Das Gleichnis von den Weingärtnern Mc 12:1–12 im Licht der Zenonpapyri und der rabbinischen Gleichnisse." *ZNW* 59.1-2 (1968) 1–39.
———. *Judaism and Hellenism*. Philadelphia: Fortress, 1974.
———. "Maria Magdalena und die Frauen als Zeugen." In *Abraham Unser Vater: Juden und Christen im Gespräch über die Bibel*, edited by Otto Betz et al., 243–56. Arbeiten zur Geshichte des Spätjudentums und Urschristeniums 5. Leiden: Brill, 1963.
Herion, Gary A. "Herod Philip." In *ABD* 3.160–61.
Herr, Larry G., and Gary L. Christopherson. *Excavation Manual: Madaba Plains Project*. Rev. ed. Berrien Springs, MI: Madaba Plains Project in cooperation with Andrews University Press, 1998.
Herrenbrück, Fritz. "Wer waren die 'Zölner'?" *ZNW* 59.3-4 (1981) 178–94.
Herz, Johannes. "Grossgrundbesitz in Palästina im Zeitalter Jesu." *PJ* 24 (1928) 98–113.
Hirschberg, J. W. "The Remains of an Ancient Synagogue on Mount Zion." *JR* 116–17.
Hirschfeld, Yizhar. "The Early Roman Bath and Fortress at Ramat Hanadiv Near Caesarea." In *The Roman and Byzantine Near East: Some Recent Archaeological Research*, edited by John H. Humphrey, 28–55. JRASup 14 Ann Arbor: Journal of Roman Archaeology, 1995. .
———. "En-Gedi." In *NEAEHL* 5:1718–22.
———. *The Palestinian Dwelling in the Roman-Byzantine Period*. SBFCMi 34. Jerusalem: Franciscan, 1995.
———. "Ramat ha-Nadiv." In *NEAEHL* 4:1257–60, 5:2004–6.
———, ed. *Ramat Hanadiv Excavations*. Jerusalem: Israel Exploration Society, 2000.
Hirschfeld, Yizhar, and Miriam Feinberg-Vamosh. "A Country Gentleman's Estate: Unearthing the Splendors of Ramat Hanadiv." *BAR* 31.2 (2005) 18–31.
Hoade, Eugene. *Guide to the Holy Land*. 4th ed. Jerusalem: Franciscan, 1971.
Hock, Ronald F. *The Social Context of Paul's Ministry*. Philadelphia: Fortress, 1980.
Hoehner, Harold W. *Herod Antipas*. SNTSMS 17. Cambridge: Cambridge University Press, 1972.
Holladay, John S., Jr. "House, Israelite." In *ABD* 3:308–18.
Holladay, William L. *A Concise Hebrew and Aramaic Lexicon of the Old Testament*. 10th, corrected impression. Grand Rapids: Eerdmans, 1988.
Homsher, Robert S. "Mud Bricks and the Process of Construction in the Middle Bronze Age Southern Levant." *BASOR* 368 (2012) 1–27.
Hopkins, Jamal-Dominique. "An Essene Filled with the Holy Spirit? Revisiting the Qumran (Dead Sea Scrolls) Hypothesis of John the Baptist Considering an Afro-Christian Pneumatological Hermeneutic." *PRSt* 48 (2021) 429–37.
Hopkins, Keith. "On the Probable Age Structure of the Roman Population." *Population Studies*. 20 (1966) 245–64.
Hoppe, Leslie J. "Caesarea Maritima." *NIDB* 1:516–17.
———. *What Are They Saying about Biblical Archaeology?* New York: Paulist, 1984.

Horsley, G. H. R. *New Documents Illustrating Early Christianity: A Review of the Greek Inscriptions and Papyri Published in 1979*. With the collaboration of A. L. Connolly and others. New Documents Illustrating Early Christianity 4. North Ryde, N.S.W.: The Ancient History Documentary Research Centre, Macquarie University, 1987.

Horsley, Richard A. "Archaeology and the Villages of Upper Galilee: A Dialogue with Archaeologists." *BASOR* 297 (1995) 5–16.

———. *Galilee: History, Politics, People*. Valley Forge, PA: Trinity, 1995.

Horsley, Richard A., with John S. Hanson. *Bandits, Prophets, and Messiahs: Popular Movements at the Time of Jesus*. 1st Harper & Row paperback ed. San Francisco: Harper & Row, 1988.

Horwitz, Liora Kolska. "The Faunal Remains." In *ETZ*, 75–96.

Huang, Pien, and Meredith Rizzo. "Tracking Health Threats, One Sewage Sample at a Time." *National Public Radio* (April 24, 2023). https://www.npr.org/sections/health-shots/2023/04/24/1171177281/wastewater-surveillance-covid-tracking/.

Humphrey, J. H., ed. *The Circus and a Byzantine Cemetery at Carthage*. Ann Arbor: University of Michigan Press, 1988.

Humphreys, Colin J. *The Mystery of the Last Supper: Reconstructing the Final Days of Jesus*. Cambridge: Cambridge University Press, 2011.

Hutchison, John C. "Was John the Baptist an Essene from Qumran?" *BSac* 159.634 (2002) 187–200.

Ilan, Tal. *Integrating Women into Second Temple History*. TSAJ 76. Peabody, MA: Hendrickson, 1999.

———. *Jewish Women in Greco-Roman Palestine*. Peabody: MA: Hendrickson, 1996.

———. *Lexicon of Jewish Names in Late Antiquity*. Vol. 1, *Part I, Palestine 330 BCE–200 CE*. TSAJ 91. Tübingen: Mohr Siebeck, 2002.

———. "Ossuaries of the Herodian Period." In *The World of the Herods*, edited by Nikos Kokkinos, 61–69. OeO 14. Stuttgart: Steiner, 2007.

———. "Premarital Cohabitation in Ancient Judea: The Evidence of the Babatha Archive and the Mishnah ('Ketubbot' 1.4)." *HTR* 86 (1993) 247–64.

Jackson, Ralph. *Doctors and Diseases in the Roman Empire*. London: British Museum Publications, 1988.

Jacobs, Andrew S., trans. "The Bordeaux Pilgrim (c. 333 C.E.)." http://andrewjacobs.org/translations/bordeaux.html/.

Jacobson, David M. "Mariam Daughter of Yeshua, Son of Caiaphas, Priest of Maʿaziah from Beth ʿImri." *PEQ* 144 (2012) 1–4.

Jarus, Owen. "This Ring Bears the Name of the Man Who Condemned Jesus to Death. Who Really Wore It?" *LiveScience* (blog), December 3, 2018 https://www.livescience.com/64217-pontius-pilate-ring-discovered.html/.

Jastrow, Marcus, comp. *A Dictionary of the Targumim, Talmud Bavli, Talmud Yerushalmi and Midrashic Literature*. 2 vols. New York: Judaica, 1971.

Jenks, Gregory C. "The Quest for the Historical Nazareth." 2013. https://www.academia.edu/3988852/The_Quest_for_the_Historical_Nazareth?email_work_card=view-paper/.

Jennings, William, and Ulric Gantillon. *Lexicon to the Syriac New Testament*. Oxford: Clarendon, 1962.

Jensen, Morton Hørning. "Antipas—The Herod Jesus Knew." *BAR* 38.5 (2012) 42–46.

———. *Herod Antipas in Galilee*. WUNT 2/215. Tübingen: Mohr Siebeck, 2006.

———. "The Political History in Galilee from the First Century BCE to the End of the Second Century CE." In *GLSTMP* 1:51–77.

———. "Purity and Politics in Herod Antipas's Galilee: The Case for Religious Motivation." *JSHJ* 11 (2013) 3–34.
Jeremias, Joachim. *Jerusalem in the Time of Jesus*. Translated by F. H. and C. H. Cave. Philadelphia: Fortress, 1969.
———. *The Parables of Jesus*. Translated by S. H. Hooke. Rev. ed. New York: Scribner, 1963.
Jevons, F. B. "Some Ancient Greek Pay-Bills." *Economic Journal* 6.23 (1896) 470–75.
Johnson, Luke Timothy. *The Real Jesus: The Misguided Quest for the Historical Jesus and the Truth of the Traditional Gospels*. San Francisco: HarperSanFrancisco, 1996.
Johnson, Marshall D. "Life of Adam and Eve." In *OTP* 2:249–95.
Jones, A. H. M. *The Greek City from Alexander to Justinian*. Oxford: Clarendon, 1940.
———. "The Urbanization of Palestine." *JRS* 21 (1931) 78–85.
Kahana, Tzipi. "Human Skeletal Remains from Wadi-Ḥalaf (Near Khirbat Ras Abu Ma'aruf), Jerusalem." *Atiqot* 48 (2004) 83–90.
Karmon, Y. "The Settlement of the Northern Huleh Valley since 1838." *IEJ* 3 (1953) 4–25.
Kazen, Thomas. "A Perhaps Less Halakic Jesus and Purity: On Prophetic Criticism, Halakic Innovation, and Rabbinic Anachronism." https://www.academia.edu/21663792/A_Perhaps_Less_Halakic_Jesus_and_Purity_On_Prophetic_Criticism_Halakic_Innovation_and_Rabbinic_Anachronism?email_work_card=view-paper/.
Kee, Howard Clark. "Early Christianity in the Galilee: Reassessing the Evidence from the Gospels." In *The Galilee in Late Antiquity*, edited by Lee I. Levine, 3–22. New York: Jewish Theological Seminary of America, 1992.
———. "Testaments of the Twelve Patriarchs." In *OTP* 1:775–828.
Keener, Craig S. "Fever and Dysentery in Acts 28:8 and Ancient Medicine." *BBR* 19.3 (2009) 393–402.
Kehati, Pinhas. *Mishnah Kiddushin*. Jerusalem: Eliner Library, 1994.
———. *Mishnah Ktebot*. Jerusalem: Eliner Library, 1994.
Kelhoffer, James A. "Did John the Baptist Eat Like a Former Essene? Locust-Eating in the Ancient Near East and at Qumran." *DSD* 11 (2004) 293–314.
Kelley, Justin L. *The Church of the Holy Sepulchre in Text and Archaeology*. Archaeopress Archaeology. Oxford: Archaeopress, 2019.
———. "The Holy Sepulchre in History, Archaeology, and Tradition." *BAR* 47.1 (2021) 34–43.
Kenyon, Kathleen M. *Jerusalem: Excavating 3000 Years of History*. New Aspects of Archaeology. New York: McGraw-Hill, 1967.
Killebrew, Ann E. "Village and Countryside." In *OHJDL* 189–209.
Killebrew, Ann E., and Steven Fine. "Qatzrin—Reconstructing Village Life in Talmudic Times." *BAR* 17.3 (1991) 44–56.
King, J. Philip, and Lawrence E. Stager. *Life in Biblical Israel*. LAI. Louisville: Westminster John Knox, 2001.
Kippenberg, Hans G. *Religion und Klassenbildung im antiken Judäa*. SUNT 14. Göttingen: Vanderhoeck & Ruprecht, 1978.
Kiuchi, Nobuyoshi. "A Paradox of the Skin Disease." *ZAW* 113 (2001) 505–14.
Klausner, Joseph. *Jesus of Nazareth*. Translated by Herbert Danby. New York: Macmillan, 1925.
Klawans, Jonathan. *Impurity and Sin in Ancient Judaism*. New York: Oxford University Press, 2000.

———. "Was Jesus' Last Supper a Seder?" *BR* 17.5 (2001) 24, 26–27, 29–33, 47.
Klein, S. "Notes on Large Estates in the Land of Israel." *BJPES* 1.3 (1933) 3–9. (Hebrew)
———. "Notes on Large Estates in the Land of Israel." *BJPES* 3.4 (1938) 109–16. (Hebrew)
Kloner, Amos. "Did a Rolling Stone Close Jesus' Tomb?" *BAR* 25.5 (1999) 23–25, 28–29, 76.
Kokkinos, Nikos. "The Location of Tarichaea: North or South of Tiberias?" *PEQ* 142 (2010) 7–23.
Kotansky, Roy D. "An Inscribed Copper Amulet from 'Evron." *Atiqot* 20 (1991) 81–87.
———. "The Magic 'Crucifixion Gem' in the British Museum." *GRBS* 57 (2017) 631–59.
Kramer, Carol. *Village Ethnoarchaeology: Rural Iran in Archaeological Perspective.* Studies in Archaeology. New York: Academic, 1982.
Krauss, Rolf. "Kritische Bemerkung zur Erklärung von ṣāraʿat als schuppende Hautkrankheit, inbesondere as Psoriasis." *BN* 177 (2018) 3–24.
Krauss, Samuel. *Antoninus und Rabbi.* Israelitisch-theologische Lehranstalt 17. Vienna: Israelitisch-theologische Lehranstalt, 1910.
———. *Talmudische Archäologie.* 3 vols. Grundriss der Gesamtwissenschaft des Judentums Hildesheim: Olms, 1966.
Lancaster, William, and Fidelity Lancaster. "Jordanian Village Houses in Their Contexts, Growth, Decay and Rebuilding." *PEQ* 129 (1997) 38–53.
Lance, H. Darrell. *The Old Testament and the Archaeologist.* GBS. Old Testament Series. Philadelphia: Fortress, 1981.
Lane, William L. *The Gospel according to Mark.* NICNT 2. Grand Rapids: Eerdmans, 1974.
Lang, Bernhard, ed. *Anthropological Approaches to the Old Testament.* IRT 8. Philadelphia: Fortress, 1985.
Last, Richard, and Philip A. Harland. *Group Survival in the Ancient Mediterranean: Rethinking Material Conditions in the Landscape of Jews and Christians.* London: T. & T. Clark, 2020.
Laughlin, John C. H. "Capernaum: From Jesus' Time and After." *BAR* 19.5 (1993) 54–61.
Le Bailly, Matthieu, and Françoise Bouchet. "*Diphyllobothrium* in the Past: Review and New Records." *IJP* 3.3 (2013) 182–87.
Leibner, Uzi. "Khirbet Wadi Hammam in the Early and Middle Roman Periods." In *GLSTMP* 2:343–61.
———. *Settlement and History in Hellenistic, Roman, and Byzantine Galilee: An Archaeological Survey of the Eastern Galilee.* TSAJ 127. Tübingen: Mohr Siebeck, 2009.
———. "Summary and Discussion: Life in a Roman-Period Galilean Village." In *Khirbet Wadi Ḥamam: A Roman-Period Village and Synagogue in the Lower Galilee,* edited by Uzi Leibner, 620–36. Qedem Reports 13. Jerusalem: Institute of Archaeology, the Hebrew University of Jerusalem, 2018.
Leibner, Uzzi, and Amir Amitzur. "A Lavish, Roman-Period Burial Cave in Tiberias." *IEJ* 72 (2022) 204–18.
Leibner, Uzzi, and Benjamin Arubas. "Area A: The Synagogue: Stratigraphy and Architecture." In *Khirbet Wadi Ḥamam: A Roman-Period Village and Synagogue in the Lower Galilee,* edited by Uzzi Leibner, 24–98. Qedem Reports 13. Jerusalem: Institute of Archaeology, the Hebrew University of Jerusalem, 2018.

Leichman, Abigail Klein. "World Malaria Experts Look to Israel's Past for Future Solutions." *Israel 21C: Uncovering Israel* (blog), December 17, 2013. https://www.israel21c.org/world-malaria-experts-look-to-israels-past-for-future-solutions/.
Leiman, Rivka Elitzur, and Uzi Leibner. "An Amulet from Khirbet Wadi Ḥamam." *IEJ* 66 (2016) 220–31.
Lenski, Gerhard E. *Power and Privilege*. McGraw-Hill Series in Sociology. New York: McGraw-Hill, 1966.
Lev-Tov, Justin. "Upon What Meat Doth This Our Caesar Feed . . . ? a Dietary Perspective on Hellenistic and Roman Influence in Palestine." In *Zeichen aus Text und Stein Studien auf dem Weg zu einer Archäologie des Neuen Testaments*, edited by Stefan Alkier and Jürgen Zangenberg, 420–46. TANZ 42. Tübingen: Francke, 2003.
Levine, Lee I. "Archaeological Discoveries from the Greco-Roman Era." In *Recent Archaeology in the Land of Israel*, edited by Hershel Shanks and Benjamin Mazar, 75–88. Translated by Aryeh Finkelstein. Washington, DC: Biblical Archaeology Society, 1984.
———. "Archaeology and the Religious Ethos of Pre-70 Palestine." In *Hillel and Jesus*, edited by James H. Charlesworth and Loren L. John, 110–20. Minneapolis: Fortress, 1997.
———. "The Synagogues of Galilee." In *GLSTMP* 1:129–50.
Levy, Nigel (prod./dir.), et al. *Smithsonian: The Real Jesus of Nazareth*. TV series. 4 episodes. Aired 2017. https://www.smithsonianchannel.com/shows/the-real-jesus-of-nazareth/.
Levy, Thomas E., ed. *The Archaeology of Society in the Holy Land*. London: Leicester University Press, 1995.
Lewis, Naphtali. *The Documents from the Bar Kokhba Period in the Cave of the Letters: Vol. 1, The Greek Papyri*. JDS 2. Jerusalem: Israel Exploration Society, 1989.
Liberatore, Stacy. "Is this the earliest drawing of the crucifixion? 1,970-year-old carving made at ancient Roman slave school lampoons worshipper of human figure with the head of the donkey that could be anti-Christian graffiti." *Daily Mail*, April 2, 2021. https://www.dailymail.co.uk/sciencetech/article-9431585/Graffiti-carved-ancient-Roman-building-1-900-years-ago-Crucifixion.html/.
Lichtenberger, Achim. "Jesus and the Theater in Jerusalem." In *JA* 283–99.
Llewelyn, S. R., ed. *A Review of the Greek Inscriptions and Papyri Published in 1986–97*. New Documents Illustrating Early Christianity 9. Grand Rapids: Eerdmans, 2002.
Loffreda, Stanislao. "Capernaum." In *NEAEHL* 1:291–95.
———. "Machaerus." In *ABD* 4:457–58.
———. "Preliminary Report on the Second Season of Excavations at Qal'at el-Mishnaqa: Machaerus." *ADAJ* 25 (1981) 85–94.
Longenecker, Bruce W. *Remember the Poor: Paul, Poverty, and the Greco-Roman World*. Grand Rapids: Eerdmans, 2010.
Luff, Rosemary Margaret. *The Impact of Jesus in First-Century Palestine: Textual and Archaeological Evidence for Long-Standing Discontent*. Cambridge: Cambridge University Press, 2019.
Lutfiyya, Abdulla M. *Baytin: A Jordanian Village*. Studies in Social Anthropology. London: Mouton, 1966.
Macalister, Alexander. "Fever." In *International Standard Bible Encyclopedia*, edited by James Orr (1915). https://www.bible-history.com/isbe/F/FEVER/.

Maccoby, Hyam. *Ritual and Morality: The Ritual Purity System and Its Place in Judaism.* Cambridge: Cambridge University Press, 1999.

Mack, Burton L. *A Myth of Innocence: Mark and Christian Origins.* Philadelphia: Fortress, 1988.

Magen, Yitzhak. "Ancient Israel's Stone Age." *BAR* 24.5 (1998) 46–52.

———. "Jerusalem as a Center of the Stone Vessel Industry during the Second Temple Period." In *AJR*, 244–56.

———. "The Land of Benjamin in the Second Temple Period." In *The Land of Benjamin*, edited by Yitzhak Magen et al., 1–28. Judea and Samaria Publications. Jerusalem: IAA, 2004.

———. "The Stone Vessel Industry during the Second Temple Period." In *Purity Broke Out in Israel (Tractate Shabbat 13b): Stone Vessels in the Late Second Temple Period*, Curator, Ofra Rimon, 7–27. Haifa: Reuben and Edith Hecht Museum, 1994.

———. *The Stone Vessel Industry in the Second Temple Period.* Judea and Samaria Publications 1. Jerusalem: Israel Exploration Society, 2002.

Magen, Yitzhak, et al. "Khirbet Badd'isa—Qiryat Sefer." In *The Land of Benjamin*, edited by Yitzhak Magen et al., 179–242. Judea and Samaria Publications. Jerusalem: IAA, 2004.

Magness, Jodi. *The Archaeology of Qumran and the Dead Sea Scrolls.* Studies in the Dead Sea scrolls and Related Literature. Grand Rapids: Eerdmans, 2002.

———. "Disposing of the Dead: An Illustration of the Intersection of Archaeology and Text." In *"Go Out and Study the Land" (Judges 18:2): Archaeological, Historical, and Textual Studies in Honor of Hanan Eshel*, edited by Aren M. Maeir et al., 117–32. JSJSup 148. Leiden: Brill, 2012.

———. *Stone and Dung, Oil and Spit: Jewish Daily Life in the Time of Jesus.* Grand Rapids: Eerdmans, 2011.

———. "What Did Jesus' Tomb Look Like?" *BAR* 32.1 (2006) 38, 40–43, 45–49.

Malina, Bruce, and Richard L. Rohrbaugh. *Social Science Commentary on the Synoptic Gospels.* Minneapolis: Fortress, 1992.

Marciniak, Stephanie, et al. "*Plasmodium falciparum* Malaria in 1st–2nd Century CE Southern Italy." *Current Biology* 26.23 (2016) R1220–R1222.

Marciniak, Stephanie, D., et al. "A Multi-Faceted Anthropological and Genomic Approach to Framing *Plasmodium Falciparum* Malaria in Imperial Period Central-Southern Italy (1st–4th c. CE)." *Journal of Anthropological Archaeology* 49 (2018) 210–24.

Marcus, Joel. *John the Baptist in History and Theology.* Studies on personalities of the New Testament. Columbia: University of South Carolina Press, 2018.

———. "Passover and Last Supper Revisited." *NTS* 59 (2013) 303–24.

Marshall, I. Howard. *The Gospel of Luke.* NIGTC. Grand Rapids: Eerdmans, 1978.

Mason, Steve. "O Little Town of . . . Nazareth?" *BR* 16.1 (2000) 32–39, 51–53.

Masterman, E. W. G. "Hygiene and Disease in Palestine in Modern and Biblical Times." *PEQ* 50.1 (1918) 13–20.

———. "Hygiene and Disease in Palestine in Modern and Biblical Times." *PEQ* 50.3 (1918) 112–19.

———. "Hygiene and Disease in Palestine in Modern and Biblical Times." *PEQ* 50.4 (1918) 156–71.

Matillah, Sharon Lea. "Capernaum, Village of Nahum, from Hellenistic to Byzantine Times." In *GLSTMP* 2:217–57.

———. "Revisiting Jesus' Capernaum: A Village of Only Subsistence-Level Fishers and Farmers?" In *The Galilean Economy in the Time of Jesus*, edited by David A. Fiensy and Ralph Hawkins, 75–138. ECL 11. Atlanta: SBL, 2013.

Mayer, Günter. *Die Jüdische Frau in der Hellenistische-Römischen Antike*. Stuttgart: Kohlhammer, 1987.

Mazar, Amihai. *Archaeology of the Land of the Bible: 10,000–586 BCE*. 2 vols. ABRL. New York: Doubleday, 1990.

Mazor, Gabi. "Beth-Shean: The Hellenistic to Early Islamic Periods: The Israel Antiquities Authority Excavations." In *NEAEHL* 5:1623–36.

McCane, Byron R. "Death and Burial, Hellenistic and Roman Period, Palestine." In *OEBA* 1:262–70.

———. *Roll Back the Stone: Death and Burial in the World of Jesus*. Harrisburg, PA: Trinity, 2003.

McClure, M. L., and C. L. Feltoe, trans. *The Pilgrimage of Etheria*. Translations of Christian Literature. Series 3. London: SPCK, 1919.

McCollough, C. Thomas. "City and Village in Lower Galilee: The Import of the Archeological Excavations at Sepphoris and Khirbet Qana (Cana) for Framing the Economic Context of Jesus." In *The Galilean Economy in the Time of Jesus*, edited by David A. Fiensy and Ralph K. Hawkins, 49–74. ECL 11. Atlanta: SBL, 2013.

———. "Khirbet Qana." In *GLSTMP* 2:127–45.

McCollough, C. Thomas, and Beth Glazier-McDonald. "Magic and Medicine in Byzantine Galilee: A Bronze Amulet From Sepphoris." In *Archaeology and the Galilee: Texts and Contexts in the Graeco-Roman and Byzantine Periods*, edited by Douglas R. Edwards and C. Thomas McCollough, 143–49. SFSHJ 143. Atlanta: Scholars, 1997.

McCown, Chester C. "The Density of Population in Ancient Palestine." *JBL* 66 (1947) 425–36.

———. "Ο ΤΕΚΤΩΝ." In *Studies in Early Christianity*, edited by Shirley Jackson Case, 173–89. New York: Century, 1928.

McGarvey, J. W. *Lands of the Bible*. Nashville: Gospel Advocate, 1966.

McNamer, Elizabeth. "Pilgrim Accounts and the Bethsaida Controversy." *Bethsaida* 2:397–411.

McRay, John. *Archaeology and the New Testament*. Grand Rapids: Baker, 1991.

Meier, John. *A Marginal Jew*. Vol. 1, *The Roots of the Problem and the Person*. New York: Doubleday, 1991.

———. *A Marginal Jew*. Vol. 2, *Mentor, Message, and Miracles*. New York: Doubleday, 1994.

Merrins, Edward M. "The Deaths of Antiochus IV, Herod the Great, and Agrippa I." *BSac* 62 (1904) 548–62.

Meshorer, Ya'akov. *A Treasury of Jewish Coins: From the Persian Period to Bar Kokhba*. Jerusalem: Yad Ben-Zvi, 2001.

Metzger, Bruce M. *A Textual Commentary on the Greek New Testament*. London: United Bible Society, 1971.

Meyers, Carol. "Archaeology—A Window to the Lives of Israelite Women." In *Torah*, edited by Irmtraud Fischer et al., 61–108. Bible and Women. Hebrew Bible / Old Testament 1.1. Atlanta: SBL, 2011.

———. "The Family in Early Israel." In *Families in Ancient Israel*, edited by Leo G. Perdue et al., 1–47. Family, Religion, and Culture. Louisville: Westminster John Knox, 1997.

———. "From Field Crops to Food: Attributing Gender and Meaning to Bread Production in Iron Age Israel." In *The Archaeology of Difference: Gender, Ethnicity, Class and the "Other" in Antiquity*, edited by Douglas R. Edwards and C. Thomas McCollough, 67–84. AASOR 60/61. Boston: American Schools of Oriental Research, 2007.

———. *Rediscovering Eve: Ancient Israelite Women in Context*. Oxford: Oxford University Press, 2013.

Meyers, Carol, and Eric M. Meyers. "Sepphoris." In *OEANE* 4:531–32.

Meyers, Eric M. "Aspects of Everyday Life in Roman Palestine with Special Reference to Private Domiciles and Ritual Baths." In *Jews in the Hellenistic and Roman Cities*, edited by J. R. Bartlett, 193–219. London: Routledge, 2002.

———. "Ceramic Incense Shovels." In *ASAWSS* 2:644–52.

———. "The Cultural Setting of Galilee: The Case of Regionalism and Early Judaism" *ANRW* II.19.1 (1979) 686–702.

———. "Galilean Regionalism as a Factor in Historical Reconstruction" *BASOR* 221 (1976) 93–101.

———. "Jesus and His Galilean Context." In *Archaeology and the Galilee: Texts and Contexts in the Graeco-Roman and Byzantine Periods*, edited by Douglas R. Edwards and C. Thomas McCollough, 57–66. SFSHJ 143. Atlanta: Scholars, 1997.

———. "Jesus and His World: Sepphoris and the Quest for the Historical Jesus" In *Saxa Loquentur: Studien zur Archäologie Palästinas/Israels*, edited by Cornelis G. den Hertog et al., 185–97. AOAT 302. Münster: Ugarit, 2003.

———. "Yes, They Are." *BAR* 26.4 (2000) 46–49.

Meyers, Eric M., and Mark A. Chancey. *Archaeology of the Land of the Bible*. Vol. 3, *Alexander to Constantine*. ABRL. New Haven: Yale University Press, 2012.

Meyers, Eric M., and Benjamin D. Gordon. "The Ritual Baths: Introduction and Catalogue." In *ASAWSS* 1:391–418.

Meyers, Eric M., and Carol Meyers. "Digging the Talmud in Ancient Meiron." *BAR* 4.2 (1978) 32–42.

———. "Holy Land Archaeology: Where the Past Meets the Present." *Buried History* 50 (2014) 3–16.

———. Introduction. In *The Pottery from Ancient Sepphoris*, edited by Eric M. Meyers and Carol L. Meyers, 1–12. Sepphoris Excavation Reports 1. Winona Lake, IN: Eisenbrauns, 2013. Meyers, Eric M., and James F. Strange. *Archaeology, the Rabbis, & Early Christianity*. Nashville: Abingdon, 1981.

Meyers, Eric M., et al. "Chronological Summary and Historical Overview." *ASAWSS* 1:14–33.

———. "Residential Area of the Western Summit." In *GLSTMP* 2:39–52.

Meyers, Eric M., et al. "The Meiron Excavation Project: Archeological Survey in Galilee and Golan, 1976." *BASOR* 230 (1978) 1–24.

Meyers, Eric M., et al. "Chronological Summary and Historical Overview." In *ASAWSS* 1.14–33.

———. "Residential Area of the Western Summit." In *GLSTMP* 2:39–52.

Meyers, Eric M., et al. *Excavations at Ancient Meiron, Upper Galilee, Israel 1971–72, 1974–75, 1977*. Meiron Excavation Project 3. Cambridge: ASOR, 1981.

Meyers, Eric M., et al. *Sepphoris*. Winona Lake, IN: Eisenbrauns, 1992.
Mi-Bartenura, Ovadiya. *Six Orders of the Mishnah*. 2 vols. New York: Shulsinger, 1943 (in Hebrew).
Milgrom, Jacob. *Leviticus 1–16*. AB 3. New York: Doubleday, 1991.
Miller, Shulamit. "Tiberias." In *OEBA* 2:429–37.
Miller, Stewart S. "New Directions in the Study of Ritual Purity Practices: Implications of the Sepphoris Finds." In *ASAWSS* 1:445–75.
———. "Sepphoris, the Well Remembered City." In *BA* 55.2 (1992) 74–83.
Minozzi, S., et al. "The Roman Giant: Overgrowth Syndrome in Skeletal Remains from the Imperial Age." *International Journal of Osteoarchaeology* 25.4 (2015) 574–84.
Misgav, Haggai. "The Ostraca." In *Machaerus I*, edited by Győző Vörös, 259–77. SBFCMa 53. Milan: Terra Santa, 2013.
Mitchell, Piers D. "Human Parasites in the Roman World: Health Consequences of Conquering an Empire." *Parasitology* 144 (2017) 48–58. https://www.cambridge.org/core/services/aop-cambridge-core/content/view/S0031182015001651/.
Mitchell, Piers D., and Yotam Tepper. "Intestinal Parasitic Worm Eggs from a Crusader Period Cesspool in the City of Acre (Israel)." *Levant* 39 (2007) 91–95.
Mols, Stephan T. A. M. *Wooden Furniture in Herculaneum*. Translated by Rob Bland. Circumvesuviana 2. Amsterdam: Gieben, 1999.
Montefiore, C. G., and H. Loewe. *A Rabbinic Anthology*. 1938. Reprint, New York: Schocken, 1974.
Moreland, Milton C., et al. "Introduction: Between Text and Artifact." In *Between Text and Artifact: Integrating Archaeology in Biblical Studies Teaching*, edited by Milton C. Moreland, 1–10. ABS 8. Atlanta: SBL, 2003.
Mossé, Claude. *The Ancient World at Work*. Translated from the French by Janet Lloyd. Ancient Culture and Society. London: Chatto & Windus, 1969.
Mull, Kenneth V., and Carolyn Sandquist Mull. "Biblical Leprosy. Is It Really?" *BR* 8.2 (1992) 32–39, 62.
Murphy-O'Connor, Jerome. "Bethlehem . . . Of Course," *BR* 16.1 (2000) 40–45.
———. "The Cenacle—Topographical Setting for Acts 2:44–45." In *The Book of Acts in Its Palestinian Setting*, edited by Richard Bauckham, 303–21. The Book of Acts in its First Century Setting 4. Grand Rapids: Eerdmans, 1995.
———. *The Holy Land*. 5th ed., rev. and exp. Oxford Archaeological Guides. Oxford: Oxford University Press, 2008.
———. "What Really Happened at Gethsemane?" *BR* 14.2 (1998) 28–30, 32–37, 39.
Nagar, Yossi, and Hagit Torgeé. "Biological Characteristics of Jewish Burials in the Hellenistic and Early Roman Periods." *IEJ* 53 (2003) 164–71.
Nagar, Yossi, and Flavia Sonntag. "Byzantine Period Burials in the Negev: Anthropological Description and Summary." *IEJ* 58 (2008) 79–93.
Nathan, H. "Skeletal Remains from Naḥal Ḥever." *Atiqot* 3 (1961) 165–75.
Naveh, Jospeh. "A New Tomb Inscription from Giv'at at Hamivtar." In *JR* 73–74.
———. "The Ossuary Inscriptions from Givat ha-Mivtar." *IEJ* 20 (1970) 33–37.
Naveh, Joseph, and Shaul Shaked. *Amulets and Magic Bowls: Aramaic Incantations of Late Antiquity*. Jerusalem: Magnes, distributed by Brill, 1985.
———. *Magic Spells and Formulae: Aramaic Incantations of Late Antiquity*. Jerusalem: Magness, 1993.
Nelson, Richard D. *Deuteronomy*. OTL. Louisville: Westminster John Knox, 2002.
Netzer, Ehud. "Cypros." In *NEAEHL* 1:315–17

———. "Domestic Architecture in the Iron Age." In *The Architecture of Ancient Israel*, edited by Aharon Kempinski and Ronny Reich, 193–201. Jerusalem: Israel Exploration Society, 1992.

———. "Herod's Building Program." In *ABD* 3:169–72.

———. "Herod's Family Tomb in Jerusalem." *BAR* 9.3 (1983) 52–59.

———. "Herodium." In *NEAEHL* 2:618–26; 5:1778–80.

———. "In Search of Herod's Tomb." *BAR* 37.1 (2011) 37–48, 70.

———. "Jericho." In *NEAEHL* 5:1798–1800.

———. "Jericho: Tulul Abu el-'Alayiq: Exploration until 1951." In *NEAEHL* 2:682–83.

———. "Jericho: Tulul Abu el-'Alayiq, Exploration since 1973." In *NEAEHL* 2:683–91.

———. "Jericho: Tell es-Samarat." In *NEAEHL* 2:691–92.

———. "Masada." In *NEAEHL* 3:973–85.

———. "Roman Jericho (Tulul Abu el-'Alayiq)." In *ABD* 3:737–39.

———. "The Synagogues from the Second Temple Period according to Archaeological Finds and in Light of the Literary Sources." In *One Land, Many Cultures*, edited by G. Claudio Bottini et al., 277–85. SBFCMa 41. Jerusalem: Franciscan, 2003.

Netzer, Ehud, and Guy Stiebel. "Masada." In *NEAEHL* 5:1935–37.

Neufeld, Edward. "Hygiene Conditions in Ancient Israel (Iron Age)." In *The Biblical Archaeologist Reader*. Vol. 4, edited by Edward F. Campbell Jr. and David Noel Freedman, 151–79. Sheffield, UK: Almond, 1983.

Neusner, Jacob, trans. *The Babylonian Talmud*. 22 vols. Peabody, MA: Hendrickson, 2005.

———. *Purity in Rabbinic Judaism: A Systemic Account*. SFSHJ 95. Atlanta: Scholars, 1994.

———, trans. *The Tosefta*. 6 vols. Hoboken, NJ: Ktav, 1977–1986.

Newswire. "New Inscription with Petition for Intercession by Apostle Peter Discovered at the Suggested Biblical Bethsaida." *Newswire* (website), August 10, 2022. https://www.newswire.com/news/new-inscription-with-petition-for-intercession-by-apostle-peter-21792135/.

Nezamabadi, Masoud, et al. "Paleoparasitological Analysis of Samples from the Cheharabad Salt Mine (Northwestern Iran)." *IJP* 3.3 (2013) 229–33.

Ngo, Robin. "Jewish Purification: Stone Vessel Workshop Discovered in Galilee." *Bible History Daily* (blog), September 7, 2023. https://www.biblicalarchaeology.org/daily/news/jewish-purification-stone-vessel-workshop-galilee/.

Nolland, John. *Luke*. 3 vols. WBC 35A–35C. Dallas: Word, 1989, 1993.

Notley, R. Steven. "Byzantine Bethsaida and the House of St. Peter." *NovT* 64 (2022) 532–51.

———. "Et-Tell is Not Bethsaida." *NEA* 70.4 (2007) 220–30.

Notley, R. Steven, and Mordechai Aviam. "Searching for Bethsaida: The Case for El-Araj." *BAR* 46.2 (2020) 28–39.

Oakman, Douglas E. *Jesus and the Economic Questions of His Day*. Studies in the Bible and Early Christianity 8. Lewiston, NY: Mellen, 1986.

Onn, Alexander, et al. "Khirbet Umm el-'Umdan." *HA-ESI* 114 (2002) 64–68, 74–78.

Osband, Mechael, and Benjamin Arubas. "Majduliyya." *HA-ESI* 134 (2022) https://www.hadashot-esi.org.il/report_detail_eng.aspx?id=26127&mag_id=134/.

Osiek, Carolyn. "What Kinds of Meals Did Julia Felix Have? A Case Study of the Archaeology of the Banquet." In *MECW* 37–56

Overman, J. Andrew. "Who Were the First Urban Christians?" In *SBL Seminar Papers 1988 Seminar Papers*, 160–68. SBLSP 27. Atlanta: Scholars, 1988.

Parker, S. Thomas. "The Decapolis Reviewed." *JBL* 94.3 (1975) 437–41.

Parkin, Tim G. *Demography and Roman Society*. Ancient Society and History. Baltimore: Johns Hopkins University Press, 1992.

Parpola, Simo. "The Magi and the Star." *BR* 17.6 (2001) 16–19, 22–23, 52, 54.

Patrich, Joseph. "Caesarea." In *OEBA* 1:147–57.

———. "Hyrcania." In *NEAEHL* 2:639–41.

Patrich, Joseph, and Shlomit Weksler-Bdolah. "Old, New Banquet Hall by the Temple Mount." *BAR* 43.2 (2017) 50–54.

Pearse, Roger. "The Crucifixion Graffito of Alkimilla from Puteoli." *Roger Pearse* (blog), January 13, 2017. https://www.roger-pearse.com/weblog/2017/01/13/the-crucifixion-graffito-of-alkimilla-from-puteoli/.

Peleg-Barkat, Orit. "Fit for a King: Architecture Décor in Judaea and Herod as Trendsetter." *BASOR* 371 (2014) 141–61.

———. "Herod's Western Palace in Jerusalem: Some New Insights." *Electrum* 26 (2019) 53–72.

Peleg-Barkat, Orit, and Asaf Ben Haim. "Monumental Ionic Columns from Areas Q and H." In *JQE* 7:68–95.

Peleg-Barkat, Orit and Yotam Tepper. "Between Phoenicia and Judaea: Preliminary Results of the 2007–2010 Excavation Seasons at Horvat 'Eleq, Ramat Hanadiv, Israel." *BAIAS* 32 (2014) 49–80.

Penner, Ken M. "Dead Sea Scrolls." In *The Oxford Encyclopedia of the Books of the Bible*. Vol. 1, *Acts-LXX*, edited by Michael D. Coogan, 173–92. Oxford: Oxford University Press, 2011.

Peterson, Brian, and Scott Stripling. "Kh. El-Maqatir: A Fortified Settlement of the Late Second Temple Period on the Benjamin Plateau." *Into the Highlands Depth* 7 (2017) 61–91.

Pfann, Stephen J., et al. "Surveys and Excavations at the Nazareth Village Farm (1997–2002): Final Report" *BAIAS* 25 (2007) 19–79.

Piper, Kelsey. Future Perfect. "Malaria Is among the World's Biggest Killers of Children. Now There's a Vaccine." *Vox*, April 24, 2019. https://www.vox.com/future-perfect/2019/4/24/18514577/malaria-vaccine-malawi-pilot-program/.

Pixner, Bargil. "Church of the Apostles Found on Mt. Zion." *BAR* 16.3 (1990) 16–17, 20–21, 23–26, 28–31, 34–35, 60.

———. "Mount Zion, Jesus, and Archaeology." In *JA* 309–22.

———. *With Jesus through Galilee according to the Fifth Gospel*. Rosh Pina, Israel: Corazin, 1992.

Porath, Yosef "Vegas on the Med." *BAR* 30.5 (2004) 24–27, 29–32, 34–35.

Preuss, Julius. *Julius Preuss' Biblical and Talmudic Medicine*. Translated and edited by Fred Rosner. New York: Sanhedrin, 1978.

Price, Jonathan J. "The Languages of the Jews in Roman Palestine: The Evidence of Inscriptions." *Orientalia* 89 (2020) 112–29.

Pryke, John. "John the Baptist and the Qumran Community." *RevQ* 4.4 (1964) 483–96.

Rahmani, L. Y. "Ancient Jerusalem's Funerary Customs and Tombs: Part Four." *BA* 45.2 (1982) 109–19.

———. "Jewish Ossuaries." In *Purity Broke Out in Israel (Tractate Shabbat 13b): Stone Vessels in the Late Second Temple Period*, Curator, Ofra Rimon, 28–36. Haifa: Reuben and Edith Hecht Museum, 1994.

———. "Ossuaries and *Ossilegium* (Bone-Gathering) In the Late Second Temple Period." In *AJR*, 191–205.
Raviv, Dvir. "The Artabba Fortress: An Unknown Hasmonaean-Herodian Fortress on the Northern Border of Judaea." *IEJ* 68.1 (2018) 56–76.
Reed, Jonathan L. *Archaeology and the Galilean Jesus*. Harrisburg, PA: Trinity, 2000.
———. "Galileans, 'Israelite Village Communities,' and the Sayings Gospel Q." In *Galilee though the Centuries*, edited by Eric M. Meyers, 87–108. Duke Judaic Studies 1. Winona Lake, IN: Eisenbrauns, 1999.
———. "Instability in Jesus' Galilee: A Demographic Perspective." *JBL* 129.2 (2010) 343–65.
———. "Stone-Vessel Assemblage." In *ASAWSS* 2:749–67.
Reich, Ronny. "Area A—Stratigraphy and Architecture: Hellenistic to Medieval Strata 6–1." In *JQE* 1:83–110.
———. "Caiaphas Name Inscribed on Bone Boxes." *BAR* 18.5 (1992) 38–42, 44.
———. "The Great Mikveh Debate." *BAR* 19.2 (1993) 52–53.
———. "*Miqwa'ot* (Jewish Ritual Immersion Baths) in Eretz Israel in the Second Temple and the Mishnah and Talmud Periods." PhD diss., Hebrew University (Jerusalem), 1990 (in Hebrew).
———. "Ossuary Inscriptions of the Caiaphas Family from Jerusalem." *AJR* 223–25.
———. "Ritual Baths." In *OEANE* 4:430–31.
———. "They Are Ritual Baths: Immerse Yourself in the Ongoing Sepphoris Mikveh Debate." *BAR* 28.2 (2002) 50–55.
Reich, Ronny, and Marcela Zapata-Meza. "The Domestic Miqva'ot." In *MOG*, 109–26.
Reinach, Theodore. *Jewish Coins*. Translated by Mary Hill. With an appendix by G. F. Hill. Chicago: Argonaut, 1966.
Reinhardt, Wolfgang. "The Population Size of Jerusalem and the Numerical Growth of the Jerusalem Church." In *The Book of Acts in Its Palestinian Setting*, edited by Richard Bauckham, 237–65. The Book of Acts in its First Century setting 4. Grand Rapids: Eerdmans, 1995.
Reinhard, Karl J., and Adauto Araújo. "Archaeoparasitology." In *Encyclopedia of Archaeology*, edited by Deborah M. Pearsall, 494–501. Amsterdam: Elsevier, 2008.
"Restoring the Church of the Holy Sepulchre." *BAR* 48.3 (2022) 17.
Rey-Coquais, Jean Paul. "Decapolis." In *ABD* 2:116–21.
Richardson, Peter. *Building Jewish in the Roman East*. Waco, TX: Baylor University Press, 2004.
———. *Herod: King of the Jews and Friend of the Romans*. Studies on Personalities of the New Testament. Columbia: University of South Carolina Press, 1996.
———. "Khirbet Qana (and Other Villages) as a Context for Jesus." In *JA*, 120–44.
Richter, Gisela M. A. *Ancient Furniture: A History of Greek, Etruscan, and Roman Furniture*. Oxford: Clarendon, 1926.
"The Ring of Pontius Pilate." *L'Osservatore Romano* 2580 (2019) 10.
Ritmeyer, Leen, and Kathleen Ritmeyer. "Potter's Field or High Priest's Tomb?" *BAR* 20.6 (1994) 22, 24–26, 28–29, 31, 33–35, 76, 78.
Roberts, Charlotte, and Keith Manchester. *The Archaeology of Disease*. Stroud, UK: History Press, 2010.
Robinson, J. A. T. "The Baptism of John and the Qumran Community." *HTR* 50.3 (1957) 175–91.

Röhrer-Ertl, Olav. "Facts and Results Based on Skeletal Remains from Qumran Found in the *Collectio Kurth*: A Study in Methodology." In *Qumran, The Site of the Dead Sea Scrolls: Archaeological Interpretations and Debates; Proceedings of a Conference Held at Brown University, November 17–19, 2002*, edited by Katharina Galor et al., 181–93. STDJ 57. Leiden: Brill, 2006.
Roller, Duane W. *The Building Program of Herod the Great*. Berkeley: University of California Press, 1998.
Root, Bradley W. *First Century Galilee: A Fresh Examination of the Sources*. WUNT 2/378. Tübingen: Mohr Siebeck, 2014.
"Roman Crucifixion in Britain." *BAR* 48.3 (2022) 16.
Roser, Max. "Child Mortality." *OurWorldInData.org* (website), July 21, 2021. https://ourworldindata.org/child-mortality-big-problem-in-brief/.
Roth, Cecil, et al. "Purity and Impurity." *EncJud1* 13:1405–14.
Rousseau, John J., and Rami Arav. *Jesus and His World: An Archaeological and Cultural Dictionary*. Minneapolis: Fortress, 1995.
Runesson, Anders, et al. *The Ancient Synagogue from its Origins to 200 C.E*. AGJU 72. Leiden: Brill, 2008.
Russell, J. C. *Late Ancient and Medieval Population*. Transactions of the American Philosophical Society, new ser., 48, part 3. Philadelphia: American Philosophical Society, 1958.
Ryan, Jordan J. "Jesus in the Synagogue." *BAR* 49.1 (2023) 34–41.
———. "What Can Recent Archaeological Discoveries Tell Us about Synagogues in the Early Roman Period?" Paper Presented to the Society of Biblical Literature, 2022, Denver, Colorado.
Safrai, Samuel. "The Temple and the Divine Service." In *WHJP* 7:284–338.
Safrai, Samuel, and Sebastian Brunner. "Home and Family." In *JPFC* I.2:728–92.
Safrai, Ze'ev. *The Economy of Roman Palestine*. London: Routledge, 1994.
Sallares, Robert. "Disease." In *OCD3rev* 486.
———. *Malaria and Rome: A History of Malaria in Ancient Italy*. Oxford: Oxford University Press, 2002.
Saller, Sylvester J. *Discoveries at St. John's, 'Ein Karim (1941–1942)*. SBF 3. Jerusalem: Franciscan, 1982.
Sanders, E. P. *Jewish Law from Jesus to the Mishnah*. London: SCM, 1990.
———. *Judaism: Practice and Belief: 63 BCE–66 CE*. 2nd imp. with corrections. London: SCM, 1992.
Schaberg, Jane. "How Mary Magdalene Became a Whore." *BR* 8.5 (1992) 31–37, 51–52.
Scheidel, Walter, and Steven J. Friesen. "The Size of the Economy and the Distribution of Income in the Roman Empire." *JRS* 99 (2009) 61–91.
Schiffman, Lawrence H. *Reclaiming the Dead Sea Scrolls*. Philadelphia: Jewish Publication Society, 1994.
Schmitt Pantel, Pauline. "Banquet: Greece." In *BNP* 2:490–94
———. "Triclinium." In *BNP* 14:915–16.
Schneider, J. "σταυρος, σταυροω," In *TDNT* 7:572–84.
Schumer, Nathan. "The Population Size of Sepphoris: Rethinking Urbanization in Early and Middle Roman Galilee." https://www.academia.edu/33894484/The_Population_Size_of_Sepphoris_Rethinking_Urbanization_in_Early_and_Middle_Roman/.

Schwartz, Joshua J. "Bar Qatros and the Priestly Families of Jerusalem." In *JQE* 3:308–19.

Searcey, Nicole, et al. "Parasitism of the Zweeloo Woman: Dicrocoeliasis Evidenced in a Roman Period Bog Mummy." *IJP* 3.3 (2013) 224–28.

"Second Synagogue Found in Magdala." *BAR* 48.2 (2022) 10.

Segal, Arthur. "Decapolis." In *The Eerdmans Dictionary of Early Judaism*, edited by John J. Collins and Daniel C. Harlow, 528–30. Grand Rapids: Eerdmans, 2010.

Seligman, Jon. "Beth-Shean: The Hellenistic to Early Islamic Periods at the Foot of the Mound: The Hebrew University Excavations." In *NEAEHL* 5:1636–44.

Serr, Marcel, and Dieter Vieweger. "Golgotha: Is the Holy Sepulchre Church Authentic?" Archaeological Views. *BAR* 42.3 (2016) 28–29, 66.

Shamir, Orit. "Mixed Wool and Linen Textiles (Sha'atnez in Hebrew) from a Nabatean Burial Cave at 'En Tamar." In *Arise, Walk through the Land*, edited by Joseph Patrich et al., 53–60. Jerusalem: Israel Exploration Society, 2016.

Sheridan, Susan Guise. "Scholars, Soldiers, Craftsmen, Elites? Analysis of French Collection of Human Remains from Qumran." *DSD* 9.2 (2002) 199–248.

Sherwin-White, A. N. *Roman Society and Roman Law in the New Testament*. The Sarum Lectures 1960–1961 Oxford: Clarendon, 1963.

———. *Roman Society and Roman Law in the New Testament*. 1963. Reprint, Eugene, OR: Wipf & Stock, 2004.

Shiloh, Yigal. *Excavations at the City of David*. Vol. 1, *1978–1982*. Jerusalem: Institute of Archaeology, Hebrew University of Jerusalem, 1984.

———. "The Four-Room House: Its Situation and Function in the Israelite City." *IEJ* 20 (1970) 180–90.

———. "The Population of Iron Age Palestine in the Light of a Sample Analysis of Urban Plans, Areas, and Population Density." *BASOR* 239 (1980) 25–35.

Shpigel, Noa, and Ruth Schuster. "The Lost City of Jesus' Apostles Has Just Been Found, Archaeologists Say." *Haaretz*, August 8, 2017. https://www.haaretz.com/archaeology/2017-18-08/ty-article/lost-city-of-jesus-apostles-may-have-been-found/0000017f-e6c1-d62c-a1ff-fefb03560000/.

Singer, Suzanne F. "The Winter Palaces of Jericho." *BAR* 3.2 (1977) 1, 6–17.

Smallwood, E. Mary. "High Priests and Politics in Roman Palestine." *JTS* 13 (1962) 14–34.

Smith, Dennis E. "Dinner with Jesus & Paul." *BR* 20.4 (2004) 30–39.

———. *From Symposium to Eucharist: The Banquet in the Early Christian World*. Minneapolis: Fortress, 2003.

———. "The Greco-Roman Banquet as a Social Institution." In *MECW*, 23–33.

Smith, Patricia. "An Approach to the Paleodemographic Analysis of Human Skeletal Remains from Archaeological Sites." In *Biblical Archaeology Today: Proceedings of the Second International Congress on Biblical Archaeology: Pre-Congress Symposium, Population, Production and Power, Jerusalem, June 1990, Supplement, Volume 2*, edited by Joseph Aviram and Allen-Paris Siddur, 2–13. Jerusalem: Israel Exploration Society, 1993.

———. "The Human Skeletal Remains from the Abba Cave." *IEJ* 27 (1977) 121–24.

———. "Skeletal Analysis." In *OEANE*, 5:51–56.

Smith, Patricia, and Joseph Zias. "Skeletal Remains from the Late Hellenistic French Hill Tomb." *IEJ* 30 (1980) 109–15.

Smith, Patricia, et al. "The Skeletal Remains." In *Excavations at Ancient Meiron, Upper Galilee, Israel 1971–72, 1974–75, 1977*, edited by Eric M. Meyers et al., 110–20. Meiron Excavation Project 3. Cambridge: ASOR, 1981.
Sobecki, Sebastian. "Saewulf's Lost Arabic Map." *Pilgrim Libraries* (blog), December 11, 2017. http://www7.bbk.ac.uk/pilgrimlibraries/tag/saewulf/.
Spathi, Maria G. "The Small Finds from the Archaeological Excavations in 2010 Underneath the Church of the Redeemer in the Old City of Jerusalem." *ZDPV* 132 (2016) 26–62.
Spong, John Shelby. *Jesus for the Non-Religious*. New York: HarperCollins, 2007.
Stählin, Gustav. "τυπτω." In *TDNT* 8:260–69.
Stager, Lawrence E. "The Archaeology of the Family in Ancient Israel." *BASOR* 260 (1985) 1–35.
Standhartinger, Angela. "Women in Early Christian Meal Gatherings: Discourse and Reality." In *MECW*, 87–108
Starbuck, Scott R. A. "Why Declare the Things Forbidden? Classroom Integration of Ancient Near Eastern Archaeology with Biblical Studies in Theological Context." In *Between Text and Artifact: Integrating Archaeology in Biblical Studies Teaching*, edited by Milton C. Moreland, 99–113. ABS 8. Atlanta: SBL, 2003.
Stauffer, Ethelbert. *Jesus and His Story*. Translated from the German by Richard and Clara Winston. New York: Knopf, 1960.
Steckoll, Solomon H. "Preliminary Excavation Report in the Qumran Cemetery." *RevQ* 6 (1968) 323–44.
Stegemann, Ekkehard, and Wolfgang Stegemann. *The Jesus Movement: A Social History of Its First Century*. Translated by O. C. Dean Jr. Minneapolis: Fortress, 1999.
Stegemann, Hartmut. *The Library of Qumran: On the Essenes, Qumran, John the Baptist, and Jesus*. Grand Rapids: Eerdmans, 1998.
Steinmeyer, Nathan. "Discovering Biblical Bethsaida." *Bible History Daily* (blog), August 17, 2022. https://www.biblicalarchaeology.org/daily/biblical-sites-places/biblical-archaeology-places/discovering_biblical_bethsaida/.
———. "Pilate's Ring Examined." *Bible History Daily* (blog), April 24, 2023. https://www.biblicalarchaeology.org/daily/ancient-cultures/ancient-israel/pontius-pilates-ring-reexamined/.
———. "Rare Evidence for Roman Crucifixion Found in Second-Century Britain." *Bible History Daily* (blog), May 3, 2023. https://www.biblicalarchaeology.org/daily/rare-evidence-for-roman-crucifixion-found-in-second-century-britain/.
———. "Restoration of the Church of the Holy Sepulchre." *Bible History Daily* (blog), March 25, 2022. https://www.biblicalarchaeology.org/daily/biblical-sites-places/jerusalem/restoring_the_holy_sepulchre/.
Stern, Efrayim, ed. "Glossary." In *NEAEHL* 4:1535–40
Stern, Menahim. "Aspects of Jewish Society: The Priesthood and Other Classes." In *JPFC* I.2:561–630.
———. "The Province of Judaea." In *JPFC* I.1:308–76.
Strange, James F. "Crucifixion, Method of," In *IDBSup*, 199–200.
———."The Eastern Basilical Building." In *Sepphoris in Galilee: Crosscurrents of Culture*, edited by Rebecca Martin Nagy et al., 117–21. Winona Lake, IN: Eisenbrauns, 1996.
———. "Nazareth." In *GLSTMP* 2:167–80.

———. "The Sayings of Jesus and Archaeology." In *Hillel and Jesus,* edited by James H. Charlesworth and Loren L. Johns, 291–305. Minneapolis: Fortress, 1997.

———. "Six Campaigns at Sepphoris." In *The Galilee in Late Antiquity,* edited by Lee I. Levine, 311–43. New York: Jewish Theological Seminary of America, 1992.

———. "Some Implications of Archaeology for New Testament Studies." In *What Has Archaeology to Do with Faith?,* edited by James H. Charlesworth and Walter P. Weaver, 23–59. Faith and Scholarship Colloquies. Philadelphia: Trinity, 1992.

———. "Sepphoris: The Jewel of the Galilee." In *GLSTMP* 2:22–38.

———. "The Sepphoris Aqueducts." In *GLSTMP* 2:76–87.

Strange, James F., and Herschel Shanks. "Has the House Where Jesus Stayed in Capernaum Been Found?" *BAR* 8.6 (1982) 26–37.

———. "Synagogue Where Jesus Preached Found at Capernaum." *BAR* 9.6 (1983) 24–31.

Strange, James Riley. "Report of the 2011 Survey and 2012 Excavation Seasons at Shikhin." American Schools of Oriental Research Annual Meeting, Chicago, IL, November 2012. https://www.samford.edu/arts-and-sciences/files/Religion/2012-Shikhin-Excavation-Report.pdf/.

———. "Kefar Shikhin." In *GLSTMP* 2:88–108.

Strickert, Fred. *Bethsaida: Home of the Apostles.* Collegeville, MN: Liturgical, 1998.

Sussman, Varda. "A Jewish Burial Cave on Mount Scopus." In *AJR,* 226–30.

Sutherland, C. H. V., and M. Hammond. "Hadrian." In *OCD.*

Sweet, Louise E. *Tell Toqaan: A Syrian Village.* Anthropological Papers from the Museum of Anthropology at the University of Michigan 14. Ann Arbor: University of Michigan, 1974.

Tannous, Afif I. "The Arab Village Community of the Middle East." *Annual Report of the Board of Regents of the Smithsonian Institution* (1944) 523–43.

Taylor, Joan E. *Christians and the Holy Places: The Myth of Jewish-Christian Origins.* Oxford: Clarendon, 1993.

———. "The Garden of Gethsemane: Not the Place of Jesus' Arrest." *BAR* 21.4 (1995) 26, 28–31, 34–35.

———. "Golgotha: A Reconsideration of the Evidence for the Site of Jesus' Crucifixion and Burial." *NTS* 44.2 (1998) 180–203.

———. *The Immerser: John the Baptist within Second Temple Judaism.* Studying the Historical Jesus. Grand Rapids: Eerdmans, 1997.

———. "Magdala's Mistaken Identity." *BAR* 48.3 (2022) 55–58.

———. "Missing Magdala and the Name of Mary 'Magdalene.'" *PEQ* 146.3 (2014) 205–23.

———. *What Did Jesus Look Like?* London: Bloomsbury, 2018.

Taylor, Vincent. *The Gospel according to St. Mark.* 2nd ed. Grand Rapids: Baker, 1966.

Tcherikover, Victor. "Palestine under the Ptolemies." *Mizraim* 4 (1937) 1–82 (in Hebrew).

"Tel Rekhesh." *The Bornblum Eretz Israel Synagogues* (website). https://synagogues.kinneret.ac.il/synagogues/tel-rekhesh/.

Tendler, Avraham S., et al. "Typical and Atypical Burial in the Late Hellenistic-Early Roman Periods at Horvat Ashun—Modi'in Hills." *In the Highland's Depth* 9 (2019) 15–40.

Tessler, Yitzhak. "Ancient synagogue discovered in Galilee." *ynetnews.com* (website), August 14, 2016. https://www.ynetnews.com/articles/0,7340,L-4841308,00.html/.

Theissen, Gerd, and Annette Merz. *The Historical Jesus: A Comprehensive Guide.* Translated by John Bowden. Minneapolis: Fortress, 1998.
Thompson, William M. *The Land and the Book.* 1877. Reprint, Popular ed. Hartford, CT: Scranton, 1910.
Tombs, David. "Crucifixion, State Terror, and Sexual Abuse." *USQR* 53 (1999) 89–110.
Touwaide, Alain. "Disease." In *BNP* 4:543–54.
Tov, Emanuel. *The Texts from the Judaean Desert: Indices and an Introduction to the Discoveries in the Judaean Desert Series.* DJD 39. Oxford: Clarendon, 2002.
Tsafrir, Yoram, and Itzhak Magen. "Sartaba-Alexandrium." In *NEAEHL* 4:1318–20.
Tsuk, Tsvika. "The Aqueducts of Sepphoris." In *Galilee through the Centuries*, edited by Eric M. Meyers, 161–76. Duke Judaic Studies 1. Winona Lake, IN: Eisenbrauns, 1999.
———. "Bringing Water to Sepphoris" *BAR* 26.4 (2000) 35–38, 40–41
Tyoalumun, Kpurkpur, et al. "Prevalence of Intestinal Parasitic Infections and Their Association with Nutritional Status of Rural and Urban Pre-School Children in Benue State, Nigeria." *International Journal of MCH and AIDS* 5.2 (2016) 146–52.
Tzaferis, Vassilios. "The 'Abba' Burial Cave in Jerusalem." *Atiqot* 7 (1974) 9, 61–64 (in Hebrew).
———. "Jewish Tombs at and near Giv'at ha-Mivtar, Jerusalem." *IEJ* 20 (1970) 18–32.
Udoh, Fabian. "Taxation and Other Sources of Government Income in the Galilee of Herod and Antipas." In *GLSTMP* 1:366–87.
University of Cambridge. Research (website). "Human Parasites Found in Medieval Cesspit Reveal Links between Middle East and Europe." https://www.cam.ac.uk/research/news/human-parasites-found-in-medieval-cesspit-reveal-links-between-middle-east-and-europe/.
University of North Carolina at Charlotte. "Ancient Parasites Show that Cleanliness May Have Been Next to Sickliness." *Phys.org/.* (website), November 13, 2006. https://phys.org/news/2006-11-ancient-parasites-cleanliness-sickliness.html/.
Urbach, E. E. "The Mishnah" *EncJud1* 12:93–109.
Urman, Dan. *The Golan.* BAR International Series 269. Oxford: BAR, 1985.
Vale, Ruth. "Literary Sources in Archaeological Description: The Case of Galilee, Galilee and Galileans." *JSJ* 18.2 (1987) 209–26.
VanderKam, James C. *The Dead Sea Scrolls Today.* Grand Rapids: Eerdmans, 1994.
VanderKam, James C., and Peter Flint. *The Meaning of the Dead Sea Scrolls.* San Francisco: HarperSanFrancisco, 2002.
Vermes, Geza. *An Introduction to the Complete Dead Sea Scrolls.* Minneapolis: Fortress, 1999.
———. *Jesus the Jew.* 1st Fortress Press ed. Philadelphia: Fortress, 1981.
Vörös, Győző, ed. *Machaerus I.* SBFCMa 53. Milan: Terra Santa, 2013.
———, ed. *Machaerus II.* SBFCMa 55. Milan: Terra Santa, 2015.
———. "Machaerus: A Palace-Fortress with Multiple Mikva'ot." *BAR* 43.4 (2017) 30–39,60.
———. "Machaerus: Where Salome Danced and John the Baptist was Beheaded." *BAR* 38.5 (2012) 30–41, 68.
Wachsmann, Shelley. "The Galilee Boat—2,000-Year-Old Hull Recovered Intact." *BAR* 14.5 (1988) 18–33.
———. *The Sea of Galilee Boat: A 2,000-Year-Old Discovery from the Sea of Legends.* Cambridge: Perseus, 2000.

Von Wahlde, Urban C. "A Rolling Stone That Was Hard to Roll." Biblical Views. *BAR* 41.2 (2015) 26, 72–74.

Walker, Phillip L., et al. "The Causes of Porotic Hyperostosis and Cribra Orbitalia: a Reappraisal of the Iron-deficiency-anemia Hypothesis." *American Journal of Physical Anthropology* 139.2 (2009) 109–25. http://www.ncbi.nlm.nih.gov/pubmed/19280675/.

Waterhouse, S. Douglas. *The Necropolis of Hesban: A Typology of Tombs.* Hesban 10. Berrien Springs, MI: Andrews University Press, 1998.

Weiss, Zeev. "From Galilean Town to Roman City, 100 BCE–200 CE." In *GLSTMP* 2:53–75.

———. "Josephus and Archaeology on the Cities of the Galilee." In *Making History: Josephus and Historical Method,* edited by Zuleika Rodgers, 385–414. JSJSup 110. Leiden: Brill, 2007.

———. "Theatres, Hippodromes, Amphitheatres, and Performances." In *OHJDL* 623–40.

Weiss, Zeev, and Ehud Netzer. "Hellenistic and Roman Sepphoris: The Archaeological Evidence." In *Sepphoris in Galilee: Crosscurrents of Culture,* edited by Rebecca Martin Nagy et al., 29–37. Winona Lake, IN: Eisenbrauns, 1996.

Wells, Calvin. "Ancient Obstetric Hazards and Female Mortality." *Bulletin of the New York Academy of Medicine* 51.11 (1975) 1235–41.

White, K. D. *Roman Farming.* Aspects of Greek and Roman Life. London: Thames & Hudson, 1970.

White, William L. "The Garden Tomb Association Responds." Queries & Comments. *BAR* 12.4 (1986) 14.

Wikipedia, s.v. "Brucellosis." https://en.wikipedia.org/wiki/Brucellosis/.

———, s.v. "Church of the Holy Sepulchre." https://en.wikipedia.org/wiki/Church_of_the_Holy_Sepulchre#Construction_(4th_century)/.

———, s.v. *"De situ terrae sanctae."* https://en.wikipedia.org/wiki/De_situ_terrae_sanctae/.

———, s.v. "Egeria." https://en.wikipedia.org/wiki/Egeria_(pilgrim)/.

———, s.v. "Ein Kerem." https://en.wikipedia.org/wiki/Ein_Kerem/.

———, s.v. "Malaria." https://en.wikipedia.org/wiki/malaria/.

———, s.v. "Saewulf." https://en.wikipedia.org/wiki/S%C3%A6wulf/.

———, s.v. "Sepphoris," https://en.wikipedia.org/wiki/Sepphoris/.

Wilkinson, John. *Jerusalem as Jesus Knew It.* London: Thames & Hudson, 1978.

———, comp. and trans. *Jerusalem Pilgrims before the Crusades.* Warminster, UK: Aris & Philips, 1977.

Williams, Faith W., et al. "Intestinal Parasites from the 2nd–5th Century AD Latrine in the Roman Baths at Sagalassos (Turkey)." *IJP* 19 (2017) 37–42.

Wingerden, Ruben van. "Carrying a *stauros*: A Re-Assessment of the Non-Christian Greek Sources." *NTS* 67.3 (2021) 336–55.

Wise, Michael O., et al., trans. *The Dead Sea Scrolls: A New Translation.* Rev. ed. San Francisco: HarperSanFrancisco, 2005.

World Health Organization. Fact Sheet: "Malaria." December 4, 2023. https://www.who.int/news-room/fact-sheets/detail/malaria/.

Wright Benjamin G. "Jewish Ritual Baths—Interpreting the Digs and the Texts: Some Issues in the Social History of Second Temple Judaism." In *The Archaeology of Israel,* edited by Neil Asher Silberman & David Small, 190–214. JSOTSup 237. Sheffield, UK: Sheffield Academic, 1997.

Wright, George E. "Israelite Daily Life." *BA* 18.3 (1955) 50–79.
———. "What Archaeology Can and Cannot Do." *BA* 34.3 (1971) 70–76.
Wuellner, Wilhelm H. *The Meaning of "Fishers of Men."* NTL. Philadelphia: Westminster, 1967.
Yadin, Yigael. *Bar Kokhba: The Rediscovery of the Legendary Hero of the Second Jewish Revolt against Rome.* New York: Random House, 1971.
———. *Masada: Herod's Fortress and the Zealots' Last Stand.* Translated from the Hebrew by Moshe Pearlman. New York: Random House, 1966.
Yadin, Yigael, et al. *The Documents from the Bar Kokhba Period in the Cave of the Letters.* Vol. 2, *Hebrew, Aramaic, and Nabatean-Aramaic Papyri.* JDS. Jerusalem: Israel Exploration Society, 2002.
Yeh, Hui-Yuan et al. "Human Intestinal Parasites from a Mamluk Period Cesspool in the Christian Quarter of Jerusalem: Potential Indicators of Long Distance Travel in the 15th Century AD." *IJP* 9 (2015) 69–75.
Yeivin, Ze'ev. "Ancient Chorazin Comes Back to Life." *BAR* 13.5 (1987) 22, 24–28, 30–31, 34–36.
———. "Chorazin." In *NEAEHL* 1:301–4.
———. "Survey of Settlements in Galilee and the Golan from the Period of the Mishnah in Light of the Sources." PhD diss., Hebrew University (Jerusalem), 1971 (in Hebrew).
Zapata-Meza, Marcela. "Domestic and Mercantile Areas." In *MOG*, 89–108.
Zias, Joseph. "Anthropological Analysis of Human Skeletal Remains." In *The Akeldama Tombs*, edited by Gideon Avni and Avi Greenhut, 117–21. IAA Reports 1. Jerusalem: IAA, 1996.
———. "Appendix A: Anthropological Observations." *Atiqot* 19 (1990) 125.
———. "Anthropological Evidence of Interpersonal Violence in First-Century-A.D. Jerusalem." *Current Anthropology* 24.2 (1983) 233–34.
———. "The Cemeteries of Qumran and Celibacy: Confusion Laid to Rest?" In *JA*, 444–71.
———. "Current Archaeological Research in Israel: Death and Disease in Ancient Israel." *BA* 54.3 (1991) 147–59.
———. "Crucifixion in Antiquity." *Century One Foundation* (website). http://www.centuryone.org/crucifixion2.html/.
———. "Human Skeletal Remains from the 'Caiaphas' Tomb." *Atiqot: English Series* 21 (1992) 78–80.
———. "Human Skeletal Remains from the Mount Scopus Tomb." *Atiqot: English Series* 21 (1992) 97–103.
———. "Human Skeletal Remains from a Second-Temple-Period Tomb in Arnona, Jerusalem." *Atiqot: English Series* 54 (2006) 117–20.
Zias, Joseph, and James H. Charlesworth. "Crucifixion: Archaeology, Jesus, and the Dead Sea Scrolls." In *Jesus and the Dead Sea Scrolls*, edited by James H. Charlesworth, 273–89. ABRL. New York: Doubleday, 1992.
Zias, Joseph, and Eliezer Sekeles. "The Crucified Man from Giv'at ha-Mivtar: A Reappraisal." *IEJ* 35.1 (1985) 22–27.
Zias, Joseph, et al. "Toilets at Qumran, the Essenes, the Scrolls: New Anthropological Data and Old Theories." *RevQ* 22.4 (2006) 631–40.

Zissu, Boaz, and David Amit. "A Classification of the Second Temple Period Judean Miqwa'ot (Ritual Immersion Baths)." In *Speleology and Spelestology*, 246–61. Nabereznye Chelny, Russia: Naberznye Chelny Institute, 2014. (in Russian)

———. "Common Judaism, Common Purity, and the Second-Temple-Period Judean Miqwa'ot (Ritual Immersion Baths)." In *Common Judaism: Explorations in Second-Temple Judaism*, edited by Wayne O. McCready and Adele Reinhartz, 47–62. Minneapolis: Fortress, 2008.

Zissu, Boaz, and Amir Ganor. "Horbat 'Ethri." *HA-ESI* 113 (2001) 101–4.

———. "Horvat 'Ethri—A Jewish Village from the Second Temple Period and the Bar Kokhba Revolt in the Judean Foothills." *JJS* 60.1 (2009) 90–136.

Zissu, Boaz, and Yuval Goren. "The Ossuary of 'Miriam Daughter of Yeshua Son of Caiaphas, Priests [of] Ma'aziah from Beth 'Imri.'" *IEJ* 61.1 (2011) 74–95.

Živanović, Srboljub. *Ancient Diseases: The Elements of Palaeopathology*. Translated by Lovett F. Edwards. New York: Pica, 1982.

Zlotnick, Dov, trans. *The Tractate "Mourning" (Semaḥot): (Regulations Relating to Death, Burial, and Mourning)*. YJS 17. New Haven: Yale University Press, 1966.

———. "Semaḥot." *EncJud2* 18:273–74.

Subject Index

Adonis (Tammuz), 13, 16, 17
Aetheria (also Egeria), xx, 67, 215, 217, 230, 231
amphitheater, 105, 106, 138, 140, 143, 204
amulet, 171–73, 260
Annas, 211, 222, 224, 232, 240, 272
Antipas (Herod the Tetrarch), 37–40, 42, 43, 54, 57, 58, 89, 98, 109–13, 137, 138, 173
Aphrodite, 6, 10
aqueduct, 56, 58, 106, 184
Archelaus (son of Herod), 42, 110, 136, 182
archisynagōs, 98, 114, 157–63
archisynagōgissa, 158, 162
ashlar, 58, 229, 230, 272, 295

balsam, 108, 181, 182, 184, 184
banquets, 37, 39, 136, 191–200, 231, 242, 256, 270
bath
   Jewish ritual (see *mikveh*)
   Roman style, 39, 121, 123, 130, 132, 137, 139, 140–42, 181, 183, 184
Bethlehem, xx, 12–19, 215, 287, 290
Bethsaida, 59, 61, 69, 70–72, 86, 109, 110, 114, 116–22, 124
betrothal, 1, 4
blocking stone (of tomb), 275, 276
burials, 83, 84, 247, 266–77, 282

Caiaphas, 53, 97, 213, 222, 232–40, 261, 262, 267
Calif Hakim, 209, 276, 284, 285

Capernaum, 61–81, 104, 109, 114–17, 153, 170, 228, 296
cardo (street), 56, 57, 60, 123, 295
carpenter (*tektōn*), 50–60
caves, 3, 16, 32, 46, 189, 220, 249, 274, 275, 285, 286
cenacle. *See* upper room
chief priests, 98, 201, 202, 204, 213
Chorazin, 81, 114, 115, 158, 162
church
   Eleona, 15, 201, 214, 215, 224, 290
   of the Annunciation, 18, 46–48
   of All Nations, 217–19, 224
   of the Holy Sepulcher, xx, 15, 209, 225, 250–255, 278, 280–290
   of Holy Sion, 225, 227, 229–31, 236, 237
   of the Nativity, xx, 14, 17–19, 76, 215, 287, 289
   of St. John, 7, 9, 10, 66
   of St. Joseph, 45, 46, 48
   of St. Peter in Gallicantu, 72, 203, 213, 237–39, 267
coins, xxix, xxx, 11, 46, 86, 92, 112, 113, 119, 121, 138, 190, 207, 230, 234, 280, 364
Constantine, 15, 215, 252, 253, 255, 279–81, 287–90
couch (*klinē*), 191–200, 219–21, 232, 296
crucifixion, 240–265
   depictions of, 257–61
   literary descriptions, 256, 257
   osteological evidence, 261–64

dates (fruit), 108, 181–86
Dead Sea Scrolls, 25, 29, 32, 33, 83, 85, 88
Decapolis, 55, 59, 105, 139, 140, 295
Decumanus, 56, 57, 295
disease, 96, 147, 164–74, 296

Egeria. *See* Aetheria
Ein Kerem, 1, 6–10, 25, 33–35, 66
El-Araj, 69–71, 117, 121
endogamy, 5
ESA pottery, 47, 154, 155, 206, 295
Essenes, 25–30, 33, 156, 189
ethnography, xxx, 295
Et-Tell, 69, 71–74, 109, 117–22, 154
Eusebius, 15, 27, 215, 217, 281, 284

female disciples, 82, 89–92, 231, 232
fishing, 64, 107–9, 116, 117, 121, 122, 124, 125

Galilee boat, 61–63
Gethsemane, 201, 203, 214, 216–23, 232, 240
Giv'at ha-Mivtar, 94, 95, 97, 179, 189, 261, 262
Golgotha, 240, 249–55, 267, 281, 285–87
Gordon's Calvary, 285, 286
gymnasium, 101, 139

Hadrian, 6, 13, 14, 21, 228, 279–81, 287, 288
Helena Augusta, 214, 289, 290
Herod the Great, 2, 11, 31, 34, 37, 38, 40, 42, 55, 105, 110, 120, 130, 170, 182, 186, 197, 204, 209, 241, 242, 283
Herod the Tetrarch. *See* Antipas
Herodium, 40, 42, 81, 151, 152, 245, 246
Hippodrome, 105, 106, 121, 123, 138, 139, 143, 181, 204
Ḥorvat Aqav, 133–35
Ḥorvat 'Eleq, 130–33
house building, 73–75
house of St. Peter, 64–71
house sizes, 71–73, 206–13, 238, 239

human remains
  latrine, 167–70
  skeletal, xxx, 5, 19–23, 52, 82, 92–97, 165, 166, 175–80, 186–91, 233–36, 259, 263

impurity (*tum'ah*), 109, 147–57, 243
inscription(s), xxix, 4, 11, 23, 45, 48, 50, 65, 70, 84, 86, 92–96, 112, 115, 122, 157–63, 176, 211–13, 233–35, 243–47, 255, 260, 262, 276

Jericho, 27, 35, 41, 81, 84, 93, 94, 96, 97, 109, 151, 152, 181–200, 268
Jerome, xx, 6, 13, 16, 226, 279, 280, 288
Josephus, 4, 11, 27, 30, 36–40, 42, 44, 55, 56, 76, 86, 91, 92, 101, 104, 110, 112, 117, 125, 129, 139, 140, 174, 186, 233, 234, 242–44, 259, 261, 265, 272, 277
Justin, xxxiii, 15–17, 51

klinē. *See* couch
kokh (pl., *kokhim*) or *loculus* tomb, 46, 48, 49, 224, 233, 272–74, 296

lamps, 46, 63, 66, 119, 121, 124, 266
large estates, 128–36, 187, 204
leprosy, 147–49, 165–67, 174, 268
lifespan (expectancy), 19–23, 177
loculus tomb. *See* kokh)

Machaerus, 37–40, 43
Madaba map, xx, 225, 230
Magdala, 45, 61, 63, 81, 99, 102, 105, 122–26, 151
Malaria, 23, 64, 170–74
Mansion
  at Ramat ha-Nadiv, 130–35
  palatial (Jerusalem), 72, 73, 205–13
  near Church of St. Peter in Gallicantu, 238, 239
Mary Magdalene, 89, 90, 98, 122, 125, 191
marriage (age at), 4, 5
menorah, 205–7

mikveh (ritual bath; pl., *mikva'ot*), 8, 26, 33, 39, 46, 107–9, 115, 125, 131, 133, 138, 146, 148–53, 155, 157, 160, 168, 184, 206, 208, 209, 223, 237
Mishnah, 1, 44, 74, 83, 101, 119, 152, 154, 196, 231–33, 249, 259
mortality (child), 175–77

Naḥal Ḥever, 3, 33, 189, 191
native informants about Palestine, 5, 16, 75, 76, 174
Nazareth, 1, 5, 12, 18, 44–51, 54, 59, 64, 104, 109, 140, 151, 153

oil press (also olive press/ olive crusher), 46, 133, 135, 219–21, 279
oikonomos, 133, 183
Origen, 14–17, 27, 59
ossilegium, 83, 271, 296
ossuary (-ies), 8, 23, 52, 53, 83–88, 91–97, 183, 198, 233–35, 246–48, 262, 273, 278, 296
osteoarchaeology, 20, 165, 175, 187, 296

palaeopathology, 167, 296
parable, 93, 97, 110, 127–45, 178, 183, 191, 199, 200
parasitic infections, 167–70, 174
pathology, 93–96, 167
patibulum, 248, 249, 257, 258, 260
Philip the Tetrarch, 37, 42, 59, 99, 110, 116, 119, 120
Piacenza Pilgrim, 15, 27, 67, 69, 219
pigs, 137, 138, 144, 145
pilgrims to Palestine, xxxii, xxxiii, 6, 27, 65–67, 69, 70, 160, 206, 219–23, 228, 236, 237, 241, 242, 276, 281, 284
polis (city), 101, 116, 121–23, 295
Pontius Pilate, 241–46, 270
Pool of Siloam, 152, 223
Praetorium (in Jerusalem), 240, 241, 267
purity (ritual), xxxi, 121, 138, 146–57, 209, 210, 223

quarry, 74, 249, 250, 251, 253–55, 278, 282–84, 287, 290
Qumran, 22, 25–33, 35, 93, 95–97, 151, 152, 168, 179, 189, 199, 274

Ramat Ha-Nadiv, 130–35
realia, xxix, xxx, 164, 174

sanitation, 76
Scythopolis, 139–45, 168, 295
Seat of Moses, 114, 115, 158, 162
Sepphoris, 5, 45–47, 54–60, 64, 72, 73, 99, 102, 112, 123–25, 137–39, 151, 153–55, 171–73
Simon of Cyrene, 246–48
shroud (burial), 166, 266, 268
skeletal remains (see Human remains)
stature, 94, 95, 186–89, 212
stone vessels, 47, 48, 119, 121, 131, 138, 150–57
stone weight, 212
swimming pools, 130, 133, 181, 184
synagogues, 44, 48, 72, 73, 77–81, 104–9, 114–16, 124, 126, 152, 157–63, 190, 225, 228, 229

Tammuz. See Adonis
Taricheae. See Magdala
tektōn. See carpenter
Tel Zahara, 144, 145
theater, 55–58, 101, 105, 139, 141–44, 204, 243, 244
Tiberias (the city), 45, 46, 54, 59, 61, 99, 105, 112, 113, 123–25, 137–40, 171, 172
Tiberius (the emperor), 31, 116, 181, 182, 186, 224, 265
tombs
 arcosolium, 274
 loculus (see *kokh*)
 monumental, 272
 trenches, 274, 275
Tomb of David, 228–30, 237, 288
Tomb of Jesus, 13, 250, 253, 266, 276–91
triclinium, 39, 43, 181, 183, 192–98, 221, 296
tuberculosis, 165–67
tum'ah. See impurity

Upper City (Jerusalem), 64, 72, 73, 121, 152–54, 201–13, 228, 231, 236, 239, 242
upper room (cenacle), 59, 89, 203, 216, 225–32, 236, 237, 267

Venus, 13, 280, 281, 287
violence, 88, 177–80, 212

Wadi Muraba'at, 3
wine press, 8, 46, 47, 133, 151
working class, 83, 84, 92–90, 125, 186

Scripture Index

OLD TESTAMENT

Genesis
18:1	215
28:2	5

Exodus
12:3	231
12:3b–4	231
20:4	119

Leviticus
11–17	147
11:7	138
11:20	148
11:23	148
11:29–30	148
11:41–43	148
13–14	166
18:16	37
20:21	37

Numbers
19	147
14:38–39	156
19:14–15	152

Deuteronomy
21:17	136
21:22	257
21:23	277
22:12	22:12

Judges
3:20	226

Ruth
4:11	13

1 Samuel
15:33	178
16:1–13	13
31:10	140
31:12	140

2 Samuel
3:3	87

1 Kings
17:19	226

2 Kings
5	166
1:2	226
4:10	226

1 Chronicles
24:10	48
24:15	50
24:18	235

2 Chronicles
26	166

SCRIPTURE INDEX

Ezra
2:21	13
2:23–24	266

Nehemiah
7:26	13
12:17	48

Isaiah
40:3	25, 27

Micah
5:2	13

NEW TESTAMENT

Matthew
1:18–19	1
1:19	4
2:23	46
3:1–3	26, 27
3:5	26
8:2	149
8:5–13	170
8:11	194
8:14–15	64, 170
8:18	61
8:23–29	61
9:1	61
9:10	194
9:18	161
9:20–22	148, 156
9:23	269
10:2–4	82
11:2–6	40
11:16–19	194
11:17	269
11:21	114
12:9–14	77
13:53–58	51
13:55	50
14:1–6	110
14:1–2	40, 111, 112
14:3–12	37, 39
14:3–6	156
14:9	194
14:13–14	61, 116
14:22–32	61
15:21–28	199
15:39	61
16:5	61
16:21	201
16:24	249
17:24–25	64
18:24–34	129
19:13	177
19:16–22	129
20:1–15	129
21	130
21:23	201
21:33–46	129
21:45–46	201
22:4	194
22:10–11	194
23:2	114
23:5	156
23:6	114, 194
23:25	149
24:3–42	214
24:30	269
25:14–30	129
26:3	201, 232
26:6	149
26:7	194
26:14	201
26:20	194
26:30	216
26:36	216, 219
26:57	241
26:59	202
27:6	273
27:12	202
27:30	254
27:32	249
27:33	249
27:55	89
27:56	89
27:59	266, 268
27:60	278
27:61	89
28:1	89, 122, 271
28:11	89

Mark

Reference	Page
1:2–4	26
1:3	27
1:4–5	26
1:4	26, 27
1:5	27
1:6	26
1:9	46
1:23	77
1:29	64, 73
1:30–31	170
1:40	149
2:1	64
2:3–4	64
2:3	64, 75
2:4	75
2:15	194
3:1–6	77
3:16–19	22
3:17	86
4:35–41	61
5:18	61
5:20	140
5:21	61
5:22	158, 161
5:25–34	148
5:35	158, 177
5:36	158
5:38	158, 268, 269
6:1–6	51
6:3	5, 50, 51
6:14–22	110
6:14–16	40, 112
6:17–29	37, 39
6:17	37
6:21	194
6:22	194
6:26	195
6:32–34	61
6:32	116
6:45–61	61
6:45	116
6:56	156
7:2	146
7:3	154
7:4	149
7:24–30	199
7:31	140
8:9	61
8:10	61
8:13–14	61
8:22–26	116
8:31	201
8:34	249
9:17–18	177
10:13	177
10:17–20	129
11:1	214
11:27	201
12	130
12:1–12	129
12:12	201
12:39	114, 194
13:3–37	214
13:3	214
14:1	201
14:3	59, 149, 194
14:8	194
14:10	201
14:12–16	59
14:14	160, 226
14:15	226, 227
14:26	216
14:32	214, 216, 219
14:37	223
14:40	223
14:41	223
14:51–52	223
14:55	202
15:3	202
15:12	250
15:16	241
15:21	246, 247, 249, 251
15:22	249, 250
15:24	257
15:25	257
15:29	254
15:34	257
15:40	251
15:46	268, 273
15:47	122
16:1–2	271
16:3	273
16:4	275
16:14	194

Luke

1:5	11, 48
1:7	29
1:26–27	1
1:39	6
1:39–56	6
1:39–40	6
1:65	6
1:80	24, 25, 35
2	19
2:1	12
2:3–4	12
2:7	160
2:22	148
2:36–37	19
2:41–52	45
2:51	45
3:1	25, 110
3:2–6	26
3:2–3	27
3:2	25, 27, 35, 222, 232
3:3	25
3:4–6	25, 27
3:7	26
3:19–20	37
3:19	110, 112
3:26	31
4:14–15	44
4:16	46
4:20	114
4:22	50
4:27	149, 166
4:31	64
4:33	77
4:38–39	170
4:38	77
5	98
5:1–3	61
5:2–11	61
5:12–14	149
5:12–13	166
5:16	24
5:18–19	64
5:19	75
5:29	194
6:1	61
6:12–16	82
7	98
7:1–10	170
7:4–5	161
7:5	77
7:11–16	269, 270
7:12	177
7:18–23	40
7:21–22	164
7:22	149, 166
7:31–35	194
7:36	194
7:37	194
7:41–43	129
7:44	194
7:49	194
8	98
8:1–3	89, 90
8:1	99
8:2–3	89
8:2	122
8:3	110
8:4	156
8:22–25	61
8:29	24
8:37	61
8:40	61
8:41	158, 161
8:42	177
8:43–48	148
8:44	156
8:49	158, 177
8:52	269
9:7–9	40, 109, 111, 112
9:9	177
9:10	116
9:12	116
9:14	31
9:22	201
9:23	249
10:13	114
10:31–32	148
10:38–42	59, 199
10:38–39	89, 90
11:37–39	146
11:37	194
11:38	149, 194
11:39	149

11:43	114	19:37	214
12:16–20	127, 129	19:47	201
12:19	194	20	130
12:37	194	20:1	201
12:42–43	129	20:9–19	129
12:45	194	20:19	201
12:46	178	20:46	114, 194
13:10–14	157	21:5–6	214
13:14	158, 159, 163	21:7–36	214
13:29	194	21:24	194
13:31	111	21:34	194
14:7–11	200	21:37	214, 216
14:7–8	194	21:39	214
14:8	194	22:2	201
14:10	194	22:4	201
14:12	194	22:7–13	226
14:13	194	22:11	160, 226
14:15	194	22:12	226, 227
14:16–24	200	22:14	194, 231
14:17	194	22:20	194
14:24	194	22:27	194
15	98	22:36–43	227
15:11–32	129	22:39	216
15:11–13	135–36	22:45	223, 224
15:12	136, 137	22:52	201
15:14–16	144	22:54–71	240
16	98	22:54	236
16:1–7	129	22:66	202
16:19–31	93, 129, 199	23:6–8	111
16:19	194, 268	23:10	202
17:7–10	129	23:11–12	111
17:7	194	23:13	202
17:12	166	23:26	246, 249, 251
17:22	149	23:27	269
18	98	23:33	249, 250, 255
18:13	269	23:34	257
18:15	177	23:35	254
18:18–23	129	23:44	257
18:35	181	23:49	251
19	98	23:50–53	276
19:1–10	191	23:53	268, 278
19:2–3	187	23:54–62	237
19:7	191	24:1	271
19:8	200	24:2	275
19:11–27	129	24:10	89, 90
19:27	177	24:20	202
19:29	214	24:30	194

John

1:23	26, 27
1:25	26
1:28	27
1:44	116
1:45–46	46
3:24	37
4:49	177
4:52	170
6:16–21	61
6:59	77
6:71	88
7:42	12
8:1	216
11	269
11:14	177
11:16	87
11:31	270–271
11:44	266, 268
11:49	232
12:2	194
12:21	116
13:2	194
13:4	194
13:12	194
13:23	194
13:28	194
14:22	88
18:1–2	216
18:13–24	240
18:13	224, 232
18:14	232
18:24	224, 232
18:28	232, 241
18:33	241
19:9	241
19:13	243
19:17	249, 250
19:20	250
19:25–27	264
19:25	89, 90
19:39–40	266
19:40	268
19:41	251, 278, 279, 284
20:1	89, 90, 271
20:6-7	266
20:12	274
20:19–29	227
20:19–25	230
20:24	87
21:2	87
21:12	194
21:15	194
21:20	194

Acts

1:3	226
1:13	82, 226, 227
1:14	232
1:15	31
2:1–4	227, 230
2:28	311
2:41	31
4:1	202
4:6	202, 222, 224, 232
4:23	227
4:31	227
5:6	268, 269
5:10	269
5:17	202
5:30	265
9:1	202
9:14	202
9:21	202
9:37	266
10:28	155
10:39	265
11:2	227
12:12	227
12:23	170
13:1	111
13:15	158, 163
15:6	227
18:8	158
18:17	158
20:8	226
21:17	227
22:5	202
22:30	202
23:14	202
23:35	241
24:1	202
25:2	202
22:15	202
26:10	202
26:12	202

Romans

16:1	161

1 Corinthians

11:23–25	194, 195
15:4	277
15:7	279

Galatians

1:14	87, 154
2:9	279

Hebrews

11:37	178
13:12	250

Revelation

1:7	269
18:9	269

www.ingramcontent.com/pod-product-compliance
Lightning Source LLC
Chambersburg PA
CBHW030431300426
44112CB00009B/949